BOSSES IN LUSTY CHICAGO

The Story of Bathhouse John and Hinky Dink

BOSSES IN LUSTY CHICAGO

THE STORY OF BATHHOUSE JOHN AND HINKY DINK

by

LLOYD WENDT AND HERMAN KOGAN

With an Introduction by Paul H. Douglas

INDIANA UNIVERSITY PRESS · BLOOMINGTON · LONDON

THIRD PRINTING 1971

Introduction

BY PAUL H. DOUGLAS
(former U.S. Senator from Illinois)

This reissue of the classic biography of "Bathhouse John" Coughlin and "Hinky Dink" Kenna, the joint bosses of Chicago's First Ward, by Lloyd Wendt and Herman Kogan, rescues for the modern generation what was enjoyed by its predecessor.

"The Bath" and "Hinky Dink" ruled politically in the vice-saturated First Ward for approximately the half century from 1890 to 1940. They were legendary characters, and Wendt and Kogan make the most of their eccentricities. The Bath was the bumbling and none too bright extrovert, while Hinky Dink was the shrewd and laconic introvert. They indeed resembled characters in the old Laurel and Hardy movies. The Bath, with his gayly colored waistcoats, his inability to speak a coherent sentence, his penchant for owning race horses which couldn't or wouldn't run, and his sponsorship of absurd songs such as "They Buried Her by the Side of the Drainage Canal" and "Dear Midnight of Love," is, in a sense, as irresistibly funny as the Keystone Cops.

But not so was his partner, Hinky Dink. "The Hink" knew the price of everything and, his opponents alleged, the value of nothing. It was charged that every saloon, every gambler, every prostitute had to come across at rates which were presumably fixed according to their ability to pay. Mike, with his aides, saw to it that this was done and that the vote was delivered on primary and election days.

I have always thought that Hinky Dink had the makings of a great idiomatic Latin scholar, for in his saloon across the longest bar in the world he had had blazoned in bold letters, "In Vino Veritas." When asked one day what that meant, he replied, "It means that when a man's drunk he gives his right name." I have never heard any of my professorial colleagues do better than that!

It was my good fortune to become personally acquainted with Bathhouse John and Hinky Dink toward the very end of their careers and I can vouch for the accuracy with which this book has caught their full flavor. I got to know Bathhouse when he was in the City Council and I was fighting Samuel Insull's efforts to take over the Chicago surface and elevated lines at a valuation of $264 million, or about twice what they were worth. The Bath had on a resplendent red flannel waistcoat. Although he disliked college professors, he unbent when he discovered that I was on the opposite side from Insull. In a lordly way he told me about all the jokers which he thought the Insull lawyers had inserted in the traction ordinance; in my innocence I thought we had an ally. But when the time for voting came, the First Ward was secretly lined up with Insull.

When I was elected to the City Council from the Fifth Ward in 1939, Coughlin had died and Hinky Dink was in his last term as Alderman from the First. Hink would sit close-mouthed and ferret-eyed at his desk, glaring scornfully at the whole assembly and casting especially chilling looks at me at my seat a few desks away. Attendants told me that at times he thought I was his old foe and my dear friend, Charles Merriam, who had returned to plague him. Merriam had served in the Council from our ward for six years, and in 1911 had been nearly elected mayor on the Republican ticket. Hink hated Merriam with all his heart and soul and concluded that I, as a professor and a despised "reformer," must either be Merriam himself or the same man bearing another's name.

I shall never forget Hink's last day in the City Council. The depression was still severe. Unemployment was everywhere; relief was scanty, the slums were spreading, and the Negroes suffered most. A Negro Alderman, Bennie Grant from the Second Ward, got up to protest the housing of his people. He was followed by the able Alderman from the Third Ward, Earl Dickerson, who told in polished English about the high percentage of Negro workers who still couldn't find a job. Hink listened to these speeches with increasing scorn and I could see that he was close to exploding. I had been carrying on a running battle to increase the food allowances of those on relief, since these had been cut to below the starvation level. As I warmed up to my demand that more money be appropriated to feed the hungry, it was too much for the Hink. He arose painfully, straightened his eighty-year-old back, took his brown derby from the top of his desk, and with great dignity slowly walked out of the Council Chamber. As he neared the door, he turned and delivered his contemptuous valedictory: "Housing, Unemployment, Relief," he snorted, " 'Tain't seemly."

He went to his house, took to his bed, and died a few years afterward. When he was buried, instead of the huge turnout that generally characterized the funerals of politicians, no large crowd came. Hink, unlike most of his colleagues, had never liked either wakes or funerals. And as one of his friends remarked, "If you don't go to other people's funerals, they won't come to yours."

Wendt and Kogan have caught many incidents like this, and I find the whole account so true to life that I can see the grotesque characters now.

But this biography, while hilarious, also provokes much deeper thought upon the nature of big city politics in the half century that preceded World War II. Here were two men of the people who rose to power not merely by brawn and self-assertiveness but also by acting as the very human friends of people in poverty and trouble. They fed the hungry and they got jobs for the unemployed. They protected those in trouble with the law. In return, like the condottieri of the medieval cities, they demanded and obtained loyalty and obedience. They ruled the central business and amusement district both within the loop and in the area immediately to the south. It was the tenderloin of Chicago and they ran it as the New York tenderloin was run in the days of Big Bill Devery. Not only did the needy and homeless flock to them, but also those who pandered to the sensual interests of an outwardly Victorian society. Gamblers set up shop so that the gilded youth of the Prairie City could find extra excitement. Whores plied their trade along the streets and in the crib houses run by the Madams, while here and there a resort such as that of the Everleigh Sisters gave an air of rococo elegance to the same transactions. The First Ward gave to the city and to the Midwest the chance to privately enjoy virtually every form of vice that was publicly condemned.

Hinky Dink himself lived a scrupulously respectable private life. He was faithful to his wife and spent his evenings with her in the quiet of their home. The Bath was a much more roisterous character and was, in a sense, the public relations man for the enterprise.

In return for the police protection that the "Lords of the Levee" accorded, the assorted community of gamblers, pimps, whores, panderers, and Madams paid money tribute and public and political fealty. One of the Everleigh sisters described the system after their place had been closed down:

> In the days when the Everleigh Club was being openly conducted with huge profits, all orders came from Hinky Dink Kenna and Bathhouse John Coughlin through the person of Sol Friedman to whom the Alderman assigned the whiskey, taxicab, groceries, and clothing privileges in the segregated district. Insurance had to be taken from Coughlin's company and a choice of four provision stores was in force.

Miss Everleigh went on to say that not only had she given the Bath a check for $3,000 to stop some threatened state legislation, but that over a period of twelve years she had paid more than $100,000 in cash. She continued, "I always entertained state legislators free in the Club," and she estimated, as Wendt and Kogan report, that $15 million in graft had been collected in the Levee.

The great annual event was the famous or infamous First Ward Ball where the resplendent Bath always led the Grand March. This was attended by all the dregs of underworld society while the thrill-seekers of the upper crust also came "slumming" to gape at the despised denizens of the deep. Here beer was sold at champagne prices and only at dawn would the haggard revelers stumble onto the street.

Thus far the picture of Hinky Dink and the Bath follows the

familiar lines that Lincoln Steffens popularized in his articles for *McClure's* and in his autobiography. But it differed in one significant respect from the Steffens formula. Most of the city bosses whom Steffens describes were the secret allies of the private utilities in traction, electricity, gas and telephones, which needed franchises to use the city streets. In the Steffens analysis, the city bosses would sell out the poor by letting the utilities charge high rates and make little or no payment to the cities for their franchise privileges. In these cases they were the connecting link between the underworld and the financial upper world, allowing each to prey upon the general public while claiming that they were protecting each from the other. This was true of Johnny Powers, the boss of the Nineteenth Ward, who was the opponent of Hink and the Bath.

Some writers have described these ward heelers as a kind of Robin Hood, shaking down the rich to give to the poor. This was in fact partially true and it was the way the ward bosses liked to think of themselves. Even in this respect, however, the commission that they charged for the transfer of income was unduly high. But a truer explanation of what happened in most cities, most notably New York, Philadelphia and St. Louis, was that the rough-and-tumble ward and city bosses allowed the private utilities and the favor-seeking men of wealth as well as the purveyors of vice to exploit the great mass of the citizens.

There were such elements in Chicago, and they flourished in the days of Charles T. Yerkes, who was the prototype of Cowperwood, whose Chicago record has been so well memorialized by Theodore Dreiser in his classic novel, *The Titan*. But the Bath and Hinky Dink differed from the pattern by being steadfast supporters of Mayor Carter Harrison and the heroic Governor John P. Altgeld as they fought to prevent Yerkes from legally stealing the streets of the city. They were, in fact, the two in the City Council who swung the decisive votes that defeated Yerkes. Bathhouse John explained his stand in typically matter-of-fact and unheroic language: "I never take the big stuff," he said.

While the two were never crusaders against Yerkes and Insull, they gave Harrison and Altgeld quiet help against the former and were never enthusiasts for the latter.

It would be wrong, then, to picture them as Robin Hoods. W. T. Stead, the English journalist, was probably right in referring to Hell as "a pocket edition of Chicago" under their regime. On some of the larger issues, however, their record compared very favorably with some of the ostensibly respectable who looked down upon Hink and the Bath but who for big fees did the bidding of the wealthy robber barons who despoiled the city. While the sturdy and self-sacrificing reformers of the stripe of George E. Cole, Charles Merriam, William H. Holly, and Harold Ickes were the best of all, I must admit that when a colleague of mine quoted some lines from John Hay's Jim Bledsoe and applied them to Hink and the Bath, I found myself nodding approval:

> He warn't no saint but at Judgment Day
> I'll take my chance with Jim
> 'Longside some pious gentleman
> Who wouldn't shake hands with him!

Fortunately the old ward bosses of the type of Martin Lomasney of Boston, Big and Little Tim Sullivan and "The McManus" of New York, and Iz Durham and Ed Vare of Philadelphia, are fast fading from the political scene. They have been largely displaced by a number of changes of which the most important have been, first, the development of social security and welfare legislation which provide protection in a relatively self-respecting manner against some of the terrible risks of industrial life—industrial accidents, unemployment, indigent old age, and many forms of poverty. These have displaced the gratuities of the ward boss and have lessened the dependence which the poor and the unfortunate used to feel toward those who at once exploited and protected them. A second factor has been the great decrease in the immigrant tide which used to run at the rate of a million persons a year. This huge influx created cultural enclaves within our cities which in turn helped to raise to power the ethnic ward bosses like Cermak, Stanley Kunz, and Moe Rosenberg of Chicago. The new migration cityward of Negroes and Puerto Ricans has created somewhat analogous groups, to be sure, but not to the same degree. A third factor that has diminished the power of the ward boss has been the great reduction in poverty and the improvement in the material condition of the people. There are still a great many poor people in the country. Probably a sixth can be fairly classified as being poor, and a fourth as poor or near-poor. But the proportion is not as high as it was, and city folk, even with the Negro migration, are not as dependent as they were. Those who can stand on their own feet do not need the protection of the ward leader as much as did their parents and grandparents. Benjamin Franklin once said that "it is hard for an empty sack to stand upright." This was one of the reasons for the power of Hinky Dink. A fourth determinant has been the growing strength of the unions. In addition to the help which they give to their members in matters of wages, hours and working conditions, they also help to protect them against unjust discharges. They act for them in civic matters and represent them before administrators of unemployment insurance, the Veterans' Administration, and other governmental agencies. All this diminishes the dependence of the voters upon the ward organizations. Finally there has been a conspicuous change in individual and political behavior. It may well be that there is far more informal experimentation in sex within the more well-to-do classes. The demand for commercialized prostitution has diminished, however, and with it most of the old red-light districts. Big Bill Devery's Tenderloin as well as the Bath's and Hink's Levee are now largely things of the past. The trade of call girl is an unhappy one, but it is not as sordid as that of an inmate in a commercialized house of prostitution, and it is voluntary rather than involuntary as it often was before.

The general level of city government has also greatly improved. The two Carter Harrisons were far better than the average American mayor of their time, but up until the final breakup they found it necessary to accept the lords of the levee as their close allies. It was a mutually protective relationship. In order for Carter Junior to check Yerkes and his successors, he had to have Coughlin and Kenna. For Coughlin and Kenna to levy tribute, they had to have a friendly mayor and chief of police.

It was, in a sense, the Victorian compromise. The upper world fed the underworld by their secret patronage while the well-to-do owners of red-light real estate pocketed high rents. The underworld gave scope to the darker passions of society at the price of being despised by those who not only tolerated but patronized them. Coughlin, Kenna, and their motley group of disreputables were the inevitable product of the dominant set of practices and social values.

Political as well as individual life has improved. Mayor Ed Kelly was no reformer, but he hated commercialized prostitution and greatly reduced it. Dick Daley has narrowed it still further, and as the older leaders have died off or retired, has replaced them with a different and improved set.

And yet there is a great continuing need for the ward political organizations and leaders, and it would be a great loss were they to disappear. For they are the vital cells of democracy. Democracy is not self-operating. It needs parties to stress issues and carry them to the voters and then to get out the vote on the election days. There are comparatively few localities where this can be done on a purely intellectual level. It can best be done by friends and neighbors who, by acts of kindness, have already proved their concern and liking for the man or family in need of help. This is where the ward organizations come in. They commonly are, and to an increasing degree should be, good neighbors. This is especially important when the citizen has to deal with the local, state, or national bureaucracy. The bureaucrat often becomes cold, impersonal and dilatory in his dealings with the citizenry. Protected by civil service, the public functionary, feeling secure himself, very frequently does not identify himself with the plight of the citizen who approaches him, hat in hand. Sometimes he is afflicted with "the insolence of office" and compels the patient suppliant to accept slurs and petty cruelties.

A political organization, in order to win votes, must be an efficient service organization and by the very nature of its being must try to be helpful. Both as an Alderman and as a United States Senator I found this to be at once the most time-consuming and yet personally the most satisfying part of my job. Every politician worthy of his salt feels the same way.

This is one of the major reasons why I would not like to see the civil service take over the whole structure of government activity. I believe it would become cold and impersonal and that we would have a privileged group of administrative mandarins who would neither know nor care how the people affected by government felt about the programs they were managing, and who would be incapable of tempering the rules to the need for mercy and justice.

A number of public-spirited representatives and scholars are now proposing the creation of salaried "ombudsmen" to represent the public before administrative agencies and officials. They are to be modelled on the Swedish system and to parallel the public defenders who now serve in the courts. Such officials could be of real service. In my opinion, however, they would be an inadequate substitute for the services of precinct committeemen, ward organizations, ward leaders, and elected representatives.

In the first place the volume of work would be so great that an "ombudsman" could only concern himself with a very small fraction of the cases where help was needed. He would, therefore, inevitably tend to confine himself to the more flagrant cases of administrative injustice or delay. The abuses, in other words, would have to be both flagrant and protracted before the ombudsman would take the case. He would come in toward the end of the incident and not in the early and middle stages, which are the crucial periods. Moreover, the chief needs of the average citizen are of a much humbler nature. He needs to know where he is to go and to be aided in filling out the necessary forms. He needs someone who will keep nudging the administrative officials to see that the papers are not lost or sidetracked and that there are no untoward delays. Sometimes he will need to have character witnesses assembled for him, and his human situation explained and defended.

In short, he needs in large numbers informed and concerned friends who can represent him in an impersonal society. This the politician can do better than a professional "ombudsman" who, after a time, is likely to become another civil servant himself and to feel more kinship with his fellow officials than with the distraught, often irritating, and highly imperfect men and women who are nevertheless imposed upon by officialdom.

It is obvious that there can be and will be abuses in this representation of the weak by the politicians. Sometimes the politicians will levy tribute and sometimes they will require political support in return for service. But they can be and are extremely useful and democracy cannot properly function without them. Those who would save politics by eliminating the local politician are like those who would throw out the baby with the dirty bath water.

This book by Wendt and Kogan is thus not only an amusing chronicle of politics at almost its lowest level, but it creates a challenge to those who abhor the tactics of Coughlin and Kenna. Can they meet the human needs which the blundering Bath and the shrewd Hink served, and do so without the corruption that they practiced? And will the prosperous and affluent abstain from taking advantage of the community and devote themselves to its service?

If this books moves large numbers of men and women to act in that spirit, it will win for itself an even higher usefulness. But this depends upon whether the readers see the deeper significance of what Lloyd Wendt and Herman Kogan have to tell us. In the meantime, let us rejoice that a new generation will now have the chance to read this sprightly story.

Contents

BOSSES IN LUSTY CHICAGO

The Story of Bathhouse John and Hinky Dink

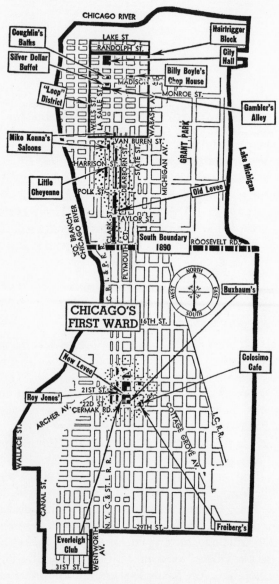

Coughlin's Baths

Hairtrigger Block

Silver Dollar Buffet

City Hall

CHICAGO RIVER

LAKE ST.

RANDOLPH ST.

Billy Boyle's Chop House

MADISON

"Loop" District

MONROE ST.

Gambler's Alley

Mike Kenna's Saloons

GRANT PARK

Lake Michigan

VAN BUREN ST.

WELLS ST.

LA SALLE ST.

WABASH AV.

STATE ST.

DEARBORN ST.

MICHIGAN AV.

HARRISON ST.

Little Cheyenne

POLK ST.

Old Levee

CLARK ST.

TAYLOR ST.

SO. BRANCH CHICAGO RIVER

C.R.I. & P. R.R.

PLYMOUTH CT.

South Boundary 1890

ROOSEVELT RD.

NORTH

WEST

EAST

SOUTH

Buxbaum's

CHICAGO'S FIRST WARD

16TH ST.

New Levee

Colosimo Cafe

Roy Jones'

21ST ST.

22D ST.

CERMAK RD.

ARCHER AV.

COTTAGE GROVE AV.

I.C. R.R.

WALLACE ST.

CANAL ST.

N.Y.C. & ST. L.R.R.

29TH ST.

Freiberg's

Everleigh Club

31ST ST.

WENTWORTH AV.

"THE LEVEE"

Chicago's First Ward

DUSTY JOHN

I

To THE snug little loft atop Billy Boyle's chophouse have come the worthy men of Chicago's Hairtrigger Block, Little Cheyenne, the Levee, and Gamblers' Alley. Sol van Praag, following rheumatic Billy up the groaning stairs, steps diffidently in as if entering at one of the 540 gates of Valhalla. But elegant Harry (Prince Hal) Varnell, immediately behind him, seems unimpressed. He sends a thick doughnut of blue smoke at the grimy ceiling, and demands of Boyle:

"Billy, why th' hell don't you clean up this old firetrap?"

The hackle at van Praag's neck stands up, and old Sol stiffens stubbornly just inside the door, his eyes a-glitter with indignation. "Why!" rasps Sol. "It was here ... !"

"Sure, sure," chuckles Varnell, spreading his delicate hands. "It was here they sent you to the legislature. It was here we made Palmer United States senator. . . ."

"For sixty-t'ree days," croons van Praag, his eyes softening, "for sixty-t'ree days th' hull hunnert an' one of us we voted. Not a man of us ud give up. Not a man! I 'member th' day . . ."

"Christ!" snorts Billy Skakel, pushing in. "I'm hungry."

It is a silent, comfortable crew swiping the plates with bread crusts while Varnell lights up a fat cigar and toys with his wineglass. Van Praag slumps back, chewing largely, his suspicious eyes wandering from the bleak walls to the handsome gambler at the head of the table and back again. Beside him Skakel sucks the marrow of his T-bone, looks up startled when Billy Boyle pads quietly behind him. Big Sandy Walters, known through the First

9

Ward as a man who has never seen a tree, hunches low to the table, keeps a careful eye on Varnell. At a corner, little Billy Mason, holding himself a man apart from the dozen gamblers, bar keeps, and brothel owners, still picks at his chicken, and smirks to himself in pleased good humor as if he knows a funny secret that will never come out.

Varnell sets his cold blue eyes upon the still ravenous Skakel, knocks the ash from his cigar, and shoves back from the table. His eyes meet the eyes of his friends, George Hankins and Johnny Condon.

"Boys," says Varnell softly, "Mike McDonald is just about through."

Skakel catches a splinter of bone in his throat, Billy Mason's eyes widen a little, Billy Boyle halts at the service kitchen and turns a thoughtful stare upon the assembly. For the rest, twelve poker faces receive the pronouncement impassively.

"It's up to us," continues Varnell. "We're payin', an' not gettin'. Mike is too God-damn busy with his upstairs railroad. Corrigan gives us th' run around. Th' flat feet give us th' run around. Th' Garfield Park boys are sick of it."

"We gotta git our own man," says Condon, fingering his diamond fob.

Skakel, persistently gnawing, looks up. "Anybody perticular in mind?"

"Yeah. Bathhouse Johnny Coughlin."

Skakel looks at van Praag, and van Praag looks at Big Sandy Walters, who suddenly starts eating again. Van Praag stretches his scraggly neck.

"Well," he says, "Skakel here is a good man. . . ."

"Skakel!" Prince Hal grins at his friends. "Hot chance we'd have electing The Clock to anything. Our man has got t' be clean, smart enough to get around, but not too smart. I been looking at Coughlin. He wants to be alderman . . . bad. He's our dish."

Varnell's eyes signal to Billy Mason, and Billy sits up obediently.

II

"I think Harry's right," he begins. "This young Coughlin has got a nice little push. He's president of th' club. He's all right with Linedecker, and ol' Joe Mackin swears by him. Now I ain't goin' into whether Mike McDonald has done right or not. But I say Johnny Coughlin will be all right with Mike. Mike gets leeched at Coughlin's, an' they talk in here lots a times. I say, let Johnny's own push start things, then you fellows pick it up. Nicky Cremer is through. Even Mike knows that. I say, let Frieberger here go out an' talk to Mike. If Coughlin is okay, then there's nothin' to worry about. If he ain't—" Little Billy's eyes rest upon Skakel—"if he ain't, well then, they's time enough t' think about that."

Teddy Frieberger is back, flushed with the importance of his errand. He halts at the door.

"Well?" snaps Sol van Praag.

"It's Johnny Coughlin!" booms Frieberger. "Mike says any son-of-a-bitch but Cremer."

2

John Joseph Coughlin had his roots in the First Ward, and never was a soil more fructuous. There Chicago itself grew up, from a ragged little slab town trestled in a swamp to a blowsy, teeming metropolis that was able, by universal consensus, to burn up in 1871 more ill-gotten damnation than any city since Sodom and Gomorrah. Chicago had a reputation. It was bad, and it was totally ignored by the good citizens who had something better to do than plant lilies in the front yard. Soul and sinew of this ill repute was the First Ward, brilliant with achievement of solid gain by day, red-lighted and lulled by the soft chatter of chips and dice by night.

To this district had come, in 1857, a ruddy, big-chested Irishman named Michael Coughlin. He was a native of County Roscommon, a firm-jawed, benevolent man who had arrived in this country as a boy of thirteen. For some years he had lived in Lake County, Illinois, near Waukegan, then a drab expanse of woods and prairie with a few farm houses and settlements scattered about. After working for years at varied laboring jobs, Coughlin moved into the rapidly growing city, settling in Connelly's Patch, an Irish district east of the Chicago River, between Adams and Monroe Streets. Here he met Johanna Hanley, a buxom colleen from County Limerick, whom he wed in 1858. Here John, their first son, was born on August 15, 1860.

Despite expenses entailed by the birth of the son, Michael saved enough to buy a grocery at Polk and Wells Streets. He began to prosper mildly, and he and his wife set about devoutly to raise a large family. Two years after John's birth came a dark-eyed son whom they named Joseph. Several years later Mary was born, a birth so difficult for Johanna Coughlin that she died a few days later.

With three youngsters to look after, Michael married Annie Whelan, a neighbor, and she, in the five years preceding the Chicago fire of 1871, bore three children, Michael Jr., George, and Kate. Over this brood the new Mrs. Coughlin ruled efficiently, and John especially was fond of her. The family was typical of Connelly's Patch domesticity. Coughlin, stern and proper, rarely smoked or drank, and in the children's presence never said so much as "damn." He was prudent, industrious and thrifty and on his way toward becoming a well-to-do man when the great fire of 1871 wiped out the store and the family home.

John went into Iroquois County in central Illinois to work on the farm of a relative for several months. By the time he returned to Chicago his father had opened a newer but smaller store at Taylor and Miller Streets. Funds were scarce, and thenceforth the young Coughlin had to earn his spending money and part of his keep. John evidently never regretted this, and in his later political life he made capital of it. Invariably in newspaper stories of later years commemorating the holocaust of 1871, Coughlin was quoted:

"Why, money didn't mean anything to me. I'm glad that fire came along and burned the store. Say, if not for that bonfire I might have been a rich man's son and gone to Yale—and never amounted to nothing!"

3

When John resumed his classes at the Jones School, at Harrison and Federal Streets, he took a job as assistant to the school janitor. Thus he acquired his first nickname—"Dusty John"—for he usually appeared in class with shirt and trousers grimy and sooty from the coal room. John took no offense at the sobriquet; he was big and agreeable and shyly happy over whatever attention he got. He responded to calls of his playmates with a cheery wave of his hand, a gesture characteristic of him the rest of his life.

Although he was definitely not an honor student, big Johnny Coughlin got along well with his teachers and the other pupils. He liked everybody, and was happy to do things for them. He made friends with towheaded Billy Lorimer, who was to progress to streetcar conductor, then political fixer and grafter, and, finally, United States senator; Joey Friedman, who would later be a saloonkeeper and political aide to Coughlin; and Andy Hoffman, the school's star ballplayer. It was Andy who became to John a symbol of all he himself was not. Andy was lively and quick of speech, and one of the brightest pupils in the school. He had a special ability to get along in the gang. He and big John, who stood a head and a half taller, became close friends, and it was Andy who lured the janitor's helper from his duties, showed him the wonders of the waterfront, took him to theaters and on bicycle trips through Lincoln Park.

This little-man-big-man team was a popular combination in Connelly's Patch. The little fellow did the thinking and planning, the big man lent his presence and took on all comers in combat. Hoffman, indispensable to the team, persuaded his mates in the Phoenix Ball Club, a neighborhood outfit, to permit his cumbersome friend to play with them. After some wrangling young Coughlin was accepted for right field, considered by the club members the least likely spot for action. In addition to that, he batted last. But John was content, and he cheerfully agreed to everything Andy planned for him.

With the members of the Phoenix Club, Johnny Coughlin passed a life of early adolescence in the pattern of the hundreds of other boys who were growing up in the Patch. There were trips to the river docks to watch the windjammers bowl in, laden with lumber, machinery, and bales of goods destined for the wholesale houses on the river's west branch. There were jaunts to Lincoln and Jackson Parks, cross-town journeys to the rapidly developing industrial areas on Goose Island. And sometimes the Phoenix gang went on embarrassed and delicious trips to the environs of the infamous Biler Avenue.

Whenever the Phoenix boys traveled they were certain to have Johnny Coughlin along, for his presence was required as the foundation of a prank favored by Chicago boys in the late seventies. This was brought off when the group boarded a rickety red and yellow horse-drawn car which, despite newspaper shrieks and civic howls, was manned by a single bobtail driver who also served as a conductor. Fares were dropped into a wooden box near the entrance. It was the delight of the Phoenix gang when they went to the baseball fields around Thirty-ninth Street and Wentworth Avenue, to hand several pennies to Big John. These, a fraction of the required five-cent fare, John would hastily deposit in the receptacle and the driver would invariably shout: "Hey, you, not enough!" But he could not very well leave his horse to argue with the ponderous passenger, even if he felt so inclined, and the boys, slapping Johnny's ample back, would yell with laughter. John laughed with them, shouting to the driver: "Th' papers say there oughta be conductors! Whyn't ya put on conductors if ya think we're cheatin'?"

Johnny Coughlin's fun with the gang was limited, for he was a big boy and his parents found plenty of jobs for him to do. Andy

Hoffman went on to graduate with highest honors, but John left the Jones School when he was thirteen years old and in the seventh grade. For two years he was a student in the Christian Brothers' Industrial School at Federal and Van Buren Streets and when he was fifteen his education was decreed at an end and he was ready to go to work.

4

At fifteen John Coughlin looked a young man of twenty. He was nearly six feet tall, with powerfully built shoulders and chest, thick, bull neck, imposing head and jaw, and hard blue eyes. He worked industriously at all sorts of jobs, once holding three at a time: butcher's delivery boy, water boy on a railroad gang and clerk in his father's store. When work was slack he went swimming in the summer with a neighborhood gang led by Billy Lorimer, and one winter when he was eighteen he joined a dramatic club which met in a second-floor hall at Halsted and De Koven Streets. Good-natured, naïve, content with whatever life offered, Johnny Coughlin was known as a boy of few bad habits, few possibilities, and many friends. Until he was nineteen, he was satisfied to work at the plentiful jobs open to one of brawn, and was happy when he could save a little money.

Black-haired Joe, his brother, meanwhile had taken to companionship with race-horse jockeys and touts who frequented the downtown saloons. Considerably sharper than John, Joe also made friends readily, but in addition he made use of them. He got a job at a race track through such friendly connections, and at seventeen, looking twenty-three, he had developed into a proficient race handicapper. Joe showed up at home flush with money and speaking of his prominent friends, and John, stirring with a new ambition, asked his brother if he could get him a job, a real, steady job. Joe was sure that he could.

Favored spots of Joe and his cronies, next to the saloons, were the city's bathhouses. To these emporiums of relaxation and cleanliness came prize fighters and jockeys, race-horse trainers and stew bums, politicians and prominent merchants. In them a man could scrub himself in an ample tin-lined tub, steam in a cabinet, take a quick shower, and get a tingling rubdown with salt or sand. Some of the bathhouses were elaborate affairs, equipped with rooms and cots on which a customer could sleep off a cold or a drunk after an hour in the steam room. Finest bathhouse in Chicago was in the Palmer House where, in addition to the wainscoted baths, was at tiny pool in which the clients could swim. The Palmer House baths were famous throughout the country, and drew the patronage of wealthy and powerful men as well as the sporting gentry. A scouring scrub at the Palmer House following a roaring night in the Levee was considered one of the grandest luxuries the nation afforded, and visiting dignitaries often availed themselves of this delightful, if enervating, experience.

The lesser bathhouses were equipped with concrete floors, makeshift showers, and crude bath cabinets, and some, unable to meet the competition of more favored places, were little more than brothels, where the customers if they so desired could receive the ministrations of female attendants.

Racing and fighting men provided the best clientele for the baths, and it was not difficult for Joe Coughlin and his friends to convince the owner of a bathhouse at 205 Clark Street, in the heart of the First Ward, that the employment of Joe's brother would bring him a healthy business.

Big John got the job, and rushed home elated. "Kid," he shouted to Kate, "I got a real job! I'm a rubber in a Turkish bathhouse. Now ain't that a real job?"

5

In the Clark Street bathhouse, Coughlin first laid the foundations for the career he would follow in the next fifty years and more. He reveled in the racy talk of jockeys and touts and quickly developed a fanatic interest in horses. He spoke fervently of the day when he himself might own a horse and enter it at Washington Park. The politicians who patronized the place also impressed him mightily. Their pompous demeanor, their ready oratory, their dress, their glib talk of election plots, and their easy spending fascinated the young rubber. The patrons liked hearty Coughlin too, for he soon learned the art of laughing uproariously at every joke and greeting each customer as if he were the most important man in town. And in time young Coughlin learned that the most prominent citizen, shucked down to the skin, is much like everyone else.

"I formed my philosophy," The Bath liked to say in later years, when he had learned the meaning of the word, "while watching and studying the types of people who patronized the bathhouses. Priests, ministers, brokers, politicians and gamblers visited there. I watched, and learned never to quarrel, never to feud. I had the best schooling a young feller could have. I met 'em all, big and little, from La Salle Street to Armour Avenue. You could learn from everyone. Ain't much difference between the big man and the little man. One's lucky, that's all."

A year later Coughlin got a job in the Palmer House baths, reaching the status of head rubber in a few months. Here came the big politicians and businessmen, the congressmen and senators traveling through from Washington, and, on rare occasions, a personage as distinguished as Marshall Field. Coughlin was a favorite with these men; he learned their whims and how to please them. They were rich, and tips were good.

Through a friendship thus formed with John Morris, a popular First Ward saloonkeeper and politician, Coughlin was able to open his own place in 1882. Morris supplemented $800 which Coughlin had religiously saved, and the erstwhile rubber purchased a bathhouse at 143 East Madison Street. At the time it seemed to Coughlin that he had attained the ultimate goal of his whole existence. Waving a receipt, he shouted to the Coughlin family, "I'm my own boss! I got my own bathhouse!" The next day he went to St. John's Church on Eighteenth Street and prayed.

Kate lost six pounds hemming dozens of towels for the grand opening.

So successful was this venture that in a few months Coughlin had made enough money to open another bath several blocks west, in the basement of the fashionable, canary-tinted Brevoort Hotel. He was now able to hire a staff of rubbers and attendants, but each morning he appeared promptly at seven o'clock at one of his establishments or the other to greet, with a boisterous jest, those patrons who had slept off all-night jags in the little white cast-iron beds in the locker rooms, or to supervise the service and bustle about, proud and happy in the endless marvel of ownership.

Coughlin was becoming a man of property. He took on more poundage, grew a full mustache and lengthy sideburns, and combed his hair in the high, fashionable pompadour of the time. To his patrons he became known as Bathhouse John and he delighted in the name, just as in his boyhood he felt that his nickname of Dusty John drew him more attention. He set out to get more business. On the walls of his bathhouses and in downtown barbershops he displayed signs reading:

GOOD HEALTH IS PRICELESS
CLEANLINESS GIVES HEALTH
HEALTH IS RICHES—HEALTH IS LIFE
THERE'S HEALTH IN COUGHLIN'S BATHS!

Quite rapidly Coughlin was establishing himself as an aggressive and promising young businessman, with a reputation for honesty. People said of him, "He's not very bright, but once he gives his word you can count on him." He was generous with his earnings, rarely failing to hand a few pennies or more to a beggar on the streets. He liked to accompany such charities with an apt homily. "That man might have been somebody once, might be somebody again," he would say. "It don't pay in this world to think you're better than th' next fellow just because you happen to be on top and he ain't."

His acquaintances among the politicians began to increase. Through Johnny Morris he met Joseph (Chesterfield Joe) Mackin,* the First Ward's dapper Democratic boss, who lived at the Palmer House and often patronized the downtown baths. Mackin liked Coughlin's homely philosophy and enthusiasm for people and urged him to become a member of his organization, the First Ward Democratic Club. Coughlin, pleased at the bid, and awed by Mackin's sartorial splendor—Chesterfield Joe habitually wore a Prince Albert coat, striped trousers, silk hat, and a red carnation—promptly joined and became an ardent Mackin man. He was soon appointed Democratic captain of the precinct in which his newest bathhouse was situated. It was an honor he prized, above all others, to his death.

Coughlin loved the loud talk and noisy friendships of politics. He began to develop his own political tenets, based on the "Live and Let Live" theory of Carter Henry Harrison the Elder, four times mayor of Chicago and Democratic hero of the First Ward. Harrison had large First Ward real-estate holdings and, like many others of his time, regarded prostitution and gambling, two of the most flourishing industries in the ward, as necessary evils.

Eternally a Democrat, Coughlin proved a vigorous precinct captain for Mackin. To voters less fervent than he about Mackin candidates, Coughlin would declaim as he made his pre-election canvasses in his precinct: "A Republican is a man who wants you t' go t' church every Sunday. A Democrat says if a man wants t' have a glass of beer on Sunday, he can have it. Be Democrats, unless you want t' be tied t' a church, a schoolhouse, or a Sunday school."

A man with such powers of political articulation could not long go unnoticed in the ranks of the First Ward Democrats and

---

*Mackin was a former saloon owner who, by giving an oyster with every beer, introduced in Chicago the saloon free lunch. In 1884 he was sentenced to five years in Joliet Penitentiary in connection with the theft of a ballot box of the Second Precinct, Eighteenth Ward from the county clerk's vault. The original ballots had been removed, and forgeries substituted in the interest of the candidacy of Rudolph Brand for state senator. Brand himself helped expose the plot. By that time Mackin had risen to the position of secretary of the Cook County Democratic central committee.

by 1883 at a nod from Mackin Coughlin was put up for his first elective office, the presidency of the First Ward Democratic Club. He was swept in without a murmur of opposition. In this new job it was Coughlin who led the ward cohorts of the Cook County Democratic Marching Club in the heated campaign of 1884. The Bath and his followers, wearing costumes of dark blue trousers, white hats and white woolen fatigue shirts with the letters C.H.H. on their chests, paraded in Chicago's streets shouting for Grover Cleveland for President and Carter H. Harrison for Governor. This first immersion into state and national politics was an exciting experience for young Coughlin. There were fights almost every night in the First Ward as Republican rooters for James G. Blaine, hearkening to the calumny regarding Cleveland's illegitimate child, invaded the precincts in mobs, caroling:

> Ma, Ma, where is Pa?
> He's in the White House. Ha! Ha! Ha!

Indignant Democrats stormed the Republican strongholds, chanting:

> Blaine, Blaine, James G. Blaine,
> Continental liar from the state of Maine!

There were speeches to be made on platforms not only in Chicago but scattered the length of the state. And, touring with the Cook County Marching Club, the handsome Coughlin, now familiarly introduced to all as "Bathhouse John," made an impressive appearance. Coughlin was sorely hurt when Harrison lost to Oglesby, but he found some solace in Cleveland's triumph.

The election over, Coughlin returned to his bathhouses, which continued to prosper. He began to live and dress as befitted a rising politician of the First Ward. He aped the loud checks and raucous colors of the racing crowd, the smooth bowlers and silk hats of the aldermen and gamblers, and added Prince Albert vests, mauve gloves, and tan shoes. Such weird getups attracted considerable attention, which Coughlin innocently attributed to his growing political importance. He began dining in expensive restaurants, at Billy Boyle's where gathered the political and gambler rulers of the city, or at Volegsang's, the Great Northern, or the Sherman House. He rarely drank or gambled, except on the horses, and never made trips to the red-light districts which thrived a brief five minutes' walk from his Brevoort Hotel bathhouse. "I wear good clothes," he told his cronies, "and you can't wear good clothes unless you're clean on th' inside."

Always fascinated by the talk of horses and betting coups, Bathhouse John soon saw his first race. With a ticket given him by his brother, he and a bartender who patronized his bathhouses drove to a running of the American Derby in Washington Park, each June the top social event of the Chicago summer season. The color and excitement of the track stimulated young Coughlin, and he vowed again to own a horse. He visited the track frequently, getting tips from jockey friends of Joe, but betting never more than two dollars on a race. He also handled bets for his friends, who assumed that the brother of one of the best handicappers in the business ought to know where hard-earned money could be placed. Bathhouse John, however, loved racing for its own sake, and in 1885 he withdrew enough savings from the bank to purchase a fine two-year-old. He named her My Queen.

"I'm naming her for Mary," he proudly told his friends.

Mary was Mary Kiley, a sweetheart from childhood whose parents, like Coughlin's, had been among the early settlers in the Patch. The two families had always been friendly, Mary's brothers John and James, owners of a box factory by the river, having been among the first of Coughlin's employers.

It was always assumed by the families that John would wed Mary, for he, in his rare romantic moments, had eyes only for the winsome Kiley girl. But John was shy and slow. On their walks together he delayed all talk of marriage, preferring instead to speak of business, of the political developments, and of the famous men whose hands he had shaken.

Mary listened, and waited patiently. She was proud of John.

He was handsome and strong and kind. He had gone a long way, and he was going farther. Politely she corrected his loose grammar, for she was studying to become a schoolteacher, and applauded his accomplishments. Her hopes rose when he told her about My Queen—it was his most romantic gesture.

It was almost a year later, however, that John Coughlin finally proposed marriage. He and Mary were wed on October 20, 1886, in St. John's Church, beginning a union which was to endure for thirty-five years. There was a wedding party in the Kiley house, and then the Coughlins rented a modest apartment on Michigan Avenue and began domestic life without a honeymoon.

THE AMBITIONS OF
YOUNG BATHHOUSE

I

FOR the next few years Johnny Coughlin, prosperous and possessed of many friends, was seemingly content with his lot. He was a cog in the political machine, delivering his precinct regularly according to the direction of the party chieftains. He was a welcome raconteur in the barrooms, a sprightly figure at the tracks, and when he took his place in the front rank of the Cook County Democratic Marching Club parades the newspapers spoke approvingly of his Sandow-like physique. He spent his money freely on costly suits and frock coats by Meyer Newfield, tailor on La Salle Street who fashioned wardrobes for the sports of the town. He bought marble statuary for Mary to set in the hall of their home, and now and then attended a horse auction to pick a likely yearling. He was treated with respect, and come campaign time the political candidates eagerly sought his acquaintance.

Then young Bathhouse grew ambitious. He yearned to sit in the inner councils of his party, to participate in the plotting and scheming. He dreamed of a new dignity. He had set his goal, he told his friends—his final goal: a seat in the city council chambers as alderman of the First Ward. When he dared express his hopes to Mackin and the other elders of the party he was advised, "We're keeping you in mind, John. You're a comer." He bided his time and offered only mild protest when others were put up as candidates. Four times he was elected president of the First Ward Democratic Club, and like a good party wheel horse he worked hard in each election. He grinned and sweated, visited bars, remembered first names, made more and more friends. "When *you* gonna run fer alderman, John?" they demanded. "We're for ya!"

Coughlin laughed shyly at the tribute, worked harder than ever, and hearkened patiently to the counsel of the party bosses: "Take it easy, Johnny. Your time will come one of these days. You're young."

2

This First Ward that Bathhouse John desired to represent—and slowly he was becoming an expert on its polyglot political population—was the nerve center of a city which at the beginning of the 1890's was still a roaring, overgrown frontier town. Only fifty years before had the pioneers sloshed the mud from the harbors, ditched the Calumet River to reach the port of New Orleans, and strung great ribbons of steel to hitch up a tough new country to the spraddling town on the flats at the south tip of Lake Michigan. In the five decades they had fought pestilence and fire to erect a city which would dominate the whole new West, from the Gulf of Mexico to Canada. They had struggled in the mud, defeated Eastern politicians and bankers who wanted their capital elsewhere, and crumpled frontier-town competitors to make Chicago the terminal of a vast, unbroken empire. They had hauled in limestone and lumber which they shaped into big buildings to supplant the huts of their notorious Slab Town. They had sent out business janizaries to capture the grain and pig trade and chased the great Illinois Central Railroad out of an Indiana terminal into their own front yard. They had built wooden roads, reared elevators, constructed warehouses, knocked together store fronts, and published newspapers and mail-order catalogues. When New York and Boston refused to deal with them, they had gone to Great Britain and Holland for money and they had even hatched a plot to trade with Canada and exclude the United States seaboard entirely until the outmaneuvered East finally came to terms.

They had been too busy fighting and brawling and working to worry much about how the city grew. All they knew or cared was that it was growing: 15,000 one year, 30,000 the next, 45,000 the next. It was going to be a million soon, and too tough and obstreperous for anyone to halt. Into this amazing city had come entrepreneurs, adventurers, carpetbaggers, hairy-chested dock wallopers and construction men, sailors and card sharps, clerks and barkeepers, gunmen and ministers and solid, hard-handed builders who saw in this juncture of lake, canal and railroads an Eden of opportunity and security. Some had failed in their ventures and had continued westward; others stayed and became laborers or millionaires, worked hard for their money or entered politics.

Within the limits of the First Ward itself, one of the thirty-five into which the city was divided, was concentrated the good and the evil, the power and weaknesses of this lush new empire. Its leading economic groups, as noted in the federal census of 1890, were businessmen and vice. In an area bounded by the Chicago River, Lake Michigan, Twelfth and Canal Streets, wealth and a vigorous culture complacently rubbed shoulders with corrupt power and viciousness. Here the leading ministers exhorted their frock-coated congregations in handsome church edifices, while around the corners the barrel-house bartenders advised their patrons. Here were luxurious Michigan Avenue mansions and the hopeless hovels of Clark Street. Near the center of the ward the magnificent Monadnock Building and the new Masonic Temple reared skyward and near by the gin mills, miserable cribs and dime hotels tilted on rickety stilts.

To the southwest was the ward's Little Cheyenne, Biler Avenue and the notorious Levee, habitat of the bums and thugs, thieves and gaudy prostitutes, crowded into a district from Wabash Avenue to the south branch of the Chicago River and south from Adams Street for more than a mile. Little Cheyenne had been named for the town in Wyoming, known as the wickedest in the nation while the Northern Pacific Railroad was being built. (Later when the Wyoming community grew large enough to have a respectable neighborhood of its own, the decent citizens there retaliated by calling its vice district Chicago.) Biler Avenue, locale of some of the fiercest dives in the country, was officially Pacific Avenue but received its more familiar name from the din of Rock Island and Lake Shore railroad boiler shops in the vicinity.

The Levee included not only South State Street but Clark Street and Plymouth Court as well. On these streets were the hop joints, concert saloons and brothels, from the twenty-five-cent bagnios to the more expensive houses operated by Carrie Watson, Mae Clark, Ike Bloom, Freddie Train and others. Off Dearborn Street, in the heart of the city, was Gamblers' Alley and near by, on Randolph Street, from Clark to State Streets, was the infamous Hairtrigger Block, lined with gambling houses of every description. And at Clark and Monroe Streets stood The Store, the extensive establishment of Michael Cassius (King Mike) McDonald, the city's gambling and political boss.

Throughout the ward were endless stretches of lesser saloons and dice and faro houses from which by night issued the pimps, piffers and pickpockets to prey upon citizens and visitors. Dime museums and concert halls, peep shows and bucket shops were interspersed among the newly built wholesale houses and commission offices. To the north and west, along the river, were great shipping wharves on which the lake boats discharged their limestone, coal and lumber, and the grain boats from Europe loaded their bins. Near them were the railroad freight houses and huge red and yellow elevators. To the east, in the center of the ward, were the office buildings and the great department stores, the fine hotels and splendid restaurants and theaters, surrounding a solemn, marble-pillared city hall.

The population of this polyglot district got on well together. The businessmen who lived clear of the ruck, on the fringes of the ward or out of it altogether, cared little how it was governed so long as the price of privilege was not too high. The bums and foreign laboring element were equally unconcerned. It was the saloon men, the keepers of brothels, the gamblers and the numerous denizens of the underworld who took the most practical interest in the ward's politics for they were at the constant mercy of the police and they had to elect, buy and hire politicians to protect them.

3

For years these elements in the First Ward and in any part of the city where gambling thrived had found their protector and overlord in King Mike McDonald. Portly and plug-hatted, McDonald was the Boss Croker of a Chicago Tammany. Reputedly the first to utter, "There's a sucker born every minute," he made splendid use of his matchless axiom. As a youth recently arrived from Ireland he had been a candy butcher on railroad trains, in which job he defrauded purchasers by selling half-filled boxes of sweets, fake prize packages and glass jewelry. After he moved northward from New Orleans in the late 1850's, he engaged in varied gambling enterprises. When the Civil War started, he readily organized an Irish regiment in Chicago, and, although he was its self-styled colonel, he never left the city for the duration of the conflict.

His gambling career was climaxed in 1875 by the opening of The Store, where he not only offered all types of gaming but where he also did business with Chicago's political rulers. He controlled mayors, senators, and congressmen. He purchased a newspaper, the *Globe,* through which he frequently influenced elections. He was treasurer of the Lake Street Elevated Railroad Company to which his gambling associates referred derisively as "Mike's upstairs railroad." King Mike was a man of great wealth, undisputed power and a friend of the perennial mayor, Carter H. Harrison, even if in each of his campaigns Harrison had disavowed any connections with the boss. In the 1880's the party of Jefferson and Jackson in Chicago was popularly referred to as "Mike McDonald's Democrats."

Toward 1890, however, King Mike McDonald, grown rich and careless and preoccupied with unhappy domestic affairs, was beginning to slip. There were those who sought his power, particularly the gamblers Harry (Prince Hal) Varnell, John Condon and George Hankins, whose Garfield Park race track was having trouble with the authorities—difficulties King Mike could not, or would not erase. Prince Hal was an experienced politician himself, and almost as wealthy as King Mike. His gambling house at 119 North Clark Street was a Chicago show place. A four-storied building, equipped at a cost of $80,000, it had Mexican onyx wainscoting on the barroom walls, a floor of Roman mosaic, and a huge bar of genuine mahogany. Neither the saloon nor the gaming rooms upstairs ever closed. Varnell had dabbled in Illinois politics for years, and in 1880 he had served as warden of the Cook County insane asylum. He promptly transformed the place into a country club for politicians, and several of the county commissioners lived there. Parties and dances were held almost every night, and rare foods and wines were served. For this lavish spending of public funds Varnell served a year in Joliet Penitentiary, but upon his release he promptly reassumed his place as a leader among the gambling fraternity.

Varnell, however, was not sufficiently powerful to challenge King Mike openly. He, Condon and Hankins clung to their chief. They agreed to his choices for aldermanic candidates. They even enlisted his aid in financing Garfield Park. But they awaited the day when they might seize his trembling scepter.

Yet McDonald, despite the reports of his growing lack of influence, gave no immediate sign that his political reign was over. Twice he rejected Joe Mackin's suggestion that Bathhouse John Coughlin be put up for alderman, and with the regulars of the Democratic party threw his support to men like Nicholas (Nicky) Cremer, a cigar maker, in 1890, and to Johnny Morris, the saloonkeeper, in 1891.

Neither Cremer nor Morris, especially the former, were proving effectual in the council in behalf of the Varnell-Hankins interests, nor were they particularly pleasing to McDonald. When Nicky failed to stop the determined efforts of the Republican mayor, Hempstead Washburne, to close the Garfield Park track, Prince Hal was prepared to act. He took note of reports that some of the First Ward regulars, led by John Coughlin's school chums, were irked by Cremer's upstage manners and were determined to obtain the nomination for Bathhouse John. This little push, which included Jake Zimmerman, Henry Carroll, Ben Barnett and Freddie Train, the latter a brothel owner who had once worked beside Coughlin in the Palmer House baths, subscribed to the sentiments expressed by Joey Friedman, the saloonkeeper.

"Nicky's no good," Joey told the others. "He thinks he's too smart for us fellas. We're going to look around for someone else. Me, I'm for Johnny Coughlin. He's a good talker, he's got a good reputation, he's president of th' club, an' everybody likes him."

While Friedman sought the approval of the regular party chiefs, and Coughlin's friends did yeoman work for their candidate about the saloons, Varnell decided that the young bathhouse owner would be a good man to back. He knew that Bathhouse John adored horses and horse racing. Here, then, was a likely politician to help him fight to keep Garfield Park track open. Coughlin, Varnell noted, was popular with the saloonkeepers, who made up most of the political working force in Chicago at the time. To become alderman, especially in the First Ward, a man needed the support of the saloonkeepers and this Coughlin seemed to have, notably that of John Linedecker, the First Ward committeeman who owned a popular saloon at Harrison and State Streets.

4

If there was any doubt in Varnell's mind as to the unsuitability of Cremer and the need of an enthusiastic horse fan on his side in the city hall, it was dispelled on December 3, 1891, when the council passed an ordinance directed at Garfield Park, one which would prevent the track from reopening for the spring and summer season. The die was cast. For Varnell it was to be Coughlin and after some earnest talking Prince Hal persuaded Hankins and the others of the race crowd to back his choice. By this time even Mike McDonald was ready to admit Cremer's utter lack of party responsibility—there were rumors that the grand jury was soon to look into boodle matters and that Cremer was one of those who would be scotched. In their gatherings at Billy Boyle's, Varnell and his associates urged and talked until finally such comparatively unenthusiastic ones as Sol van Praag, a former state representative, and Billy (The Clock) Skakel, a Civil War veteran, gambling-house proprietor and bucket-shop operator, decided to help elect Coughlin. Skakel even agreed to contribute $700 to the campaign fund. At the same time Friedman, Carroll, and other cronies of Bathhouse John had organized most of the precincts for Coughlin, and this preparation, plus the approval of McDonald and the support of the Garfield Park gang, was virtual assurance of a victory at the nominating convention.

5

Once it was determined that Coughlin would be the party's candidate in the spring elections, he was accepted more readily into the inner councils of the Democrats who met at luncheon daily in Billy Boyle's chophouse, just off Gamblers' Alley. Here the leaders of the party gathered to exchange political gossip, engineer plans and make and unmake minor party chiefs as they chewed on Billy Boyle's lamb chops and hung beef, and sipped his excellent coffee.

This famed eating place was the favored haunt of King Mike McDonald, who twice weekly ordered Billy's chef to prepare for him huge helpings of salt pork with truffles. He would sit at a corner table, stuffing himself with food, and talking with such men as A. S. Trude, a brilliant criminal lawyer and strategist of the Cook County Democrats; Gray Tom Gallagher, Curt Gunn, Sam Doll, Congressman William (Billy) Mason,* Teddy Frie-

---

*Mason was elected United States senator by the Illinois assembly in 1897.

berger, all of them important in politics, the gambling or saloon businesses; Frieberger was a power in the brothel district.

Boyle's chophouse was severe in its furnishings, the dark wood-work everlastingly wreathed with blue tobacco smoke and the rime of deep-fat cookery. Billy ruled his guests with a heavy hand. He wanted dignified conversation, heavy eating, and no drinking. If he disapproved of a customer, he hauled out his special menu card, à la carte, and presented it to the unwelcome visitor with a snarl. It read: Pigs' feet, an order, $4.30; Ham and eggs, $4.40; Rum omelet, $4.50; Raw oysters, $5.40; French peas, $1.25; Potatoes, $1.10; Coffee, 50 cents. Once when two Negroes entered, Billy handed them the special menu, at which they gazed without flinching. They ordered a full meal, paid a check of $32, and, to Boyle's astonished gurgling, bought two black cigars at $1 each. Then, puffing grandly, they stalked out.

It was in this restaurant that the famous scheme for electing John M. Palmer, the first Democratic United States senator from Illinois since Stephen A. Douglas, had been concocted. For sixty-three days, early in 1890, the 101 Democratic members of the Illinois Assembly, who had been pledged to Palmer at a meeting of their leaders held in Boyle's loft, persistently cast their votes for Palmer, while leaders among their Republican and Farmers' Alliance opponents struggled, took sick, died, and eventually lost their battle. Hero of this affair was Charles (Big Sandy) Walters, a First Ward peanut-stand proprietor, who as Democratic sergeant-at-arms of the House repeatedly saved the day for his party by carrying to the chambers on his back ailing Democrats whose votes were needed.

In Billy Boyle's place Coughlin now strengthened rudimentary acquaintanceships. He grew more friendly with Johnny Condon, another of the triumvirate ruling the Garfield Park gang, and he had long conferences with Hankins, Varnell, van Praag and Skakel. He lunched with Friedman and Freddie Train, and sat and talked occasionally with McDonald, who seemingly had over-come his earlier aversion to the bathhouse owner. Two of Billy

Boyle's habitués eventually became Coughlin's close and valuable friends. One was Trude, who would in future provide useful advice on political strategy, and the other Congressman Mason, earthy and practical.

"Never take anything big," Mason advised young Coughlin. "Stick to the little stuff. It's safer."

At home when Coughlin finally confided to Mary that he was going to sit on the city council, she began industriously to prepare him for the honor. Her daily assaults upon his grammar were intensified. When her husband had finished his usual breakfast of thick slices of ham and a half-dozen fried eggs Mary carefully surveyed him, scraped the traces of yolk from his cravat, or forbade his departure until he had changed his vest.

"John," she'd tell him, "if you're going to be an alderman you must talk and act like one."

Mary was proud of her rising young husband. She slipped out secretly and bought him a gift, a big porcelain spittoon. This she carried to a near-by art school, where she inquired of the director: "Could one of your girls decorate it with some pretty flowers? Some red and blue ones? Mr. Coughlin is very fond of flowers."

6

"You're gettin' th' ax!" was the warning shouted to Cremer by his hirelings as the boom for Coughlin gained momentum. Desperately Cremer attempted to stem the drive. But the meetings of the First Ward Democratic Club had been turned into campaign rallies for John Coughlin, and Cremer was thwarted in every step he took. At one of these meetings, soon after Coughlin's cronies and the Garfield Park crowd had joined forces, Cremer was booed heartily when he tried to make a speech and he left in a huff.

But Nicky was not finished. Realizing that most of the delegates to the forthcoming ward convention could be instructed to vote for Coughlin, Cremer directed his helpers to circulate about the ward buying up as many proxies as possible, exchanging $10 for the signatures of bona fide delegates who would be relieved of the necessity of attending themselves. This was a corporation method new to politics and was destined to fail.

Cremer and his boys came to the convention armed with proxies, which were duly presented to Tom McNally, a Coughlin well-wisher who was chairman of the meeting. McNally twisted the proxies into a compact bundle and shoved them into his pocket.

When the meeting started and the name of the first absent delegate was called, one of Cremer's followers arose and announced, "I represent this man."

"Where are your credentials?" demanded McNally.

"The chair has the credentials, all properly signed. The chair has 'em!" shouted Cremer.

"Th' chair don't know what you are talkin' about," was McNally's bland reply. "Let's get on with th' meetin'."

This was repeated several times and the ensuing rumpus nearly broke up the convention. Cremer and his followers were thrown into the street. They stood outside and howled until the police chased them away. Then the Cremerites, noted a *Tribune* reporter, went off to the Levee where they got drunk and told the bartenders and the prostitutes their troubles.

Inside, the convention proceeded in routine and dignified fashion. The votes were taken, counted, and the result, decided upon weeks earlier, was announced:

Bathhouse John Coughlin would be the Democratic party candidate for the city council.

THE CONTINUOUS CRY OF BOODLE

I

THE lawmaking group into which Bathhouse John craved entry had about it, in 1892, an especially unsavory odor. The city's major legislative unit, the council, had deteriorated as Chicago had grown. Each ward elected its aldermen in alternate years for two-year terms and every twelvemonth, when half the aldermen were up for election, the city usually witnessed an influx into the council of inept burghers who more often than not joined the money-wise incumbents in sharing the copious graft. The ministers scorched the aldermen from their pulpits, the newspapers raved "Boodle! Boodle!" and on each election day called for aldermanic purges, but the councils grew steadily worse.

The opportunities for "tainted money" were limitless. In the First Ward alone in the three decades preceding 1890 the city fathers had disposed of twenty-five per cent of the streets to various railroads. Sixty companies, including department stores, junk shops, foundries, laundries and factories, had taken possession by city ordinance of 175 of the ward's thoroughfares. Eight new streetcar companies and elevated lines had come to the city to organize transportation. Three gas and electric companies had been formed and there were innumerable lesser groups shouting for rights in, under, and over the streets.

Few aldermen took the trouble to deny receiving money for backing ordinances which surrendered exclusive street rights to this railroad or that streetcar line. In the collective council mind these physical properties of the city were the aldermen's own and could be sold as they saw fit. When the public howled "Graft!" the city fathers responded loftily that their votes for various franchises encouraged a flow of capital into the city, greater transportation facilities, more jobs.

The irksome aspect of boodling to the civic-minded was not only that the vicious system corrupted the whole of Chicago politics but that the city gained from the passage of boodle ordinances hardly a cent in compensation. Even the grafting aldermen, receiving as little as $100 or as much as $25,000,* actually were being paid only a small fraction of the real worth of the privileges they were selling. Big business was the beneficiary of this system, for it needed such favors to expand and grow rich. Once having created the system, business had no choice but to deal with the aldermen, and it was happy to do it under prevailing prices.

Boodle technique was simple. A favored method of securing passage of a graft measure was first to see to it that the ordinance was referred to a committee on which sat one or more influential boodlers who were susceptible to at least an occasional bribe. The promoter of the enterprise would send his representatives to these aldermen, who soon would suggest that the company hire one or more lawyers to "explain" the ordinance to the committee. The company then hired a member of the boodle gang's legal battery and paid an immense "fee" which would be apportioned among counsel and the boodlers. Should a rare honest alderman expose the scheme to the public, the company officials would profess to be as shocked as the voters. All they had done, these innocent-eyed gentlemen would protest, was to employ an attorney to straighten out difficulties the aldermen might have in expediting the ordinance. Usually there was a brief civic hullabaloo and the matter would be forgotten.

The small businessmen of Chicago might grumble at the vir-

---

*This latter amount was the price paid to each of four aldermen in 1890, according to exposés of the time, for their support of a measure giving valuable privileges to a railway corporation. Some others who joined them were said to have received $8,000 each. The all-time high, according to Chicago political legend, was the payment of $100,000 and two pieces of property to a high city official who insured passage of a boodle ordinance.

tual extortion practiced by the aldermen, but they paid. They paid for ordinances which would allow them to expand and they paid to smother shakedown ordinances which might harm them. The aldermen, rewarded at a rate of only three dollars a council meeting, owned mammoth houses, country places, racing stables, and when questioned publicly they insisted they were able to maintain these because of "good investments."

There were few in 1892 to dispute C. C. Thompson, of the city Chamber of Commerce, when he moaned: "If you want to get anything out of the council, the quickest way is to pay for it—not to the city, but to the aldermen."

2

There was one man in Chicago who wanted plenty and was willing to pay for it.

He was Charles Tyson Yerkes, emerging rapidly as the czar of midwest traction and the financial boss of municipal Chicago. Yerkes had come to Chicago in 1882 after a flashy rise—resulting in a prison term—in his home town of Philadelphia.

The son of a Philadelphia bank president, Yerkes had started his business career as a clerk and in 1859 had opened a brokerage office. Three years later he started his own banking house and soon became known as a financial genius. In 1868 he gained considerable fame throughout the nation through his operations in municipal bonds, and by 1871 he was recognized as a financial power in Philadelphia. In the panic that year which followed the great fire in Chicago, however, Yerkes was caught short when called upon to deliver money he had received from the sale of some Philadelphia bonds. Tried and convicted of embezzlement, he was sentenced to two years and nine months in prison but was pardoned after serving only seven months.

Yerkes went to Chicago. Supplied with funds by Philadelphia bankers, he invested in Chicago transportation, and soon won control of several traction lines. Early in his Chicago career, he incurred the enmity of Joe Dunlap, publisher of the Chicago *Dispatch,* a paper notorious for its scandalous exposés. Dunlap sent a reporter with a pressroom proof of an article exposing Yerkes as an ex-convict.

"The boss wants you to look this over and see if it's all true," the reporter stated.

Yerkes' sharply etched face went livid. "You're damn right it's true," he snorted. "And you tell that God-damned Dunlap that if he ever publishes a line or tells a soul I'll kill him the first time I see him."

The story was not used.

It was this ruthless, forceful Yerkes who, by devious means, by rich payments to the aldermen, grew to a position of power. When he arrived in Chicago the city's transportation had been in a woeful state. Although Chicago was expanding rapidly, it still depended for the most part on tiny stretches of car lines which served limited neighborhoods. It took almost as long to get from the city limits to the city hall as from Chicago to Milwaukee by steam train.

Borrowing more money from A. B. Widener, the Philadelphia traction king, Yerkes had organized his own traction line, the North Chicago Street Railway, and using the stock of this company as collateral for further loans, had built an empire of subsidiary transportation companies from which, by complex juggling and watering of stocks and bonds, he derived great profits while stockholders invariably were left with ornate stock certificates and little else. A builder as well as a plunderer, he had, in the decade since his arrival, replaced horsecars with cable lines, had added 500 miles of track to the city and applied electricity to some 250 additional miles, and was building Chicago's famous Loop.

Arrogant, contemptuous of the public, Yerkes' theory, simply expressed, was: "Buy old junk, fix it up a little, unload it on the other fellow." Once, when a group of passengers smashed up a streetcar in protest against the poor service, he stopped all cars on the line until the public begged that service be resumed. When a friend suggested that he ought to run more cars on his lines, Yerkes replied, "Why should I? It's the straphangers who pay the dividends."

To expand and maintain his financial realm Yerkes needed special favors from the councils. Whether his mercenaries were Republicans or Democrats mattered little to Yerkes. He cared nothing for a man's political beliefs; all he craved was results. His payments to Republican hirelings were made through William Lorimer, one of Coughlin's boyhood friends, and by now a Republican chieftain popularly called "The Blond Boss."

Yerkes' man in the Democratic ring was John (Johnny de Pow) Powers, the alderman from the Irish-Italian Nineteenth Ward, who doted on funerals and reveled in the title, "Prince of Boodlers."

Of Johnny de Pow, the *Times-Herald* once wrote:

Powers has piloted, either openly or covertly, nearly every boodle ordinance in the city council since the embodiment of the pernicious influence that has dictated municipal legislation for many years. In the Nineteenth, Mr. Powers is not called the Prince of Boodlers. He's called the Chief Mourner. The shadow of sympathetic gloom is always about him. He never jokes; he has forgotten how to smile. He never fails to visit the bedside of the dead, nor to distribute Christmas turkeys to the poor.

Those who know Powers best will tell you that no meaner miser ever rivalled Shylock. The only way he can get votes is by hypocritical posing as a benefactor by filling the role of friend in need when death comes. He has bowed with aldermanic grief at thousands of biers. He is bloodless, personally unattractive. His demeanor is one of timid alertness and anxiety to please, but he is actually autocratic, arrogant, and insolent.

Like Coughlin a former grocery clerk, Powers later opened his own grocery and then went into the saloon business, a sure step toward a political career. In 1888 he was elected alderman and became a follower of Billy Whalen, then boodle boss of the council. Two years later when Whalen was killed in an accident, Powers staged a coup which set him up as Billy's successor. Whalen a few weeks prior to his untimely death had collected some $30,000 to be split with his associates as booty for a freshly passed franchise. The money was in a safe in Whalen's saloon and none but Powers knew this. He immediately purchased the entire furnishings of the saloon at a high price, moved out the safe, and a few days after Whalen's burial each of the aldermen in on the deal was paid his share. This deed established Powers as a "square guy" among his roughneck fellow legislators.

It was Powers who kept the boodlers in line and prevented them from selling out to two or more opposing interests simultaneously. He devised varied boodling refinements, one of them a system of granting a franchise a street block at a time so that the syndicates desiring such measures should ever be at the aldermen's mercy. He also worked out the plan of selling rights to a street not once but many times. If a transportation company, for example, had a horsecar franchise and decided to improve by installing cables, a new franchise became necessary. Similarly, council action was essential to substitute pony engines* for cable, or electricity for pony engines. Further, a company might obtain surface rights to a street at an exorbitant price only to find that the air rights above had been sold to an elevated line and the earth beneath transferred to a gas, electric, or tunnel firm.

· Powers saw to it that Yerkes and his other benefactors received many favors. A favorite adjunct to the regular services was the fixing of personal property assessments which a powerful councilman like Powers, by greasing a palm here and there, could easily manage. Thus in one year, although Yerkes maintained a stable of fine horses and owned jewels and a lavish home containing a Japanese Room, a Yellow Room, an Empire Room, a palm garden, an art collection later sold for $769,200, a private museum and a library, his property for taxation purposes was assessed at only $1,337.

---

*Steam engines, carried aboard the cars experimentally for several years. They were later discarded.

Yerkes' manager, D. H. Louderback, once publicly boasted that his chief controlled the city elections. The reform groups shouted this was so. And Johnny Powers, explaining to his constituents his friendship with Yerkes, once said, "You can't get elected to the council unless Mr. Yerkes says so."

Powers' explanation possibly was more shocking than it was true. For some, like Coughlin, had other backers, and many honest men occasionally became aldermen constituting a minority which was kept in check by Powers. One of these was John H. O'Neill; another, Martin Madden, later a distinguished United States congressman. Sometimes even such aldermen as Madden strayed. "I round up the boys and Madden talks to them," Powers is said to have boasted. But if some of the honest aldermen did find themselves often aligned with the boodlers, it was from necessity rather than conviction or greed. The golden rule of the council was reciprocity. "Either you go along with us," Powers would warn an alderman balking at a particularly heinous ordinance, "or you won't get a can of garbage moved out of your ward till hell freezes over."

3

Even while Bathhouse John was preparing joyfully his campaign to join this assemblage, the newspapers were resuming their annual clamor against the boodlers, concentrating this time on Alderman Edward (Smooth Eddy)* Cullerton, a Powers aide, and his connections with recent ordinances of doubtful civic value.

The newspapers poured vitriol into their descriptions, and even the *Herald,* a Democratic newspaper, expressed its nausea at council affairs stating:

The average Democratic representative in the City council is a tramp, if not worse. He represents or claims to represent a political party having respectable principles and leaders of known good

---

*Another sobriquet of Cullerton's was "Foxy Ed."

character and ability. He comes from 25 or 30 different wards, some of them widely separated, and when he reaches the City hall, whether from the west, the south, or the north division, he is in nine cases out of ten a bummer and a disreputable who can be bought and sold as hogs are bought and sold at the stockyards. Do these vicious vagabonds stand for the decency and intelligence of the Democratic party in Chicago?

The *Inter-Ocean* remarked that in spite of the fact that aldermen drew only three dollars a meeting in pay, a healthy crop of 115 candidates was out to serve the city in the council chambers. The paper observed:

Even if they met every day, the law prevents them from making more than $1,100 a year. Why are so many men eager to become aldermen? Do they wish to serve two masters?

And the *Graphic,* a weekly magazine, complained:

It has been an open secret for many months that the council is controlled by a gang of corruptionists and that municipal franchises are as clearly matters of bargain and sale as goods at a bargain counter. For years the character of the men elected to the Chicago council has been below the average in moral sense and intelligence, but from year to year men of notorious official and political corruption have been reelected as lawmakers for the people. A cleanup is needed.

This familiar cry was echoed by the other newspapers. The sitting aldermen chose to ignore them, but on March 17 the council was jarred from its complacency by the announcement of State's Attorney Joel Longnecker that he was summoning a special grand jury to investigate a whole series of malodorous ordinances passed in the current term.

"We're going after this strong," promised Longnecker. "We'll have strong indictments and forceful prosecution. This will be a big exposé. We want the little fish and the big fish, the little ones first, and then the big ones."

General Herman Lieb, a fiercely bearded Civil War veteran who was named jury foreman, was more concise and forceful. "We have the rascals," he told reporters, "where the hair is short."

Longnecker's move evoked a furor among the reformers and the public was eager for action. They anticipated a genuine cleanup. But the aldermen shrugged and Nicky Cremer, with calm guile, commented, "It's news to me. I don't believe much in this continual cry of boodle. I can't imagine what aldermen they're after."

Details of the grand-jury inquiry, which had been gossiped about for weeks over Billy Boyle's tables, now crept into the newspapers. There were reports of aldermen receiving $200 to $300 every time they voted for minor ordinances of the boodle gang. Some papers told of envelopes passed from utility-company attorneys to various councilmen, of messengers who had left bundles of currency at aldermen's homes.

One after another, the members of the council passed into the hearing rooms, where the grand jurors gathered information on ordinances benefiting such firms as the Economic Gas Company and the Chicago Power Supply and Smoke Abating Company. The Chicago Power Supply and Smoke Abating Company measure, termed the "Cyclone" ordinance, was, according to the *Inter-Ocean,* "the most nefarious deal and most infamous ordinance ever passed by the council." It allowed the CPS, as the papers called the company, to lay pipes in every street, alley, or public place for the purpose of supplying compressed air to homes. Although company officials insisted that compressed air was a wonderful source of power and would help to eliminate the smoke menace, the newspapers called it a complete robbery.

From those who voted for the Cyclone ordinance, a unique explanation was offered to the public by Alderman John Dorman. The alderman, recalling his early days as a struggling butcher, noted: "Why, compressed air would be great. Every man can be his own sausage maker. When the CPS has its pipes laid all over the city, all the housewife will have to do is turn on compressed air, drop a piece of meat in the slot, and breakfast sausages will be ground out while she waits."

Such an explanation evidently failed to convince the grand jury of the worth of this Utopian ordinance, and on March 21 that body handed down an omnibus indictment charging Alderman Dorman and six others with conspiracy to commit bribery. Nicky Cremer, despite his seeming ignorance of what all the shouting was about, was one of those indicted. There was a great scurrying by professional bondsmen to furnish bail for the unfortunates and Mike McDonald, as one last gesture, sent one of his croupiers to secure Cremer's release on bond.

Although the grand jury labored on to name two minor city-hall characters as go-betweens in the bribery, public interest now focused on the aldermanic election itself. Only a few of the boodling leaders, all of them unscathed by the inquiry, were up for re-election—Cullerton, Charles (Broad) McAbee and one or two others. Against them the newspapers hurled their broadsides.

The notorious First Ward was almost ignored in the city-wide fray. Such newspapers as did comment sporadically with brief items on the campaign in the First summarily rejected the bid of Bathhouse John Coughlin for public office and urged the election of Dr. Albert E. Ebert, who had owned a drugstore at Polk and Clark for forty years. Dr. Ebert, a gaunt, venerable pharmacist with a long braided beard, was the nominee of the Independent Republicans, a candidate whose political experience had been limited to casting his ballot on election days, but whose reputation was beyond suspect. A vote for Lester Hills, the regular Republican, or William Pomeroy, the Labor party champion, the newspapers warned, would merely be a vote for Coughlin.

The papers simply would not take Bathhouse John's political effort seriously. From the august *Tribune* to *Mixed Drinks: The Saloon Keepers' Journal,* they predicted his defeat.

"Bathhouse John Coughlin cannot fire the popular heart in the First Ward," intoned the *Tribune.* "The voters are for Ebert."

The *Mail,* dealing Bathhouse the additional indignity of a misspelled name, claimed that Ebert had an excellent chance to win, and noted, with considerable insight, "Coughlin has the sporting and saloon circles behind him and among this element there is a belief that Bathhouse John would use his vote and influence so as not to interfere with the gamblers."

Mixed Drinks even printed a handsome picture of Dr. Ebert atop a commendatory biography, and the *Journal* remarked succinctly: "Coughlin, the Democratic candidate, is in every way unfit."

4

On April 5, election day, voting in the First Ward was "exceptionally light," according to the *Tribune*. It soon became evident, however, that a busy little organization was hard at work in the First, rounding up voters to cast their ballots for the hefty young man who would not turn the city council into a Sunday school. By afternoon the evening papers reluctantly admitted that Coughlin was likely to win, although they did not expect him to equal the record plurality established by Cremer in 1890. When the polls closed, however, Bathhouse John had been carried into office with 1,603 votes, a plurality of 768 over his adversaries, and a new record. Hills was second, and Dr. Ebert trailed a bad third.

The newspapers found cause to exult over the trend of the election. Cullerton, despite his boasts, last-minute threats and an offer of $10,000 to his foe, Fred Rhode, a saloonkeeper, to withdraw, was beaten. He stormed about the ward, threatening to sue. McAbee, also defeated, went wild and roamed the Twenty-fourth Ward with his brother, threatening to fight anyone who had voted against him. James A. Quinn, a hat-store owner, accepted the challenge, and his skull was fractured by the brothers McAbee. Billy O'Brien was retired from the service, despite the influence of his partner, Johnny de Pow. Altogether, the newspapers concluded that it was an improved council and a triumph for the good citizens.

A PINCH AND AN OUTRAGE

I

INTO the egg-shaped council chamber of the city hall, some thirteen nights after the election, strode the newly elected aldermen, the incumbents, and a throng of special guests. Among them Bathhouse John, the new alderman from the First Ward, stood splendidly forth. In the days following his election Coughlin had spent a great deal of his time at Newfield's. Bathhouse had his ideas of how an alderman ought to dress, and Meyer Newfield was ingenious in his own right. Between them they evolved a debut outfit.

For his first appearance in the council chamber Coughlin had donned a coat of delicate gray with trousers to match. His waistcoat was a darkish green, checked with white, his racing colors. His shoes were a bright tan and he wore a shirt of brown silk. The ends of his waxed mustache jutted out like those of a grand vizier, and his closely cropped hair thrust stiffly up like that of a Prussian general. Altogether, towering above his colleagues, Bathhouse John was a striking and a prepossessing figure. He swept the sweat from his forehead as the eyes of the spectators focused upon him, then drew a large silk handkerchief and daubed delicately at his cheeks and chin.

Along the aisle to his desk he lumbered, gave Aldermen Johnny Morris a friendly clump across the back of the neck, and dropped beside him into his seat. The packed galleries, awed to silence for a moment, craned for a better view. "Then," reported the newspapers, "there was a good-natured merry cheer for Bathhouse John."

The evening's business was swift and curt. A brief and dull

message from the mayor, some routine ward affairs, and then the naming of committees, whose composition had been determined in advance. Coughlin found himself placed on two—the committee on railroads, wharves and public grounds, and the one dealing with problems and administration of the Bridewell, the city jail. The first of these was a good post for anyone with boodling inclinations—or was there to be no graft now that the "venal elements" had been purged?—and his place on the Bridewell committee could be valuable too, for from that vantage point an alderman could facilitate the speedy release of any faithful constituent who might have been luckless enough to draw down a jail sentence.

2

During his first two weeks in the council Coughlin was content to sit quietly, listening to the veterans, watching Powers and Tommy Gahan, one of the Democratic sages, as they deftly lined up votes for this or that minor ordinance. As was customary in the beginning weeks of a new term, there was no attempt to introduce unsavory ordinances, but Powers was keeping his eye out for likely recruits to fill the places of those whose careers had been cut short by the recent grand-jury action. The Longnecker inquiry had expired conveniently, the indictments against the grafting aldermen had lingered and died, and Powers well knew that the public would soon forget about the "little fish" snared in the grand jury's net. He could then make firm once more the lines which had been shattered by the election. The various interests would stand ready as usual to empty their moneybags into the aldermanic palms.

Coughlin shied away from Powers. He intended to have his own independent place in the city's lawmaking. His first chance to offer legislation came about during his third week in the council. Mayor Washburne had been informed that many women of uncertain repute had been ministering to male patrons in the cheaper bathhouses and massage parlors, and he instructed Corporation Counsel Miller to prepare an ordinance which would "cope strenuously with this distressing situation."

Such an ordinance, barring women of spotless character or otherwise from employment in these establishments, was duly drawn and Coughlin, as the council's foremost representative in bathhouse enterprise, was chosen by the mayor to introduce the measure. This, after a guiding word or two from Gahan, Bathhouse John did quite handily and he beamed with satisfaction as the ordinance was passed without a dissenting vote.

There was little else for Coughlin, nor indeed any other alderman, to do in those spring and early summer months, for Chicago was in feverish preparation for the forthcoming Columbian Exposition. While Bathhouse John occupied himself in obtaining a permit for Prince Hal Varnell to open a string of bucket shops—an action that won him the everlasting enmity of Billy Skakel, who previously had held a monopoly in this field—Chicago spruced up for the expected influx of World's Fair visitors. The council defeated Alderman Madden's proposal to limit the number of saloons in the residential district, and let it be known that Chicago would be a wide-open town in 1893. General N. A. Miles started a shuttle bicycle race to New York to advertise the exposition. The South Side "Alley L" put a new twenty-eight-ton locomotive on its tracks and announced the dawn of a new era in public transportation. New downtown buildings were erected. Frank Parmelee, first in the city to operate busses, added seventeen coaches to his fleet to celebrate his fortieth year in business. Committees of all sorts were being named, sites on the south-side midway were being cleared for the marble-white buildings of the great fair, the saloons and brothels were preparing for the expected glut of trade. Only the nomination of Judge John Peter Altgeld as Democratic gubernatorial candidate to oppose the current governor, Joseph (Private Joe) Fifer, and the national Democratic convention in June, succeeded in diverting some of the public's attention from the pre-exposition excitement.

For the first event 150 picked members of the Cook County Democratic Marching Club, led by Jimmy Farrell, stuffed themselves into a railroad special and went off to Springfield. There—with Mike McDonald and Sol van Praag and Johnny McGillen, chairman of the Cook County Democratic Central Committee, whooping it up for the bearded judge—Altgeld was named on the first ballot.

In Chicago, meanwhile, the final touches were being applied to the specially built $35,000 Wigwam on Michigan Avenue, off Washington Boulevard, in which an expected 15,000 delegates and spectators would gather to name a candidate for the coming Presidential election. Somehow the contractor building the Wigwam made an error, and when the rambling structure was completed it was found to contain 19,500 seats, 4,500 more than had been ordered by the national Democratic chiefs.

Immediately a frantic hubbub about the disposition of the extra tickets developed. The Chicago Democrats had been allotted 3,000 tickets, and the outside delegations feared, quite logically, that the local politicians would attempt to keep the extra tickets for themselves and cram loud-voiced rooters into the added section to cheer for Grover Cleveland, who had supplanted Senator John M. Palmer as the favorite of the Illinois delegates.

The loudest protests came from Boss Richard Croker, who, heading a proud and potent New York Tammany crowd, hoped to snare the nomination for his choice, Senator David N. Hill. He complained to the national committee of the obvious coup planned by the Chicago bosses, and the strict order went out that the 4,500 tickets for the extra section would be distributed proportionately among the states. But Illinois Democracy, gracious hospitality notwithstanding, was determined to support its man with as much vocal power as possible, and the word was issued to the Chicago leaders to thwart Croker's plan.

To Bathhouse John Coughlin was assigned the task of helping to gain this objective. He promised complete success and promptly selected as doormen and ushers for the new section a corps of the most formidable of First Ward precinct captains, led by Big Sandy Walters who weighed 275 pounds and was known throughout the city for his physical prowess. Walters on each day of the convention stationed himself and his squads, with Johnny O'Brien and Jack Brown, two political toughs acting as lieutenants, before the entrance to the special section. There they yelped: "This way to Secshun C, gents, this way!"

Those who held tickets for Section C, but who possessed no special penciled notes from Bathhouse John, or those whom Walters and his aides did not recognize as loyal constituents of Coughlin, were refused entrance and hustled to other gates. There they were shunted back to Section C, where their efforts to enter again were defeated. Each day these thwarted citizens, many of whom had come miles to the convention, ranged themselves on the sidewalks outside Section C and shouted insults at Walters. He was unruffled, however, and quietly requested the police to chase the "troublemakers" away. "They're good fellows," Walters told the policemen, "but the alderman don't want them in there."

The galleries, thus packed with Cleveland adherents, shouted for their favorite so lustily that after Cleveland had been nominated for the Presidency and General Adlai E. Stevenson of Illinois for Vice President, several newspapers about the country deplored the "mob methods" at the convention and speculated on the possibility of barring spectators at future conventions.

3

This triumph at the convention brought Bathhouse John to the attention of loyal Democrats throughout Illinois, but his sudden glory was dimmed by trouble developing within the city. Former Mayor Carter Harrison, long a friend of King Mike McDonald, lashed out suddenly in his *Times* against Chicago racing interests generally and King Mike in particular, and Republican Mayor Washburne, not to be outdone, served notice that he intended to close the Garfield Park race track. This of course would prove a direct assault on Alderman Coughlin, who had entered the council especially to protect the Garfield Park interests.

Day after day, Harrison's *Times* railed against the track and especially against McDonald. "Mike McDonald," read a typical editorial, "is an unscrupulous, disreputable, vicious gambler, a disgrace and menace to the city. He should be driven from the city and the race tracks closed forever."

Simultaneously, Mayor Washburne stepped up his campaign against Coughlin's backers. At the council meeting of July 18, Alderman John Cooke, an administration spokesman, rose to present an ordinance to enforce the closing of the tracks in the west division of Chicago—specifically the Garfield Park track.

"This is a residential district," he declared, "and the residents complain that the betting pools cause disreputable men and women to loiter in the neighborhood. I want to see that no further license is issued to Garfield Park."

Coughlin was the first to clamber to his feet.

"You can't do that!" he yelled. "You can't do that! You can't shut up a man's property. You can't do it. It's unfair. It's . . . it's . . . un-American, that's what! Why, gentlemen, think of the money racing brings to Chicago, the millions of dollars. You can't get an order like this through the council and I tell you, Mr. Maar, I'm going to vote against it and I know every man here will do the same!"

In the ensuing vote, Cooke's proposal to close the track and make permanent the anti-Garfield Park ordinance was referred to the council judiciary committee, which a week later reported that such an ordinance would be unfair to the owners of Garfield Park track and suggested that other tracks be included.

Gleefully Harry Varnell bustled into the city collector's office and applied for a ninety-day license, but he was denied any consideration. Refused this permit, the Garfield Park crowd sued to compel the city to issue the license, but Judge James Horton, with a blistering denunciation of all race-horse betting, and especially that at the west-side track, turned down the plea.

This created a stalemate, and, although Johnny Condon insisted to reporters that the track would continue to operate, no races were run that week. At Hawthorne, however, the turnstiles clicked merrily and Varnell fumed that the entire drive against the Garfield Park track had been forced on the city by Ed Corrigan, the affluent Hawthorne owner. Coughlin huffed and puffed and charged that Carter Harrison was behind the drive, but he was at a loss to know how to help in the council.

But Johnny Powers was not. Near the end of July he told the council sweetly, "It's very plain what the mayor wants. He wants the tracks regulated, and I'm for that. Therefore I'm going to offer a new ordinance to the effect that a track cannot run unless it pays to the city clerk a license fee of fifty dollars a day."

"Make it a hundred a day!" shouted Alderman O'Neill, completely taken in by the Powers ruse.

"You vote for it and we'll make it a hundred!" countered Powers. O'Neill nodded; so did most of the other more honest aldermen and the ordinance supplementing Cooke's was passed. All this moved entirely too fast for Bathhouse John to comprehend but he obeyed the edict from Varnell: "Keep your mouth shut and vote for the ordinance."

On the afternoon of the following day, even Coughlin could see the significance of the temporary coup scored by Powers. For King Mike himself hurried to the city hall, $3,000 for a thirty-day license clutched in his hand. Had McDonald been able to get a permit, the Powers move might indeed have been a great victory, but Washburne, detecting the intent behind the Powers proposal, had vetoed the entire ordinance several hours after its passage. So, City Clerk Ambley informed McDonald of the mayor's action and refused a license.

Despite this brief setback, Powers had acted with foresight. In the same meeting at which he proffered his ordinance the council had voted to adjourn for the summer, thus suspending any further aldermanic deliberation on the measure. Varnell, Hankins, and Condon, certain that the mayor would make no effort to act before the council reconvened later in the summer, reopened the race track and soon the announcements were appearing in the newspapers:

RACING TODAY!
RAIN OR SHINE!

4

Coughlin had failed his backers, but none of them at the moment seemed to realize it. Racing at Garfield Park got under way with a flourish, and huge crowds jammed the enclosure, wagering freely. As befitting a man supposedly representing the track in the city council, Bathhouse John had his own box, and he daily brought his cronies to the meeting. They were a jolly crowd, free with money, loud in their conversation, resplendent in their "brown dicers," checked suits and gleaming tan shoes with fawn-colored spats. Bathhouse was gayest of all. His rugged form was pinched into a bright powdery-gray frock coat, tailored exactly to his sturdy torso, and whipping with a grand flourish just above the knees of his checkered pants. His thick neck was lashed with a silken cravat of dazzling purple, from which gleamed in surpassing radiance a huge diamond horseshoe. Over his shoulder hung a pair of German-made glasses, contained in a case of tooled leather. The Bath was noisily full of facts and figures on the racing business, for he himself was a sportsman and owner of a promising stable. He had just overpaid for a pair of yearlings—Jay-Jay-Cee and Jake Zimmerman, the latter named for one of his political henchmen—which he stabled outside the Garfield Park course. Life seemed good to Bathhouse John once more; the sun was warming, the races thrilling, his backers were happy and prosperous, and the fact that his horses rarely won did not discourage him.

This bubble burst suddenly on the afternoon of September 2. The last race at the track was not more than a minute over when two patrol wagons rattled through the main gates and a score of policemen, clubs swinging, piled out. Bathhouse John was standing near the judges' box, engaged in earnest conversation with an official, when the raiders swooped down. The Bath loosed a bellow of wrath, leaped upon a step of the box, and howled to the thousands leaving the stands: "It's a pinch! It's an outrage! It's constitutional!"*

It was indeed a pinch. Inspector Lyman Lewis, in charge of a hundred policemen who had completely surrounded the enclosure, ordered the nine Pinkerton guards hired by Varnell removed from the gates and into the wagons. The thirteen jockeys were allowed to weigh in so that the last race would be legal, and then they too were piled into patrol wagons and carted away to the Desplaines Street station. The bettors were ordered to leave the track. The furious alderman and his friends were not molested.

Coughlin and Varnell scurried to the station, where they spent the rest of the afternoon and evening furnishing bonds for the prisoners.

"Ed Corrigan did this!" cried Bathhouse. "He's in with the mayor. An' he's in with Harrison. That Harrison owns part of Hawthorne. That's why we was raided."

Varnell was equally indignant. "This is against the law," he told Inspector Lewis. "Tomorrow we'll run those races just the same."

"We'll stop you at all hazards," retorted Inspector Lewis.

The police department meant business. On the following day, with 8,000 persons in the stands, Inspector Lewis and 150 patrolmen appeared just as the races were scheduled to start. They rolled down the smooth track to the starter's stand and there they remained for the next three hours. Ben Fly, the jolly little track manager, was the only calm one as he directed the track band to play over and over, "Ta Ra Ra Boom de Ay." Coughlin, Varnell, Hankins and Sid McHie conferred desperately to find a way out of this unhappy situation.

Finally Hankins angrily yanked the starter's bell and the police

---

*Coughlin later explained he meant "unconstitutional."

went to work. They threw Hankins himself into a wagon, then seized as many track employees as were within reach. They ignored Coughlin, however, who fumed about them and dared anyone to put him under arrest. Even Varnell was dragged to a wagon when he attempted to battle a policeman who was smashing a railing. "You may arrest me peaceably," shouted struggling Prince Hal, "but I don't propose to see you destroy property. There is a limit to one's endurance."

King Mike McDonald, who had himself come out to witness the excitement promised by the morning newspapers, was appalled by the activity of the police. In spite of a recent distaste for the Garfield Park crowd, he leaped on a chair in the box, purpling with rage, and yelled curses at Chief of Police R. W. McLaughry: "He's an interloper, a crook. You can't give the people a break under the Republicans. Vote Democrat! Vote Democrat! It's that rotten Ed Corrigan. He's got the mayor and the chief fixed!" After this outburst McDonald was cheered and hoisted to the shoulders of admirers and carried to his brougham.

The racing fraternity and the politicians, the gamblers and even a good number of the ordinary citizenry talked about little else on the Sabbath but the situation at Garfield Park. The newspapers, unanimous in their dislike of the west-side track, upheld Chief McLaughry, who insisted that he was only acting on the petition of west-side businessmen and church leaders who wanted their neighborhood rid of the evils that had consistently accompanied racing at Garfield. To all he denied that there was any other objective in mind, either to accommodate Ed Corrigan or to institute a general campaign against race-horse betting.

"We know better," railed McDonald, thoroughly fearing that the police might establish an unwholesome precedent. "We know Corrigan is in good with McLaughry and there'll come a day when we can prove it."

Alderman Coughlin went about repeating this charge, and, being so advised by Varnell and Hankins, announced that there would be racing on Monday. "Entries are being received for tomorrow," he said, "and, if there is any law in the land, and I think there is, there will be racing on that day!"

On Monday the track swarmed with horse fans. The Pinkerton men closed and bolted the gates as soon as the crowd was in and the first two races were run off without mishap. Then at three o'clock, five wagonloads of police stormed up to the locked gates.

"Break 'em down!" shouted Inspector Lewis. "Everybody in the park is under arrest."

Hankins and Varnell were grabbed at once. Hapless jockeys again were dumped into the wagons, and as many patrons as could be rounded up, about 800 in all, were held prisoner by a cordon of police. Most of these were sent home, but about 125 who stopped to argue were hustled off to jail.

From his box, where he was entertaining his father, Alderman Coughlin shouted insults at the raiders. The policemen balked at laying hands on Bathhouse himself, but they seized Michael Coughlin and threw him in with the others. The alderman was in a frenzy.

All that night Coughlin, with money supplied by Al Hoffman, a brewer, stomped about the Harrison Street police station, where most First Ward prisoners had been taken because of the overflow at Desplaines, bailing out those arrested. In all his anger he did not forget to shake the hand of each prisoner released, saying: "I'm Alderman Coughlin. It's a shame you got pinched!"

The raid, one of the biggest in the history of the Chicago police department up to that time, still failed to stop the track operators. On the following day Garfield Park was open again, with fewer than 1,500 spectators in the stands. One of these was James (Sheriff Jim) Brown, a horseman who, during his term as sheriff of Lee County, Texas, had killed a dozen men. Just before the races started Brown left his friends in the stands and climbed to the roof of a barn where he kept his horses. There he took his stand, twirling a big .44 caliber revolver and yelling: "By God, these police ain't goin' to stop these races no more!"

When, shortly after three o'clock, the police again swarmed

through the entrances, Brown leaped up and down on the roof, howling threats.

"Come down here!" called a policeman. "We want you."

"You got no warrant, you sons-a-bitches!" replied Brown.

Several policemen fired shots into the air. Brown leaped to the track and ran toward an entrance. Six policemen went after him. Halfway down the track Policeman John Powell caught him, but Brown squirmed free, turned, and shot Powell through the head. The ex-sheriff ran on for two blocks beyond the track, pursued by other policemen. Around a corner, Brown crashed into Officer William Jones. He pulled the trigger, but his gun failed to fire. Jones shot twice, killing Brown instantly. In his pockets police found extra bullets and $7,420 in cash. On the handle of his gun were twelve notches.

5

The police gunplay and the murder of Powell aroused a barrage of public fury. Businessmen, women's clubs, ministers, and newspapers called for a final shutdown of Garfield Park track. "The fringe of Garfield Park is a disgrace to civilized mankind," preached the Reverend D. F. Fox, a leading minister. "I know of nothing so ghastly, so degrading, so criminal. Why should Chicago endure such a curse?"

At the moment neither Chief McLaughry nor Mayor Washburne were able to offer an adequate answer. Both had become enmeshed in the investigation which followed the deaths of Brown and Policeman Powell.

At the inquest before Police Magistrate Jarvis Blume, Washburne testified that during the early summer, before the agitation against Garfield Park had begun, Chief McLaughry had reported to him that Ed Corrigan and Jimmy Burke, Corrigan's secretary, had offered to pay $50,000 to the Republican campaign chest if the Garfield Park track should be closed.

"I told McLaughry," the mayor said, "that even if we should need the money very badly we certainly would not take it from any source such as that and that under no circumstances would we entertain any such proposition."

McLaughry, Corrigan and Burke immediately denied that any such incident had occurred. "Why, I'm a good Democrat!" protested Burke. "What would I be doin', givin' dough to th' Republicans?"

The uproar continued, loud and sharp. Hourly the rumors spread that Washburne, angry at being called a liar, would ask for McLaughry's resignation, but the chief, backed by reputable businessmen, remained at his post. The newspapers overlooked the Washburne statement and urged the mayor and McLaughry to continue to work together for the downfall of the track. Jubilant Democrats launched an inquiry into McLaughry's background, but the only taint of scandal they found involved his use of convict labor to build his house when he was warden of Joliet Penitentiary some years earlier.

The council reconvened, and the battle against Garfield Park moved to the city-hall chambers. On September 12 the aldermen met to consider Washburne's veto of the licensing ordinance. The Garfield Park supporters made a last effort to save the track. To test their strength before a vote on the veto was taken, Alderman Henry Ellert offered a resolution praising Sheriff Brown as a brave man and demanding an investigation of the police, Mayor Washburne and Chief McLaughry. Coughlin rose for one last try.

"I am very much in favor of this resolution," he said, "and I am in favor of the police guarding Chicago in a proper way. We want them to guard the burglars—I mean, we want them to guard us from the burglars. Jim Brown was a good man and I don't think he meant to shoot those policemen. This thing that happened the other day is a—a—a onslaught on a perfectly law-abiding amusement. This thing that happened was one of the worst outrages ever preepeetrated on a community. My father, my own father, got hurt and he's still sick!"

But the council, for once cognizant of the public's anger, rejected the resolution and called for consideration of Mayor Washburne's veto. Coughlin was loyal to his backers almost to the very end. He voted with twenty-one other aldermen to delay consideration of the veto. The motion lost. He voted with six other aldermen for reconsideration of the entire measure, which would have nullified the veto, but again the motion was lost, this time 59 to 7. When both these efforts had failed, there was a third vote on whether to uphold the mayor's action. The veto was approved, 60 to 3, and Coughlin was not among the three still steadfast to Garfield.

"The reign is ended!" sang the newspaper headlines. "This really winds up Garfield Park," lamented the racing fans. Varnell and the brothers Hankins filed $100,000 damage suits against Mayor Washburne and Chief McLaughry, but the gates of Garfield Park stayed locked. The mayor and his chief of police shook hands and forgot they had called each other liars. Mike McDonald shrugged and started mending his fences with Carter Harrison. Ed Corrigan piled up profits in his strongbox in the Wellington Hotel and announced that he would keep Hawthorne track open through the winter. John Condon and Paddy Ryan kept busy denying they had anything to do with a new track opening in Roby, Indiana, in November.

The spirits of Bathhouse John were low. The defeat of the Garfield Park crowd threatened to drive him from politics. His best source of financial support was gone. Only five months after that glorious first night in the council Alderman Coughlin appeared certainly on the way out. He blamed his troubles upon Washburne, McLaughry, Harrison and even Johnny Powers.

"Johnny started this with that ordinance of his about a hundred bucks a day," he lamented. "I knew it was no good, and I wanted to say so, but they wouldn't let me."

Coughlin brooded and vowed vengeance. His opportunity was not long in coming, for a boom for Carter Harrison as World's Fair mayor was under way. Bathhouse John, despite his approval of the Harrison "Live and Let Live" philosophy, determined to cast his fortunes with the anti-Harrison forces.

TIN HORN MIKE
AND HIS ORNERY LIKE

I

CHICAGO during the closing months of 1892 was in excited preparation for its celebration of the four-hundredth anniversary of the discovery of America by Christopher Columbus. On the south side the sandy tracts along the lake shore were being transformed into a city of magic. Splendid white palaces, lovely lagoons, wide avenues of trees, a magnificent Court of Honor with a gigantic figure of The Republic at its head, were built with unbelievable wizardry near the mud flats where Professor William Rainey Harper was industriously constructing his University of Chicago. The attention of the world had been focused upon the noisy, overgrown frontier town in mid-United States, and visitors, more than had first streaked to the Philadelphia Exposition in 1876 or even to Paris in 1889, were preparing to pour into Chicago to ogle this fantastic White City within a city and to determine for themselves whether Chicago was really as wicked, as blowsy, and as tempestuous as world repute had it. The natives, stripping themselves of money and energy to make the World's Columbian Exposition the greatest extravaganza in all history, put out their chests and shone with pride as they read the newspaper accounts of the international interest they were exciting.

Against such a background, Carter Henry Harrison frankly asserted his right to be mayor of the city in its greatest hour. He submerged all other political considerations in his zeal to regain the job he had once forsaken forever. In his *Times* daily editorials urged his nomination by the Democratic party and frequent stories chronicled the earnest pleas by citizens' groups that "Our Carter" be again the party candidate. What if Harrison had bolted the party in 1891 to run against Washburne? He was ready, claimed the editorials, to resume his strong place at the head of the party and to make Chicago the proverbial city second to none. Who, demanded the Harrison adherents, was better fitted than Carter Henry Harrison, both by breeding and experience, and even tradition, to be World's Fair mayor?

The Republican journals, sparked by the *Tribune,* might sneer at Harrison's aspirations, but his backers were zealous, active and numerous. With the approach of 1893 there was a strong "Harrison for Mayor" drive throughout the city. Everywhere sprang up Carter H. Harrison Associations, supposedly of non-partisan origin. The Democrats themselves divided sharply into two camps, the Harrisonites, and those who would find anyone else more acceptable. In the First Ward Bathhouse John Coughlin would have no portion of the Harrison boom. Billy Skakel seized the opportunity. He organized some 100 political sluggers and saloonkeepers into the Carter H. Harrison Club of the First Ward. In the Briggs House staunch Harrison supporters conferred with certain of the party leaders—Johnny Powers, fat Stanley Kunz, Martin (Irons) Butler, and roly-poly, scheming Robert E. Burke. Coughlin, still smoldering over the defeat of the Garfield Park gang, remained aloof. With John Patrick Hopkins, a smart young lawyer, and Tom McNally, he deserted the faction known as the regular Democrats, and took up the standard of Washington Hesing, the fiery young German who was editor of the *Staats-Zeitung.* Hopkins became Hesing's campaign manager, rejecting an offer of an appointment as commissioner of public works if he would join the Harrisonites. Bathhouse likewise refused a lucrative city-hall job, disregarded the threats of the party regulars, and openly pledged to the German editor the votes of the First Ward.

The Democratic schism spread wide, until even the ordinarily cohesive Cook County Marching Club was embroiled in the fight. When Captain Jimmy Farrell, grizzled, energetic marshal of the club, proclaimed his loyalty to Harrison, half the members refused to travel with him to Washington for the inauguration of President Cleveland unless he retracted. All the newspapers except the *Times* scoffed at Harrison's chances, the *Tribune* and the *News* labeling him "the playfellow of the Corrigan racing crowd who will permit gambling, wide-open saloons, and keep visitors away from the Columbian Exposition." Harrison's *Times,* substituting Hesing's name for that of Mike McDonald, assailed the gambling element, and charged that the editor of the *Staats-Zeitung* was "the candidate of the Garfield Park gang and the management of their race track."

Of former mayor Dewitt Cregier, the only other Democrat under consideration, the newspapers wrote little. The real contest, they agreed, would be between Harrison and Hesing.

2

"It'll be our Carter Harrison on the first ballot, boy!" predicted Alderman Powers on the afternoon of February 28 as some 2,000 delegates and spectators surged into Central Music Hall for the Democrats' mayoralty nominating convention. His confidence was based on the party primary of the previous day, in which the Harrison forces appeared successful. There had been innumerable fights—Billy Skakel and Big Sandy Walters had staged a vicious battle amid the crowds on State Street—and there was likely to be a stiff tussle on delegates' credentials. Still, Powers thought it was "in the feed bag."

Despite the prospective Harrison triumph, Alderman Coughlin and his fifteen First Ward delegates, including McNally, Walters, and Jake Zimmerman, marched bravely in to their front-row seats prepared to battle to the end for Hesing. They were cheered by delegates from the German wards, who sang German songs and hissed every mention of Harrison.

For an hour after the convention was called to order, the Harrison delegates kept up such a clamor for their candidate that the proceedings could not begin. It was obvious that the convention was for "Our Carter," but Hesing insisted on having an opportunity to speak. Three times he was shouted down, but on a fourth attempt he pushed A. W. Green, the chairman, away from the speakers' platform, and out-yelled his foes.

"I wish," Hesing called out, "before these Democrats here assembled, to announce my allegiance to the Democratic party and to Democratic principles . . ."

Bathhouse Coughlin jumped to his feet, shrieking: "Three cheers for Hesing! Three cheers for a real Democrat!"

A boisterous clamor, mingling huzzahs and catcalls, was the response. Hesing threshed the smoking air with his arms and went on:

". . . my allegiance to Democratic principles when that party and those principles are backed by honest methods and decent men, when the Democratic party can boast of honest and incorruptible primaries. I know already this convention is packed against me. I know already that this convention is packed against me by the corrupt use of money!"

Deafening boos answered Hesing. The general turmoil renewed. Bathhouse John Coughlin strode up and down the front aisle, shouting, "Hurrah for Washington Hesing!" DeBaugh's band played a gay Irish tune and at the rear of the hall Mike McDonald and Sergeant-at-Arms Tom Cooper danced a merry jig.

Hesing screeched for quiet, for his right to the floor. Carter Harrison himself sought to come to his aid. Hesing, mistaking his purpose, turned fiercely on him. "No power on earth can move me from this platform except brute force!" he yelled. "I am here as one of the standard bearers of Democracy!"

Coughlin turned to the delegates, waved his hands above his head, and shouted: "Democrats of the convention! It's only fair that we should listen to what Mr. Hesing has to say!"

"G'wan, sit down, Bathhouse!" yelled the delegates. "Hi! Yi! Hi!"

"It's a disgrace to Democrats," Coughlin continued, "to choke off any man entitled to a hearin'! It's a . . ."

A crowd of Harrison backers surged forward and crammed Bathhouse into his seat. The entire Coughlin delegation arose, and there was a flurry of fisticuffs. Fights in other sections of the hall broke out, and the noise could be heard, as one newspaper reported, "as far away as the city hall." DeBaugh's band, with rare whimsy, played seven choruses of "Oh Dear, What Can the Matter Be?" and A. C. Hesing, the editor's aged father, stood trembling at the edge of the platform, his heavy cane ready for action. Cregier joined in the appeal for quiet.

"Let me say a half-dozen words," he demanded. "Democrats, don't you value free speech?"

"Aw, g'wan home!" retorted the delegates.

Through a half-hour of this, Hesing kept his place on the platform. But no one heard his plea that the convention should nominate anyone but Carter Henry Harrison. Finally, Hesing fled. As he boarded his carriage, he could still hear the shouts, inside: "Go home, Hesing! Go soak your head!"

With Hesing gone, the convention sped along quietly. Colonel Harry Donovan, friend of Harrison, rose and recounted the "great former exploits of my candidate."

"The name I shall present to you is encircled with a diadem and a corona of honor," he declared.

"And a bolter!" called out Tom McNally, from his seat beside Coughlin. "Put that in the speech. Harrison's a bolter!"

Colonel Donovan disregarded the interruption. "The city government was in his time the best we ever had. I give you the name of . . ."

"Yah, yah, a bolter!" shrieked Coughlin. "He ain't a good Democrat! Bring back Hesing!"

For a moment the hectic scene threatened to repeat itself. But Colonel Donovan, a man of lusty voice, shouted: "I desire to name you the man who found Chicago with wooden block pavements in its business district and who left it with granite blocks, finer than any other pavement on earth!"

"Whose money was it? Whose money?" Bathhouse John asked. "Who paid for it?"

"I name to you a man who has made the fire department of Chicago the best on earth. I name to you a man that the taxpayers delight to honor! I name to you Carter H. Harrison!"

Bathhouse John's delegation and the German contingent mocked and shouted, but the Harrison sentiment was unmistakable as the majority of the delegates rose to cheer. Harrison smiled and bowed, but declined to speak. A few minutes later, Cregier's name was placed before the convention to the accompaniment of polite applause. The first vote was taken then. Harrison received 531 votes to 91 for Cregier and only 57 for Hesing.

Immediately Hesing, in his newspaper office, issued a strong statement denouncing Harrison and charging his rival with spending $30,000 illegally to win the nomination. Cregier announced that he would run as an independent candidate of the labor organizations. And a few days later the Republicans, led by William Lorimer, Martin Madden and one-legged Henry L. Hertz, gleeful over the prospect of victory as a result of the Democratic split, nominated Samuel Allerton, the millionaire founder of the Union Stockyards, and offered him to the public as a sound businessman and a militant reformer.

3

Bleating philosophically about "family quarrels," most of the Democrats who had so strenuously opposed Harrison now clambered aboard his bandwagon. But not Bathhouse John. He truculently stood aloof as the symbol of rebellion. Defying the advice of such leaders as Trude and van Praag, he threw his support to Cregier, and for the first two weeks of the month preceding the election he managed several rallies for the labor candidate and introduced in the council a series of minor resolutions in behalf of Cregier's chief backers, the Trade and Labor Assembly of Chicago.

Coughlin's recalcitrant stand, however, attracted slight interest in the ranks of the more realistic Democrats. Billy Skakel took notice of Bathhouse John's stubbornness by ordering his club to withhold endorsement of Johnny Morris, who, in a half-hearted way, still clung to Coughlin. By remaining silent the club tacitly endorsed the Republican aldermanic candidate, Louis Epstean, who owned a wax works and freak museum at Randolph and Clark Streets.

One after another, the gamblers and other underworld gentry shrugged, mumbled, "A guy's gotta eat," and offered their services and funds to Harrison's managers. Harry Varnell, subdued since his unsuccessful attempt to unseat Mike McDonald immediately as ruler of the gambling world, summed up his associates' thoughts in a statement to a *Tribune* reporter: "Harrison may give us the double-cross, but we've got to take our chances. We've got no show with the other people."

Alderman Johnny Powers, now actively managing the Harrison campaign, brought into the fold no less a personage than Mike McDonald himself, and the erstwhile "scoundrel without honor or character" set himself up in an office in the Harrison headquarters at 137 West Monroe Street, on the door of which was painted in gold letters, "Committee on City Organization." To this room trekked the gamblers, summoned by notes from McDonald which caused Harrison no end of embarrassment. These missives, dispatched by messenger two weeks prior to the election, were on the stationery of the "Democratic Party of Cook County" and read:

Dear Sir:
    I wish you would come to 137 Monroe st. to see me as soon as possible on important business.
        Very truly yours,
                M. C. McDONALD

The newspapers, increasingly hostile toward Harrison, made much of the messages, predicting a wide-open town of gambling, crime, graft and corruption if he should be elected. The *Herald* headlined its account of the incident, "DENIALS WON'T AVAIL!" and the *Tribune* angrily editorialized:

Shifty denials do not meet the issue. Mike is working for Mr. Harrison. He does not work for love but to benefit himself. But that which will be for his advantage will be for the disadvantage of the community. Therefore the latter must steer clear of a candidate who is willing to accept McDonald's support and will not drive him away. Mr. Harrison is so anxious to be elected he will not denounce anyone. He does not protest against tough aldermanic or town candidates. He does not object to McDonald bossing his headquarters. And if he were elected these are the men who would dictate his policy, control his appointments and manage the city finances.

In the *Daily News,* a poet columnist was inspired to write:

> No days like the old days,
> With me in the Mayor's chair.
> When Tin Horn Mike
> And his ornery like
> Ruled like kings
> With his banks and things
> Wide open everywhere.

McDonald smiled blithely at the fuss. "The exposure of my connection with the campaign," he boasted, "will bring 5,000 extra votes to Harrison." Candidate Harrison himself, however, continued to deny that he was allied with the notorious "King Mike."

"Mike McDonald," he roared to his audiences, "voted against me in the convention, and when Hesing made his crazy speech McDonald was in the center aisle dancing with glee! He will not gain a thing from my election!" Then Harrison went on to recount the benefits of his previous administrations and invariably ended: "If you elect me, I will fulfill my duties, keep the streets and alleys clean, and uphold the city's fair name."

Despite Harrison's protestations, the gambling clique worked quietly and efficiently, with the Hankins brothers, Skakel and Condon, as McDonald's prime lieutenants, gathering up financial contributions for the Harrison campaign chest. Some said that the gamblers' fund was $100,000; others, $500,000.

One effect of McDonald's entry into the political struggle was that Bathhouse John, finally convinced that further opposition to the party chiefs was futile, deserted Cregier. He tried desperately to make up for lost time, and boasted to reporters that "we got 2,300 new names on the registration lists."

"But you don't mean to say," he was asked, "you've really got that many new voters in the ward?"

"Well," The Bath replied candidly, "it's like this, see? It don't make no difference whether they're new votes or no, see? We got the names on the books and the names goes election day."

The Harrison crowd welcomed Bathhouse with only a mild show of enthusiasm, and Skakel, annoyed at this turncoat tactic just when he was preparing to deliver a knockout blow to Coughlin, blurted: "That ain't gonna do Johnny no good, comin' over now. We got the ward organized for Harrison without him. Johnny's a dead pigeon."

Coughlin's defection from Cregier, however, especially after his recent labor activity in the council, did enable the Harrisonites to emphasize to on-the-fence voters that the laboring man's best friend was "Our Carter."

"A vote for Cregier is a vote for Allerton and strike-breaking," they told stockyard and steel-plant workers.

The appeal was successful. Howl though they did about Harrison's frank attitude toward vice and gambling, the newspapers and the Allerton campaigners could not overcome the former mayor's great personal appeal, his vigorous campaigning, his promises to labor, and the very effective aid of the underworld. "Our Carter" was rolled into office with 113,929 votes, 20,000 more than Allerton received, and the biggest majority in his political career. Cregier was a pitiful third and in the First Ward Johnny

Morris felt the lash of Skakel's organization, running 3,000 votes behind the victorious Republican, Epstean.

Harrison, worn with the fatigue of a hard campaign, hastened off with an entourage of well-wishers for a vacation in French Lick, Indiana, traditional political spa. Bathhouse John, despite his conversion, was not on the special train. "When I am elected," Harrison promised, as he lolled in the baths, "I will have the best administration. Mike McDonald? The gamblers? I am for the people. I will not have anything to do with bummers."

4

The days were bleak now for Bathhouse John.

He shared little in the general elation of the Democrats over the decisive outcome of the election. The triumphant inner circle remembered his efforts in behalf of Hesing and Cregier, and pointedly refused to forget. He chafed in silence while the thoroughly loyal prepared for a heyday of favoritism in the fifth reign of "Our Carter." Coughlin glumly attended the council meetings in the city hall, and squirmed and pouted as Johnny Powers led the eager council boodlers through the final weeks of the Washburne term.

Swiftly Johnny de Pow called up a measure handing over to a make-believe firm known as the Midland Rapid Transit Company the greater portion of the city's west side, from Jackson Boulevard to Madison Street, and from Lake Michigan westward to the city limits. The men behind the company were not named, their investments were not disclosed, and there was the trite rumor that this was another of the fictitious companies through which the boodlers and their overlords worked their complex and lucrative schemes. There were many who insisted that the man behind Midland was Yerkes, seeking to push the ordinance through the council so that, on some later day when public attention was diverted, he might buy the franchise at small cost and expand his traction empire. The anti-Yerkes men tried to defeat the measure, but the promise of sharing in a boodle fund reputed to be $100,000 held a great appeal for the aldermen and the ordinance passed 40 to 22.

Coughlin dutifully cast his machine vote for the measure, and hoped for some peace and quiet, if not spoils. But he was denied such solace. Powers, evidently in sly rebuke for Bathhouse John's failure to back Harrison from the start, seduced him into an action that made Coughlin the principal scapegoat for the malodorous Hyde Park Gas ordinance.

At Powers' instruction Coughlin brought before the council this distasteful piece of pending legislation at a time when the public had been thoroughly aroused against it. The Mutual Gas Company, a small firm, had been organized early in the year by Henry Watson, a stone mason and contractor from Alton, Illinois, who sought, by the ordinance, gas-pipe rights to the south side. Having gained such privileges in a strategic area, Watson and his backers proposed to wholesale gas supplies to other companies at exorbitant rates. But since the ordinance had first been introduced, Watson's company in some manner had erred in its gas mixture and several persons on the south side had been asphyxiated.

Public feeling ran high against the measure, and there seemed little doubt that the ordinance was doomed. Bathhouse John, too dull or disinterested to realize that wily Powers had set a trap, called up the measure and urged its passage. He was met with a howl of indignation from a majority of the aldermen, and, led by Henry Stuckart, the measure's original sponsor, the council smothered the ordinance. Powers, smirking at Coughlin, declined to vote, and the following day unhappy Bathhouse was denounced in the newspapers as the very worst boodler of all.

Shortly thereafter came another blow, directed again by Powers. The Nineteenth-Ward alderman piloted through the council a seemingly innocent ordinance extending Homan Avenue from Jackson Boulevard to Fortieth Street. The extension split Garfield Park race track exactly in two! Bathhouse John pleaded for time, and indignantly refused to vote. The measure passed handily, apparently dooming racing at the track forever.

Johnny de Pow was again riding high as absolute lord of the council. He reached the apex of his boodling effrontery when, during the last days of Mayor Washburne's tenure, he chose to push forward his astounding Hygeia ordinance. Here, proposed the lugubrious Powers, was an ideal civic project: "Why not pipe into the city of Chicago during the World's Fair good, clear, cool spring water from the famous springs at Wisconsin's Waukesha?"

In a fervid plea to his eager colleagues at the April tenth council meeting, Powers described the directors of the Hygeia Mineral Springs Company as the most altruistic of men, ready to risk their money and effort in a truly glorious plan for the benefit of the common people. "If this ordinance passes, we'll all be drinking spring water," proclaimed Johnny de Pow, "drinking spring water right in our own homes, from our own kitchen sinks! The people of Chicago demand the ordinance. I want Waukesha water in my house, and so will you!"

"How many men supporting the ordinance ever drink water?" inquired Alderman George Swift. "What one of those aldermen drinks water?"

His sally went ignored. Enough aldermen were eager to taste spring water—or to dip into the boodle bag held outstretched— and in its first test, Powers' ordinance passed. Powers rushed to the Wisconsin legislature where, from a gallery seat, he supervised the efforts to obtain that body's approval of the project. Although protesting delegations of Waukesha citizens marched in picket lines around the capitol singing: "Throw Out the Pipe Line," in parody of the old hymn, "Throw Out the Life Line," the legislature voted to allow the laying of the pipes.

But the charming plan was destined for failure. Governor George Peck promptly vetoed the action of the legislature, and a day later Mayor Washburne did likewise with the council's approval of the Hygeia ordinance. Neither group of legislators could muster enough votes to override the vetoes, and, despite the avowals of Hygeia Mineral Springs Company officials that they intended to carry out their plans without official sanction, the project soon lapsed and the aldermen and World's Fair visitors were compelled, as in the past, to drink the waters of Lake Michigan.

5

On April 17 "Our Carter," refreshed and vigorous after his vacation, was inducted into office. Coughlin applauded Harrison's speech, but in his heart he was low and spiritless. Nor did the committee appointments assuage his gloom, for he was pointedly omitted from the more remunerative positions and assigned to but two committees, one on fire and water, and the other on harbors, wharves, and bridges. Even the Republican newcomer, Epstean, exceeded him in fruitful committee jobs.

On the very next morning after Harrison's induction more troubles were heaped upon the hapless Bathhouse John. To the utter surprise of the lesser gamblers, who thought that Coughlin's last-minute espousal of Harrison would save them, detectives from Chief McLaughry's office invaded their meager establishments and back-room dice parlors, seizing bettors, proprietors, and even mere spectators. Only the larger places that had made an early peace with Mike McDonald, notably those of the Hankins brothers and Harry Varnell, were untouched and operating in full force. When asked by reporters if they knew of any orders issued by Mayor Harrison to close all the gaming rooms in the city, these gentlemen, according to the *Tribune,* "pointed to the crowded tables and disclaimed all knowledge of the fact."

The harried little fellows went with their woes to Bathhouse John, but he was powerless to help. It would be useless, he realized finally, to attempt to approach Harrison. Mike McDonald kept the bewildered alderman at a good arm's length. Harry Varnell had long since lost his enthusiasm for Bathhouse John. Billy Skakel was more ferocious than ever, warning Coughlin: "I'm goin' ta get you one of these days, Johnny."

As the raids continued, fewer and fewer of his followers remained to comfort Bathhouse John. He went mournfully from one friend to another, seeking advice and help. Finally, in desperation, he told his cronies that he would withdraw entirely from political life and devote his time to his handsome string of horses and his prospering bathhouses. But in this dark moment he was drawn into closer acquaintance with a mite of a man whose curt words of political wisdom had won him respectful hearing far beyond the bounds of his precinct. This man was absurdly tiny, an inch above five feet, with a pair of cold blue eyes and an eternally bland expression, inscrutable in poker and business; a skinny saloonkeeper and political dabbler who continually chewed an unlighted cigar. His name was Michael Kenna, but everyone called him Hinky Dink.

ENTER HINKY DINK

I

Michael Kenna, like Bathhouse John, was another noble product of the First Ward. His birth, in 1858, was on a wintry day in a frame shack at Polk and Sholto Streets, just east of Halsted Street at the edge of Connelly's Patch. His little Irish mother, fiercely defiant of her neighbors' criticism of the puny babe, carried him across the sleet-covered prairie to be baptized in the tiny church at Eleventh and May Streets, built the previous year by Father Arnold Damen.

All formal education came to an end for young Michael when he was ten. His mind was nimble enough, but he could not relish the schoolroom regimen. He found his way eastward to State Street where he took to hawking newspapers. A fellow salesman was the future Republican boss, Billy Lorimer, who was a play-mate of young Coughlin's. But swimming and play and boyish sports were not to the liking of this midget of a boy with an old man's face. He darted in and out of saloons and restaurants, sell-ing his newspapers, running errands for saloonkeepers and porters, striking up valued friendships with saloon hostesses and brothel madams and their charges. At twelve he felt the need for greater profits, and with fifty dollars loaned him by a bartender he pur-chased from an older boy the rights to a newsstand at Monroe and Dearborn Streets, just outside the old *Tribune* building. So rapidly did he prosper that he repaid the loan in less than a month.

It was then, according to insistent First Ward legend, that Kenna got his nickname, from none other than Joseph Medill, august *Tribune* editor, who liked to discover what his newsboys

73

thought of the way the dispatches of the night were being handled.

"What's your name, boy?" Medill is said to have asked of the newsie.

"Kenna's my name," the lad replied. "Michael Kenna, from over on Polk Street."

"That's a good Irish name," Medill replied, "but I'm going to call you Hinky Dink because you are such a little fellow."*

Nickname and all, young Kenna continued to make money. His rasping voice outshouted and his short legs outran all the other newsies. He was first to sell his quota of papers each night, and soon he had made enough to buy another stand a block or two from the first. Always he worked alone. He shunned all attempts by less successful newsies to form partnerships, replying to such proposals with a succinct: "I ain't crazy."

Even the great fire of 1871 failed to burn out little Hinky Dink's passion to succeed. A few months after the venerable Matteson Hotel, at Randolph and Dearborn Streets, had been destroyed, Kenna, then thirteen, rented a shack erected on the site and hired a man ten years his senior to run a coffee and lunch counter in the dilapidated structure. The "Little Matteson" was a failure almost from the start, however, because, as Kenna commented years later, "cash registers hadn't come into style at the time and the man who worked for me knew it." It was the first and one of the rare times anyone had been able to get the better of Hinky Dink.

Unlike Coughlin, who, except for his trip to his relative's farm after the fire, was a stay-at-home, Kenna left the city early for adventure elsewhere. In 1880, when Leadville was the largest and most lawless town in all Colorado, Hinky Dink withdrew his bank account and headed west. He had no wish to prospect for gold; he wanted a speedier and less arduous way of making money. He armed himself with a letter from Joseph Medill, recommending him for a position as circulation manager of the *Lake County*

---

*Robert Lee, late managing editor of the *Tribune,* doubted this story. Kenna himself said he got the nickname at "th' old swimming hole."

Reveille, a Leadville paper, but he confided to cronies that he might instead follow in the steps of several former Chicagoans who had made their way to the boom towns of the mining district and were growing rich running roulette wheels, faro games, and saloons. Shortly after his arrival in Leadville a furious shooting fray took place in a gambling establishment, in which three miners were killed instantly and three others were fatally wounded.

Kenna decided to take the newspaper job. He remained in Leadville nearly two years, but the constant violence in that brawling town upset him. Hinky Dink had no desire to carry a gun. He preferred his facile brain as a weapon. So finally he muttered his excuses to his employer, packed his carpetbag, and scurried back to his home town where he could deal with problems in a more familiar way.

By 1882, when he was only twenty-four, Kenna had become a successful saloonkeeper and political underling, aiding Chesterfield Joe Mackin and the First Ward Democrats thereafter in the frequent elections. His yeoman work in the fight to secure Cleveland's victory in the memorable 1884 presidential campaign won him sufficient notice to gain his appointment as captain of his saloon precinct, in the vicinity of Clark and Van Buren Streets, an honor Joe Mackin was able to bestow before he went off to jail for his part in the county-vote frauds. For the first time, Kenna's political activities brought him close to the ward's other political neophyte, Bathhouse John, but there was no great comradeship between the two, even in the years immediately preceding 1893.

Their differences were vast. Coughlin was bluff and hearty; Kenna was the glummest little man in the entire ward organization. Coughlin was the accomplished backslapper; Kenna cared little for gay companionship and was aloof almost to the point of snobbery. Coughlin laughed at everyone's jokes, asserted his friendship for every man, and sought votes in his bathhouse precinct by knocking on doors and personally extolling the multifold attributes of the party candidates; Kenna spoke sparingly, rarely smiled, counted only a picked few as his friends, and organized the saloon hangers-on as a corps of assistant precinct captains to make door-to-door calls and offer promises of free beer and lunch. Coughlin was all sound and fury; Kenna was silence and action.

But there were similarities too. Both were young and avid for gain, whether money or power. Both hated Billy Skakel. Both saw in the gradual decline of Mike McDonald the great chance for assumption of command in the prosperous First Ward. Both had sprung from the same social and economic background, and even their wives were strikingly alike. Kenna had married Catherine Devro, of the Irish settlement. She, like Mary Coughlin, remained aloof from the sordid aspects of the ward, collected fancy statuary, was a devout church and temperance worker. Mary Coughlin was, perhaps, a little cannier, a little more dominating, a bit more strait-laced. She shuddered when anyone called Coughlin by his nickname, and always insisted that he was a gentleman. Catherine Kenna often referred to little Mike as "The Boss," and made no attempt to improve his grammar.

In the whirl of fast-changing politics during the decade preceding the World's Columbian Exposition, Coughlin and Kenna were on good enough terms, but neither made any special effort in behalf of the other. Both took orders from Chesterfield Joe, and when the organization offered Coughlin as the aldermanic candidate in 1892, Kenna merely carried out orders with his customary effectiveness. Indeed, there had been considerable strain in the Kenna and Coughlin relations when Democratic solidarity was shattered during Harrison's final campaign. Kenna had been among the first to offer his support to Harrison, Coughlin the last.

But Kenna's ready offer to the party regulars failed to benefit him. When Harrison's police began harassing the gamblers, Kenna's little gaming parlor above his saloon suffered with the rest. Kenna frankly and vehemently liked gambling. It was his boast that he always conducted an honest game. The betrayal by the Harrison crowd infuriated him. He was one who never went back on his word, and he despised anyone who did. The gambling raids, and the rising importance of detested Skakel in the ward, prompted Hinky Dink to consider an alliance with Coughlin. Pleas to Mike McDonald brought no surcease. King Mike was moving farther and farther from the politico-underworld arena and he refused to act, just as he had declined to help the friends of Bathhouse John. McDonald, Kenna mused glumly as he chewed up cigars, had lost all claim to the loyalty of the little fellows in the First, and it was time for an effective organization to get into action. Kenna saw not only a chance to save his own stake in the ward, but to gather under a Coughlin-Kenna protectorate the gambling-house owners whose establishments were beset by the raiders. He needed a council spokesman, and certainly Bathhouse John Coughlin needed him.

Kenna summoned Coughlin to his saloon and bluntly laid the proposition before the alderman. "John," growled little Mike, "things are movin' fast. Mike McDonald can't do anything for us. That damned Skakel and his kind are gettin' the dough. You're th' alderman, and you've got another year to run. We'll get you elected again. Now all you want to do is behave and soft-soap Carter. We got a good thing and we want to hold on. Let's stick together and we'll rule this roost some day."

It was one of the longest speeches Michael Kenna ever made. Its direct and simple logic appealed to Coughlin. He suddenly had an enormous faith in this little man who said flatly: "We'll get you elected again." The Hink knew his politics. Coughlin remembered once, in a meeting of the First Ward Club, when the Ninth Precinct was under consideration, Kenna had settled a discussion of Republican strength in the area with but a single sentence: "There are fourteen saloons, twelve lodging houses, nine five-cent restaurants, four opium joints, and six livery stables in the Bloody Ninth, and if any Republicans got in they're colonizers to be bought at fifty cents a throw." Bathhouse recalled his boyhood partnership with little Andy Hoffman.

"I'm with you, Mike, I'm with you," blustered Alderman John sententiously. "Why together . . ."

"Can that stuff," said Hinky Dink. "We got work to do."

2

The World's Columbian Exposition brought Chicago unprecedented prosperity and international acclaim. Visitors thronged the White City, gaped at exotic exhibits gathered by intrepid commissioners from over the earth, ogled the exhibitions of Little Egypt and the wonders of Sol Bloom's Streets of Paris, and, by night, packed into the protected brothels, concert saloons and gambling hells of the city's speedily expanding Levee. Bathhouse John in haste made peace with Mayor Harrison. He and the Hink needed the blessing of the administration if they wished to talk protection to the First Ward's little fellows, and they needed it quickly and publicly. Kenna heard that Harrison was considering a campaign for a seat in the United States Senate, and he dispatched Bathhouse to pledge support.

"I have to be sure of a man's loyalty, Mr. Alderman," said the skeptical Harrison.

"I'm loyal, I'm loyal!" cried Bathhouse. "I promise loyalty to you, Mr. Maar. We're getting an organization that's the best. It can't be beat. The organization is all yours, Mr. Maar."

The mayor seemed impressed with the sincerity of the supplicant. Coughlin hastily pressed his advantage.

"And I got a complaint, too, Mr. Maar," he moaned. "You take the Fair, now. I ain't on a single Fair committee. I'm used to meeting people down here in the First, and I think I ought to be on some of them reception committees."

"I'll see that you get on some committees," smiled Harrison. "I welcome your support, Alderman."

"All I want, Mr. Maar, is to keep on doing my work without getting into no trouble."

Mayor Harrison smiled again, the significance of the remark perhaps escaping him.

"You do your work, Alderman, and there'll be no trouble."

To Bathhouse John, this meant only one thing: the administration would ease up on those who were going to pay gambling and brothel tribute to him and Kenna.

"Go ahead," he told Hinky Dink.

Kenna proceeded eagerly, but slowly. There were many McDonald foes and Skakel haters to choose from. Into his little organization The Hink drew one-time political greats, such as Chesterfield Joe Mackin, fallen, since his jail term, from secretary of the county organization to unofficial protector of Carrie Watson's expensive bawdyhouse; sluggers and political gangsters from Mackin's old organization, panders and pickpockets who previously had possessed little political standing, and such energetic worthies as Andy Craig, a tough safe-blower; Isaac Gitelson, better known as Ike Bloom, a sharp-eyed habitué of the red-light district; Samuel Tuckhorn, a disgruntled brothel owner; Freddie Train; Buck Moriarty and Frank Wing. These men formed the nucleus of the new organization. Kenna chose and chose, discarded and discarded. All he asked of the men was firm loyalty and closed mouths.

Kenna began, too, to lay the groundwork for an extensive benefit system that would attract supporters and knit his organization together. He proposed the establishment of a defense fund in which a percentage of the protection money paid by the brothel keepers and the gamblers should be pooled for the assistance of all Kenna-Coughlin followers who got into trouble. Prostitutes suffering from tuberculosis would be sent to Denver sanitariums. Hoodlums arrested for slugging other hoodlums, or for acting in the line of duty under any circumstances, would have legal counsel provided from a defense fund. Coughlin made arrangements to retain, at some $10,000 a year, two lawyers who would be prepared to spring immediately into the courts with writs of habeas corpus should anything untoward happen to the Kenna-Coughlin cohorts. This first $10,000 Hinky Dink and Bathhouse paid themselves. Such rising young attorneys as John Caverly, protégé of Kenna and later a distinguished judge, earned their first fees from this First Ward defense fund.

Some dubious gamblers and saloonkeepers made initial payments to the new organization, and when they discovered that their lookouts and barkeepers were promptly defended against any charge from spitting on the sidewalk to rape and murder, a few grew enthusiastic. Too, the number of gambling raids decreased, and Bathhouse and Kenna promptly took the credit. Actually the raids stopped because Mayor Harrison discovered that out-of-town visitors were as anxious to patronize the Levee as they were to visit the Fair, and public opinion, always following practical economic thought, no longer demanded reform.

So the wheels clicked merrily and the brothel doors stood ajar. Concert saloons blossomed out with extravagant shows, panel houses opened in the principal streets, freak shows and dime museums pandered to the lowest of public tastes, new bordellos and crib shacks sprang up, and hundreds of sharpers, pimps, and strong-arm men lurked in every Levee street and alley to separate the visitors from their money. The entire Levee seethed with the most abandoned orgy of vice and crime the city had yet seen. Elaborate new saloons and brothels were built up in an area south of the Levee proper, between Eighteenth and Twenty-second Streets, which came to be known as the Tenderloin and which shortly exceeded the old Levee itself. Thousands of dollars poured over the gaming tables every hour, day and night, and one syndicate, headed by Tom O'Brien, known as King of the Bunko Men, was able in a few months to net in excess of $500,000. In the brothels beer flowed, champagne corks popped, the "professors" and Negro bands played gay tunes and the girls worked in double shifts. Bawdyhouse shutters came down, and women exhibited themselves to the potential trade, or solicited in the streets. Never had the quarter-mile stretch of infamous Customs House Place, from Harrison to Twelfth Streets, been busier. Vina Fields, whose staff of forty girls was already the largest in the city, now employed from seventy to eighty. In Carrie Watson's brownstone establishment, the show place of the Levee, sixty girls, clad in shining silk, worked night and day, while Carrie's amazing parrot croaked in its cage by the door, "Carrie Watson. Come in, gentlemen." In the doorways of the less expensive houses, the whores—black and white, from sixteen to fifty years, of every nationality, and clad in anything from purple tights to Mother Hubbards of mosquito netting—stood and called to the men. Chicago again was earning its reputation, and earning it fast, as the wickedest wide-open town in the nation.

3

The underworld was incredibly prosperous, and Coughlin and Kenna, having perfectly timed their alliance, found themselves in possession of a thriving little syndicate. The alderman, his fears dissipated, his political future seemingly assured, began to enjoy the excitement of the Fair. He even felt benevolent toward his enemies and took his string of ponies to Ed Corrigan's Hawthorne race track, where his three-year-old, First Ward, promptly brought him a delicious triumph by outrunning Corrigan's entry and smashing the course record for the mile. Toward the end of the summer another of Bathhouse John's ambitions was fulfilled. Mayor Harrison appointed him to the World's Fair reception committee which did honors before the visiting dignitaries. The Bath, beautifully attired in tailcoat and top hat, his breast spangled with magnificent badges, his mustaches trimmed with surgical perfection, was a brave sight as he waited upon the station platform, or swept the crowds with his glasses from the officials' stand at the exposition grounds. "There's The Bathhouse!" awed visitors would exclaim, and the spectators cheered him happily as he shook the hand of a visiting potentate.

Bathhouse rose to his opportunity. Inspired at the sight of ribbons and braid and epaulets, he sported louder and louder vestments, until he almost rivaled the spangled military escort of the Enfanta Eugenie, come to represent the government of Spain at the festivities.

Coughlin took the advice of Kenna and gave his allegiance

where it would obtain the most good. Bathhouse stood so stead-fastly by the detested Johnny Powers that the newspapers soon began referring to Powers, Coughlin, and Little Mike Ryan* as the official council spokesmen for the mayor, despite the fact that all three united to override Mayor Harrison's veto of the Yerkes-sponsored Midland ordinance.

At the tenth running of the American Derby in Washington Park, the social and sporting event of Chicago's summer season, Bathhouse Coughlin appeared in a box adjoining that of Lillian Russell, and delighted the crowds when he rose and bowed grandly to her, extending to her the facilities of the city, which she had previously received from Mayor Harrison himself. A group of girls from Ike Bloom's, watching near by in their picture hats and pristine organdy gowns, giggled and clapped their hands at this gesture, and reported to their customers that night that Alderman Coughlin was, indeed, Chicago's first man after the mayor himself.

Frequently the alderman appeared in the Levee, though in quest of no more than further acquaintanceships. When he strode the Levee streets in his dazzling raiment, natives and yokels alike cheered his name, or, not knowing, made immediate inquiry as to who this magnificent fellow might be. Coughlin, usually surrounded by a noisy crowd of friends, delighted to dash upon open-mouthed strangers. "I'm John Coughlin," he would shout. "I'm th' alderman of this ward. Come on, I'll buy you a glass of beer." Whether the startled visitors accepted the invitation, they rarely forgot to tell the folk back home of the amazing Bathhouse John.

Hinky Dink had no penchant for exhibiting himself. He remained quietly at his bar, persistently expanded his little "push," and sought to convince as many gamblers and vice mongers as possible that he and Coughlin were to become the new leaders of the Levee. Impassive, soft-voiced young men called periodically for money. Some of the underworld barons sneered and ordered their

---

*The alderman who once, opposing the purchase of six gondolas for the Lincoln Park lagoon, shouted at his colleagues: "Why waste th' taxpayers' money buyin' six gondolas? Git a pair of 'em, an' let nature take its course."

bouncers to throw the collectors into the gutter. The more timor-
ous paid without objection. They had discovered that even if
Coughlin and Kenna were not sufficiently powerful to afford complete protection, they would provide legal help in a hurry when it
was needed.

The organization, Kenna remarked, was getting along. Bathhouse John was jubilant. Only five months earlier he had considered abandoning his political career forever.

4

Politically, the city was in the doldrums throughout the
World's Fair. The council concerned itself merely with routine
business, for most aldermen had some special duties to perform in
connection with the great show. Mayor Harrison was busiest of
all. He hustled about the city, attending receptions, welcoming
dignitaries, dining with royalty, making speeches. He extended
the hospitality of his own home to many notables and generally
conducted himself in such a manner that even the *Tribune* remarked that he carried himself "with a dignity and frankness of
spirit and action which wins him the respect of Chicago's guests
from abroad and the approval of her citizens."

As the end of the memorable exposition approached, Harrison
was saddened not only by the prospect of forthcoming routine, but
the financial problems menacing Chicago as panic began to sweep
in from the East. Still, he made his plans for the future of the city,
and, although he was nearly seventy years of age, toyed with the
idea of campaigning for the United States Senate. On October 28,
in the last week of the exposition, before a convention of mayors,
he made a great, confident speech. It was to be his last. That
night, as he rested in the library of his Ashland Avenue mansion,
the doorbell rang. The mayor himself leaped up. Opening the
door, he smiled at a pale man on the stoop, and started to speak.
The intruder drew out a revolver and fired. Harrison fell across
the doorstep, mortally wounded. Eugene Prendergast, whose frus-

trated ambition to be city corporation counsel had led him to commit murder, waited until the police arrived and surrendered calmly.

The terrible news spread swiftly through the city. Bathhouse John had been drinking one of his rare glasses of beer with several cronies in Kenna's saloon when an excited First Ward citizen ran in shouting: "Mayor Harrison's moidered!" When the news had been verified and the milling crowd had left, little Hink grew thoughtful.

"He was a good man, Carter," Kenna said. "But now we gotta think of the future."

THE RIGHTEOUS WRATH
OF WILLIAM T. STEAD

I

THE proper civic elegies had been sung and Prendergast lan-
guished in a cell, resigned to death on the gallows. The politicos
shed another tear or two and turned to the fight to name a mayor
to serve till December, when a special mayoralty election would be
held.

For a brief period the latent rivalry between Johnny Powers
and Bathhouse John came to life again. Powers began whipping
up Democratic support for John McGillen for mayor *pro tem,*
while Coughlin, reflecting on the setback of the previous spring,
once again proposed Washington Hesing as the logical candidate.
But Powers was still the Democratic chief in the council, and his
wish prevailed. The Republicans, in numerical control of the
council, named George Swift, the somber alderman from the
Eleventh Ward, as their candidate.

Coughlin's pleas in behalf of Hesing went unheard in his party.
Powers, working feverishly to unite the Democrats behind the
candidacy of McGillen, knew also that it would be necessary to
overcome the Republican majority if he ever hoped to elect his
man. He bluntly informed his party chieftains that he would seek
to influence some of the wavering Republicans if sufficient cash
could be raised. Enough money, Powers promised, would assure
McGillen's election over the "reformer" Swift. A few of the big
gamblers, including one of the late mayor's staunch backers, Joe
Martin, opened their purses, and Bobbie Burke, expert campaigner
and original Harrison adherent, offered sage advice.

With his pockets filled, Powers approached more than a dozen

Republicans. Five—enough to swing the election to McGillen—
were reported to have accepted $5,000 each in return for their
promise to favor Powers' man. A meeting of the council was
hastily called, and a vote taken. One traitorous Republican double-
crossed Powers by casting a blank ballot. The result—Swift 34,
McGillen, 33—threw the meeting into an uproar. Shouts of
"Fraud! Illegal!" came from the Democrats. Powers, exploding
with rage, shook his fist at as many Republican aldermen as he
could see. So insistent was his charge that the election, which he
had helped to call, had been conducted without proper notifica-
tion of the aldermen, that a new election was held the following
day. The second vote was even more disastrous for McGillen, for
many Democrats, disgusted by Powers' tactics, switched their votes
and Swift won by a big majority.

"Ah, here comes Deacon Swift," sneered McGillen as the new
mayor was escorted to the rostrum. "Now we can have the doxology."

"What was that?" inquired Coughlin.

"Doxology."

"What track's he runnin' on?" asked The Bath.

Coughlin gloated over Powers' humiliation, but in the only
eventful week of Swift's stay in the mayor's office, Powers wiped
away the stain, and Bathhouse John helped him to do it. At
Yerkes' command, Powers sought to win approval of ordinances
providing permission to electrify the traction baron's lines. While
admitting the need of such improvement, Swift sought to attach
compensation clauses to the measures, so that the city might gain
some needed revenue. But Powers disdained the proposal, and
even Coughlin spoke strongly against the inclusion of such clauses.
Both men might disagree on political choices and other council
matters. They knew better than to fight each other on any issue in
which Charles Tyson Yerkes was interested.

But the coalition was temporary. In December, with the special
election approaching, Powers and Coughlin were again at odds.
The leaders of the Harrison organization, including Johnny de

Pow, Captain Jimmy Farrell, Aldermen Austin Doyle, Tommy Cusack, Little Mike Ryan and Stanley Kunz, announced their support of Frank Wenter, president of the Drainage Board and a deserving Democrat. Emissaries were sent to Coughlin and Kenna, but neither gave immediate notice they would either back or buck Wenter.

A meeting of party bosses was called by Powers in a hall at 44 West Lake Street to launch the Wenter boom. Farrell, Preston Harrison (the late mayor's son), Tommy Gahan and other strong Wenter supporters were present, and, unfortunately for Powers, so were Alderman Bathhouse John and Hinky Dink.

Little Mike Ryan, his goatee twitching as he spoke, made an impassioned oration for Wenter. "Frank Wenter," he yelled, "is a good Democrat, a man after our own hearts and he knows what deserving Democrats want. He'll make a great vote getter."

Powers was about to call for a vote making the selection of Wenter unanimous, when Bathhouse John arose.

"Just a minute, Johnny," he objected. "There ain't any point in getting in a rush about this. The little fellow, Hinky Dink, and me, we been thinkin' hard about it. This Wenter, he's a nice fella, but he ain't got no public sentiment. Over in our First Ward we don't think he'd have a chance. Over in our First Ward we want Johnny P. Hopkins, and he's th' man we're gonna back."

Powers glowered at the big alderman and grunted in disgust. Hopkins, according to rumors, was backed by Roger Sullivan, the Cook County probate court clerk who had visions of becoming head of the party, a post Alderman Powers coveted. He tried to belittle Coughlin's choice, but Bathhouse John's brief speech had done its work. Stanley Kunz and a few others admitted there was reason in what The Bath had said and Powers was forced to defer a vote on the candidates until a later meeting.

But on the next day the Hopkins group met in the office of Sam Chase, county recorder, and the young lawyer announced his candidacy. Immediately, some of Powers' strongest associates, notably Tommy Gahan, swung over. Wenter denounced Hopkins as the man who had attempted to wreck Carter Harrison by threatening to run against him as an independent, and he and Powers labored mightily to keep the old Harrison forces together. The Republicans named Swift, and by the time of the Democratic convention Hopkins' strength had grown so that he was nominated by acclamation.

On December 2 Hopkins was elected by a scant plurality of 1,290 votes. In the First Ward the Coughlin-Kenna organization had given him an excess of 1,326 votes, more than his ultimate margin of victory. Chicago Democrats took proper notice. Bathhouse John and Hinky Dink had done their job well. They hoped Johnny Hopkins would not forget.

2

Mayor Hopkins came to the city hall with excellent intentions but almost from the start his term was marked by events which political historians have described as beginning "a period of incredible corruption."

No sooner had Hopkins cleared his desk than Yerkes besought his aldermanic representatives for new rights to bring his West Chicago railway into a "loop" about the main business district and to electrify his north and west-side lines. As usual, he offered to pay the city $50 for every car run 300 days of the year. This clause was a hoary joker, for it was simple—and legally proper—to operate the cars 299 days and avoid compensating the city for the street privileges. Flagrant as were the ordinances, at the first public outcry the council seemed to stiffen stubbornly, as usual. A minority among the aldermen and several of the newspapers renewed their interminable cry against Yerkes' highhandedness. They declared that the West Chicago line had a net profit of $1,400,901 out of gross earnings of $5,233,982 and could well afford adequate payment. But the aldermen, who knew well enough that Yerkes was paying compensation even if their modest tribute could not be shown on the books, paid no heed. Again, Coughlin and Powers forgot their differences. The whip cracked, the herd lined up, and the czar's wishes became law.

The boodle ordinances came thick and fast, with the council granting illimitable favors to anyone who cared to pay for them. Then Coughlin, who learned little but forgot nothing, decided to attempt passage of the original Henry Watson ordinance, this time as the Metropolitan Gas measure. He asked Little Mike Ryan to introduce it, and Little Mike, whose hide was as thick as his skull, assented.

Alderman John O'Neill promptly sprang to the attack.

"This is a sandbagging ordinance!" he cried. "It's the same gas company that wreaked death on the south side last summer. Name the promoters if the ordinance is on the level."

"You're one of the men that has stock in the Gas Trust," retorted Bathhouse John. "We want to put men to work and you want them to starve. This is a good ordinance. We'll name the promoters when the time comes."

Amid newspaper charges that $175,000 had been collected to be paid out at the rate of $2,000 each to the fifty aldermen in the gang with $75,000 left over for other officials who needed convincing, the ordinance passed by a vote of 50 to 10.

Mayor Hopkins hearkened to the criticisms of the press and vetoed the measure. When the newspapers collectively vowed to whip every man who voted for Metropolitan Gas over the mayor's veto, some of the boodlers became frightened and the ordinance was lost.

But the following week redoubtable little Mike had another ordinance, this time for the old Hyde Park Mutual Fuel Company. The same monotonous charges were raised again, but Ryan insisted that the company intended to offer lower gas rates and would light Chicago streets at seventy-five cents for 1,000 cubic feet, considerably under the one-dollar rate of the Gas Trust. Yerkes saw fit to announce that he had no connection with this ordinance, and subsequent investigation disclosed that the Henry Watson, of two prior defeats, was again the promoter. He had only $200,000 to back his company, a wholly inadequate amount, and the press shouted that here was another fictitious company, organized for the sole purpose of sandbagging the seven companies which formed the Gas Trust.

Bathhouse John accused the trust of prompting the tornado of criticism, a charge undoubtedly true, but Mayor Hopkins again threatened his veto if the ordinance passed. "How can we win in the spring election?" Hopkins pleaded with the Democratic councilmen. "Every Democrat is backing this ordinance. If it stands we won't have a chance." He read a blistering new veto message and Coughlin, Kunz and Powers sought frantically to override the action. But, before the final vote was taken, Mayor Hopkins and Coughlin had a curt conference, where important matters regarding the spring election were discussed. Hopkins reminded the alderman that Billy Skakel had been boasting around town that he was ready to blast Bathhouse John out of politics. The fight was likely to be a hard one, cautioned the mayor, accompanied by copious flowing of both money and blood. Bathhouse John might need the help of a friendly administration.

When the veto discussion came up on the council floor, Bathhouse John was conspicuously silent, and he ignored Johnny Powers' suggestion that he get busy with some wavering aldermen. He could not go entirely the mayor's way, however, and he cast his pledged vote with the boodlers. But the gang lost, four votes shy of the two-thirds required to beat the veto, and Alderman Coughlin breathed more easily. Technically he had saved face, and at the same time he might count on help from Mayor Hopkins on some dark future day.

While Coughlin floundered about in the council, Kenna was busy in the Levee. His own dice game over the saloon, with Johnny Ryan in charge, was doing splendidly. Seventy of the hundreds of gamblers who had come to operate during the Fair remained to keep shop in Chicago permanently, and Hinky Dink added some of them to his organization. But much of his activity now was hardly of an illicit nature; it was, rather, humanitarian.

For all his hard-lipped demeanor, Kenna, like Coughlin, was a benevolent man. In the dire depression that swept the entire country that winter, the whole of Chicago was beset with the jobless, and the First Ward was particularly troubled. Some finally straggled off southward, others joined with General Jacob Coxey's "Commonwealth of Christ" army and marched off to Washington, but great hosts of the unemployed roamed the streets, begging jobs and food. The city-hall corridors were thrown open and each night 1,500 of the unfortunates slept there, depending for their food on saloon free lunches. Hinky Dink fed more than any other. In one week, at the height of the misery, he cared for 8,000 destitute men and he fired a bartender who demanded five cents from a vagrant who had helped himself too freely from the counters. Kenna's activities that winter were those of the Good Samaritan, but they also gave him an idea. Every one of those men, however impoverished, could vote. There was always a plentiful supply in Chicago, come panic or prosperity. It would be simple, and inexpensive, at election time to house and feed the multitude, and instruct them in the principles of the franchise.

3

This black scene, the destitution, the council boodling, the squalor of the working sections, the gambling and the vice, starkly contrasting with the splendor of the exposition, had all been surveyed by the blazing eyes of a bearded English editor named William T. Stead, who had arrived in the city on the day of Mayor Harrison's assassination. No sooner had he alighted from the train than Stead began to compare critically the magnificence and misery of a city he later called "one of the wonders of the nineteenth century." Chicago fascinated him with its evils and possibilities for good. He envisioned a metropolis that might hold in its sturdy hands the future of the American republic, with space enough for millions of happy citizens, and energy sufficient to refashion the hemisphere. He was dismayed at the dissolute treatment being accorded such a heritage. The time had come, he decreed, for reformation, and he sought to launch a genuine movement for betterment among the community's most stable population.

Stead was no ivory-tower reformer. He dined with the wealthy who dwelled in the Prairie Avenue mansions, but he also visited Hinky Dink's saloon, Hank North's famous bar, and the lesser establishments along Customs House Place and Clark Street, talking with the bums and bartenders and brothel madams, and interviewing the girls in their squalid cribs. He lunched with boodling aldermen and obtained their open admission of guilt; he examined the tax records and property assessments, heard the plaints of preachers and professional reformers. He asked impertinent questions of civic dignitaries. He examined the schools, the jails and the churches. He looked upon the balance sheets of prospering business houses. Then he descended upon a startled Chicago like an Isaiah, mantled in righteous wrath. From a platform in Central Music Hall he bombarded avid crowds with descriptions of their iniquities; he shocked ladies' clubs, upset luncheons of businessmen, out-Heroded the ministers and howled down the few puny defenders who rose to dispute him.

Out of Stead's horrendous revelations evolved a new civic conscience that launched the first Chicago reform movement of any importance, the Civic Federation. It was a child of the better element, but based its structural organization on no less a reform antithesis than New York's Tammany Hall.

"Tammany is a brotherhood," declared the perspicacious Stead. "Tammany men stick together and help each other. The members may be corrupt, their methods indefensible, but the question for Chicago is whether or not the Civic Federation can organize a brotherhood that will work as hard to make Chicago the ideal city in the world as Tammany has been successful in organizing a party which practically holds New York in the hollow of its hand. In other words, are there as many men and women in Chicago who will work as hard for the Kingdom of the Lord in Chicago as there are men who will work for the rule of Tammany in New York?"

There evidently were. Laborers, housewives, businessmen, lawyers, social workers, journalists and not a few politicians clamored for admission to Stead's organization. Among the leaders were Marshall Field, Lyman Gage, Sarah Hackett Stevenson, and Jane Addams. There were some who scoffed and pointed to the names of men prominent for boodle payments and tax fixing on the Federation's executive board, but the new brotherhood filled its ranks with enthusiasm and shook Chicago with a reform fervor.

The Civic Federation announced to the Chicago aldermen that henceforth it would keep its eye on each councilman's activities and would issue reports on actions it considered against the public welfare. But its immediate task was to care for the jobless. Some $200,000 was raised at once to deal with the pressing distress, and shelters were erected about the city. A horde of 3,000 men were given jobs cleaning the city's streets. The newspapers called it "Stead's Brigade" and the crusading journalist donned a suit of ragged workman's clothes and labored with one of the gangs for several hours.

Stead did not limit his shocking Central Music Hall meetings to the honest reformers and the prurient-minded respectables. He hired a detective agency to distribute tickets on Saturday nights to the lowest vice haunts, gaming halls, saloons and dance pavilions. The denizens of the Levee were urged to come and state their grievances. Few ever appeared. But the reformers and the municipal leaders marched to the hall and what they heard sent them roaring back to their pulpits and clubs. The call sent out by Stead and the Civic Federation for a genuine reform movement became a tumultuous shout that reached even to the lairs of the gang politicians.

Then, on February 24, 1894, along with the official incorporation of the Civic Federation, came Stead's most sulphurous blast. In a sensational book of more than four hundred pages, bearing on its cover a lithograph figure of Christ with one hand raised in re-buke against a score of Chicagoans rising from a gaming table with gold-laden arms, the daring Englishman set out for public exhibition all Chicago's filthiest linen. The startling volume, closely packed with data to raise high the most worldly eyebrow, was strikingly titled: *If Christ Came to Chicago*.

Stead left nothing to the imagination. Immediately under the cover was a map of the city's vilest section, the Ninteenth Precinct of the First Ward. The brothels along Customs House Place, designated by red squares, were located for all to see, together with the saloons, the pawn shops and the disreputable lodging houses. Stead printed a Black List of owners, renters, tenants, and taxpay-ers of "property used for immoral purposes." He told of the wan-dering and homeless thousands who were housed in the smelly Harrison Street police station and fed by the saloonkeepers. He analyzed, criticized, and eulogized the Chicago Trinity—Marshall Field, the merchant; George Pullman, the railroad magnate; and Philip Armour, the packer. But he also belabored the wealthy, rip-ping into Charles Tyson Yerkes, detailing the methods by which the traction tycoon had acquired overwhelming privileges through graft payments. He exposed the links between gamblers and poli-ticians and saloonkeepers, accusing the late Mayor Harrison of accepting regular tribute from the underworld. There were re-ports of interviews with Carrie Watson—"She has made a fortune out of her trade in the bodies of her poorer sisters"—and Vina Fields—"The rules and regulations of the Fields house enforce de-corum and decency with pains and penalties which could hardly be more strict than if they were drawn up for the regulation of a Sunday School." He reached the blunt conclusion that most girls sought brothel employment because of low wages and horrible liv-ing conditions. He upbraided the police for their lawlessness and despotism. He wrote glowingly of young Mayor Hopkins, whom he had supported in December. To the particular annoyance of Bathhouse John, who was beginning to dabble in this kind of racket, Stead exposed the tax fixing which was so widespread that the city's assessed valuation was lower than in 1873, when the population was fewer by a million.

For the city council Stead had nothing but scorn. In thousands of indignant words devoted to "The Boodlers and the Boodled" he described the various obvious boodle ordinances, the frank blackmail and sandbag measures, told of the political racketeers, described politicians who sold out to big business and noted the circumstances of the frequent distribution of fat little envelopes in Alderman Powers' saloon on West Madison Street.

"The boodling aldermen," he wrote, "are indeed the swine of our civilization but unfortunately there is no Antiochus to offer them as sacrifices to the offended gods." Therefore, Stead urged, a purge was essential and he avowed that the citizenry was "justified in turning to the April polls with the hope that they will show Chicago has at last wearied of being represented and governed by the vilest of her citizens."

4

The furor created by the publication of the book was worldwide. Other cities had only praises for Stead's exposé, the St. Paul News predicting a "social earthquake not only in Chicago but throughout the country." The local newspapers did not dispute the accuracy of Stead's facts, but none was enthusiastic in appraisal of his work. Most bitter of the comments came, surprisingly enough, from a Presbyterian journal, The Interior:

Mr. Stead has signalized his departure by leaving for publication a guide book to the brothels and other places of evil resort in Chicago. It is filled with pious nastiness and abuse of the Church and of respectable people out of which he manufactures his sensations. The very worst that can be said of Chicago is that such a man made his way into church circles and attracted public attention.

Both the book and the Civic Federation, roared many, were

nothing less than a Republican plot to destroy the Democratic party. Stead was denounced as a sensationalist, and lauded as a great leader. He was threatened with harm if he remained in the city and he was urged to stay and assist in the rising reform movement. Stead departed, but the Civic Federation, issuing pamphlets in his support and disdaining the sneers of the cynical, continued to enroll members and adopted a bold slogan: "No scoundrel need apply for the position of alderman in the City of Chicago!"

BENEVOLENCE, ORGANIZATION,
AND BRASS KNUCKLES

I

THREE weeks to the day after Stead's account of civic rottenness burst upon the city, the top Democrats of the First Ward shuffled to the bar of Mike Kenna's saloon for a political conference. They gulped their beer and gorged themselves on the free lunch and discoursed, meanwhile, in subdued tones. Then at a shout from Tom McNally they left and trooped to a meeting hall at 224 West Van Buren Street, around the corner from Hinky Dink's, to name the aldermanic candidate for the coming term.

Here they fretted and stamped about. Finally Bathhouse John rolled in and there was a great cheer. Then, to begin the briefest political convention in Chicago's history, Johnny Morris leaped to a chair.

"Johnny Coughlin!" he yelled. "Johnny Coughlin! It's Johnny Coughlin we want for alderman again!"

Others joined in the cry and The Bath grinned and waved his hands above his head. Tom McNally, serving as chairman, rapped with his gavel, a bung starter he had picked up at Hinky Dink's, and Morris formally and with great dignity placed Coughlin's name before the assemblage.

"Any further nominations?" asked McNally.

There were none. McNally whacked the gavel once again. The meeting was adjourned and the delegates filed out hastily, still calling, "Hurray for Johnny Coughlin! Hurray for Bathhouse John!"

Again Bathhouse waved his hands and shouted his thanks; then he strode off with McNally and Hinky Dink to a hack stand.

97

The *Herald* reporter present returned to his office and wrote for the morning's edition:

John J. Coughlin was renominated for the council last night by the Democratic convention of the First Ward. The convention session lasted only a few minutes as the delegates were in a hurry to get away to attend a prize fight.

2

Two of the leading members of First Ward Democracy were absent from the gathering. Sol van Praag and Billy Skakel had sulked at Billy Boyle's, telling all who paused at their table of their intention to put an end to the political career of Bathhouse John.

Skakel's hatred stemmed from the early days of the young alderman's term, when, with the sanction and protection of Coughlin, Prince Hal Varnell had opened two bucket shops, one at 126 West Washington Street, and another at 116 West Monroe Street, which had cut heavily into the monopoly enjoyed by Skakel with his four similar establishments.* Coughlin had ignored Skakel's demand that he call on the authorities to stop Varnell, and The Clock, who was far from being the most even-tempered man in the First Ward, thenceforth had regarded The Bath as a mortal foe. Van Praag's interest in defeating Coughlin was more impersonal, but no less impelling, for he envisioned himself and Skakel, rather than Bathhouse John and Hinky Dink, as the fit rulers of the flourishing realm of gambling houses, saloons and bagnios.

Early on the morning following the nominating convention Skakel summoned the newspaper reporters.

---

*Skakel's operators daily drafted a list of stock quotations presumably based on bona fide trading in western mining shares. Actually, the quotations were completely fictitious. They were listed on a huge blackboard every fifteen minutes and the bucket-shop players bet on their ability to guess whether the next figures would be higher or lower. Since about 300 deals in each of five stocks were "quoted," there were 1,500 chances for action each day and the house took twenty-five cents for each two dollars played.

"Coughlin's no good," he bellowed. "I asked him to do a few t'ings fer me an' he never done them. He never done a t'ing fer th' party. I'm runnin'. I'm gonna smash him. That bathhouse rubber ain't gonna never be alderman no more. I'll beat that dirty bum!"

With their Carter H. Harrison Club of the First Ward as a nucleus Skakel and van Praag formed the Independent Democratic party and began working with a fury that sent The Bath running fretfully from McNally to Morris to Kenna.

McNally and Morris were as glum as Coughlin, but Hinky Dink's gimlet eyes blinked rapidly and his jaw set. "We ain't gonna be beat by that Billy Skakel, boys," he assured them. "He won't win."

Skakel scoffed at the midget Hink and boasted of his huge campaign fund. He blandly admitted that he was making offers of five dollars a vote where that kind of money was needed, and he told delighted newspapermen: "We're gonna spend money like water. We got plenty."

The political reporters, coming away from the thronged meetings of the Carter H. Harrison Club of the First Ward with the shouts of the Skakel enthusiasts still pounding in their ears, convinced themselves that Coughlin's aldermanic career was approaching its finish.

One newspaper, the *Herald,* even predicted that The Bath would garner fewer votes than the First Ward's Republican candidate, J. Irving Pearce, the mild-mannered owner of the Sherman House. The *Herald's* political editor forecast:

Alderman Coughlin is apparently hopelessly beaten. As matters now stand, he will do no better than third at the finish.

All the other publications, and notably *Mixed Drinks: The Saloon Keepers' Journal,* were voluble in their praise of Bathhouse John's foe. In a front-page column, adjoining one offering a prize rum-drink recipe, that periodical impressively characterized Skakel as

. . . the patriotic soldier who fought to preserve the union and who is now one of the most progressive business lights of our proud Chicago. His election will crush the most infamous autocratic rule that is now threatening to disrupt the Democratic party.

Coughlin paid close heed to the newspapers and what he read appalled him. Refusing to be cheered by Kenna's calm insistence that Skakel would not win, Coughlin hustled to Mayor Hopkins to plead for help. The mayor called Skakel to his office.

"Billy," he said, "I'm asking you to get out of the race. You're hurting the party."

"Nuthin' doin'," retorted Skakel. "I'm th' next boss in the First Ward an' you might as well know it now."

The much-disturbed Bathhouse then sought aid from his attorneys, and Moses Salomon, the erudite state senator from Chicago's First District, plunged into his law books. A week before election day he came forward with a device which he thought might thwart the gambler. He had uncovered a city law which barred any man convicted of a crime from municipal office. Skakel, it was promptly recalled, had been arrested a few years back for gambling and had been fined.

Coughlin and Salomon rushed to the election board, bearing a petition for the erasure of Skakel's name from the ballot. Without granting Skakel a hearing the Hopkins-controlled board, after solemnly considering the charges, held the petition to be legal and proper, and ordered the deletion of Skakel's name.

The action enraged the Skakelites. It was adjudged a blow below the belt. "That fat bathhouse rubber!" blubbered Billy The Clock. "He'll never be alderman again. Sure, I'm a gambler. I don't deny that. But I'm a better man than Bathhouse was or ever will be. I never took a bribe! What can Bathhouse say about that, eh?"

"He never had the chance," countered Bathhouse John. But his seeming blitheness did not reflect the general gloom in his camp over the possibility of his defeat. The election-board trick was not well taken in the First Ward, where men were sensitive concerning their pasts and where political ethics demanded that no public display be made of a man's relations with the police department. Faithful supporters of Coughlin were alienated. Big Sandy Walters was the first to leave.

After a tussle with his conscience, Walters sought out Coughlin in the campaign headquarters and lamented: "Johnny, I didn't ever t'ink you'd do a t'ing like dat, tell on a guy what got t'rowed in th' bink. I ain't wid you no more. Billy an' Sol, they're gonna finish you off. Billy'll be back on th' sheet t'morrow, an' we're gonna give you a trimmin'."

And on the next morning a battery of seven attorneys, including young Clarence Darrow, appeared before County Judge Frank Scales with Skakel and van Praag and a throng of subordinates in the rear. The striking of Skakel's name from the ballot, argued the legal staff, had been improper, illegal, and unconstitutional.

"Yeh, Judge," the gambler chimed in. "It was unfair. Sure I was convicted for gamblin', Judge. But it was only a small fine. It really didn't amount to nothin'."

Judge Scales, a virtuous Republican, nodded sympathetically. "Since when," he demanded, "is a man deprived of the right to serve the people merely because of some forgotten misdemeanor? I believe the election board has overstepped its authority. The petition of Mr. Skakel is granted and the board of election commissioners is restrained from removing his name from the ballot."

The Skakel followers greeted this decision with joyous acclamations. They hoisted Billy to their shoulders and carried him in triumph to the street. Coughlin followers spied the procession and hastened to report to Bathhouse John, who morosely complained that it was a trick of the Republican party. He moped about headquarters until the exasperated Hinky Dink finally exclaimed: "Cut it out, John. That Skakel ain't gonna get elected. Don't be a pansy."

3

While Bathhouse John had been seeking to destroy Skakel before the board of election commissioners, Hinky Dink, with a fine distaste for the involved legal processes, had been more practical. He had evolved an elaborate plan for the re-election of his bulky friend, a plan born as he observed the hungry shuffling before his free lunch counter in the winter of '93.

He knew humans, this little Hinky Dink, and he readily perceived that the favors he had done for the thousands of bums and tramps and respectable homeless men could be easily returned in the field of political action at the cost of no more than the slight effort of balloting. Moreover, the men whose votes were solicited would be grateful and flattered, for they were thereby given standing in the community. Hinky Dink had a simple and basic political philosophy: favors and benevolence produced votes; organization brought them out. While Bathhouse John had been running from Mayor Hopkins to the election board, from adviser to adviser, Hinky Dink had been busily at work, perfecting his organization, issuing calls to the sans-culottes, putting his theories to practical test.

Into the ward from all parts of the city had poured the grateful dregs. They were housed and fed and supplied with plenty of beer. They scorned the glib Skakel promises of five dollars a vote on election day for the snug security of a sawdust-covered floor, fifty cents for their vote, and all the sausages, bread, cheese and lager they could hold. Into The Bath's own precinct Kenna piled 300 additional voters to be registered. Some slept in Coughlin's bathhouse, on the benches or in the steam rooms. Precinct captains like Mike Lawler and Joe Friedman rounded up hundreds of others and transformed their saloons into lodging houses. Cheap hotels, flop joints, deserted buildings, brothels, saloons, empty warehouses, even railroad freight stations—these were the forts where Hinky Dink marshaled the Coughlin voting forces, to await the time when they should march out in the interests of their benefactor. When registration day was over, the First Ward had 8,397 voters on the books—almost twice the number that had balloted in the previous mayoralty election. Skakel howled to the election board, but his protests were ignored.

There was more to Kenna's plan than the mere colonization of voters. He advised Coughlin, as election day approached, to pay another visit to Mayor Hopkins. "The mayor oughta be reminded how we helped him in the election," he suggested. This Coughlin hastened to do, and on the afternoon preceding the election the mayor made his final appeal to Skakel.

"NO!" Billy roared.

Mayor Hopkins shrugged. "There might be a lot of trouble tomorrow, Billy, and I might not be responsible."

Shortly after Skakel departed, Captain Jack Hartnett, head of the First District police, conferred briefly with Mayor Hopkins. That night, at the Harrison Street police station, Lieutenant Charles Holden summoned a group of stalwarts slated for election detail in the First Ward.

"Listen, boys," said the lieutenant, "I don't want you to be taking any part in this election, but the man who always looks out for the First Ward police over there in the city hall needs our help."

The squads went to work that very night. Men wearing Skakel buttons were heaved into cells. Saloonkeepers who displayed Skakel campaign pictures were forced to close promptly at midnight. Equipment in gaming houses owned by pro-Skakel gamblers was confiscated and destroyed. Into the south end of the ward, the district of colored voters hostile to Bathhouse John for aiding in the defense of Policeman Tom Kinsella who had killed a Negro several months back, went plain-clothes detectives. "Either you line up behind the Bathhouse," they told the crap-game operators, barrelhouse proprietors and panders, "or you get closed up."

While the police were doing their share to create a Coughlin victory, Kenna sought to assure himself further that his loyal voters would go unmolested to the polls the following morning. Besting van Praag, who had a similar idea, by only a few hours, Kenna acquired the services of the dread Quincy Street gang, composed of some of the toughest strong-arm men, bouncers and rowdies in the First Ward. These hoodlums, led by Johnny Dee, a professional slugger, were directed to serve as a roving squad for the protection of Coughlin voters. The police, Dee was informed, would be looking the other way should self-defense entail the application of billies, blackjacks or brass knuckles on bellicose Skakelites.

4

Shortly after dawn on election day, an hour before the polls were to open, a carriage rolled away from the saloon headquarters of the Quincy Street gang. Aboard were Dee and his brother Dave, a State Street saloon bouncer; Louis Rabshaw, a punch-drunk prizefighter; Jack McCarthy, gambler and slugger; Thomas Kerwin, a big-muscled bridge tender; and Thomas Hanon, a neighborhood tough. Through the precincts the carriage whirled, its occupants on the lookout for anyone wearing a Skakel button or daring to hoist a Skakel banner.

"Coughlin's men," read a report later in the *Tribune,* "went after Skakelites like hungry hyenas in a traveling circus at an evening meal of raw steak. Nowhere was any man wearing a Skakel badge safe from the onslaught of the Quincy Street boys and their cohorts."

The first of the many encounters occurred in the McCoy Hotel on Clark Street, owned by Colonel William McCoy, a friend of Bathhouse John and a rabid Irish patriot.* At the entrance Dee's men perceived five Skakelites, doubtlessly bent on evil, for McCoy was a vociferous Coughlin backer.

---

*Years later McCoy was forced to sell the hotel, and the new owner called it The Victoria, after the Queen of England. This latter humiliation, it was said, hastened Colonel McCoy's death.

The carriage halted and Dee and the others leaped out after the Skakel men, who fled into the hotel lobby. Clubs and blackjacks began swinging, furniture was overturned, and a banister crashed to the floor. Colonel McCoy appeared, glanced quickly at the damage, and with an awful cry of rage joined in the fight. Some combatants drew revolvers, and bullets smashed into the gleaming woodwork. In ten minutes the quintet of Skakelites lay in a semi-conscious state on the floor while Dee's gang kicked them. When the police finally arrived, they glanced at the two sets of badge-wearers, seized the Skakelites and dumped them into the waiting patrol wagon. The Quincy Street Boys moved on.

At a polling place in the Fifth Precinct Rabshaw, eager to display the fistic talents that had brought him indifferent success in the ring, challenged the wearer of a Skakel button. The Skakelite was Solly Smith, who, unfortunately for Rabshaw, was a professional fighter himself. He knocked out his assailant with a single punch. The rest of the gang was about to beat Smith to insensibility when a policeman appeared and took him to jail.

As the voting began, the battle grew wild throughout the First. In the Sixteenth Precinct Toots Marshall, a Coughlin worker, and Sam Phelps, both colored, met and drew pistols. After blazing away for a few minutes both were wounded severely and were hauled away to the Bridewell hospital. In other sections of the ward each time the carriage of the Quincy Street Boys passed a wagon carrying Skakel supporters there was a furious exchange of revolver fire and the terrified pedestrians raced for safe cover.

The members of the Kenna army of floaters were roused from their sawdust beds, and they, along with ordinary citizens courageous enough to venture into the streets, hastened to the polls to exercise their democratic privilege. Lesser members of the Quincy Street gang, traveling in groups of four or five, came out to afford them protection. They prowled the streets, chasing Skakelites into hiding or into the safety of the police stations. Some of the men in the flying squads bore six-shooters, others baseball bats, and they used both frequently. Early in the afternoon one squad of the gang drew up to Hinky Dink's establishment, beat a colored Skakel watcher unconscious and handed him over to the police. Another Negro Skakelite known as Jumbo fled into the saloon, followed by the Quincy Streeters. He ran about in circles, jumped on the bar, broke several bottles, and finally sped back to the street, straight for a near-by police squad. The police clubbed him down and hauled Jumbo to the Harrison Street station, where he was charged with disturbing the peace.

Despite the terrible beatings and the odds against them the Skakel men were not weaklings. One group invaded Hinky Dink's saloon in a surprise onslaught and smashed beer barrels and whisky bottles. Coughlin sluggers came to the rescue and by late afternoon the floor was a foamy sea of beer and liquor. Skakel himself came to the saloon to plead with Hinky Dink for a respite from the slaughter. There was a grim silence when the gambler was blocked at the door by a drunken Quincy Street braggart named Pinky Kerwin, brother of Thomas. The two men eyed each other.

"I licked fifteen men today," sneered Kerwin.

"You touch me," stormed Skakel, "an' you'll die in that swill."

Kerwin backed away and Skakel was permitted to enter. Hinky Dink was elsewhere in the ward, however, and not only did the attempted armistice fail but in every precinct the fighting grew even more desperate. In the saloons those bouncers not yet enlisted for active street battle were kept busy chucking demonstrative Skakel men into the gutters. In one Clark Street polling place five Quincy Street Boys were beset by a pair of Irishmen named Joe Kelly and Tom Connors. Both were good fighting men, but the gang's fury sent Kelly reeling into the street with a shattered jaw, and Connors against a doorpost, his skull split open. At the Eleventh Precinct polls on Harrison Street twelve Skakel men were arrested after a free-for-all.

Even after the polls closed the struggle continued. A quartet of Negro brothel bouncers named Butterface Jones, Make A Fuss Wilson, Sporting Billy Johnson, and Slick Sam Phillips had been armed by the Coughlin hoodlums with guns and baseball bats in addition to their usual razors. In Harmon Court, just off State Street, during the late-afternoon rush hour these worthies encountered a Skakel gang led by Fighting Billy Marshall, a notorious tough. The voting was over, but blood was hot. The two gangs charged. A crowd collected and soon grew to 3,000 persons. Slick Sam and Marshall began shooting at once while the others engaged with ball bats in hand-to-hand fighting. For blocks along State Street the cable cars were stalled while the rival gangsters beat, cut and shot at one another. A policeman fought his way through the throng, but was unable to halt the battle and turned in a riot call. Three squads of police responded and rushed into the crowd, clubbing indiscriminately. They provided the colored fighters a needed respite, and soon Marshall and his gang lay inert on the cobblestones. They were dumped into the patrol wagon and hauled off to jail, but the wounded Slick Sam was placed in another wagon and taken to the county hospital.

This was the final battle of the day except for minor barroom brawls. By evening, while election judges and clerks were busily tallying the votes, the newspapers made up casualty lists. They discovered that forty Skakel men had been wounded, two of them critically, and hundreds were in cells. Only six men in the Coughlin camp had been seriously injured; none had been arrested.

And out of the brawling and shooting and rioting and fighting, Alderman Coughlin emerged the victor. He collected 2,671 votes while Pearce ran second with 1,261 and Skakel trailed third with 1,046. Whether the rest of the 8,379 registered voters were some of Kenna's floaters who failed to do their duty or duly qualified First Ward residents who feared to visit the polling places, no one, not even the astute Hinky Dink, could determine.

5

Chicago, accustomed to violent election days, generally agreed that the carnage in the First Ward had exceeded all previous horrors. The *Tribune's* comment summed up the general feeling:

There have been elections in Chicago and there have been elections, but yesterday's fight between the followers of Bathhouse John and Billy Skakel was a world beater. Clubs were trump, and the police carried the clubs. Bathhouse John's election was secured by methods which would have disgraced even the worst river parishes of Louisiana.

The men of the Civic Federation and the Union League Club shook their heads and deplored "the grossness and illegality of yesterday's election in the First Ward." Mayor Hopkins was attacked and accused of ordering the partisan conduct of the police, and although he was firm in his denials, few believed him. Even gang aldermen in other wards shuddered and looked upon Bathhouse John as some sort of wild man.

But Alderman Coughlin was unmoved by the horrified criticism of press and pulpit. He had been re-elected. There were great days in store for him, he told his followers, and he hugged little Hinky Dink in a maudlin display of gratitude.

"You're a great little guy, Mike, you're a great little guy," chortled The Bath, his eyes filled with tears. "We're goin' places, you an' me."

Kenna was not one to become emotional, but he smiled wryly once or twice and slapped Coughlin's ample back. "We'll see, John," he answered. "You're in again; now get goin' in the council."

Although Coughlin was indisputably victorious in the First Ward, his position in the council had not been enhanced greatly. Twelve other gang aldermen, judged by their votes on the Watson gas ordinance, had been ousted, although Johnny Powers and one or two others survived. The Republicans had twenty-two new representatives in the council and with Billy Lorimer shuffling about in the background they desired to obtain and keep control.

In spite of the fact that the Republicans were solidly against him and many of the Democrats were angry because they believed

Mayor Hopkins had helped the First at the expense of other wards, Bathhouse, at the second meeting, undertook an often-defeated project still dear to his heart. The ordinance extending Homan Avenue, thereby cutting in two Garfield Park race track, had not yet been carried out. Alderman Coughlin petitioned Mayor Hopkins to grant a permit which would allow Garfield Park race track to reopen.

Several new aldermen, elected under reform auspices, quickly offered resolutions entreating the mayor not to issue such a permit.

"Why don't you include Washington Park?" shouted The Bath. "If you're gonna close one, let's close 'em all and keep horse money out of Chicago."

"We'll kill one snake at a time," retorted Alderman Ballard, newly elected and aspiring to be spokesman for the Civic Federation.

The leader of the Republican aldermen took up the fight. "This track is operated by an infamous and disreputable gang," said Alderman Madden. "It menaces the peace of the West Side."

"What about Washington Park? What about the South Side?" yelled Bathhouse John. "Why pick on the West?"

He won a temporary victory. Although the council went on record as opposing the reopening of Garfield Park, it did not pass any formal resolution denying Mayor Hopkins the right to issue the permit.

But pressure on the mayor came from other quarters. The meetings of west-side religious and civic organizations were resumed and the press and preachers renewed their thunder against the iniquities of the track. Coughlin and George Hankins pleaded with Mayor Hopkins. "Just give us a permit for thirty days," they begged. "That's all we need, thirty days." They pointed out that the property leased for the track was owned by Lambert Tree, wealthy and loyal Democrat, who received a rental of $58,000 a season when the track was running. But Tree's lawyers informed the mayor that their employer, then vacationing in Europe, had sent word that he'd prefer to see the track closed.

This final development seemed to make up Mayor Hopkins' mind. He declined to issue the permit and ordered the street extension to be carried through as soon as possible. This was finally the end of the track, for a street was extended. Years later a section of the track served as a roller-skating rink, and ultimately as a site for apartment dwellings and yellow brick bungalows for solid west-side citizens.

THE PATH OF REFORM

I

Bathhouse John was a lone but lusty figure in the city council the next few months. Eschewed by reformers and grafters alike, he trod a tenuous path between the two opposing camps, startling his colleagues by uttering loud brays in behalf of decency at one meeting, and by leaping vociferously upon the boodlers' bandwagon the next. He was as articulate as he was perplexed during those council meetings, and despite Hinky Dink's exhortations that he ought to remain comfortably quiet until they could determine which way the wind was blowing, he insisted upon introducing measures and passing public judgment upon even the most trivial business to come before the aldermen. The newspapers, however, discovered in him no inconsistency. They sneered or remained cynically silent when he plumped for honesty. They roared and painted him a boodler anew when he and the graft fraternity triumphed.

In no instance was Coughlin's unpredictability more striking than the renewed efforts of the boodlers to sandbag the companies in the Gas Trust. In July 1894, while state and federal troops patrolled Chicago as a result of the Pullman strike and the citizens shuddered before the strong words of Eugene V. Debs, the council was busy with a boodle problem. It was the hoary Watson gas ordinance called up again, this time in the guise of an act giving to a Universal Gas Company the privilege of installing gas mains everywhere.

The eternal cry, "Fictitious! Boodle!" was promptly raised by the habitually good men of the council, like John O'Neill and

Blind Billy Kent. And it was echoed by what other alderman? Why, the esteemed burgher from the First Ward!

"This order," boomed Alderman Bathhouse John as the roll of the council was called for the first vote on the ordinance, "is a dishonest order, Mr. Maar!"

His colleagues gasped. Mayor Hopkins, in whose mind Roger Sullivan already had planted an idea for forming a utility company of their own for the purpose of beating the Gas Trust, and who therefore opposed the Watson measure, nodded gratefully.

"There's no difference between this and the Watson ordinance," Bathhouse John yelled on. He glared angrily at aldermen who called reminders that he himself had once attempted to obtain passage of the original Watson ordinance, and continued: "This order, Mr. Maar, is a specul'tive order to extend dishonest privilege! Who are the promoters? Why don't they come out in the open and say what they want? There ain't nobody going to believe this franchise ever will build a genuine company! It's gonna be sold down the river!"

The Bath swept his arm in an indicting arc. "You all know this order ain't good," he lectured severely. "Me, I'm goin' to vote No."

He sat down heavily. The roll call proceeded and, despite the stirring sentiments of Coughlin, the Universal Gas measure won. Alderman Bathhouse John alone of the boodle gang had voted against it.

Public indignation rose swiftly when newspaper accounts of the ordinance appeared. The new council was denounced in familiar terms as "the worst in Chicago's history." Eagerly Bathhouse John scanned the papers for a laudatory word or two concerning his efforts to save Chicago from the terrible evil. He discovered no mention whatever, but members of the boodling corps approached to tell him he was an utter fool. He fretted and considered that his loyalty to Mayor Hopkins had called for futile, needless and excessive sacrifice.

When Hopkins vetoed the ordinance, he sent for the council

leaders he expected to support him in the action. Coughlin reluctantly appeared with the others.

The mayor was brusque and brief. "Boys, I need your votes and as many more as we can get to beat this ordinance."

All nodded sharply, but Bathhouse John mumbled, "I already give you my vote, Mr. Maar."

"You mean you're not going along?"

"I already give you my vote," Coughlin whined. "You ain't got a chance getting sustained. I been in politics a long while now, Mr. Maar, an' a man's gotta live. Live an' let live, I say. Now, what I want . . ."

"All right, John," snapped Hopkins. "I see how it is."

"Aw, Mr. Maar, I voted against it first, but I see now it's th' Gas Trust fighting it. The Gas Trust that's bleeding th' poor."

So the Universal Gas ordinance passed over Mayor Hopkins' veto, to be snapped up soon by the Gas Trust at a reported $170,000. And Bathhouse John, who had been the first to thunder "No" was now the first to shout "Aye!"

2

Still, all through the hot summer, Bathhouse John continued to follow what he considered was "the path of reform." He backed action forcing the streetcar companies to clean the thoroughfares in which their tracks were stretched, voted for a measure providing for a municipal lake-front area east of the Illinois Central Railroad tracks, blocked the same railroad's efforts to bar citizens from crossing its tracks to the lake, and pushed through a law requiring a score of factories and warehouses to pay for policemen watch service which the city previously had furnished without cost.

No words of praise resounded in his ears for these good deeds. Indeed, when he proposed to drive opium dens from the city by raising their fines from three dollars to one hundred dollars, Finley Peter Dunne, whose Mr. Dooley was even then hacking away at the evils of the city council, snorted editorially in the *Post:*

We welcome this amiable statesman to the army of reform. We commend his illustrious enterprise. But we should be more enthusiastic in our applause if we were sure that the statesman was unselfish in his undertaking—that he was not indirectly aiming to divert the drab procession of vice from the hop to the hot room.

Coughlin's brief flight with reform ended abruptly in mid-summer when the fledgling Civic Federation, solemnly incorporated the previous February and already armed with a plethora of evidence against gamblers, declared open war on the monarchs of roulette and crap tables. It hurled spiteful accusations against the politicians, told of fat protection envelopes passing from gambling-house owners to police captains and important city-hall bosses, and it particularly directed its ire upon the First Ward, where most of the gamblers were situated. A typical statement read:

We are led to believe that a regular monthly stipend of from $9,000 to $30,000 is collected by intermediaries and paid over to certain municipal, county and state officials. Gambling is going on with the doors wide open and cappers and stool pigeons are plying their vocations to catch the unwary, while the heads of the police department are giving these places ample protection from arrest.

They wanted action, these stern zealots of the Civic Federation, and they stormed Mayor Hopkins' office to demand it. But Hopkins, in spite of his rancor against Coughlin for the Universal Gas desertion, was as great a realist as his predecessors, and he deemed the official suppression of gambling virtually impossible. His police, nevertheless, began raiding many of the houses, although Mayor Hopkins denied issuing any orders. As fast as the places were shut they reopened. Such chicanery did not fool the vigilant Civic Federation. Week after week grim committees, headed by indignant ministers, called on the mayor and thrust upon his desk long lists of gambling houses in operation. The harassed mayor tried to evade their direct demands for a complete shutdown.

"Why, some of the businessmen in this city want such places open," he once blurted. "It's surprising how many reputable businessmen want gambling to continue."

Among such businessmen was Hinky Dink Kenna, who sought desperately to carry out his promise that the Coughlin-Kenna organization would protect the little fellows. The Civic Federation, however, would not be appeased. In a bold move the reformers engaged Matt Pinkerton operatives and invaded Gamblers' Alley and its environs, crashing into back-room dice parlors as well as the rich establishments of Prince Hal Varnell, Johnny Condon and Billy Fagan. Equipment was smashed, dragged into the streets and there chopped to bits by angry crusaders. The gamblers retaliated with damage suits and mandamus actions and for weeks the forces of alleged vice and alleged virtue battled in the gaming houses, the courts and the streets.

Finally it became obvious that protection from Mayor Hopkins was not forthcoming. Several gamblers repaired to near-by Hammond and other wide-open Indiana towns, a few into obscure retirement, and some took up other illegal enterprises. Many remained behind, hopeful that this frightening display of reformers' arrogance and strength soon would subside. The Hink, meanwhile, pointed out to bewildered Bathhouse the needless cost of fighting the administration.

Late in the year, with the few remaining houses opening and closing with irksome regularity, the Civic Federation, flushed with its successes, prompted its Republican spokesman in the council to demand a huge investigation into the police department along the lines of the Clarence Lexow probe which had agonized Tammany Hall in New York.

Alderman Bathhouse John, having learned his lesson, rose in

the city hall, as he would countless times in future years, to fight the reformers.

"I'm heartily in favor of an honest investigation," he sneered. "But I don't think we'd get one, considering the direction from which it comes. Chicago can't afford to pay the three thousand dollars such an investigation would cost. We got city employees yelling for pay and these reformers want to waste money looking into a police department that's good the way it is. Reformers! I can smell 'em a mile away."

A majority of the aldermen agreed with Coughlin, and the proposal was shunted aside. Slight as it was, this defeat of the Civic Federation furnished the signal for an attempted gambling resurrection in the First Ward. Small gaming hells venturesomely opened their doors. The raids were resumed. The gamblers closed down again, only to pop up a few days later in inconspicuous rear rooms, lofts and basements. The small fry desperately needed protection, aside from that afforded by the Coughlin-Kenna defense fund.

Quick and decisive action was needed, for Hinky Dink was looking forward to the spring elections with a view to running for alderman himself. Bathhouse again wended his way to Mayor Hopkins' office, this time abjectly desirous of peace. Hopkins had a project in mind that would require a steadfast aldermanic vote. He relented, and while the Civic Federation relaxed, the gambling raids suddenly ceased.

The Hink began patiently to rebuild his lines. Now, and definitely, the reign of King Mike McDonald was over. He had had no part in the final salvation of gambling, and the Civic Federation had insolently demonstrated for months how puny the King had become. It was Coughlin and Kenna who had eventually averted disaster, and henceforth they would essay the roles of protectors and would forever engage the Civic Federation in combat. They had come out of the struggle weakened, but the Civic Federation had cleared the way for their eventual resurgence by loosening from the ward the last aging grasp of the erstwhile czar.

3

By the time the new year arrived, Mayor Hopkins had had enough of the city hall. He announced he would not seek re-election in the spring. Chicago was soon to learn that dapper Johnny was out for bigger game.

Local Democracy was in a fragile state, its ranks threatened by the strife between Governor Altgeld and President Cleveland over the dispatch of federal troops during the Pullman strike. Washington Hesing, elevated to the position of Chicago's postmaster by President Cleveland, offered to save the party by breaking the deadlock, but the leaders recalled his enmity toward the sainted "Our Carter," and frowned anew on his mayoral ambitions. They swung behind Frank Wenter, while the Republicans, blatantly confident of victory, nominated austere George Swift, the alderman, to whom the so-called decent vote was pledged.

In the First Ward Kenna sought feverishly to rebuild his harried organization. He revealed to Coughlin his ambition to enter the council. The big alderman solemnly promised him that the election was in the feed bag, and at the First Ward Democratic convention Kenna was nominated by whooping acclamation. Among those not present, however, were Sol van Praag and the irascible Billy Skakel.

Kenna's response to the cheers of the organization was characteristic. "If I am elected," he told his supporters, "I will try to show the people I am not as bad as I am painted on account of the name Hinky Dink."

But while Kenna and other Democratic hopefuls were proceeding with campaign plans, those sterling party leaders Mayor John Hopkins and Roger Sullivan staged the audacious coup which was to gain them riches but spell disaster to the party candidates.

Sullivan had organized his plans carefully. Only five experienced aldermen—John Powers, Tom Gahan, Tom Byrne, Little

Mike Ryan and the sometime candidate for mayor, John Mc-Gillen—knew what was afoot on the eve of the council's meeting, February 25, 1895. The others, including Bathhouse John, had been forewarned, however, that vital events were impending, and they made certain not to be absent from the council chamber.

That session proved a nightmare for the honest council minority. Mayor Hopkins presided for five minutes, then excused himself and hustled from the chamber. Little Mike Ryan climbed into the mayor's chair and promptly recognized Alderman Mc-Gillen. That worthy rose and droned out a substitute for an electric-power ordinance which had been introduced in 1893 and since placed on file. This, he announced, was the Cosmopolitan electric ordinance, and, since it was a routine substitute, there was no necessity to read it aloud. Ryan agreed and called for a speedy vote and the ordinance was rushed through, 61 to 4.

Aldermen Kent, James R. Mann and O'Neill, who knew nothing of the intent of the ordinance but were suspiciously certain that no good was embodied in it, demanded more time for a careful study of the terms. They were shouted down by the boodlers, but O'Neill seized a copy of the measure for inspection. A hasty perusal disclosed a daring boodle franchise, awarding to a fictitious company rights to build electric power plants and to construct conduits anywhere in the city to supply not only light and power, but heat and signal communications for fifty years. A heat, power, telephone and telegraph ordinance all rolled into one, not only encompassing the entire city, but doubling the usual life of such privileges!

The three aldermen sputtered and fumed but their cries soon were muffled by new developments. The time for Sullivan's greater coup had arrived and the steam roller was ready for action again.

Alderman McGillen had now taken the chair and was asking pleasantly of Little Mike Ryan, "What is your pleasure, alderman?"

Blithely, Little Mike offered another ordinance to substitute for an old gas measure. Alderman Mann spouted objections without even knowing the terms of the ordinance, which involved an Ogden Gas Company. Bathhouse John, anxious to do his bit, sprang to his feet, and, though he knew as little about the measure as Mann, hailed it as a thrust against the Gas Trust and orated in behalf of the people who were being robbed by excessive gas prices. His needless tirade wasted valuable time, irritating Alderman McGillen, who yelled, "Oh, shut up, John, and sit down!"

Bathhouse subsided and cast his vote. The Ogden Gas ordinance, like the Cosmopolitan Electric measure, passed, 61 to 4.

The next morning the good citizens of Chicago awakened to discover that their council not only had authorized a mystery firm called the Cosmopolitan Electric Company to dig up any part of Chicago but also had granted to an equally vague Ogden Gas Company similar rights to make, pipe, and sell gas for half a century. The Ogden Gas ordinance called for a ceiling of 90 cents per 1,000 cubic feet as compared with the $1.20 rate charged by the Gas Trust, but this fooled nobody. It was part of the sandbagging technique to force the Gas Trust to buy up the ordinance, or, if the Ogden Company ever actually went into business, the ceiling could readily be removed by amendment. Both measures looked to the public exactly what they were, brazen shakedown ordinances.

The Civic Federation immediately called a mass protest meeting. The newspapers spread their blackest print. Even the loyal *Times* lambasted the council. On its front page, the irate *Tribune* printed a mocking advertisement:

> FOR SALE—ONE GAS FRANCHISE COVERING ALL OF the earth within the corporate limits of Chicago: guaranteed sound and court proof: a bargain at $250,000. Apply early and avoid the rush!
> ALSO
> ONE FRANCHISE, ALLOWING OWNER THEREOF TO build and operate (if he so desires) electric lighting plants, telephone systems, telegraph lines,

etc., etc., etc. This is a copper bottomed, riveted
cinch and this is cheap at $500,000.

Apply THE GANG

City Council Chambers, Chicago.

The thunder raised was of such violence as to continue to
reverberate for years afterward. The sixty-one guilty aldermen
prudently retired to their saloon storm-cellars and piously hoped
that the thing would soon blow over. Although some of the sinners occasionally emerged from their sanctuaries to plead that the
ordinance would help to break the high prices charged by the
utility firms, the uproar did not abate, and indignant executives
of the companies in the Gas Trust shouted more loudly than anyone about "flagrant shakedown measures." The prices, evidently,
had been set too high. Only one of the Ogden firm's incorpora-
tors, who were discovered by the newspapers after some difficulty,
seemed a man of reputation. He was John Lanehart, cousin of
Governor Altgeld, and he insisted that the measure had been
drawn up in good faith.

The Civic Federation turned its attention to Hopkins, but the
wily mayor refused a veto. It was a case of get and run with Hopkins. The Democratic party was dead for the time being, and
Roger Sullivan and his Chesterfieldian satellite in the mayor's
chair had laid a decorative wreath on its grave.

4

Such was the heat that neither the Gas Trust nor the utility
barons would have connection with the ordinances. In a few years
the Ogden Gas Company actually became a reality, and it built
and operated a plant with Roger Sullivan as president* until its

*The Ogden Gas shares were distributed as follows: Hopkins, 2/11; Sullivan,
1/11; Powers, Gahan, Thomas Byrne, Ryan, Levi Mayer (attorney for Yerkes),
McGillen and Lanehart, 1/11 each. A 1/11th share was split for various aldermen,
including Coughlin, who is reported to have received little. In later years these 1/11th
shares were worth $166,666.66 each. On the death of Lanehart, Governor Altgeld
inherited his shares.

eventual absorption by the People's Gas Light and Coke Company. In time, the burning issues of 1895—the steam-roller technique, the chrematistic gluttony of the city fathers, the cries of graft and boodle were forgotten.

But the instant effect of the ordinances was disastrous for the aldermanic aspirations of Michael Kenna. Until the Ogden Gas affair had burst he had cherished reasonable hope of election, in spite of the insalubrious state of Democratic affairs generally and the recent incursions against the gamblers. For little Hink had among the election judges of the First Ward no fewer than six professional gamblers, six bartenders—three of them his own: John Ready, Charlie Kurf, and E. J. Barry—plus twenty confidence men and brothel bouncers and fifty-three loyal rooming-house lodgers.

Such was the public indignation over Ogden Gas that reaction against Democrats generally seeped even into the First Ward. The Dink was first to perceive it. "I don't think a gent like me's got as much chance of bein' elected as a snowball in hell," he mourned to Bathhouse John.

Kenna faced opposition from many sources. The speakers of the Civic Federation were in a frenzy of righteous wrath, and they drew big audiences even in the First where they particularly excoriated the boodlers and all associated with them. Those aldermen and their friends, shouted the orators, were jackals, hyenas, harpies, parasites, thieves, sandbaggers, bloodsuckers, vultures, wolves, vampires, thugs, pirates and rapacious beasts.

From other quarters came treachery. Billy Skakel and Sol van Praag, fortified by the presence of still truculent Big Sandy Walters, were out to upset Coughlin's apple cart by doing evil to Kenna. They attempted unsuccessfully to gain the party support for Nick Cremer, and then determined to back a certain Colonel Babcock, until they learned his election petitions had been signed in Hinky Dink's saloon. Finally they committed the most vile of political sins: they pledged their support to the Republican candidate, Francis (Paddy) Gleason.

In the high ranks of the party also treachery and crookedness sent Hinky Dink's hopes falling. A few days before the election it was discovered that $100,000 of the party's campaign fund, containing much of the First Ward's vote-buying money, had been filched, reportedly for the purpose of buying council votes in behalf of Ogden Gas. Coughlin then grimly realized that he had been paid off, in effect, with his own money. He and The Dink made desperate last-minute efforts to raise new funds.

Van Praag, however, seemed to have plenty of money and he staged pompous rallies at which the downfall of Kenna and Coughlin was freely predicted. Mayor Hopkins, moved finally by the hysterical plaints of Bathhouse John, did at last make an effort for Hinky Dink. He ordered van Praag before the party's central committee and sought to reason with him. But the keeper of the Owl Saloon was hot to be avenged for Skakel's defeat in 1894.

Avenged he was. He borrowed Kenna's technique of paying the floaters and increased the rates to fantastic proportions—some of the bums claimed to have been paid as much as five dollars a vote—and Kenna was unable to fight back with similar weapons. It was a quiet and sad election day in the First Ward, and when it was over Gleason had won, although by a meager plurality of only 346 votes. Alderman Swift carried the ward and the city for the mayorship against Wenter, and was sent into office with a 41,000 majority. The Hink was far from being alone in his political woe. Nine aldermen who had voted "Aye!" on the Ogden Gas and Consolidated ordinances were now ex-aldermen, and the new council was to have fifty Republicans and only twenty Democrats.

The newspapers cruelly gibed Hinky Dink in his defeat, the *Tribune,* on its editorial page, dedicating to him the following poem:

> "I t'ink,"
> Said Hink-
> Y Dink,
> "I'll take a drink."

"At this writing," commented the publication, "it looks as if there would be nothing else for him to take."

"The Honorable Hinky Dink has gone to West Baden to boil out," remarked the *Tribune* a few days later. "Has he lost faith in the efficacy of Chicago's bathhouses?"

Following the election it was discovered that van Praag and Skakel had assisted Gleason by revealing to the Republican organization the names and addresses of hundreds of dead men and repeaters registered to vote by the Coughlin-Kenna organization. The Republicans in turn had forced the board of election commissioners to remove the names from the polling lists. When the source of this noisome double-dealing stood revealed Kenna summoned the press and issued a statement: "If ever Bill Skakel sticks up his head again in this ward, jist you watch me put a hump on it."

5

In less than a month Bathhouse and Kenna had their first opportunity for revenge. Van Praag and Walters, regarding themselves as the new leaders of the ward, thought to celebrate their ascendancy by picking up a few thousand dollars promoting a prize fight in Battery B Armory on the lake front. To circumvent the city ordinance barring bare-fist battles, they announced the fighters would wear gloves.

As soon as Coughlin heard of the impending show he drew up an ordinance prohibiting all types of fights. He did not introduce it at once, but waited until the night before the battle, after tickets had been sold and all preparations completed. The aldermen passed the ordinance without much argument, but Mayor Hopkins, who had already issued a permit for the fight, refused to sign the measure, which in any event could not become effective until the expiration of ten days.

The Bath worked speedily. He consulted attorneys and received the legal opinion that a fight was a fight, gloves or not. The old ordinance could be invoked to stop the contest. Coughlin sought out Police Chief Brennan, secured his promise of co-operation and obtained warrants for Tommy Ryan, Jack Wilks, Will Mayo and Frank Childs, the top fighters on the card. They were to be arrested at the ring just before the start of the semifinal bout, an action certain to precipitate a riot, with the promoters the victims of the mob.

The manager of the show was Parsons Davies, an experienced old-timer in Gamblers' Alley who once had managed Mike McDonald's Store. When he heard of the plot he checked with Brennan and learned that the police would certainly serve the warrants as directed. Without even consulting van Praag and Walters, Davies called off the bouts and left the ensuing financial worries to the promoters.

"I ain't got a chance with the police against me," said Davies. "I must've have made a mistake. I seen the wrong people, I guess. I should've seen Alderman Coughlin, huh?"

The bad feeling in the First became murderous. Choleric Skakel, who knew that his faction had become the laughing stock of the Levee, was completely inarticulate. Bathhouse John proceeded grandly through Clark Street, crowing to his friends:

"I tell you now I stopped that fight. I stopped it all by myself. I did it because I thought certain people interested in this affair had no right to run a show in this ward, such people as Sol van Praag and Big Sandy Walters, fellows that are no possible good on earth. I was after Walters and van Praag, and I fixed 'em!"

Van Praag was furious, but he lost little of his equanimity. "It was just the kind of dirty trick a dirty mind would think up," he said. "It don't hurt me none, but think of poor Parsons Davies. I guess Bathhouse won't amount to much among the sports after this, eh?"

As for Walters, erstwhile friend of Coughlin, he was so enraged he could barely talk. But he approved the following sentiment as prepared by a reporter: "I read in a natural history book that the lowest form of animal life is a thing called a bathybius. And that's what John is. He's a bathybius."

SPLITTING A POT

I

LIKE a ruffled phoenix Bathhouse John rose from the ashes of the First Ward disaster to lunge into the affairs of the council. Hinky Dink, not one to brood over the past, had seen in the ruins of political defeat a remarkable opportunity. In spite of the efforts of Charles Tyson Yerkes, who collaborated financially in the campaigns of many of the boodlers, the gang had been riddled all over town by the reform barrage. Most of them were Democrats, and few remained at the very moment Yerkes was planning the greatest expansion of his traction career. Kenna saw at once that Coughlin's aldermanic vote would be vitally needed, not only to forward the ambitions of Yerkes but to do battle with the Republican mayor and the Republican majority in the council. Nor had the realities of the situation escaped Johnny Powers. He and the Coughlin-Kenna organization proceeded immediately to form an alliance. It was not an easy thing to accomplish, after the unspeakable duplicity of Hopkins, Sullivan and Powers in the Ogden Gas affair, but Yerkes' interests and the Republican menace transcended internal Democratic squabbles.

While Kenna grimly began reorganizing his shattered First Ward forces with a view to personal vengeance in 1897, the new boodle combination, with Bathhouse John one of the acknowledged leaders, prepared for action. The panic of 1893-1894 had passed, and business was in a mood for privilege. Yerkes desired to electrify streetcars through the entire downtown area, standing ready to buy the First Ward, block by block. The elevated lines—Lake Street, Metropolitan, Northwestern and South Chicago "Alley L"—were moving downtown, all desperately anxious for

125

ordinances and permits allowing them to complete a loop about the First Ward business section.

No sooner was the new council sworn in than the boodling resumed. Not a week passed without a chance for the aldermen to share in a profitable ordinance. The public soon discovered that however indignantly Mayor Swift might protest, the Republican-dominated council was fully as bad as its predecessors. When there was money in sight the new councilmen forgot partisan differences and eagerly accepted the leadership of Coughlin and Powers. The newspapers saw the boodle laws coming, reported and condemned them. The pulpits shook with the thunder of the clergy's cries. The Civic Federation ranted and threatened. But the plunder mill ground on serenely. Many an alderman bought a country estate, Yerkes built a $2,000,000 mansion in New York and added the works of more masters to his fabulous art collection, and the First Ward treasury grew fat. The steady sale of franchises over the city-hall counter was, if anything, more open than ever, and it was common knowledge that the gang collected and split in the Powers & O'Brien saloon according to the might wielded for the measure and the wards affected. Sneered the *Tribune:* "These aldermen are honorable men. They never cheat each other in splitting a pot."

Since the bulk of the boodling interests centered in the First Ward, it was Bathhouse John who sponsored and guided many of the measures. His alliance with Powers created a tight ring of veteran conspirators able to control the Republican majority almost at will by merely loosening the purse strings. Wealth and power were suddenly thrust upon The Bath, and he rose magnificently to his opportunity. No ordinance, however trivial, could pass without a speech from Bathhouse John, harangues the newspapers contemptuously dismissed as "long and rambling." As his power grew, Coughlin took delight in making himself obnoxious to Mayor Swift, for whom, in the mayor's aldermanic reform days, The Bath had conceived a petulant dislike. It became commonplace for Coughlin, in a single session, to sponsor a blatant boodle law and with rare whimsy to produce unquestionably useful reform measures designed to irk the mayor.

On the evening of June 3 Bathhouse John and his friends undertook to run through the council the famous Calumet and Blue Island Railroad ordinance. This railroad was a child of the Illinois Steel Company, which sought a right of way from the Indiana state line to Ninety-fifth Street, a route which would shut off the far south side of Chicago from Lake Michigan. The entire district had arisen in wrath when the ordinance was first contemplated, but the aldermen were deaf to the protests. It was a project too hot for the south-side councilmen to handle, but Bathhouse John had nothing to fear. His constituency rarely visited the lake in any part of town, and was supremely indifferent to neighbors beyond its boundaries. So Coughlin undertook to debate the measure himself.

Dressed in his already famous black silk frock coat, the lapel agleam with his diamond aldermanic star, primed with arguments by the steel-company attorneys and glowering fiercely at Mayor Swift, Bathhouse puffed his cheeks, thrust out his lower lip, shoved his right hand into his flowered waistcoat in the approved oratorical style of the day, and commenced:

"This ordinance is going to make Chicago! It's goin' to put waste property on the tax rolls. Where would Chicago be if it wasn't for industry? We've got to get industry where we can get it, and we've got to get money where we can get it." There was a tittering in the gallery, but The Bath ignored it. "What good is a lot of swimmin' in th' lake goin' to do us?" he demanded contemptuously. "I tell you, we got to have this railroad!"

"There is grease behind this ordinance!" shouted Alderman John O'Neill. "Grease!"

"Well," inquired The Bath blandly, "what are we here for?"

"I know what you are here for!" yelled Alderman Hambleton. "You——" Hambleton was cut off by cries of "Vote! Vote!" from The Bath's associates. Mayor Swift rapped ineffectually for order, and then wearily ordered the clerk to call the roll. Coughlin led off with a defiant "Aye!" and forty-two other aldermen followed him. Twenty-one, supporters of Swift, stood by the mayor.

But Coughlin had by no means finished for the night. He had planned his strategy and advised friends that he intended to pick a personal fight with Mayor Swift. Then, when Swift vetoed the Blue Island ordinance, The Bath could yelp that it was a personal attack on him, born of vengeance; weak-kneed boodlers whose votes were needed would not be frightened out of passing the measure over the veto. Coughlin assumed a risk, for Swift, at least nominally, controlled the First Ward police, and the Coughlin-Kenna organization always needed the police. Still, The Bath hit hard and he found a sore spot, even if it was one created by the loose regime of Mayor Hopkins and simply inherited by the hapless Swift.

"Mr. Maar," said Coughlin, "there's a lot a talk goin' around about the stuffin' of city pay rolls with politicians. Now I don't like that sort of thing. I understand there is a lot of department heads just waitin' to confess. I move that Billy Kent,* the commissioner of public works, be directed to prosecute all these persons concerned with the alleeged stuffin' of public pay rolls." He lingered in sinister fashion on that word "alleeged" and sat down, winking at his friends.

Swift, aware of the truth of the charge and startled by the alderman's proposal, recovered slowly. "I support the alderman from the First Ward in his desire," he said, with all the sarcasm he could muster. "I congratulate him! Any stuffing of pay rolls will be found to be left over from the previous maladministration. I think that the evidence to be uncovered will be interesting. If this order is a challenge, this administration is ready to meet it!"

Alderman O'Neill was quickly on his feet. "Alderman Coughlin must have deserted the Democratic party! Surely he cannot want any further exposure of the most corrupt administration this or any other city has ever been afflicted with! I'm glad it's the

---

*Not "Blind Billy" Kent, the alderman.

leader of the Democratic minority who has introduced this order!"

Coughlin glowed as O'Neill affixed the title "leader of the Democratic minority" to him. He had few qualms about the "exposures" of which O'Neill shouted. He knew well that most of the high politicians, whether Republican or Democrat, could hardly afford any serious investigation into boondoggling and pay-roll stuffing. But now he would be able to charge that Swift would veto the Blue Island ordinance in retaliation for the exposure of corruption in his regime. He saw the measure pass handily. No one dared oppose it.

Then Coughlin rose once more. "Another thing," he declared. "There have been lots of complaints about the waste of water. Everybody knows that water is wasted because the administration hasn't instructed the chief of police to stop it. I move that the chief of police prosecute all people wastin' water."

This aroused considerable merriment among the councilmen. "I move," quipped Alderman Lammers, "that, in view of the scarcity of water the saloons be allowed to stay open all night!" But the council knew again that Coughlin's charge was just, for there was a genuine threat of a water shortage. Again the motion passed. Then the "leader of the Democratic minority" rose for his fourth major motion that night.

"This Chicago Economic Gas Company," said he, "is supposed to be payin' the city five per cent of its earnings, but it ain't. I move the corporation counsel be told to take steps to cancel this ordinance."

This was something the boys could appreciate and a quick vote sent the measure to the gas committee, where appropriate pressure could be quietly applied to the remiss company. The Bath's work for the night was over.

For the next few weeks the newspapers were busy with stories about the water shortage and the prospective prosecutions in Kent's department, a great outcry arising when a street foreman confessed that he had 194 more men on his payroll than the department required. In a month Swift vetoed the Calumet and Blue Island ordinance, and Coughlin promptly responded with charges that the mayor had acted from malice, to punish those who had exposed his corrupt administration. Thus exculpated in advance, fainthearted boodlers rallied to The Bath, passed the ordinance over the veto of the bewildered mayor, and gave a grateful Illinois Steel Company not one route along the lake front, but a choice of three.

2

Coughlin's arrogance in the council soon undid him. He had forced the newspapers to agree that his "reform" measures were good ones, he had handily defeated Mayor Swift, and he was fast becoming a hero among the boodlers. Late in the summer, after a series of successful and profitable railroad ordinances, he elected to do battle with the press.

In the spring the *Tribune* had opened a campaign for a lake-front park from Randolph Street south with "splendid buildings, large playgrounds, noble statuary, graveled walks, macadamized drives." Most of the other newspapers joined in support of the park project, but the Illinois Central Railroad was filling in the land, which lay east of its tracks, and proposed to keep the area for itself. The Illinois Central had First Ward precinct captains on its pay roll, and Coughlin set out to discharge his obligations. He sounded his favorite theme: the only way to get more taxes was to put more land into production.

The *Tribune* was irate and printed a page-one cartoon depicting a politician, unmistakably the pompadoured Coughlin, kicking the lake-front park into Lake Michigan. "The pig in the parlor does what might be expected of him," read the caption. The Bath was lashed with all the blistering invective eight daily publications could muster. His colleagues grew frightened, and he was forced to bear the attack alone.

Nevertheless, Coughlin was determined to win for the railroad. So one warm night he rose in the council, armed with the usual arguments about property and taxes. But his opening words doomed him.

"We," boomed The Bath, with a wave of arms to take in the whole of the council, "are heartily in need of funds . . ."

There was a storm of laughter, catcalls, and jeers from the gallery. Even the aldermen began hooting, to disassociate themselves from that brash beginning. Johnny Powers chuckled quietly. Friends of the mayor on the rostrum wiped tears of laughter from their eyes, and the newspapermen yelped delightedly in their cagelike press box. The Bath, his mouth agape, stood helplessly at his desk, sweat streaming from every pore. Coughlin was unnerved, and would have given one of his best horses if Hinky Dink were at his side to advise him. Unable to find words to explain his statement, he tried to shout above the uproar and demanded that Mayor Swift clear the chamber. Swift tapped daintily with his gavel and said something that sent his friends into a paroxysm of mirth. The Bath flopped into his seat and wiped his brow. Five minutes later the lake-front ordinance was sent to a committee sure to report it favorably. Coughlin sat silent, glaring straight ahead oɪ him, until near the end of the meeting, when, amid a noisy demonstration in the gallery, he secured a routine permit to allow Hinky Dink to install a covered entrance for his saloon at Clark and Van Buren Streets.

3

Coughlin's humiliation in the council was quickly forgotten in the excitement of new events. Governor John Peter Altgeld, an ardent liberal who was still furious with President Cleveland for federal intervention during the Pullman strike, determined to seize the Democratic party of Illinois and make it a part of the Free Silver boom then rumbling on the prairies of the West. The governor called a special convention of the party in Springfield, and among the sterling Democratic leaders he invited to participate were John Coughlin and Michael Kenna of Chicago's First Ward.

Altgeld's action split Chicago Democracy, but he had with him the ward leaders, saloonkeepers and less affluent party men who remembered well the rigorous winter of 1893-1894, when a large part of the laboring population fed at the free-lunch counters of the corner saloons. These supporters were rounded up in Cook County by Tommy Gahan, state warehouse commissioner, aided nobly by Gahan's personal friends, Bobbie Burke and Alderman Bathhouse John.

Through the influence of Burke, Captain Jimmy Farrell and his Democratic Marching Club and the First Regiment band were called out, and a special train was chartered to carry 437 marchers and delegates to Springfield. Bathhouse John superintended the bar and beer barrels in the baggage car, and newspaper artists accompanying the expedition drew cartoons of him drinking a glass of water. "Say, it's great!" said The Bath in pleased surprise, according to the captions.

The enthusiasm of the Chicago Silverites was probably more than Altgeld expected. They fetched a cargo of skyrockets, roman candles, blue fire and nigger chasers, marched their noisy legions through the streets, accidentally exploded a whole barrel of skyrockets, frightened the horses, turned in false police alarms, and engaged in a free-for-all fight with Springfield citizenry. They were going to march in triumph to the statehouse, but desisted when Governor Altgeld sent word he wasn't there.

"These Chicago Democrats," reported a correspondent, "are for 16 to 1—sixteen parts whisky and one part water."

At a banquet prior to the opening of the convention Bathhouse John led the delegates in a cry that was to become famous throughout the land:

"Rah, rah . . . sixteen to one!"

The Bath's voice was not heard in the convention proceedings, although he was elected a delegate to the national Free Silver convention, should one be called, but he received a good deal of attention from the press.

"It would have done your soul good to have seen Alderman John Coughlin," said the *Tribune*. "He was made up for festive scenes. He was attired in a summer suit faultless in fit and cut, linen in keeping with the season, and on his head he wore a yachting cap of white flannel. It would be unnecessary to add that on the bosom of the alderman's shirt was a four-carot [sic] diamond that would put a locomotive headlight to blush. Beside him sat Mike Kenna. Coughlin chewed gum. Kenna chewed a toothpick."

The final day of the convention an ambitious young man from Nebraska asked for an opportunity to address the delegates. He was William Jennings Bryan. His "Cross of Gold" speech was yet to come, and he made little impression on Altgeld, but he won a ready convert in Bathhouse John. When Bryan's new Chicago disciple returned to Clark Street he opened a saloon, calling it The Silver Dollar. This establishment, in which former Alderman Johnny Morris owned a part interest, was dedicated with ceremonies on July 23, 1895. Coughlin confided to friends that he had always wanted a saloon. "It was this way," he explained to reporters. "There were three of us and we were all drinking beer an' I went home an' dreamed I was a brewery, and th' next day I owned a saloon."

The grand opening attracted most of the aldermen, including even John O'Neill. They were welcomed at the door by One-Eyed Jimmy Connelly, already famous as a gate-crasher. "Dis is de proudest moment dat me an' de city of Cheecago has ever witnessed," Connelly assured the visitors. "Here's to de Silver boufay an' to de constitooents of de Silver King, once known as Bat'ouse John."

The Bath had commissioned a South Halsted Street artist to paint huge silver dollars on the ceiling and walls of the buffet. They were larger than beer-barrel heads. In place of the dates were legends: Silver Money, Your Money, Easy Money, Matrimony, Long Money, Short Money, Farmer's Money, Pension Money, Workingman's Money, and, in a conspicuous place in the center of the ceiling, My Money. Each dollar, of course, bore the inscription *E pluribus unum*. "He brews us new rum," translated One-Eyed Connelly.

When the guests had assembled, The Bath stepped out among them. "Boys, she's open!" he cried. "The Silver Dollar. . . . Sixteen to one! The silver dollars in the floor," he added, "are at a ratio of one to 725. Everybody have a drink!"

4

The summer was quiet politically, although the Free Silverites were marshaling their forces, and Coughlin remained in Chicago to watch over his new saloon and to aid the beginning Free Silver campaign. There were rumors that the gang was planning a real coup in the fall. Mayor Swift was in New York, studying traction problems. Coughlin was devoting some of his time to his bathhouses, for it was recorded that Tim Hogan, state representative of the Fourth District, visited the alderman in his bathhouse for the administration of a pair of leeches after his left eye had been closed by Daniel (Montana Kid) Egan in a fight at the stockyards.

The coup came on October 7, and, after the debacle of the lake-front-park ordinance, Alderman Powers was selected to direct it. Powers called up for passage a fifty-year franchise for the Union Elevated Company, which was to operate all of the four loop elevated lines then being built. This was a Yerkes project, with D. H. Louderback, president of the Lake Street and Northwestern elevated companies, collaborating.

The joker in the ordinance was that, while the four companies—Lake, Northwestern, Metropolitan, and Chicago and South Side (The Alley L)—had franchises for only twenty years, requiring the payment of three and one-half per cent of gross receipts to the city, the Union Elevated ordinance provided for control of the city's loop for half a century with only three per cent of the gross as remuneration.

Coughlin was angered by the fact that Powers exclusively had been assigned to obtain passage of the measure. He attempted to knock out a provision of the ordinance that would permit the company to carry the United States mails at a good profit, but he was unsuccessful. Alderman Mann led a fight to prevent passage unless the compensation should be increased, but he likewise failed. Big business was with the boodlers in this measure. "Compensation or no compensation," said Robert C. Givens, head of a delegation of businessmen who called on Mayor Swift, "we want a downtown loop. To stand in the way of this ordinance and load it down with obligations at the present time would be unjust to the public."

The ordinance passed, and Bathhouse John, hoping for crumbs, was among the aldermen voting for it. But the rift with Johnny de Pow was opening again.

5

Coughlin, in November, brought out perhaps his least known yet most enduring ordinance. Many men make a feeble swipe at immortality by erecting great monoliths in the graveyards of the land, only to have them dwarfed up by other monuments. But The Bath can never be forgotten in Chicago, for he is responsible for the twelve-foot stone and brick walls about many of the cemeteries.

"I am going to introduce an ordinance for twelve-foot stone walls around all the cemeteries," announced Alderman Coughlin. "This is no bosh. Cemeteries are bad places at best. They have a deadening affect on the neighborhoods and I want them covered up as much as possible. I want the walls ornamented on the outside and it might be a good idea to sell the space to advertisers. What's the use of spoiling a whole neighborhood by having a joblot of woozy tombstones in sight when you can just as well fence them in? I'm in dead earnest about this matter, and I'll spring it in the council as soon as my lawyer gets the bill ready."

The ordinance was never passed, but several of the cemetery associations surprisingly accepted Coughlin's idea as a good one, and walls were erected. They remain today, but they are appropriately blank, and are rarely confused with the city's multitudinous billboards.

REPRESENTING THE PEOPLE

I

As December of 1895 approached, and the politicians began to think of the spring campaign, the tether binding Coughlin and Johnny de Pow abruptly parted. The Bath was enraged by his exclusion from inner council deliberations on the Union Elevated ordinance and the liberal franchise for the Yerkes-owned American Gas Engine Electric Company that quickly followed. It became clear that Yerkes and Powers had executed an arrangement in which Bathhouse had little part. The slick Nineteenth Ward statesman had welcomed Coughlin back in April, when Democratic fortunes were low and it was impossible to forecast the predilections of the new Republican majority, but since that time Powers found the Republicans fully as venal as his own gang, and far less expensive. So Powers elected to dispense with the services of the costly and noisy Bathhouse, and Yerkes' ordinances, which ought by custom to have originated from the First Ward, which they largely concerned, instead went into the council hopper by way of the Nineteenth. It was an indignity no alderman should be expected to endure, and Coughlin, fuming anew at his recollections of the Ogden Gas affair, furiously refused to do so.

His opportunity for vengeance on Powers came the night of December 2. The lugubrious councilman from the Nineteenth aspired to the chairmanship of the Cook County Democratic central committee, a position that would make him boss of the party in Cook County. Coughlin and Kenna, with Tommy Gahan and Bobbie Burke, had undertaken to carry Chicago Democracy into the Free Silver camp of Governor Altgeld, and they boldly determined to capture the central committee chairmanship themselves.

136

They advanced Gahan as a candidate, and of course had the support of Altgeld. Powers, supreme on the west side, had the assistance and advice of Hopkins, Sullivan and Mike McDonald and he boasted that the chairmanship was tucked snugly away in his vest pocket.

For their showdown fight both Coughlin and Powers abandoned the meeting of the city council that night,* and The Bath rose majestically in the committee meeting to deliver an impassioned oration for Gahan. Powers and his gang threatened flatly to withdraw completely from the Democratic party unless their candidate should be elected. There were recriminations and fist fights, and the worst Democratic split in Chicago's history appeared in the making. But the influence of Altgeld was formidable, and the saloon-keeping delegates from the workingmen's areas knew what the common man was demanding. Gahan and Free Silver won, 72 to 35. He promptly named Burke the committee secretary, and the Silver forces found themselves in control of the party machinery.

Flushed with this victory, Bathhouse John decided that the time had come to trip up Powers in the council, and Yerkes with him. The traction baron was just preparing the final links in his extensive west-side streetcar system. And he was having trouble. He proposed to bring his lines together in Jackson Street, to feed them into the loop, but the property owners along Jackson stubbornly refused to give him the frontage consents necessary to the passage of an ordinance.

The situation was discussed at the Silver Dollar and in Hinky Dink's saloon. Finally it was decided that circumstances were auspicious for another shakedown coup, in the manner of Ogden Gas. Only this time there would be no doubt that the victim would be ready to buy at a good price. Yerkes couldn't refuse. Coughlin and Kenna took into the scheme Perry Hull, boss of the Third Ward, and two La Salle Street entrepreneurs, Lucius

*Noted the *Tribune:* "The council session was tame and brief. Alderman John Coughlin wasn't there."

Clark and Charles L. Stinson. They incorporated the General Electric Railway Company and began getting frontage consents for streetcar lines on the southwest side, adjacent to the Yerkes territory. They carefully stayed away from Jackson Street.

On the night of January 9, 1896, Bathhouse John plumped the General Electric ordinance into the council. A few hours before he had presented to Public Works Commissioner Kent his list of frontage consents for verification, as required by state law. The petitions had come in too late for investigation however.

As chairman of the committee on streets and alleys, south, Coughlin called up for passage the General Electric ordinance. It provided for streetcar privileges in Dearborn Street north to Fourteenth, east to Fifth Avenue, and then south to Forty-third Street and west to Western Avenue. In other words, it covered the whole of southwest Chicago and provided for a loop near the business district. The aldermen in on the game were anxious to pass the measure and reap the benefits.

"I call for passage of this order," said Bathhouse. "The necessary frontage consents have been obtained and inspected by Commissioner Kent."

Alderman Mann was skeptical. He wanted the measure referred to committee so that a proper investigation might be made. This annoyed Bathhouse. "If it ain't right, let th' mayor investigate and veto," he said. "Th' thing to do now is pass it."

The clerk called the roll and the ordinance passed. Then Coughlin called for a reading section by section. This was normally done before the ordinance was passed and the council was puzzled at the curious reversal of procedure. The Bath, chuckled his enemies, had tangled himself up in parliamentary methods and they gleefully anticipated the outcome. They agreed to hear the ordinance section by section.

As the reading progressed, Bathhouse John rose innocently and offered to amend the section regarding the route. His amendment would bring the line east on Fourteenth Street to Plymouth Court, north in Plymouth Court to Jackson, and then run in Jackson to

Customs House Place and back to Fourteenth. So Alderman Coughlin was proposing that General Electric should have a loop downtown, in the heart of the business section, a loop that even the powerful Yerkes couldn't obtain over the embattled Jackson Street property owners!

The aldermen quickly saw the significance of the move. With a foothold in Jackson, the General Electric Company would control the key to all west-side transportation and could demand a tremendous price from Yerkes, or his one powerful competitor, the City Railway Company, entrenched on the south side, which was also effectively blocked if Coughlin got his way.

"This brings in a lot of new frontage no one knows about," stormed Alderman Blind Billy Kent. "We've got to get the consents."

"The consents are here!" Bathhouse assured him, waving a pack of papers.

"Let us examine them," demanded Kent.

"There's no need to examine them," said Bathhouse. "They're here. We've got to pass this ordinance."

"Who wants this ordinance?" cried Alderman O'Neill.

"The people!"

"I can amend that by saying that Alderman Coughlin wants it," said O'Neill.

"And I," roared Bathhouse, "I represent th' people!"

There were a few cheers from the gallery and the councilmen awaiting a kill called anxiously for a vote.

The opposition aldermen were taken by surprise and they had no opportunity to organize. Desperately Alderman Hambleton called for adjournment.

"Mr. Chairman, that ain't fair!" yelped Bathhouse in sudden fear. He was cheered by a roar of anger from his followers for the night. Roll was called on the adjournment motion. It lost, 50 to 18.

Alderman Kent returned to the attack. "Why look at this ordinance! It provides for overhead trolleys. Why, only two weeks ago you tried to pass an ordinance right in this council forbidding the use of overhead trolleys!"

"Well," said Bathhouse airily, "we don't know if a third rail will work. We got to leave in the overhead trolleys."

Alderman O'Neill, seeking time, offered an amendment to reduce the fare on the lines from five cents to three cents. That was defeated. Kent suggested that the aldermen consider a compensation provision, requiring that the company should pay one per cent of its gross the first five years, two per cent the second five years, two and a half per cent for three years, and three and a half per cent for seven years, the remaining life of the franchise. Bathhouse John had no objection to that—he had not really hoped to get the ordinance through without compensation, and the inclusion of the amendment would take some of the fire out of the mayor's veto message. Hambleton attempted to force in a provision that the company should pave the streets it used from curb to curb, but this was rejected.

Having exhausted a store of amendments and parliamentary obstructions, the opposition aldermen began attacking the frontage consents, insisting that action should be delayed until they could be investigated. But the mood of Coughlin's backers was growing ugly, and The Bath readily convinced them that the council itself was judge of whether the necessary frontage consents were had. The cries of "Vote! Vote!" were renewed. Finally Mayor Swift had no choice but to put the ordinance to vote.

It passed 53 to 18.

The news fairly exploded upon Chicago the following morning. Here was a steal so vast and obvious as to make Ogden Gas seem trivial. The newspaper editors were beside themselves.

"This ordinance is disclosed to be of vital importance to the great streetcar corporations," said the *Tribune*. "It permits any kind of motive power. The chief objection is the shameful, lawless manner of its passage by the venal gang which is supreme in the council. The state law prescribes that the frontage owners must petition for a line. The dulled and disciplined majority under Alderman Coughlin jumps when he cracks the whip."

"This council," mourned the *News,* "is a remorselessly venal one. Cannot the Augean stable be cleansed of men who laugh the public to scorn?"

It was rumored that Coughlin was offered $75,000 for the ordinance even before it was passed and that the figure would be at least quadrupled if he should be able to carry it over the mayor's veto. Word got about that the Chicago and Englewood Company, a small independent, would buy the franchise and that it then would be sold to Yerkes. President McCann of that company admitted he was ready to buy. "We've got to, if we want to get uptown," he declared, a hint to Yerkes.

The more the *Tribune* thought about the matter, the more incensed it got. "What caused this infamous steal?" the paper demanded editorially on January 13. "The aldermen may have been hypnotized. Bathhouse John may have fixed them with his glittering eye and forced them to vote as he wished, not as their constituency wished and honor and decency demanded. If there are aldermanic Trilbys, the victims of aldermanic Svengalis, the sooner they are dropped from the council the better. Certainly the aldermen were given no chance to examine this ordinance. The bundles of papers were tossed in by Ringmaster Coughlin, and when he cracked the whip, they performed."

Mayor Swift vetoed the General Electric ordinance, and Coughlin called it up for passage over the veto. Blind Billy Kent and Alderman Judah rose to assail him. The Bath listened impatiently, and then jumped into the battle. He knew he was certain of victory.

"The Chicago City Railway doesn't want this ordinance," he sneered. "They want the south side to themselves. Who is this Kent? I'll tell you. Why, his family is wealthy and owns stock in th' City Railway Company. And who is this Judah? Why, he is the man who's interested in th' South Side Railway Company!" The Bath turned fiercely and his little eyes belligerently swept the council. "I want a quick decision on this ordinance!" he barked, and sat down.

"It's a lie! It's a lie!" Kent was shrieking, but he was drowned out by shouts of the boodlers and the vote was ordered. The measure passed over the veto 50 to 18, four votes to spare above the required two-thirds. Friends rushed over to congratulate The Bath. He beamed shyly and protested that it was nothing, but now and then he whirled about to glare furiously at his defeated enemies. He had won the greatest business triumph of his aldermanic career. He turned a cold eye upon Johnny Powers. "Johnny," said Bathhouse, "put that in your pipe an' smoke it."

2

The latest railway steal aroused Chicago and brought about a joint meeting of reform organizations at the Masonic Temple. Former Judge Louis C. Collins summoned the gathering, aided by Lyman J. Gage of the Civic Federation, Walter C. Newberry, Franklin McVeagh and others. Coughlin and his colleagues were damned on all sides. It was agreed that united action by all reform groups was necessary. Judge Collins proposed that a new political party be established to do just one thing: elect twelve more honest aldermen in the spring elections to prevent further steals over the mayor's veto. The Civic Federation called a meeting of its executive committee and pledged itself to the movement. Other organizations followed. It was decided to call the new alliance the Municipal Reform party.

Bathhouse, apprised of the reform activities, invited reporters to his saloon, struck a position, and read a prepared statement:

"This new movement is the mist which rises skyward before one's eyes, and while it may become thick enough to make a cloud and look scarlet and silver and gilt edged in the sunlight, it will yet be the cloud that will blind good political vision.

"That means," The Bath amplified, "that the Municipal party is a Jonah, an orphan, a child without parents which will cry for a little while an' die. It means I count myself too wise to associate with 'em. Honest, I'd ruther be a Republican—put that on record—than associate with such a party that stands for nothin' but a dream, a regular dewy mist. Rise above th' mist an' look for th' earth. You can't see it, but keep on lookin'. Th' sun comes out an' drives th' mist away, an' you see the solid bedrock of Democracy an' th' sands of Republicanism still stickin' close to ground. That's me. I want my feet on th' earth. Th' Municipal party is in th' air."

"What will it accomplish?" asked the reporters.

"What will it accomplish?" repeated Bathhouse grandly. "It will live through one election, poll maybe eight hundred votes, elect nobody, an' then quit."

3

Every newspaper and decent citizen in town was vociferously against Bathhouse, but that worried him not half so much as the fact that Billy Skakel had once more reared his ugly head. Skakel, still burning from his defeat in 1894, was quietly organizing such gamblers as had refused to join the Coughlin-Kenna organization. They raised a purse of $10,000, picked George H. Williams, a Republican, as their candidate, and announced they would permanently retire Coughlin from political affairs. "We're gonna run him right outa th' ward," proclaimed Skakel. "We're gonna mash him, that bollix washer!"

Hinky Dink had been unable to save himself the year before, but still Bathhouse had unlimited faith in the Little Fellow. Furthermore, the First Ward organization now had money, and Alderman Coughlin had learned a few things about political manipulation in the council.

He rose at a meeting of the aldermen late in January to point out indignantly that the gas companies were violating the state law forbidding them to hold the meter deposits of their customers. The companies for years had been taking five dollars, ten dollars, and twenty dollars from each gas customer and simply keeping it, although the depositor was supposed to get it back at some indefinite time.

"Why is this law violated?" thundered The Bath, thoroughly lathered by his feeling for the people. "I tell you, some of this money's got t' be refunded! Th' rest, an' it's about $5,000,000, Mr. Maar, has got to go into th' city treasury, cause you can't find th' owners. Th' gas companies get five-per-cent interest off this money. They use it to run their business. Th' city can do th' same thing. Let's get this money!"

Mayor Swift blinked. The Bathhouse had something. The city desperately needed funds and it would be a windfall for the customers they would never forget. It would be political suicide to oppose Coughlin. The council passed the order unanimously, and Mayor Swift made haste to sign it. Coughlin got little credit in the newspapers for his coup, but in the First Ward, where the prospect of a few dollars really mattered to citizens fortunate enough to have gas, he received plenty.

4

The reform elements, discouraged from their plan to organize a third party, formed instead the Municipal Voters' League. They made president one George E. Cole, thickset, bandy-legged proprietor of a printing and stationery shop who, personally and with little help, had brought about the prosecution and conviction of a group of boodlers in the county commissioner's office. Cole was a fiery little man with angry eyes, a snarling goatee, and a bulging jaw that reporters described as "threatening as the ram bow of a ship." Born in Jackson, Michigan, he fought in the Civil War with the Tenth Michigan volunteers, and then settled in Chicago to develop his stationery business. When he accepted the leadership of the MVL, he demanded $10,000 and a free hand. He got both, and went into action with such vigor that he quickly became the white hope of the decent citizens.

"In Cole," Judge Murray F. Tully told a reform rally, "we've got a little sawed-off giant of reform. He is our machine, tireless and fearless. He has X-ray eyes, and can look right through a candidate and see whether he is a boodler at heart or not. George E. Cole is a human buzz saw."

Thereafter he was "Buzz-saw Cole." He demanded the support of a united citizenry, and the newspapers, ministers and organizations rallied solidly behind him. The *Times-Herald* particularly took the reform campaign seriously, pouring vitriol upon the crooked council, publishing daily cartoons showing little Cole as a scrapping fellow who was going to beat the gang. One of these, on March 28, depicted a sprawling collection of lodging houses and decrepit saloons resting on rocks which bore the likenesses of several aldermen: Bathhouse John, Johnny de Pow, Little Mike Ryan, Handsome Maurice O'Connor, and Edward Stanwood. Cole, in overalls, was at one side, waiting with a dynamite pump to blow the whole thing up. Near by were kegs labeled: "Reform powder." Other cartoons showed Cole as a reaper cutting down the evil aldermen, or as a lion tamer, cracking his whip over the council tigers. Buzz-saw Cole had captured popular imagination.

The Municipal Voters' League chose the First and Nineteenth Wards in which to concentrate its barrage. Coughlin and Powers, the league concluded, symbolized the whole of Chicago's political viciousness.

The Republicans nominated Charles H. King in the First Ward, and sought to rally such decent citizens as were available behind his candidacy. But George Williams, also a Republican and backed by Skakel, caused the MVL unending embarrassment when he filed as an independent. He claimed to be a reform candidate, at least insofar as franchise matters were concerned, although Hinky Dink swiftly exposed him as the tool of a clique of gamblers. Mayor Swift demanded that Williams withdraw from the race, in the interests of King, but the Skakel crowd refused to listen.

While Bathhouse poured sheafs of relief orders into the council, all designed to attract the support of the numerous indigent in his ward, the reformers beat their drums at angry meetings in Central Music Hall. Finally, on April 3, the long-awaited report on aldermanic candidates by the new-born Municipal Voters' League came out, signed by Cole.

"First Ward," said the report, "all candidates utterly unfit.

"John J. Coughlin (Democratic candidate) lives at No. 165 Van Buren Street; the notorious 'Bathhouse John'; born near Waukegan, Ill., about 1854; been a leader in politics of his ward for many years; was elected to the council in 1892 and 1894; voted for all questionable ordinances; conducts a bathhouse at No. 145 East Madison Street patronized chiefly by gamblers and racing men; runs the 'Silver Dollar' saloon at 169 East Madison Street, owned by ex-Ald. Johnny Morris; saloon is a resort for prostitutes, gamblers, thieves: is uneducated and coarse in conduct, the friend of toughs and thugs, a disgrace to his ward and city; is supported by Hinky Dink and Johnny Morris."

The Bath was furious about this report, published in all the newspapers. Early the following morning, Coughlin, with Hinky Dink beside him, invaded the headquarters of the Municipal Voters' League and demanded to see Cole. Cole, busy with his secretary, Hoyt King, knew neither Bathhouse nor Hinky Dink by sight. He strode to the high banking counter that formed a wall of his private office. Coughlin towered above it, but Cole and Hinky Dink could just see over, to bore into each other's eyes.

"Mr. Cole, I am John J. Coughlin."

"Glad to meet you, Mr. Coughlin."

"This is my friend, Michael Kenna."

"How do you do, Mr. Kenna."

"Now, Mr. Cole, I have come to see you as man to man, to say you done me a very great injustice in your report."

Coughlin handed Cole the report, and the little stationer read it carefully. "This is all true, Mr. Coughlin," said Cole firmly. "We have checked every word of it. You voted for all those ordinances. You associate with thieves and thugs."

"That is not the point, Mr. Cole," said Bathhouse. "In this record you say I was born in Waukegan. That ain't true. Mr. Cole,

I was born right here in Chicago, and I want that corrected."

The reformers and others charged that Coughlin and Kenna had brought thousands of colonizers into the ward to cast their votes on April 6. This was undoubtedly true, for the evidence piled high in the offices of the board of election commissioners.

The Saturday night before election The Bath strode up and down the rows of saloons on Clark Street, with as many as five hundred men at his heels, going from one barrel house to another, buying beer until the supply ran out. The procession was led by a fife and drum corps and two buglers. Coughlin started from his headquarters just north of Van Buren and Clark, rounded the inner section of the ward, and proceeded to Hinky Dink's.

"That's a rummy push you've got there, John," grinned little Hink, "but every one of them has a vote, and that's what counts."

Then they moved to Ben Samuel's big saloon at 335 South Clark, where The Bath made one of his few campaign speeches. While shouts of "Three cheers for Bathhouse," and "Set 'em up ag'in!" resounded, Coughlin addressed his constituents:

"All I ask of you fellows is that you do your duty Tuesday. Remember that I'm your friend and I'm with you from soda to hock. Now be good fellows an' we'll put Billy Skakel an' his push in th' bink."

Sunday was Easter, and the ministers were forced to forego comment on the campaign. But that night Billy Skakel got into action. As crowds emerged from the theaters, they were confronted by huge posters with big red letters, which read:

ATTENTION, VOTERS OF THE FIRST WARD! READ THIS!

This election day will recall the bloody 3rd of April two years ago when four hackloads of ruffians traveled this ward armed with pistols, billies, loaded canes, beating into insensibility voters who dared exercise their rights to vote for whom they pleased under the constitution. What has this Coughlin, the friend of thugs and thieves, ever done for the Democratic party of the First Ward?

VOTE FOR GEORGE WILLIAMS!

The posters never saw the light of day. As fast as they went up Hinky Dink's men busily yanked them down. There were quarrels and fights as some Skakel workers opposed them, but nothing serious enough to interest the police. The Civic Federation had put up posters offering a reward of $100 for any information convicting a person suspected of vote fraud, and these were unmolested.

Monday night the First Ward and the Levee rang with jollity as the faithful prepared for their labors of the morrow. Beer and whisky were plentiful, and most of it was free, and there was evidence that plenty more would be available election day. Toward midnight a tally-ho full of The Bath's supporters, thirty-five red-blooded citizens howling and cheering for the free exercise of franchise, upset at the intersection of Hubbard Court and State Street, and one man was taken to a hospital.

On election eve the papers freely predicted the defeat of the boodlers, Coughlin and Powers among them. "GANG'S DARK DAY!" ran the headline in the *Times-Herald*. "BEAT THE BOODLERS!" urged the *Tribune*. But The Bath was quietly confident. The Skakel supporters had begun to desert, among them Big Sandy Walters, who secretly visited Hinky Dink and made his peace. Kenna sent him back whence he came, to his job as field captain of the George Williams election forces, but he was pledged to Bathhouse John.

Election day was a riotous affair, and the First Ward was worst of all. Saloons did a heavy business from 5:30 to 6 A.M. In and out walked red-nosed citizens, all beautifully happy and purposeful as they made their way to the polling places. When the bars shut down at six o'clock, the saloonkeepers and their bartenders rolled down their sleeves and went out to help the Hink and Bathhouse.

Coughlin also was out early. His overcoat, the *Times-Herald* reported, was so heavy at 6 A.M. that it made him round-shouldered. The right pocket was loaded with quarters, the left with nickels and dimes. Wherever he went crowds followed, and he poured out silver like water.

Every cab driver in the First wore a badge of white ribbon, termed ironically by the *Times-Herald* an "emblem of purity," on which was inscribed, "Our Friend, John J. Coughlin." A stage-coach ran up and down the main streets with Bathhouse John shouters piled over it. Williams adherents wore blood-red badges. No one saw any King badges.

There was trouble, to be sure, but this was settled by what The Bath, with a dash of inspiration, had called the "honest hearts and willing hands" of his boys. In the course of the work of the "honest hearts, etc." several Coughlinites met violence—William Bull Hickey, a thug, was shot in the wrist, Charles Seymour was beaten with a revolver butt, and Big Sandy Walters, the double-dealing terror of the First Ward, was beaten up by a one-armed man he thought he could whip.

The moment the polls closed it was evident the Williams clan had not been in too great earnest. "The reds and the whites," the *Times-Herald* reported, "shook hands in mutual satisfaction, shouted 'Hurrah for Johnny Coughlin,' and broke for the saloons."

The results of the election: Coughlin, 2,462; Williams, 1,257; King, 1,197. Vincenzo Rossi, an Independent, and H. N. Wooley, People's party, split 326 votes between them.

In the Nineteenth Ward Johnny de Pow was also victorious. He was said to have spent $10,000 to win narrowly. "Nobody will ever beat Johnny Powers as long as he has a dollar in his pockets," he told his cronies. But outside these wards, the new Municipal Voters' League had won an impressive victory. Among some twenty-three politicians whose defeat the league sought, eighteen were retired, including Handsome Maurice O'Connor and Little Mike Ryan.

George E. Cole, who had not expected so much, said that a new day had dawned in Chicago.

WORKING FOR FREE SILVER

I

RIGHT and left the boodlers had toppled, but as the new council came in there was Bathhouse John, swinging grandly in his new swivel chair, and across the aisle his enemy Johnny de Pow. The chamber was gay with flowers and bunting, and officials of the Municipal Voters' League had prominent places on the rostrum. The Bath teetered back and forth at his desk as these visitors pointed him out and whispered among themselves. He waved gaily at friends in the gallery and grinned at the glum aldermanic losers, come to surrender their seats to the reformers.

The gallery and corridors were thronged when a delegation of cab drivers from the First Ward pushed their way to the council floor, bearing a massive floral horseshoe on whose silken banner was embossed in golden script:

HONEST HEARTS AND WILLING HANDS
FOR OUR FRIEND, JOHN J. COUGHLIN
Plurality, 1,205

Alderman Bathhouse John thanked the hack drivers, waved again as the gallery cheered, and winked at Johnny Powers. He was in a jesting mood. Gripping the flowers, he rose and addressed his colleagues: "I am touched by this little tribute from the Municipal Voters' League! But I'm still the same. The vote was for me. And I'm still plain Jawn!"

2

Cole's hopes for the new council were borne out immediately, although he postponed indefinitely his planned retirement from

150

the league in order to keep his eyes on aldermen who might stray. Yerkes made several attempts to obtain a portion of Jackson Street, but his ordinances were voted down. When he demanded a section of Van Buren Street in order to complete his Union elevated loop, the aldermen insisted that he must pay compensation to the city.

"If we are going to be loaded down with compensation clauses," Yerkes threatened, "we will not build the south-side loop at all. We have been held up often enough already," he added, leaving the remark poignant with meaning.

Cole urged Mayor Swift not to yield an inch to Yerkes. He now had an honest council behind him. But Swift insisted that a compromise would profit the city and appease the traction czar. He scorned Cole's demands for a high rate of compensation, and in June signed what he called a "victory" franchise. It gave Yerkes control of the Union loop for thirty years. It provided that the city be paid a graduated scale of compensation, from five per cent of the gross profits during the first five years to twenty-five per cent the last fifteen.

The Bath watched silently while Swift maneuvered with Yerkes. He knew that he was *persona non grata* with the traction man since the General Electric Company squabble, and he knew too that boodle profits had temporarily ended. But again the Free Silver campaign kept him from slipping into the political doldrums.

Governor Altgeld was preparing for the Democratic state convention, to be held in Peoria, and desired both the endorsement of his candidacy for re-election and the official espousal of the "16 to 1" principle. In Cook County the Altgeld supporters got busy, Coughlin and Kenna, Burke, Joe Martin, the gambler, and A. S. Trude, all laboring with Chairman Gahan to take a solid Cook County delegation to Peoria. The Bath and Hinky Dink sought jobs as delegates to the convention, and with only one polling place in the ward, drew more votes than any other of the county's candidates, and praise from Bobbie Burke. "They made a showing that was astounding," glowed Bobbie. "Those boys really know how to work."

A pre-convention gathering of Cook County Democrats in Turner Hall confirmed a new split in the party. The Gahan forces, proudly wearing "16 to 1" sashes across their bosoms, voted to adopt a Free Silver platform and endorsed Altgeld for re-election. Powers, Hopkins, Roger Sullivan and their followers quit the meeting in disgust and held their own "Gold Bug" convention at the Palmer House. Crowed the *Tribune:* "Never has the Democratic party been so torn to pieces as it is now."

Altgeld handily won the nomination at Peoria, and Coughlin and Kenna returned to Chicago more enthusiastic than ever for the Free Silver movement. Yerkes' financial pressure on the council became terrific, and even Bathhouse yielded and cast his vote for the Union loop franchise. This did not, however, repair the rupture with Powers. Chicago had won the Democratic national convention, and Kenna and Coughlin aided Gahan in his efforts to set the stage for an endorsement of Altgeld's Free Silver platform, while Powers and his Gold Bugs sought to sabotage the movement. In Philadelphia Mark Hanna put up his good friend, William McKinley, as the Republicans' presidential candidate. Three weeks later William Jennings Bryan, thundering, "You shall not crucify mankind upon a cross of gold!" took the Democratic convention by storm and was named the Free Silver candidate.

The Bath, whose affection for Bryan never had wavered since the Free Silver convention of 1895, was deliriously happy.

"I am not going to take a vacation this summer," he promised. "I'm goin' to stay in town an' work for Free Silver." This remark was variously interpreted by the press, but it was true that of all the aldermen, Coughlin alone endured Chicago heat that summer.

3

The summer and autumn passed quickly enough. Bryan, hero to Bathhouse and half the nation as well, was nevertheless destined to defeat. Little was saved in Illinois but the Free Silverites' control of the Cook County Democratic machinery. In the council the franchise business, to George Cole's sorrow, was renewed as viciously as before, and Blind Billy Kent of the Fifth Ward charged openly on the council floor that Yerkes, through Johnny Powers, was paying from $1,000 to $2,000 per alderman for his ordinances. The citizens yawned or clucked their tongues. The reform crusade had ended. Bathhouse, again suppressed by the ruling clique, found the sessions boring and unprofitable. Only once could he strike fire. That was with an ordinance providing that all policemen should be paid in cash. Explained the proprietor of the Silver Dollar, "When the coppers get their checks it's too late to go to a bank, so they cash 'em in saloons, and that ain't a good influence on 'em."

The subject of cash was continuously in the alderman's mind. A few months hence a new aldermanic election was scheduled, and while the First Ward organization was strong in its friends on the central committee, neither Coughlin nor Kenna wanted to be caught again with insufficient funds. The stream of graft was thin. The gamblers, harried by drives which the reformers pressed upon Mayor Swift, were making less money, and they either paid less for protection or chased the Coughlin-Kenna collectors from their establishments.

The big man and the little man had surveyed the possibilities for raising revenue. The solution came to them in an inspired moment one day in Hinky Dink's saloon, shortly before the approach of the Christmas season. They were bewailing the fact that this year, unlike the fifteen years preceding, there would not be the annual party for Lame Jimmy, the crippled pianist and fiddler in Carrie Watson's parlor house. In the late 1880's and early '90's these affairs had been held in the once respectable *bierstube* and waltz palace now known as Freiberg's Hall on East Twenty-second Street. Saloonkeepers and brothel madams vied in the splendor of their tributes to Lame Jimmy, the flow of champagne was copious, Lame Jimmy sang and played his lachrymose ballads, high-lighted by his favorite, "The Palms," and at the end he led the jolly assemblage in a discordant "Auld Lang Syne." At each affair police captains and patrolmen were present as honored guests, mingling with the thugs and sluggers, who, in recognition of the occasion, always left their brass knuckles and blackjacks in their overcoats. It was an occasion of camaraderie and happy reunion, Lame Jimmy's party, and always joy, as Carrie Watson liked to put it, "reigned unrefined."

But at the 1895 party a drunken Harrison Street detective, braving the high indignation of other guests at his lapse in Levee decorum, grew boisterous and shot and critically wounded a fellow officer. This evoked a great civic outcry, demands were made upon the high police command for immediate action, and not even the intervention of Bathhouse John, who had attended many of the affairs, could save Lame Jimmy from the order: No more balls.

As he lamented the passing of the Lame Jimmy festivities, Bathhouse Coughlin came suddenly to the realization that the little brothel professor's misfortune was a great opportunity for the First Ward Democratic organization. Lame Jimmy's parties had been held in a small hall; tickets sold for one dollar each; three hundred attended. Why, if a ball—a real ball, a lavish ball, a gigantic ball in a gigantic hall—were to be held, who would know how much its sponsors might make? Coughlin and Kenna had friends willing to contribute wines and liquors, the madams and their girls would come. . . .

"We take it over, Mike, we take it over!" The Bath yelped joyously. "Why, done right, there's thousands in it, tens of thousands!" Hinky Dink was not too enthusiastic, but he knew it was best to let the Big Fellow go when he thought he had something. So Alderman Coughlin began to plan, and the wonders of such an affair grew larger and larger in his mind.

4

Word spread swiftly through the First Ward of the ball to be held under the auspices of Bathhouse John and Hinky Dink, and for the benefit of persons then unknown. The place: Seventh Regiment Armory. The time: eight o'clock till—?

Aldermanic couriers carried the information to the First Ward faithful. They visited saloons and cigar stores and dropped into every parlor house with blocks of tickets and a glowing verbal prospectus. They met few objections.

The saloonkeepers and brothel owners and purveyors to the pleasures of the Levee either genuinely welcomed the projected frolic, or possibly saw its deeper significance. Whatever the stimuli, they bought tickets, lots of tickets. Waiters, apprised of what they might expect in tips, eagerly shucked out five dollars each for the right to serve at the fete. Brewers and wine merchants and whisky distillers knew without being told that it was to their benefit to provide stocks of liquors at moderate prices and at unlimited credit. One could always be certain there might come a day when a favor from the First Ward overlords might be needed.

Tickets sold speedily. All the prospective participants in the festivities were allotted places in the general floor plan. The tavern owners and madams and wine sellers were to be allowed to decorate their boxes—at their own expense—and the brewers were assigned wide sections in the corridors and basement. The Bath subdivided the armory with the sagacity of a real-estate broker and the money rolled in. Throughout the ward it was considered wise to be co-operative and enthusiastic. No parlor house was too grand, no ten-cent crib too lowly to be represented.

This first of the First Ward balls was to be like nothing ever before seen in the Levee. It captured the imagination of the *souteneurs* and the *filles de joie,* and when they heard that Alderman Coughlin was preparing a special costume for the event, they rushed out to do likewise.

It was clear at the very beginning that the First Ward ball surpassed Lame Jimmy's parties as completely as Carrie Watson's house eclipsed a Clark Street crib. The Bath's love of garish pomp had found amazing expression. The bizarre decorations were like freshly painted nightmares from Tommy Wong's hop house. But these were exceeded by the alderman's startling personal splendor. Even the girls from the expensive brothels, some of whom had spent as much as $200 for their costume gowns, bemoaned the poverty of their ingenuity when Coughlin stepped from his personal box at midnight to lead the Grand March.

His tail coat was a crisp billiard-cloth green, his vest a delicate mauve. His trousers were lavender, as was his glowing cravat, and his kid gloves a pale pink. His pumps shone a gleaming yellow, and perched on his glistening pompadour was a silken top hat that sparkled like the plate-glass windows of Marshall Field's department store.

This sartorial elegance, even more than the ball itself, was the attraction of the evening. The glowing descriptions recounted the next morning by wide-eyed reporters were reprinted in newspapers of other cities and editorials sneered at the Chicago council not only for its reputation for boodle and graft but as the stamping grounds of a statesman in green coat and lavender pants. The effete East saw in this outfit the supreme symbol of wickedness in the Chicago government. The reformers at home were aghast at this "open display of vice and debauchery" as they read of the gambols of the frisky brothel girls, the numberless drunken assaults in the armory basement, the almost unanimous attendance of the residents of such choice districts as the Black Hole, the Bad Lands, Bed Bug Row, and Hell's Half Acre, the mingling of pimps and pickpockets with political leaders, policemen with burglars and confidence men.

Churchmen raised their hands to heaven and wailed that organized vice, at which all the city had winked and whispered, had gone on public display. "It has," they said, "pushed beyond all bounds of decency and offered insolent challenge to the rest of the community." They hurled colorful epithets, "a Saturnalian orgy," a "vile, dissolute affair," a "bawdy Dionysian festival," "a black stain on the name of Chicago."

But Hinky Dink called it a lalapalooza, and spent a day totaling the $25,000 in profits. Alderman Bathhouse John went about promising those unfortunates who did not attend that there would be other balls to follow. There were, for a decade or more, and each one wilder than the last, each a signal for a renewed hue and cry from reformers who demanded the political extinction of "that infamous pair of vicious men."

IN VINO VERITAS

I

THE horrified citizens might shudder at the name of Bathhouse John, but when Lucy Page Gaston bustled into Chicago a few months later it was the handsome alderman from the infamous First Ward who assisted in the anti-cigarette fight in the council. For more than a year the women's clubs had clamored for legislation curbing tobacco sales, and now it was Bathhouse John who took up their cause.

In March he presented to his amused colleagues a measure requiring a license fee of $100 for all shops selling cigarettes and barring their sale entirely within 200 yards of schools. This was really only a sop to the anti-cigarette crusaders, and part of The Bath's general scheme for annoying Powers, but the followers of Lucy Page Gaston grabbed for it and demanded that the other aldermen back Bathhouse John. Without a whimper, and with many a cynical smirk, the aldermen cast their favorable votes. The "Tobacco Trust" railed, but the newspapers threw out a few crumbs of praise for The Bath. Even the *Tribune,* which habitually held its nose when speaking of the First Ward, commented editorially:

By this measure he [Coughlin] will drive from the school areas the petty peddlers in death who have been inviting the children to ruin.

Tobacco salesmen, musing on the incongruity of sponsorship of an anti-cigarette law by Bathhouse John, thought the whole incident farcical and advised their clients to ignore the new statute.

But the council was not fooling. Dealers who violated the law were thrown into jail, stores without licenses or near the schools were shut down, and the license fees began to come into the city treasury. It was at this time, ironically, that the state law calling for fines of $200 against saloons kept open on Sunday was being ignored by the police.

Whatever his motives in sponsoring such an obvious reform ordinance, The Bath stilled temporarily some of the violent criticism against himself, Kenna and the late ball. It was more than necessary that he do so. For he wanted to get Kenna elected in April, and some citizens of the First were becoming irked at the constant animadversion. Too, both Bathhouse and Little Mike were being drawn into the orbit of a new and purely shining political star: Carter Henry Harrison the Younger, son of the martyred mayor.

2

One looked at young Carter Harrison, heard him speak in cultured tones and in any of several languages, and found it difficult to believe that he, like rough Coughlin and uncouth Kenna, also came from the First Ward. But his stay there had been brief, and his early years were spent far from the canyons of the Levee or the ramshackle houses of the river front. For Carter Harrison there had been no hawking of newspapers nor stoking of schoolhouse stoves.

The Harrisons had settled in their exclusive Ashland Avenue mansion when "Cato"—so the elder Harrison called him and the young Harrison detested it—was still a boy. Much of his schooling he acquired in Germany and other parts of the continent. When the aging "Our Carter," possessed with the ambition to be mayor again in 1893, had purchased the dying *Times,* young Carter and his brother, Preston, had been placed in command, editorially and financially. Their reign had been brief but vigorous. Through the mayoralty contest, the Pullman strike, the Altgeld campaigns, the brothers had maintained a forceful attack on the newspaper's foes. And its foes were among the wealthy and privileged, many of them, interestingly enough, members of the Harrison social circle. But the paper drew less and less profit, and in 1895 the brothers Harrison had sold it. Carter sailed off on a world cruise, and when he returned a year later he interested himself lightly in Democratic politics and devoted some time to managing his inherited estate, some of which, through no fault of his own, was on wicked old Biler Avenue.

There were many who had been his father's supporters who welcomed young Harrison into the party's councils. There were other Democrats, like A. S. Trude and John Hopkins, who disliked the handsome young man for a meddlesome dilettant. But friend and foe alike had to agree that he was loaded with political possibilities. His name was a household word in the city—when critics said he was but the shadow of a name, he would retort, "Yes, but I am the shadow of a good name!"—and he had immense personal presence; a fine figure of a man with blazing eyes, a clean-cut jaw, a trim mustache, the guise and comport of a theater matinee idol. He was well enough liked by men, adored by women. He was at ease in any element. He was a liberal who had backed Altgeld, he had friends in the silk stocking and Gold Coast districts, entry into the world of the Potter Palmers and the Marshall Fields. And he was strong for the paternal philosophy of "Live and Let Live" and dedicated to the theory that saloons should remain open on Sunday. He was all that Bathhouse John Coughlin and Hinky Dink Kenna found to admire in a man, and when the party began thinking of a mayor in 1897 these two had already made their choice.

There were distressing problems, though. Trude, to whom Bathhouse John owed much for political teachings, considered his long and worthy service to the Democratic party and yearned to be mayor. The decision was difficult, for Trude was his friend, but Bathhouse John determined to stand by young Carter as the man to beat the Republicans. He advised Harrison's chief backers,

Bobbie Burke and Joe Martin, "If Trude runs he'll split th' party. He ain't that kind of Democrat. I'll handle Mr. Trude."

Confusion thrived in the early weeks of the behind-the-scenes campaign. Trude lined up Tommy Gahan, thus inferentially the blessing of Altgeld, and began making experimental appearances in the outlying wards. But Altgeld turned thumbs down on Trude, thus inferentially favoring Harrison. Trude, persistently heckled by The Bath to give up, for the good of the party, his dream of being mayor, first insisted he was a candidate, then said he was not, then reversed himself again. Finally Gahan fled to Mexico on a "business trip." Trude went to Hot Springs, Arkansas, "for a rest." Before leaving he indicated he might be willing to be drafted, but added that in the interest of harmony he preferred the candidacy of Judge John Barton Payne, rich and reactionary.

Burke and Martin, Coughlin and Kenna—although Little Mike was somewhat preoccupied with his second attempt to snare a council seat beside The Bath—steadily built their Harrison for Mayor organization. When Trude returned and sniffed about, he detected among the party regulars an increasing ardor for Harrison, and his friends beseeched him to dispel it by formally announcing his candidacy. But Trude's taste for the job had been dulled by Altgeld's continued coolness and by Bathhouse John's flat statement that he could expect no aid from the First Ward and other vital centers.

So the venerable Democrat capitulated, but not without rancor. The peace meeting between him and Harrison was far from affable, a cold, formal affair at which Harrison arrogantly refused to offer any share of the patronage, and Trude grumbled: "I don't like the cut of this young man's jaw. Look out for him!"

While this fence was being mended, the Populist party, in convention assembled, came out for Harrison, an action that promptly branded him a radical. This last was too much for Washington Hesing, who hated Altgeld, radicals, Free Silver and the name of Harrison. He rose once again to list his own rights to the mayor's chair. His backers were a strange crew—the "clean aldermen," such boodlers as Johnny Powers, the stern executives of the Municipal Voters' League, and political manipulators like Johnny Hopkins and Roger Sullivan.

3

But Bathhouse John and Messrs. Burke and Martin managed the nominating convention far too skillfully to give Hesing even the slightest show. Harrison himself was absent, as the delegates trickled into Turner Hall, but Hesing was on hand early in full and righteous display. The battle in the offing promised to be as lively as that unforgettable one four years earlier when Hesing and "Our Carter" had sent the Democrats into a frenzy. There would be fireworks, that was certain.

It was Bathhouse John who produced the fireworks, in one big blast. Amid the confusion and uncertainty he launched a real torpedo—A. S. Trude to deliver the nominating address for Carter Henry Harrison.

And Trude outdid himself. He extolled Harrison, eulogized the Democratic party nationally and locally, and gave fulsome approval to all Democratic platforms present and past. He discoursed on the scenic and cultural beauties of Chicago and on the staunch histories of the nationality groups in the city, lauded big business and praised little business, expounded the fundamental philosophy of a free democracy, and wept for the workingman, at the same time predicting a happier future for that inarticulate fellow under a benign reign of Democrats. He wound up with a snappy account of his own sacrifices in stepping aside for Harrison.

"The event of the day," recorded the *Tribune,* "was the speech of Mr. Trude putting young Mr. Harrison in nomination. The selection of Mr. Trude for this office is one of the bright ideas which occasionally come to Alderman Coughlin of the First Ward, and after the speaker had done, everyone who wishes for the election of Mr. Harrison wished the First Ward statesman had been drowned in one of his own bathtubs before he gave the lawyer from the Thirty-second Ward the chance to make the speech he did."

Opprobrious though Trude's speech may have seemed to the *Tribune's* scornful political reporter, it stampeded the convention for Harrison. The delegates, weary but impressed by the ardor of this loyal party man and good loser, began to whoop and continued to whoop so that poor indignant Hesing had no chance to speak at all. Bathhouse John, in honor of his Trude coup, was named with John C. Schubert and Patrick White to the committee to notify Harrison of his selection. They hustled from the chamber and soon brought the beaming candidate back with them, Bathhouse John leading him by the arm to the platform. Many of the hardened politicians wept unashamedly as they saw in the features of the son those of the revered father, and the crowd shouted with joy and even Johnny Powers reversed his stand and led the clamorous huzzahs from the west-side delegation.

Harrison bowed graciously. Although Trude had implied in his prolix oration that Carter the Younger would relish a wide-open town, the candidate refrained from this topic.

"I promise," he said simply, "to have a clean and efficient government. It will be a government far superior to that of the present administration which is hopelessly, unequivocally and characteristically Republican."

Harrison was still bowing to the applause when a group of First Ward galleryites, at a signal from Bathhouse John, rose and released their whisky tenors in song:

We'll elect Carter and we won't do nothing wrong,
He will have gambling and let the races run!
Now rich men will spend their money and give the
    poor their share,
So think no more till April 6, and elect young Carter
    mayor!*

---

*The rhyme scheme of "share" and "mayor" suggests that this lyric may have been the first poetical work of Coughlin himself.

Again and again they sang the verse and the delegates marched from the hall with the happy ballad on their lips.

4

There was no dearth of other candidates.

A respectable jurist and art lover named Nathaniel C. Sears, with the big newspapers behind him, was named by the Republicans. John M. Harlan became the candidate of the Independent party as a fierce foe of the traction interests. The irrepressible Hesing gripped the banner of the Gold Democrats, a force sadly riddled by general defection to Harrison, while the Prohibitionists nominated an obscure anti-saloon crusader, T. D. Reynolds. The respective supporting lines were well drawn: for Sears, the press, the big money, the respectable elements, the traction group; for Harlan, the reformers and the MVL, which frowned on Harrison for his failure to embrace the new state civil service law; for Harrison, his father's reputation, his renown as a bright young man and ardent cyclist,* a good labor vote, and the power of the Chicago saloonkeepers.

Not the least of Harrison's political assets was the organization Hinky Dink was bringing to perfection in the First Ward. The lessons of 1895 had been learned. There was now plenty of money as well as plenty of voters, and the Republican snoopers be damned. The members of the First Ward Democratic Club, ruled by Bathhouse John and Hinky Dink, were loyal to a man, and when they were told to back Harrison they backed Harrison. More important, they were going to put Hinky Dink in the council. Never before had the First Ward been so well colonized with floaters. Daily the Republicans screamed that four thousand bums had moved into the district for the election, and their Special Committee for the Detection and Prevention of Vote Frauds bustled about, horrified at what they presumed to find in the lodging

---

*Chicago's cycling population was enormous. No census of wheels was kept, but in 1895 the police reported 13,068 bicycles stolen.

houses. But Hinky Dink and Coughlin and Tom McNally and Ike Bloom paid these complaints little attention. Even Sol van Praag and Billy Skakel were taken back into the fold, and they worked with the zeal of those who know they have been conquered. Sol took a leading part in organizing shock troops known as the Star League, composed of seven hundred policemen who had been fired by Mayor Swift for no other evident reason than that they were Democrats. Harrison endeared himself to these men by opposing the new civil service law, under which they could not regain their jobs. He promised work for the Star Leaguers when he should come to power.

It was in the First Ward, at Tattersall's hall, amid an uproarious demonstration, that Harrison began his speaking campaign.

"Boys," he shouted above the tumult, "I was born in the First Ward and I know what the First Ward wants. Look me over, boys, look me over, so you'll recognize me."

Hinky Dink, on the platform with him, pulled Harrison's coat-tails. "You'd better cut that out," he warned. "There ain't a one of them that won't be after you tomorrow morning, touchin' you for two bits."

The campaign had its serious and farcical moments. Harlan and Harrison largely ignored each other in their campaign speeches, but young Carter lit out after Sears as a "representative of the Republican machine and all its corporate influence and associates." Harlan boasted of his football prowess and those who listened named him the "Center Rush" candidate because he threatened to tackle any of his detractors. Not to be outdone in this appeal to sports enthusiasts, Harrison had campaign photographs taken of himself on a bicycle, and had printed on them: NOT THE CHAMPION CYCLIST BUT THE CYCLISTS' CHAMPION! He proved that he had inherited his father's flair for showmanship as he spoke in their native tongue to the German voters in the northside wards. After these meetings young Carter always invited leaders in his audience into the nearest *bierstube,* where he bought beer for the house and joined in German songs.

5

Ten days before election every vacant room and office in the First Ward was stuffed with registered Democrats and more than a few Republicans, who helped to keep the registration totals respectable but who would also plump for Hinky Dink and Harrison. Still Hinky Dink kept bringing more into his precincts. Seventy-five men were kept under lock and key at 51 Fourth Avenue and carted each day to Kenna's saloon on Van Buren Street for food and drink. A lodging house at 335 North Clark Street, normally housing 24 boarders, had no less than 161 citizens. The Eye and Ear Infirmary at 227 West Adams Street had 57 residents in addition to its staff and patients. Six tiny shop spaces along South State Street each held twenty to thirty well-fed and bibulous voters.

Finally Congressman Lorimer, who was directing the Republican campaign and knew a thing or two about vote colonization himself, acted. He sped to the Harrison Street police station after a parley with Mayor Swift, and demanded three hundred John Doe vagrancy warrants from Captain Frank Kock. Hinky Dink, Bathhouse John and Charles Thornton, an adviser to Harrison, having been apprised of the plot by friendly policemen, were on Lorimer's heels. Bathhouse John railed at his boyhood friend and at Captain Kock, but the "Blond Boss" merely smiled and the captain tearfully said that it was necessary for him to do his duty. Out of the station dashed Lorimer, accompanied by a squad of policemen. They struck first at the headquarters of the Afro-Democratic First Ward Club at 474 South State Street, where eleven drowsy Negroes were seized and charged with vagrancy. The Little Fellow stormed.

"I'll arrest every Republican precinct captain and watcher in the First Ward!" he threatened. But Lorimer found no more vagrants. Other police had preceded him, and the colonists had disappeared. Kenna was cheered when forty-four new voters, hearing favorably of the largess in the First, marched over from the west side and presented themselves at the First Ward headquarters. Kenna grunted and set them up in Coughlin's Wabash Avenue bathhouse.

Dwight L. Moody came to the city near the close of the hectic campaign to hold a revival in the Auditorium Theater, within the confines of the First Ward. Asked to comment on the election, he pontificated: "I don't know about your mayors, but God has forsaken this part of Chicago. Elect a saloonkeeper to the city council and he'll sell whisky to your son. You sow whisky and you'll reap whisky!"

This blast reached Kenna only indirectly, for few First Warders attended the Moody services. But he was too busy to reply, for he was fighting off a terrific threat before the election board, where the Sears forces were attempting again to knock out the Kenna voters. He and other indignant Democrats had come to the hearing rooms to demand that Republicans cease the nefarious practice of sending out suspect notices.* R. S. Iles, in charge of the Republicans' vote-fraud committee, complained that five of his investigators had been arrested a dozen times during the day as they were issuing notices. They could not appear to testify, said Iles, because they were languishing in jail cells.

"Hah!" snorted Bathhouse John. "That shows you what we think of our voting rights in the First. When you serve one of them suspect notices, the citizens get so mad they go right out and get a warrant!"

On the Saturday preceding election the anti-Harrison forces thought they had damning proof of young Carter's unsavory connections. Harry G. Darrow, ex-hoodlum and proprietor of The Fashion, a First Ward drinking place, built a new saloon, The Bon

---

*Cards were left at addresses from which voters were registered but where it was suspected no such voters lived. Citizens thus notified were required to come to the election board and prove a right to vote.

Ton, at 68 East Randolph Street, and issued the following en-
graved invitations to the grand opening:

> You are invited to a political-social reception at 68 East
> Randolph Street. The Hon. Carter H. Harrison, John
> Coughlin, and Michael Kenna will be on hand to greet you.
> Good music, a fine lunch, and a delightful time to all. Open
> all night.
> P. S. A handsome souvenir will be presented to each
> lady present.

The invitations aroused as much fuss as the notes King Mike
McDonald had sent in the days of Carter the First. Here, asserted
the MVL, was conclusive proof. Here is where Carter Harrison
would lead Chicago—"to the all-night saloons!"

The reporters descended upon the Bon Ton and outdid themselves in describing the lavish setting for the reception. They wrote
of the "long rosewood counter, just high enough for a man to lean
one elbow while bending the other." They told of the "row of
round tables which fills a side of the room, together with a brass
chest out of which protrudes brass faucets." They described the
decorations, and noted that above the brass chest were portraits of
Messrs. Kenna and Coughlin. "The general effect," they concluded, "appears to have been for the production of what is technically known in Levee society as a beer tunnel, and as such it
should be recognized by all, including Mr. Harrison, Mr. Coughlin, and Mr. Kenna."

All this unpleasant publicity kept Harrison and Kenna away,
if, indeed, they had ever intended to come, but undaunted
Coughlin was present, sipping only clear water, milling among the
guests, shaking all the hands he could and exhorting all to vote for
his candidates.

William Jennings Bryan passed through the city a few days
later and put to rest any talk of Harrison's desertion of Free Silver.
"If Harrison is elected," he declared, "I will proclaim the result far
and wide as a victory for Free Silver at 16 to 1."

George Cole's Municipal Voters' League issued a thundering condemnation of all gang candidates, called for the defeat of Harrison, and of Hinky Dink wrote:

Michael Kenna is a Democratic candidate commonly known as Hinky Dink. Runs a saloon at 120 East Van Buren Street. Said to be intimately associated with the gambling element; a standing candidate for the council for a number of years; utterly unfit for the position.

Shrugged Hinky Dink at the pronunciamento: "Sure, I associate with gamblers. Why shouldn't I? I like a good game myself."

6

Election eve was a riotous one in the First Ward. Members of the Star League paraded through the streets with blazing torches, pausing for a last orgy of speeches and prophecy in front of van Praag's Owl Saloon. The bars were open all night and the brothels were jammed. By ten o'clock the next morning, though, the saloons were shut down, not in concession to the reformers, but because many of the bartenders and owners were needed to staff the First Ward field organization. The Bath, Hinky Dink and their aides ran busily from polling place to polling place, silver bulging their pockets into which they dug frequently and deeply.

The effort was not in vain, and the outcome was gratifying:

Harrison, the Younger, at 36, mayor by a majority of 77,756 votes, receiving five times the Sears vote in the First Ward.

Kenna, alderman, by 4,373 votes to the 1,811 of the Republican incumbent, Paddy Gleason.

The Levee went wilder than usual. Gangs of men and women crowded the streets. Boxes, barrels, stairsteps and portions of store fronts were torn free and smashed along Clark Street and used in huge bonfires set by Star League men. Young ruffians produced zinc torpedoes and exploded them under the wheels of streetcars, the flying particles making that part of the district a veritable no man's land. Gamblers and harlots, thieves and bums came into the crowded thoroughfares and cheered for their little hero or jeered as they strode past the darkened Republican headquarters. One hilarious group decided to pay victorious Hinky Dink a visit, but found his saloon was closed, the blinds down, the lights out. The Hink had gone to the Harrison headquarters, having completely forgotten, sneered the empty-handed *Tribune,* "that free beers might have been in order."

7

But his triumph had not transformed Hinky Dink from a man of benevolence into a miserly one; on the contrary. Less than a month after the election, Little Mike purchased and set up on Clark Street, just south of Van Buren, the Workingmen's Exchange, where for more than three decades the bums and tramps, hobos and hungry jobless could come for free lunch, and, if they had a nickel, a glass of beer which, proclaimed a big beer-glass sign out front, was "The Largest and Coolest in the City." Above this establishment was the Alaska Hotel, a flophouse which could accommodate three hundred men, and during elections twice that number.

Shortly after his induction into the council Hinky Dink opened still another saloon across the street, at 307 Clark. Here his more favored visitors were received, to confer in Hink's little rear office or to sip spirits at Hink's bar while studying the inscription in Latin above the bar-length mirror, *In Vino Veritas.* Such visitors would roar with laughter at Hink's favorite joke. He'd nod at the sign, withdraw his cigar, spit, and explain: "That means when you get your snoot full you'll tell your right name."

THE TORTUOUS ROAD
OF CIVIC RIGHTEOUSNESS

I

The election of Carter Harrison the Younger as mayor of Chicago moved Bathhouse John Coughlin near the pinnacle of his political career. The Bath had become a veteran in the Chicago common council. He was one of the first on the Harrison bandwagon, and entitled to the perquisites of priority. But, more important, Harrison was going places, and Bathhouse followed him with the complete, dogged affection of a punch-drunk prize fighter for his glib and brainy manager.

Harrison was all things to The Bath. He had the physical prowess that had never failed to impress and please the erstwhile rubber. He possessed an elegance of person to which The Bath aspired. He spoke the kind of language Coughlin sought constantly, and quite unsuccessfully, to employ. Harrison was liberal in his attitude toward the saloon, which Bathhouse regarded as an indispensable fixture of Democracy. He knew the ways of practical politics, and was forbearing and sympathetic. Furthermore, Harrison Democracy was not Powers Democracy, nor Sullivan Democracy. He ran the circus himself, and permitted John Coughlin and Hinky Dink to conduct the First Ward side shows as they wished.

Yet Harrison, in his youth and enthusiasm, was in many respects a reformer. He saw as the greatest menace to Chicago the traction titan, Charles Tyson Yerkes. He was again eye to eye with The Bath, although their reasons differed vastly. Coughlin wanted vengeance upon Yerkes for the fight against General Electric.

As the battle between Harrison and Yerkes developed, it be-

172

came obvious that the young mayor was whipped hands down unless he could subvert some part of the boodle gang. For Yerkes still was the man who controlled the council and he was moving in for the final coup. The owner of twelve traction companies in addition to his gas and electric interests, with handsome privileges in the outlying regions, Yerkes wanted now the complete control of the Chicago streets. He wanted it quick, and he wanted it cheap.

Yerkes was weary of the block-by-block purchase of privileges. One company alone had been forced to take out seventy-nine ordinances between 1859 and 1897 in order to complete its lines. Every time the reformers raised a new fuss the aldermen got more expensive. Besides that, they were becoming unreliable, and it was no longer safe to put up a franchise measure just before an election. The defection of Bathhouse John was a prime example. He was beginning to introduce utterly needless reform measures, and to clamor for compensation like a Mann or an O'Neill.

Yerkes knew that the boodle aldermen were impatiently awaiting his final, blanket ordinance, and he knew that they would ask fantastic prices for its passage. So, a few days before Harrison's election, he suddenly determined to go to the state legislature instead, and have it over with. It has always been a strange anomaly of Illinois politics that a legislator can be bought cheaper than an alderman. Senator John Humphrey introduced three bills in the legislature, which would create a state commission empowered to grant street franchises in all cities of the state. In lieu of taxes the companies receiving these rights were to pay the state three per cent of their gross earnings.

The bills were full of jokers. They robbed Chicago of home rule. They reduced compensation one-half of one per cent, as compared with many recent Chicago ordinances, in addition to omitting taxes completely. Most important, compensation was to be paid on gross earnings and not gross receipts, a difference of millions of dollars. Although Yerkes was supported by such important stockholders in his companies as Erskine M. Phelps, Levi Z.

Leiter, Marshall Field and Samuel W. Allerton, Chicago almost unanimously leaped upon the Humphrey bills as soon as they were presented.

The reformers charged that Yerkes was preparing to rob the city in the most dastardly fashion in history. The boodlers saw their graft bonanza vanishing. Both forces joined to fight the Humphrey bills, led by the combined press.

Immediately on taking office Harrison seized the leadership of this united movement. Bathhouse John, in his new mantle of white, wanted to lead with him. The Bath had become a power now: he was the Harrison spokesman who presented administration measures in the council, and he and Hinky Dink between them held the choice committee spots in that body.*

But Harrison knew that genuine and traditional reformers must direct the attack on Yerkes. He rejected The Bath's proffer of services on the special council committee to fight the Humphrey bills, and gave him instead a place on a special committee to beat the Gas Trust frontage bill.

This was an excellent sop. The Gas Trust, numbering seven companies including Roger Sullivan's Ogden Gas, had caused to be introduced in the legislature a bill which would permit a combination of the seven firms into one unit. This would create a monopoly and it would relieve some of the newer companies, such as Ogden Gas, from the ninety-cent ceiling on their prices. The new combination could jump prices to the $1.25 maximum which had been granted to the older companies. In addition, by requiring a high percentage of frontage consents, the bill would prevent the organization of new companies, keeping competition out of Chicago.

The Bath leaped to his work with a will. Here was a remarkable opportunity to shine as a Harrison reformer. The Civic Federation, a Special Committee of One Hundred, the press and the

*Coughlin's committees were: finance; health; wharves and public grounds; streets and alleys south (chairman); harbors; viaducts and bridges. Kenna had railroads; gas, oil and electricity; police (chairman); water department; elections; and markets.

pulpit were belaboring the Gas Trust as much as Yerkes. Further-more, it would be an excellent chance to repay Sullivan and Powers for virtually counting him out when the Ogden Gas franchise was passed.

Harrison, Coughlin and the members of the two committees journeyed weekly to Springfield to battle Yerkes, who was person-ally directing his legislative forces and spending an estimated $190,000 to get his bills passed. Week ends the Chicagoans would return to whip up anger at home and attend the Monday council meetings.

In these Monday meetings Bathhouse John demonstrated that he was not fooling in his new reform role. When Johnny Powers called up the Garfield Electric Light franchise, Bathhouse John fought it vigorously because it failed to provide for sufficient re-muneration to the city. It passed 57 to 8, with Bathhouse alone of the gang aldermen joining the seven veteran representatives of purity. Hinky Dink could not bring himself to vote.

John Harlan, archfoe of graft, seemed uncomfortable with his new companion. "I want to express my joy that the First Ward representative is converted to the idea that the city ought to get payment," cracked Harlan. Coughlin was fighting mad at this gibe and was about to reply when Mayor Harrison caught his eye. The mayor beamed upon his disciple, Bathhouse grinned back and resumed his seat without a word.

Kenna made his bow in the council with an order for an ambu-lance division in the police department. The measure was read by the city clerk. Kenna was determined not to make a speech if he could possibly avoid it.

Many of Coughlin's ordinances in this period won the grudg-ing admiration of the uplift organizations, particularly his order forcing an investigation of business houses which, he asserted, were stealing city water. It was this probe that later resulted in the dis-covery that the packing plants had been systematically thieving for years, a sin for which they atoned upon discovery by paying a quarter of a million dollars in back water bills. The Bath also won the gratitude of organized labor by passing a measure requiring that all city printing must bear the union label.

But Coughlin did not wholly espouse reform. He maintained his independence. While the Humphrey bills were being debated in Springfield he launched a drive to restore the ex-policemen of the Star League to the city pay rolls. The reformers, in their exuberance, were putting pressure on Harrison to declare for strict civil service under the terms of the new state civil service law.

The Bath railed at the civil service commission, a body appointed to administer the few civil-service positions created by Mayor Swift. He introduced an ordinance requiring that the commission be made subservient to the city council and conduct no business beyond making periodical reports.

"Look at what they've got here!" cried Bathhouse. "Two governments: the council and th' civil service commission. It's a fallacious fallacy. It's un-American. Here we've got honest policemen with loyal hearts and willing hands, kicked out by a corrupt Republican administration, who want to get back their jobs. I say, put these policemen to work, and do it now."

Coughlin won a partial victory. The council refused to limit the civil service commission illegally, but the chief of police was ordered to take back the Star Leaguers.

2

The furor against the Humphrey bills resulted in their defeat. The redoubtable Yerkes promptly caused to be introduced the Allen bill. It passed quickly, and Governor Tanner, Billy Lorimer's man in the state house, promptly signed it.

This piece of legislation recognized the right of Chicago's aldermen to sell the streets. It empowered the council to issue franchises for a period of fifty years, instead of twenty, and it eliminated any consideration of compensation for the city. The *Tribune* estimated Chicago would lose $150,000,000 in revenue if the council acted under the Allen law.

The councilmen were quick to see that if they gave Yerkes a blanket franchise for fifty years the era of small-time, block-by-block sales was ended. No one had objection to that. Few aldermen could be sure of re-election in any event. The time to make money in politics was always *now*. Still, obviously, if Yerkes planned to buy his security for half a century, he would have to pay high.

The inflated values the council members placed on their votes startled even Yerkes, who had been accustomed to generosity. He decided to let the council cool off, and in a huff departed suddenly for a vacation in Europe. The greedy burghers, their tongues hanging over their cravats, were forced to depart to their own summer playgrounds without any slight idea of what the traction baron intended to pay.

Bathhouse and Hinky Dink put in a profitable summer at the tracks. With Coughlin firmly established as lord of the First Ward, John Condon, Harry Varnell and others of the boys had scraped together savings and set up the Harlem race track, in competition with Ed Corrigan's Hawthorne. There Coughlin raced his ponies, sojourning week ends with Hinky Dink, who had become fond of the baths at Mount Clemens, Michigan.

All was well in the best of all possible worlds. Bathhouse and Hinky Dink had money. Coughlin held his box regularly at Washington Park, where he entertained the big shots of the town and daily demonstrated his sartorial inventiveness during the brilliant Washington Park season. Billy Skakel and Sol van Praag were docile—Billy paying readily for the privilege of re-establishing his famous Clock, Mike McDonald was content to watch over his Eleventh Ward, Ed Corrigan was being forced to the wall (he gave up in September, selling his interests in Hawthorne), the mayor was with them, the Silver Dollar, the bathhouses and Hinky Dink's saloons were doing a thriving business.

There was just one thing more Bathhouse John wanted: the humbling of Johnny Powers.

When the council reconvened in September, Bathhouse was

set for battle. He strode pompously into the chambers wearing a Prince Albert coat, a big red carnation, wing collar and a purple cravat. His hairbrush pompadour stood up like a rising vote of thanks. The Bath was in splendid humor. He stomped about the floor, slapping his friends on the back, waving at enemies, chuckling and guffawing, and receiving compliments on the performances of his horses. He surveyed his forces with whom he had conferred frequently in the summer. They were all stalwarts from the gang—Brennan, Mulcahy, Martin, Wiora, Carey. These, with the Little Fellow, would be enough to bring Powers to terms.

The battle was joined when Powers offered an ordinance to establish a system of ward superintendents to direct the cleaning of streets and collection of garbage. This would provide much new patronage for the hungry aldermen and should, of course, gain unanimous passage. The Bath was first on roll call, and he loudly voted "No!" Powers jerked to attention at such heresy. He knew well enough that Coughlin wanted his scalp, but he expected no test on such an ordinance. He bit angrily at his mustache, looked warningly about at his friends, and then bent forward to watch the vote. One after another the members of the gang lined up behind Bathhouse. The reformers were with them, and the measure lost.

In a rage Powers held a quick conference with his loyal followers.

"Johnny says you'll never get another peanut stand in the loop if you try that," whispered Alderman Brennan to The Bath.

"You tell Johnny that he ought to be runnin' a peanut stand himself," replied Coughlin, loudly enough for his friends to hear. There was a round of laughter. Powers rose angrily. The Bath's friends booed him. Then Coughlin took charge of proceedings.

He resumed his attack on the new civil service law, calling it unconstitutional, and offered a resolution requiring the city clerk to pay out no more money to the civil service commission. This would put it out of business immediately, in spite of the fact that civil service for Chicago had been approved by a majority of 45,000 citizens two years previously. The Republicans and reform aldermen were on their feet immediately. The measure was sent to the finance committee.

Coughlin then introduced a measure to require all insurance companies doing business in Chicago to pay three per cent of the premiums collected to support the city health department. This was the first evidence of The Bath's interest in insurance, and briefly preceded his establishment of his own insurance agency, wherein he represented virtually all existing insurance companies and had a monopoly on property damage in the loop. This ordinance was referred to committee, as Bathhouse expected it would be, and there was buried, after leading insurance men had come in to reason with the committee members.

The third Coughlin ordinance would require Mayor Harrison to appoint personally all city employees. This was to circumvent further the civil service law, but the measure failed to pass.

Coughlin's ordinance number four that night would empower the mayor to remit fines for infractions of city ordinances. This was a project dear to a politician's heart, but Johnny Powers could no longer stand it.

"I'm ag'in' that ordinance!" shouted Johnny de Pow. "It puts too much work on th' mayor."

Derisive laughter from Coughlin and his friends, and Powers quickly sat down.

"The alderman from the Nineteenth wants this ordinance as much as any of us," said Bathhouse, undisturbed. "I hope it passes." It did.

The Bath wound up an impressive evening with an ordinance to establish a new cab stand in the loop. "Let the hackmen make an honest dollar just like th' aldermen," he said.

Powers, smarting under the gibes in next morning's newspapers, refused to let Coughlin get away with it. His alternative was difficult, but he accepted it. He joined the reformers and went out in support of the civil service law! As chairman of the finance committee he prevailed upon the members to recommend an appropriation of $12,000 for the maintenance of the civil service commission. Coughlin brought in a minority report opposing the appropriation. The showdown was to come in the council meeting of October 7.

The men with Coughlin were ready for it. They believed, like The Bath, that Johnny de Pow had taken much money and given them little. His big flashing diamonds, his huge gold chains, and his noisy, ruthless manner of shutting them off in debate had aroused them beyond their sense of fear. If Coughlin could bait Powers and attack him in open council, they could follow.

When Powers entered the council chambers the night of October 7 he was greeted with resounding boos. He sulked to his seat, snarled at Bathhouse, but then sat back confidently, drumming his fingers upon his desk. He could take it. He was certain to win. He had the reformers with him.

The civil service ordinance was duly introduced. But Bathhouse John insisted on consideration of his minority report, and the council was deadlocked in the voting, 33 to 33. The argument was held over for another week.

By October 14, Powers had rounded up sufficient supporters to pass the civil service appropriation. He called it up.

"I do not like the civil service law," Powers admitted. "I don't think it should have been enacted. But we've got it, and the law says that we must provide funds for th' commission."

"The law is unconstitutional!" bellowed The Bath.

"What are you, th' Soopreme Court?" challenged Powers.

"Th' law is unconstitutional, and un-American," continued Bathhouse. "The law is an enemy of th' Poles, the enemy of th' Bohemians, the enemy of th' Germans, the enemy of th' Irish, the enemy of th' Americans in America. It ought not be tolerated!"

"Th' Irish can take care of themselves!" someone yelled. The Bath beamed and bowed.

"Vote! Vote!" shouted the Powers gang and the reformers.

But there were more speeches. McInerney, Martin and Brennan attacked the proposal. Madden, Mann and O'Neill joined Powers in its support. These latter made a telling argument. After all, the council had no right to determine whether it would provide funds. The law said it must. The question was how much, and $12,000 was an absolute minimum.

The vote was ordered. Powers was victorious, 42 to 20, and Bathhouse admitted it was one of the worst defeats of his life.

3

The war between Bathhouse and Powers was halted temporarily in mid-November when Richard Croker, Tammany boss of New York, called upon Chicago Democrats to assist him in his whirlwind fight to elect Robert A. Van Wyck as mayor. Croker wanted Harrison and the Cook County Democratic Marching Club, but particularly he required the services of Alderman Michael Kenna, whose ability as a political organizer was becoming known about the country.

The Chicago Democrats, Powers among them, journeyed to New York for a series of meetings. When they departed, after Mayor Harrison had made several speeches, little Hink remained behind to assist Croker with his strategy. The "Napoleon of the Levee," as the Gotham newspapers called him, proved useful, for Van Wyck won with a plurality of 86,000 votes.

Only one bit of legislation arose during December on which the contending aldermen were able to get together. Coughlin and his friends had been repeatedly blocked in their attempts to vote themselves a salary. Then one of the rebels had a happy idea. "Why not authorize each alderman to hire a secretary at $1,500 a year?"

Such an obvious solution did not require a second thought. The ordinance was forthwith introduced and passed. Most of the aldermen pretended they really were going to hire secretaries. Powers employed one, his son, John Powers, Jr.

But Bathhouse had no patience with such evasion. "I'm not th' Supreme Court," he said, "an' I don't know if this law is legal, but do you know what I'm gonna do? I'm gonna hire Mr. Kenna for my secretary, an' he's gonna hire me."

4

During the early months of 1898 nothing went through the council but routine business, and a sorry business it was, for Powers saved himself from annihilation only by his unholy alliance with the reformers, and Coughlin, as a Harrison disciple, was also committed to the tortuous road of civic righteousness. No one dared put up a franchise measure, good or bad, for it would be doomed from the start. Nothing was sufficiently harmless to escape fire from one camp or the other, and the notorious Chicago council became positively antiseptic.

Bathhouse, nevertheless, made a further attempt to restore the jobs of his Star League police. The council had ordered them back to work, but reform organizations had dug up an old city ordinance which provided that discharged policemen could not be re-employed and had gone into court for a writ of mandamus to enforce it. Coughlin went to the council with a resolution calling for the repeal of this law. The alderman was in a gay mood, for it was perfectly obvious that Powers and his gang, as good Democrats, would have to back it.

To the horror of the rebels, Powers voted with the Republicans and reformers against the resolution and beat it. "Powers thereby pressed home the point that no alderman can get a permit to erect a barberpole in his ward so long as he follows the leadership of Coughlin and McInerney," commented the *Tribune*.

Bathhouse John was in a rage. He visited Mayor Harrison, and the mayor sent him to Corporation Counsel Charles S. Thornton. Thornton and Bathhouse searched the law books together, and found a solution. It appeared in Section 1481 of the Revised Ordinances that the law had been previously amended to provide that a policeman could not be re-employed only if he had been discharged for malfeasance, intoxication, or conduct unbecoming an officer. Unquestionably the Star League police had been discharged for possessing the wrong political faith. That night Chief of Police Kipley summarily dismissed four hundred patrolmen who had been given jobs by Republican Mayor Swift, and employed a similar number of Star Leaguers to replace them. They whooped it up at the Silver Dollar.

Elated, the Bathhouse went lustily back to his attack on Powers. He blocked an attempt by Yerkes to obtain downtown connections for his new Union Loop, and kept all Powers-sponsored track-elevation ordinances from passing. He let no opportunity pass to prove that he was ruler of the council. An alderman introduced a track-elevation ordinance while Coughlin was conferring on the floor. All he heard was the name "Indiana and Western."

"Streets and Alleys South," bawled The Bath loudly, calling for the assignment of the legislation to the committee of which he was chairman.

There were protests from over the floor. The ordinance had nothing to do with streets and alleys, and it was in the north part of town. Clearly it should go to the special track-elevation committee.

"Streets and Alleys South," howled Bathhouse, still not knowing what it was all about. There it went, despite the fuming of Powers.

Having set this precedent, Coughlin sought to make the most of it. When the Northwestern Elevated Railroad Company got its franchise in 1893, it was required to complete the elevated structure within five years, or lose the franchise. The five years were almost up. Yerkes, meanwhile, had bought Northwestern, and he wanted an extension of time. So Powers was commissioned to get it, and the order had to be passed immediately.

This legislation was the legitimate property of Streets and Alleys North. But there Powers had friends. Coughlin determined to have the measure himself. When the extension resolution was introduced, Coughlin shouted:

"Streets and Alleys South!"

"It's north!" yelled Powers.

"Streets and Alleys South!"

Mayor Harrison ruled with Coughlin, and Streets and Alleys South, with The Bath chairman, got the resolution. When Coughlin reintroduced the order a few weeks later Powers was so enraged he voted against it. But it passed, 36 to 17.

At the next meeting the Powers gang was again in the middle. The Twin Wire Telephone Company franchise was one of Johnny Powers' favorites. The company, organized in 1893 by Perry Hull, was purely speculative, and several aldermen were interested. Powers had put through the franchise, but to obtain passage he had left in a requirement that a plant must be built within five years or the franchise would lapse.

Of course none of the promoters behind Twin Wire ever intended to build a plant. The right to lay conduits under every street and alley in town had been granted to shake down Bell Telephone, or to provide a handsome sale to a competitor. But Bell had refused to shake, and no competitor appeared.

Late in 1898, however, a syndicate of New York men decided to go into the Chicago telephone business and they wanted an ordinance. There was Twin Wire. Shares were worth $3 each, and the Powers gang bought them up, expecting to sell at $100. All that was needed was the extension of the plant time limit.

News of the expected coup got about the saloons, and Bathhouse was primed for Johnny Powers when the extension came up. There was no time for the usual council procedure, and Powers moved for suspension of the rules.

With the rules suspended it would require a favorable vote of two-thirds of the aldermen to pass the extension. The rebels were warned to think several times before they attempted to block Johnny de Pow on a windfall of such proportions.

Bathhouse John was first on roll call. *"No!"*

Twenty-three of his followers were with him. The extension was lost. The shares, grabbed up so greedily, were utterly worthless.

"Come on, boys!" yelled the jubilant Bath. "We got 'em licked. Now for Yerkes!"

THE STREETCAR FRANCHISE WAR

FOLLOWING the spring election, in which several new Yerkes supporters were victorious,* Johnny de Pow was once again in control of the council. He promptly ended his romance with the reformers, and went out for vengeance upon the followers of Carter Harrison. In his role as organizer of the aldermanic caucus to name the members of committees, he saw to it that choice Powers men landed on vital committees where they might smooth the path of Yerkes-directed legislation, and, in jest, he put leading Harrison supporters on an obscure Committee on City Hall. This body rarely met, had no prescribed duties, and little notion of its jurisdiction.

Powers had lined up the Yerkes cohorts with considerable foresight, for in June the Cook County Republican convention called for repeal of the Allen law at next January's session of the legislature, and a poll of the members of the Illinois assembly pointed definitely to a triumph there for the anti-Yerkes groups.

The traction king's hand was forced. He must either bring forth and pass the all-important council legislation now, or retire in defeat. Yerkes had no intention of quitting. Day after day his attorneys met with the heads of the various transportation systems to plan their strategy, and Powers, fortified by the return of Foxy Ed Cullerton to the council, held parleys with that parliamentary wizard and with Mike McInerney, who had deserted the banner of Bathhouse John. The city had not long to wait for the first glimmer of action.

On July 11 the rumor started that the Yerkes measure was

---

*Coughlin also won easily, defeating Patrick S. Reilly by 3,200 votes.

ready. At once traction stocks soared $1,830,000 in that single day, and Powers and his closest cronies bought heavily. Their greed aroused others of the purchasable aldermen who had been left in the cold on this transaction and these men angrily demanded, according to the *Tribune,* that payments for their votes on the forthcoming ordinance be doubled and tripled to $50,000, and as high as $75,000. If the stocks could rise that fast in one day on a mere rumor, the higher prices for votes, they reasoned, were fair enough. They could well afford to be arrogant. Yerkes needed this ordinance more than he had ever needed any other council favor. He needed it quickly, before the swelling opposition had a chance to form a solid front.

But the report had been premature or the Yerkes representatives were unwilling to raise the antes, even if Joseph Medill did assert in his newspaper that Yerkes would gladly pay as much as $1,500,000 to get his monopoly. When the council met two nights later not a word was uttered about the ordinance. The traction issue was still in the air and no one could predict when the opposing legions would clash.

On the next day Yerkes streetcar stocks dropped $2,358,000.

Powers, snared in a trap of his own making, consoled his disgruntled followers as best he could, and went off on a vacation trip to his native Ireland. When he returned a few months later, having conferred en route with traction men in New York, he bore in his right hand a shillelagh and on his lips a vow to win for Yerkes.

2

All that summer Yerkes prepared his offensive. He loosened his purse-strings and purchased the *Inter-Ocean,* a staid Republican journal, and imported George Wheeler Hinman from the New York *Sun* to write brilliant and vicious diatribes against the Chicago "Trust Press" opposing the Yerkes ordinance. Hinman was a fierce antagonist who could stab with sharp adjectives and flay his foe with trenchant verbs. He had a special grievance against Victor Lawson, owner of the *News* and *Record,* who had been founder of the Associated Press, anathema to the *Sun*. Harrison, stung by Hinman's blasts, rallied Lawson and the city's other important editors and publishers to his side: Medill and Robert W. Patterson of the *Tribune,* and Herman H. Kohlsaat of the *Times-Herald* and the *Post*.

Soon the opening barrage began. Hinman screeched that the newspapers were blackmailing Yerkes because he had refused to pay each "Trust Press" publisher $50,000 to remain silent. He declared that Lawson, "sanctimonious churchgoer," owned interests in the Harlem and Roby race tracks and that both the Lawson newspapers were controlled by gamblers. He charged that Kohlsaat had sold his soul to bankers fighting Yerkes, and even called the mighty Medill, who practically had driven Altgeld out of office for pardoning the Haymarket rioters, an anarchist.

The "Trust Press" replied in kind, and the aldermen ran for the nearest shelters, and into the offices of the Yerkes managers. There tempting offers were dangled before them: contracts to furnish coal to power houses, contracts to supply motormen and conductors with uniforms and caps, promises to employ aldermanic brokers in the purchase of insurance and real estate. Some succumbed; others balked, seeking more. Chicago awaited the outcome of the dickering.

By November the time was short. But the battle lines were shaped and both sides expected soon the head-on collision. Harrison continued to plead with the people to stand by him. Yerkes' *Inter-Ocean* yowled that it was the citizen's true friend, and provided ingenious moral arguments by which Yerkes aldermen could justify their stand. Streetcar lobbyists swarmed about the city hall and the meetings in Johnny de Pow's saloon office were numberless. M. K. Bowen, president of the Chicago City Railroad Company, spoke every other day to skeptical reform aldermen at the Union League Club, pleading that a fifty-year franchise was vital to insure a fair return to investors. But the skeptics demanded a bigger return for the city and held fast before the Bowen pleas.

There was nothing left to do but fight it out on the floor of the council.

3

On the night of December 5 there came an end to rumor and speculation and doubt. Alderman W. H. Lyman, a Yerkes stalwart, presented the master's ordinance: an extension for fifty years, with meager compensation, of all Yerkes railway rights after the expiration of existing franchises in 1903.

The Yerkes machine rolled into action and the ordinance was sent not to a single committee but to a joint body made up of three committees—those on streets and alleys north, south, and west. This was an adroit and well-planned step, for the committees held a large number of the aldermen sympathetic to Yerkes and in the recesses of the committee room itching fingers could quietly receive the special Yerkes analgesic.

The clamor which arose had been expected by the Yerkes crowd. No one, not even the boodlers, had anticipated passage of so flagrant an ordinance, so they smoothly added an amendment as a peace offering: a compromise providing that the companies pay to the city one per cent of gross receipts for all lines earning $7,500 a mile per year and increasing one and one-half per cent for every additional $2,500 per mile earned until $20,000 a mile was reached, when a three-per-cent maximum on gross receipts would be forthcoming. The people fighting Yerkes quickly saw through the forest of figures. Many of the lines were already paying three to three and a half per cent regardless of earnings. No line would ever earn more than $15,000 a mile. Besides that, Mayor Harrison and some of the reform aldermen had estimated that the companies could well pay ten or twelve per cent of gross receipts. So Harrison said "No!"

And what of Bathhouse John and Hinky Dink? Had the cry "Now for Yerkes!" been only an impulsive gesture? Was the precious pair going to cut itself out of the greatest melon of the boodle age? Would their loyalty to young Mayor Harrison survive? The first hint of their stand came when both voted against the compromise ordinance on the theory that the worse the ordinance, the easier it would be to defeat. Yet, just as Harrison and the anti-Yerkes men rejoiced in the evident determination of Coughlin and Kenna to stand with the mayor, Bathhouse John, with his rare talent for speaking out of turn, stated to reporters his position on the traction problem and started Harrison worrying again.

"I," said Alderman Bathhouse John, "am in favor of the streetcars paying the city a fair compensation for franchise privileges. I shall look into the present measures and consider them carefully. I am not against fifty-year franchises under proper restrictions."

Kenna was even more obscure and ominous. "I have no opinion to express," he snorted.

The Yerkes crowd exulted. The pair seemed to be wavering. One emissary was rushed to Kenna's office, another to the Silver Dollar. There were conferences, whispered words, thumpings on tables. The Yerkes offer was $150,000 to be split equally between the two, all the money needed at election time, jobs for ward heelers on the streetcar lines, opportunity for rakeoffs on supply contracts. More heated and angry words. And soon the messengers returned to their chiefs: "They won't say nothin'."

This was the last peaceful overture. The war began in earnest now. Mayor Harrison announced plans for meeting after meeting, mostly in wards whose aldermen were known to be Yerkes adherents. The city was aroused. Joseph Medill reasserted that Yerkes was trying to steal $150,000,000 from Chicago and pledged his *Tribune* to a finish fight.

"It will not be easy," said Medill. "Yerkes spent a million dollars to put the Allen law through the legislature and he will spend as much or more to get his measures through the council. Now is the time for the people to act!"

But the *Inter-Ocean* scoffed that the fight was already won, with a majority of ten aldermen for Yerkes. "The aldermen who have decided to settle the railway controversy equitably and reasonably need not fear Medill," scribbled Yerkes' journalists. And in ebon type on several pages of each issue they printed the warning:

THE ALDERMAN WHO VOTES AGAINST A FAIR ORDINANCE FOR THE STREET CAR COMPANIES IN ORDER TO HELP THE TRUST NEWSPAPERS EXTORT MONEY FROM THE TRACTION COMPANIES THEREBY BECOMES ACCESSORY TO BLACKMAIL AND EXTORTION. HIS NAME WILL BE PLACED IN THE PILLORY AMONG THOSE WHO PROSTITUTE THEIR CONVICTIONS TO THE INTERESTS OF BLACKMAILERS AND CORRUPTIONISTS. THE BRAND OF DISHONESTY AND COWARDICE WILL BE UPON HIM FOR LIFE!

Against Coughlin and Kenna Editor Hinman unloosed a host of harsh accusations, further evidence that they were showing no warmth to the Yerkes offers. The Official Red and Green Lottery Game, running wide open in the First Ward and owned and operated by the Coughlin-Kenna lieutenants if not, as the *Inter-Ocean* averred, by the aldermen themselves, received its share of abuse. This policy game had stations at 273 Dearborn Street, the rear entrance of 24 Plymouth Street, 350 State Street, 1441 State Street, and 162 Van Buren Street. Each branch had its runners, ready to service any part of the city. Players purchased red and green cards bearing several columns of numbers, with winners keyed to either treasury-department reports or stock-market quotations. The game exceeded even Billy Skakel's clocks for great profits, for it was played by thousands every day and yielded estimated returns of as much as $25,000 on some days.

Hinman did not limit his charges against the First Ward bosses to operating a numbers racket. Bathhouse John and Hinky Dink, the *Inter-Ocean* went on, held domain over "a vast illicit empire of 400 opium resorts, 100 gambling dens, 7,000 saloons and other haunts of sin and over a population which is 18 per cent criminal."

"Aldermen Coughlin and Kenna," Hinman wrote, "are bribed with the promise of protection in their various schemes of robbery. They are bribed with money they make and expect to make out of their Official Red and Green Policy Game, their gambling dens and the profits assured them by the mayor's promise of immunity to their panel houses. They are paid for their votes with the money which came to them through the violation of the law with the knowledge, consent, and connivance of the mayor."

Thus the trials and tribulations of honest men seeking only to serve their city well. The newspapers belaboring Yerkes were well aware of the temptations set before The Bath and The Hink and they knew, too, that Bathhouse had not only been a Harrison enthusiast from the beginning but had helped to engineer the election of the man leading the fight on Yerkes. They might have replied to the *Inter-Ocean* that Coughlin fought and flouted Mayor Swift, who, like Harrison, had controlled the police who presumably could end all vice and sin. Yet, in the columns and columns about the furious Franchise War, not one word appeared to encourage the erstwhile boodlers in their effort to be, for one of the few times in their lives, on the side of civic righteousness.

But if the newspapers were wary of Coughlin's ultimate intentions, Mayor Harrison was not. Working like a demon, the mayor sped from hall to hall in every ward represented by a Yerkes alderman, but he never appeared before the voters of the First Ward. It was a diplomatic move, for The Bath and The Hink thus were not subjected to the indignity of telling their constituents how they intended to vote before the time came for them to cast their ballots.

Rallies, to which came men and women from all parts of the city, were staged in every large downtown auditorium; in the Central Music Hall, in Turner Hall, in the Rink, and in the headquarters of the Democratic party, but none of them were designed to reach the followers of The Bath and The Hink. At these meetings Aldermen Charles Walker, Billy Kent, and MVL's George Cole shouted themselves hoarse, the little stationer almost undoing all of Harrison's good work by listing Coughlin and Kenna as "doubtful" when he enumerated those aldermen certain to oppose Yerkes in a future vote.

The city seethed with excitement. Page one, column one for weeks was devoted to the traction question and the cartoonists and editorial writers dipped deep into their supplies of denunciations and imprecations. Each morning the *Times-Herald* lampooned Powers and Yerkes with grotesque cartoons, the *News* and *Record* ran screaming headlines, the *Post* exhorted in dignified page-one editorials, and the *Tribune* carried on its front page in bold type: "BULLETINS OF FRANCHISE WAR NEWS!"

In the north-side wards there were reports of threats by excitable citizens to lynch any council member who voted against the mayor. Aldermen received letters threatening the kidnapping of their children and wives and the dynamiting of their homes. The newspapers of the country predicted a civil war in Chicago after Harrison in a special interview declared boldly: "The people will have to beat gold by any method they can find. I hope that 150,000 persons will descend upon the city hall when the ordinance is being considered and show the aldermen they mean business!"

"Harrison and the anarchistic Trust Press," countered the *Inter-Ocean,* "want blood to flow in Chicago streets!"

The eastern newspapers, ever ready to herald calamity in Chicago, echoed the cry of "Anarchy!" and published reports that the governor was preparing to call out the state militia to prevent bloodshed. This roused residents in downstate Illinois counties, who protested: "We will not send our sons to die for an ambitious Chicago mayor who wants to be President!" Harrison was supplanting John Peter Altgeld as "the nation's Number One Anarchist" and even staid *Harper's Weekly* called him a "dangerous demagogue."

With the charges flying about him, Mayor Harrison summoned the two aldermen from the First Ward. He needed to be certain of their support. His private polls indicated that two votes, or perhaps even one, might determine the outcome of the battle. The newspaper polls still branded Coughlin and Kenna as waverers and the mayor had to be sure.

"Boys," he told Bathhouse John and Hinky Dink, "now is the time to finish Yerkes. I'm depending on you to help."

Coughlin stared vacantly out of the window. Kenna paid polite attention.

"John . . . Mike," the mayor continued. "I hope you're going to be loyal to me. I need your help. Your name will be remembered forever if you fight with me."

Bathhouse rose and faced the mayor. "Mr. Maar," he said, "I was talkin' a while back with Senator Billy Mason and he told me, 'Keep clear of th' big stuff, John, it's dangerous. You and Mike stick to th' small stuff; there's little risk and in the long run it pays a damned sight more.' Mr. Maar, we're with you. An' we'll do what we can to swing some of th' other boys over."

Fortified with such a promise, Mayor Harrison pulled out all the stops. On the Sunday before the council meeting at which the Lyman ordinance would be up for decision, he staged one last rally in Central Music Hall. Even Altgeld, who was on the verge of announcing his candidacy for mayor against Harrison, appeared on the platform and made a brief speech.

"The question," said the ex-governor, "is whether a few powerful men can dictate terms to Chicago!"

Harrison predicted: "We will win a major victory. I think we have enough aldermen to defeat them. I have the pledged word of many of them and only yesterday I talked with two who promised to fight corruption to the finish. It would warm your hearts if I could tell you the whole story. These are trustworthy and honorable men who are going to stand by me. We are going to win the fight!"

The ministers, ever ready to inveigh against the corrupt, were fierce in their Sunday sermons. "Any alderman who will take a bribe must be hunted down and sent to the penitentiary," stormed Bishop Samuel Fallows of St. Paul's Reformed Episcopal Church. "The evil aldermen are the devil's dogcatchers!" was the sentiment of the Reverend P. S. Henson of the First Baptist Church.

4

Determined citizens fell upon the city hall as the traction debate began. The chambers quaked with noise when the aldermen convened the evening of December 12. In the galleries men sat two in a seat along the rugged benches, and among them were many First Ward hoodlums. They yelled insults at the Yerkes aldermen. In the front row sat a dozen grim-faced constituents, each holding a noose that dangled ominously over the railing.

When Alderman William Mangler, who ironically had been supported by the Municipal Voters' League, shouted in the heat of discussion, "We need all we can get from the traction companies!" the boys in the galleries guffawed and yelled: "How much are you getting?" Mangler turned angrily upon his tormentors, shaking his fist. "I dare you to come down here and talk that way!" he challenged.

In the tightly packed corridors outside, a German Hungry Five band and a drum and bugle corps tramped through the moiling crowd, blasting "Battle Hymn of the Republic" and other incidental music. When a newspaper photographer in the chambers set off his flash powder, Alderman (Hot Stove) Jimmy Quinn quipped: "The Dutchies up north just shot an alderman who won't vote on th' mayor's side," and Alderman Abe Ballenberg quietly paled, slid beneath his desk and for some moments took no further interest in the proceedings.

Mike McInerney railed against the Trust Press. "I say to you that all this claptrap is brought about by the newspapers of Chicago——" Hisses sounded in the galleries. "I come," yelled McInerney defiantly, "from a country where only snakes hiss."

Mayor Harrison, calmly puffing a cigar, tapped with his gavel. "This is not a debating society. The gentlemen in the gallery will preserve quiet."

A semblance of order finally prevailed. There were preliminary skirmishes and then Alderman Augustus Maltby, who had cut short his vacation on a Colorado ranch to rush into the fight, rose with a motion to suspend the rules and delay all consideration of a Yerkes franchise until the legislature had an opportunity to pass on the proposed repeal of the Allen law.

This appeared to be a vital moment. If two-thirds of the aldermen supported the motion, Yerkes was definitely beaten in the council. The clerk called the roll: "Alderman Coughlin!"

Bathhouse John rose, stared directly at Harrison and called out, "I vote yea!"

Like a jack-in-the-box, Kenna was up before his name was called: "Yea!"

The galleries cheered and people stomped anxiously about in the corridors, attempting to hear what was going on. The clerk droned the names. When the roll call was over, Maltby's ordinance had lost. Thirty-eight aldermen, only a few short of the number needed, had backed him.

But, if those thirty-eight stood steadfast with Harrison, it would be impossible for the Powers gang to pass any traction ordinance over the mayor's veto. The anti-Yerkes crowd whooped it up. In this temporary defeat they saw an ultimate victory. In the corridors the visitors, supposing Yerkes finally beaten, began a tremendous celebration.

Harrison attempted to restore order in the council. Tom Carey, normally one of the council's silent men, who had been won over to Harrison's side by his hatred, personal and political, for Mc-Inerney, arose and shouted: "I wanna make a speech."

His eyes shone and he gazed long upon Bathhouse John before he began. "We've had a good fight," said Carey, when the noise subsided. "A good fight. And there is one man here who deserves special credit for this here fight. I want to say to you, John Coughlin, that you placed yourself on record tonight and you will hear from the people of Chicago in the future. All of Chicago will be your friends because you stood up as you did in the interests of the City of Chicago by upholding the mayor in his position."

The First Ward boys in the galleries whistled. The band in the corridor struck up a tune. Carey held up his hand for silence. "They say the mayor is looking to be the next governor of Illinois," he continued. "But I expect to see him the next President of the United States!"

A new and more furious demonstration was loosed. Again Carey waved for quiet. "Yes!" he roared. "I expect to see Carter Harrison President of the United States, and when the people elect Carter Harrison as their leader in Washington, I expect to see John J. Coughlin as the next mayor of Chicago!"

Again the weary galleries went wild with delight. Harrison beamed and saluted Coughlin. The Bath glanced up shyly at Carey, with an almost beatific look upon his broad face, and the two erstwhile Gray Wolves, covered now in their mantles of white, smiled righteously into each other's eyes.

But while the Harrison men were congratulating one another and Carey was making his impassioned oration, Powers and Cullerton had rallied their forces. There had been no need, in the initial fight, for them to expose some of their weaker members to the pressures of public criticism. When the final test came Powers and Foxy Ed knew where their votes lay. Cullerton rose, asking that the Lyman ordinance be given to the Committee on Railways. This committee was packed with Yerkes adherents. This time the vote was more significant, 40 to 23 for the Cullerton motion. Yerkes was saved, although there was no definite indication how the final battle might come out.

On Clark Street, though, the followers of Bathhouse John and Hinky Dink celebrated. "John J. Coughlin, th' next maar of Chicago!" they shouted, far into the night.

5

The awakening for Bathhouse was quick in coming. True, the *Tribune* called the night's action a "black eye for the ordinance," but it sneered at Tom Carey's glorious speech: "The Hon. Bathhouse John will never be elected mayor unless the city goes daft."

Too, Medill and the other publishers had no illusions about that initial vote. They feared a final drive by Yerkes in the Committee on Railways. Said a *Tribune* editorial:

There is reason to believe that some of the aldermen who seem to have voted right will not stick when the final and decisive vote is taken.

Johnny Powers pooh-poohed the decision on Maltby's motion as being of no consequence. "All we needed was th' one-third to stop passage an' th' rest we let them have," he boasted. "We're as strong as we were before. Th' only thing that's happened is that the ordinance is in a good committee."

But Powers failed to consider one member of the Committee on Railways: Hinky Dink. This silent little man now became as loquacious as his big associate. The Dink jammed the committee hearings and discussions with baffling questions and parliamentary obstructions. He passed out subtle hints that the mayor was contemplating grand-jury action against the aldermen who were accepting graft—if Yerkes won. So well did Kenna tie up the sessions that Powers, fuming in frustration, despaired of accomplishing anything there and maneuvered a sudden meeting of the Joint Committee on Streets and Alleys, where a substitute ordinance was drawn up.

The new measure seemed Utopian when placed side by side with the Lyman ordinance. It was designed to placate an indignant public. It recommended the extension of the franchises for twenty-five years only, called for payment of three per cent of all receipts the first ten years, four per cent the next five, and five per cent for the rest of the life of the franchise. Fares were to be five cents, twenty-five for $1. There was a provision also that pointed toward ultimate municipal ownership.

Surely, said a pleased public, this was an astounding Harrison victory. Yerkes had yielded and now appeared to be seeking only half of what he originally wanted. But the mayor was adamant.

A relaxation of public vigilance was exactly what he feared. He insisted that any franchise must be for no longer than twenty years, he demanded a flat ten to twelve per cent payment on gross receipts, and he insisted that no ordinance should be passed until action had been taken in Springfield on the Allen law. He was more determined than ever to drive Yerkes completely out of power.

Once again he called Bathhouse John and Hinky Dink. The Bath had been hurt when the newspapers mocked Carey's suggestion that he would be the next mayor, but he and Hinky Dink promised to stand by their word. What was more, Bathhouse John, who as a member of the Committee on Streets and Alleys had sat at every session, disclosed to the mayor the precise details of how Johnny Powers hoped to push the ordinance through the council at the next meeting. Harrison, together with Alderman Charles Walker, devised a counter plan.

On the following Monday night, the aldermen gathered again. Compared with the previous week's meeting, this was a solemn affair. But the tension and suspense were far greater.

It was Johnny de Pow's plan to reverse the calling of the roll, so that Coughlin and Kenna would be last to cast their votes and make their speeches. Halfway down the roll call, as the wards of the Yerkes stalwarts were reached, Alderman S. S. Kimbell was to introduce the new substitute measure. Then the gang aldermen would stack up a big pile of votes before the Harrison men could get into the fight, thus giving extra courage to the men who might waver. It was this strategy Bathhouse John had outlined to the mayor. The roll call never got to Kimbell, for when the name of Alderman William Mavor was reached that staunch Harrison man bounded to his feet with a surprise for Powers.

"I move," he said, "that we reconsider the vote by which the Lyman ordinance was referred to the Committee on Railways."

Powers was puzzled, but he made no objection. Let the Harrison men, he smirked, have their fun. The Lyman ordinance was no longer good anyway. His silence was a signal for his followers to agree to this seemingly unimportant step. It won, 40 to 23.

Then Mavor shouted: "I now present a motion to take the bill from the Committee on Railways."

Again Powers remained silent. He could not understand these weird maneuverings. Why pay attention to the Lyman ordinance when Kimbell held in his inner coat pocket a brand new ordinance certain to pass without much opposition? This motion was passed too, by a vote of 36 to 27, Bathhouse and Hinky Dink, of course, supporting it.

Mike McInerney was more wary than Powers. "What kind of child's play is this?" he demanded. "An ordinance must go to some kind of committee. Let's have a little common sense around here. If you take this ordinance from the Committee on Railways you must send it somewhere. I can't see the point of all this."

In a moment he did. Mavor wet his lips, smiled at Harrison, who rolled an unlit cigar in his teeth. "I wish," said Mavor, "to present a motion to refer the Lyman ordinance and all subsequent ordinances dealing with the traction problem to the Committee on City Hall!"

There was an uproar on the floor. Powers finally saw the meaning of the crazy actions of Mavor. The Committee on City Hall! That group of Harrison men he had personally put there! Most certainly they would not meet until after the legislature had voted on the Allen repeal in January! That bunch of do-gooders whom Johnny Powers himself had put out of the way with such a rare Machiavellian touch!

Johnny de Pow rushed into action. "What is this, Mr. Mayor? These ordinances can't go to the Committee on City Hall! What have streetcars to do with the Committee on City Hall? This whole proceeding is illegal an' a fraud. We did not object, Mr. Mayor, when these measures were called up from their proper committees, for it was obvious they must be returned to these committees! But the Committee on City Hall! It's outrageous. It's crooked. We have an ordinance here"—he pointed to the bewildered Kimbell—"an' we got a right to go ahead!"

Harrison replied softly, "That is not for the chair to decide. There is a motion before the council. Let us vote on the motion." He signaled the clerk to call the roll, and the clerk began with the First Ward.

Bathhouse John rose grinning. It was another great moment as he shouted: "Yea! Yea!" Alderman Kenna followed with a low, firm "Yea!" and Mayor Harrison smiled his blessing upon them.

One by one the remaining aldermen arose to announce their votes. The totals teetered back and forth. Six for the motion, five against it. Ten for the mayor, ten for Yerkes. Powers sputtered an angry "Nay!" and Mangler followed him loudly. Maltby and Kunz, Carey and Wiora, for the mayor.

Finally, the end of the roll call. In the hush, Harrison received the clerk's tally and announced the result:

For the motion, 32.

Against the motion, 31.

6

That night of December 19 marked the end of the era in which the word or threat or the purse of Charles Tyson Yerkes would control an aldermanic vote. Three weeks later the legislature met and killed the Allen law.

Even Johnny Powers, still fuming over the way in which he had been outwitted, admitted that any monopoly traction ordinance was dead. "It's all over," he lamented.

As the newspaper reporters crowded upon the aldermen in ensuing days for their statements, most of the councilmen spoke their hearts out. But Bathhouse John delivered himself with unaccustomed curtness.

"I," said he, "have recently joined the church."

RIVER OF GOLD

I

DIRE and woeful was the political future of Bathhouse John and
Hinky Dink, if the editorials in the newspapers could be believed.
The press freely predicted that the Powers gang would exact ven-
geance for the defeat of Yerkes. The *Tribune* professed to see a
crisis in the aldermen's careers. Discussing the ire of Johnny de
Pow at the First Ward chieftains, it said:

It was Alderman John Coughlin and his understudy, Alderman Mike Kenna, both of the First Ward, who came in for the
full share of objurgations and stigmas. It was the desertion of these
two which left their oldtime friends in the lurch.

In the case of Coughlin, a boycott will be established in the
council. The First Ward alderman has had a habit of introducing
connecting bridges and other favors for merchants in his ward, all
of which are allowed to go through without objection. It has been
understood that the alderman acted more as attorney than alderman in these matters and found the practice profitable. Now the
word has gone out that every order of this kind he introduces shall
be sent to committee, there to be buried.

Bathhouse John shrugged arrogant shoulders, and little Hink
was unperturbed. Let the soreheads in the council stew in the juice
of their fury. Let Johnny Powers and Foxy Ed curse and rave
against their perfidy. Let the committees balk them. Carter Harrison was the victorious mayor and Carter Harrison was the true
and good friend of Bathhouse John and Hinky Dink. Had he not
praised them publicly for their steadfastness, calling them "the two
rocks ... the rocks of Gibraltar"? Was not the police department

most co-operative? The little rivulets of gold which had been streaming into the First Ward money bags from the Levee, the First Ward balls, the gamblers and the petty rackets were swelling into rivers. The First Ward aldermen, realists that they were, had stood by Harrison. The mayor was a realist too. There was, they thought, likely to be little interference with the sources of these rising streams.

At a time when Harrison's chief of police, Joseph Kipley, told the Baxter investigating committee, "There is not a gambling house in Chicago, and the city is freer from gambling today than it has ever been in its history," an estimated two thousand professional gamblers were happily plying their trade within the boundaries of the First Ward, and paying handsomely for the privilege. The Official Red and Green Policy Game, its popularity increased by the *Inter-Ocean's* campaign against it, was doubling its profits. The madams and the whoremongers, though driven from North Clark Street on the orders of the mayor, were setting up elaborate new establishments at the south end of the ward, where they prospered mightily. A few, like Carrie Watson, who took her parrot under one arm and her bankbooks under the other and departed to the dull respectability of a suburb, were able to retire, but eager newcomers took their places. They settled about Twenty-second Street and Dearborn, and wherever the madams went, the First Ward collectors followed.

The field workers in the collection machine were directed by jolly Bill Gaffney, to whose saloon they brought the receipts. The "little push" which Kenna had begun organizing in the dark days of 1894 was functioning smoothly and efficiently. Swarthy Ike Bloom was already "King of the Brothels," directing his domain from his grimy little office in Freiberg's dance hall, which he operated with his brother-in-law, Solly Friedman. To this little office Bathhouse John came nightly to get reports on the previous day's business. Inside worked the syndicate's bookkeepers, totaling the receipts. Outside were the dancing girls and the waitresses who worked along with the women guests in soliciting trade, which they took to Freddie Buxbaum's hotel around the corner, in which Bloom owned a share. Friedman controlled the liquor trade in the district, and levied upon the grocers, peddlers and wine merchants who sold their wares to Levee customers. Freddie Train and Sime Tuckhorn were busy too. And Andy Craig was rising in the organization, acting as fence and broker for thieves in his saloon on Customs House Place, where he sat and boasted: "Any thief or murderer is safe when he's in my place. No copper dares go past my door." Andy had a soft spot in his black heart for thieves, having spent eighteen months from February 1891 to September 1892 in Joliet penitentiary for robbing a store.

Into the river of gold flowed brooklets of profit from the tax-fixing racket, in which most of the bad aldermen and more than one good alderman shared, the same racket that Stead had denounced on his memorable visit. In a joint exposé by the *Daily News* and the *Journal,* it was found, to the horror of plodding, steady taxpayers, that many a rich Chicagoan was derelict in payment of personal property assessments. One man, J. Z. Palmer, a suit manufacturer in the First Ward, said he paid two representatives of the First Ward machine $500 to effect a lowering of his assessment. "They came to me and told me they knew the assessor would fix it so I could save $1,500," said Palmer. "All I had to do was pay $500. I agreed and another man came later and made out my tax schedules and I signed them."

The exposé caused the Board of Review to open an inquiry into assessments. A real-estate dealer testified he had paid $2,500 to have his property value reduced from $2,300,000 to $1,700,000. The Chicago City Railway Company was found to have been taxed on an assessment of $800,000, whereas the true worth of its property for tax purposes was $4,000,000. Wilson Brothers, shirt manufacturers, complained that they had been assessed at $1,119,542 while a competitor in the First Ward who had buildings and equipment of identical value had been rated at only $27,000! Even such an untouchable as Franklin Head, a high and mighty capitalist-reformer, was found to have profited from the system, and the indignant

Board of Review promptly raised the amount of his assessment from $2,000 to $100,000. Head cabled from Europe that he had no connection with the racket, and that he was not responsible for his property managers' actions. When the anger of the public showed signs of dying down the Board of Review closed its inquiry by adding $3,000,000 to the assessment rolls and, in the state of trauma induced by innumerable instances of graft and delinquencies, municipal criticism was soon stilled.

2

Carter Harrison might laud the two aldermen from the First Ward as "The Rocks of Gibraltar" but George Cole and the men of the Municipal Voters' League had no illusions. When the talk turned to the spring elections there was no sentence of praise for little Mike Kenna's good vote against Yerkes. But the stern recommendation that Kenna be defeated evoked a pleased comment from Hinky Dink. "Good," was his sentiment. "Whenever I see a reformer, I hold to my hat and keep my hands in my pockets. I'd lose my ward if they supported me."

Hinky Dink had no intention of losing the ward. His nomination was a routine affair, enlivened only by Jake Zimmerman, who, groggy from celebrating the victory of his equine namesake at a New Orleans track, thought that The Bath was up for re-election and insisted on nominating him for mayor. "Bathhouse John Coughlin is the next mayor," boomed Zimmerman. "He is the Julius Caesar of the First Ward and the Bismarck of the city hall." When Jake had been quieted Kenna received the unanimous vote of the convention, and he buckled to the job of organizing the campaign. The precincts were soon generously arrayed for registration day and the stew bums and floaters were bedded and fed in the saloons and lodging houses. No less than 12,224 names appeared on the poll lists and the jeremiads of the Republicans rang out over the city.

When William H. Bell, a Kenna worker, was arrested on

charges of fraudulently registering men in the Twenty-second Precinct, he protested: "I was appointed captain here by the Big Fellow and the Little Fellow. They told me if I didn't help, my saloon wouldn't get to stay open after hours."

But the Bell incident was only a footnote to the story of the night of March 27 when the objectors to the mass registration in the First Ward marched to the offices of the election board in the city hall to voice their protests. There, packing the office and corridors, they found Coughlin, Kenna, Tom McNally, Andy Craig, two hundred toughs and thirty constables armed with John Doe warrants furnished by a Democratic justice of the peace named Thomas Edgar. F. B. Barr, a Republican worker in the First Ward, had come with evidence of fraud, but he got only as far as the top of the stairs. There several Coughlin-Kenna sluggers lunged toward him and Deputy Sheriff W. H. Brainard who accompanied him. Barr escaped, but Brainard mistakenly was seized and driven to the office of Justice Edgar, who reluctantly informed him: "You're not the one we wanted. We wanted that other gentleman." Edgar held Brainard, nevertheless, in $5,000 bail.

Another Republican, a Negro named Richard Hardeman, attempted to push his way through the First Ward thugs. He was seized, beaten and dragged down three flights of stairs. He staggered to the detective bureau and secured a warrant charging Bathhouse John with assault with intent to murder, claiming the alderman had grabbed him by the throat and had punched and kicked him in the abdomen. Then, with deputy sheriffs at his side, Hardeman was whisked to the Cook County Hospital. Deputy Sheriff Mike Jones searched in vain for Coughlin, then gave up. The next morning Coughlin strolled into Justice John Richardson's court, posted a $10,000 bond, and denied touching Hardeman.

"The man's mistaken; I wasn't even near him," he said. "I didn't choke, I didn't kick him. I don't know who did. Ask Andy Craig, ask Tom McNally. They'll tell you."

Those worthies doubtlessly would have so testified, but their glib tales were never told. Hardeman suddenly disappeared from his room in the hospital, and the Republicans yelled: "Kidnapping! Kidnapping!" Robert J. Gould, Kenna's opponent, rallied a group of Negroes in Quinn chapel, Twenty-fourth and Wabash, and raised the race issue, urging a vote for himself to "bring equality between black and white, between every creed and race." The day before election, however, Hardeman showed up at his rooming house on Customs House Place, gay and smiling and forgiving. "It was jest a p'litical argument," he grinned. "I'm droppin' charges. No use makin' trouble." The charge was shelved and the police took little interest in the story of Henry Carson, Hardeman's fellow roomer, that Hardeman had received a gift of $500 from some friends of Bathhouse John.

Otherwise the campaign, both in the First Ward and the rest of the city, was tame. Waving the banner of his victory over Yerkes, Mayor Harrison was seeking another term. His fame was nationwide and the national party moguls were said to be considering him as Presidential timber, a development that irked John Altgeld, who feared that Harrison would sell out the Free Silver plank of the Chicago platform of 1896 to obtain Tammany support. The valiant Altgeld, ill and weary of politics, announced himself as independent candidate for the mayoralty and promised to put candidates into the aldermanic elections in every ward. This was received gleefully by the Republicans, who believed they had a winner in Zina R. Carter, former alderman and president of the Board of Trade. Although the *Tribune* predicted that none but anarchists would support Altgeld, it was overjoyed at the prospect of organized opposition against Hinky Dink. Altgeld's First Ward candidate was Fitzgerald Murphy, who labeled himself a "Man of the People." "There is a big revolt among the Democrats against Kenna," exulted the *Tribune,* "and an Altgeld candidate will draw the vote from him."

The newspapers had a genius for being wrong in their guesses about the First Ward. For Kenna, after a quiet and serene election,* collected 5,349 votes, almost five times as many as Gould and ten times those of Altgeld's "Man of the People." The papers were wrong in their guesses on the mayoralty fight too. Harrison won by a 40,000 plurality over Carter, and Altgeld received only 47,000 of the 304,000 votes cast.

The First Ward demonstration that followed was a rousing one. Torpedoes and aerial bombs exploded in front of the saloons and panel houses, red fire smoked luridly among the marching processions, and tar barrels blazed the length of Clark Street. One gang set fire to the floating oil scum on the Chicago River, starting a conflagration that called out the downtown fire departments. With Clark Street lurid from flames on the river, the First Ward boys gathered in Pat O'Malley's saloon at Polk and Clark Streets to hear Kenna acknowledge his thanks. Both his saloons and Coughlin's Silver Dollar were closed because, as The Bath laughed, "We're reformers like Mayor Harrison."

"There were two things done it," Hinky Dink explained. "I was a model alderman and the boy Carter Harrison was on top of the slate. You see, there was two that wouldn't be flagged."

The *Tribune* sneered: "That high souled and immaculate statesman, The Hon. Bathhouse John, regards the Harrison victory as a personal vindication," and added, "The Honorable Hinky Dink is of the opinion that there will be plenty of wide openings for business now."

3

Scoff though they might, the newspapers were forced to admit that Coughlin and Kenna were the men who, with Bobbie Burke, had brought victory to Harrison and presumably held his future in their hands. A few days after the election there appeared a cartoon in the *Tribune* showing the three preparing to touch off skyrockets labeled governor, senator, President, while a fourth rocket, bear-

---

*One of the few arrested was George Silver, bartender in Coughlin's saloon, seized for illegally soliciting votes for Kenna.

ing a tag, "Mayor of Chicago," had already exploded over the city. "Does everything go or only one?" asked the caption.

At the moment it seemed that the Presidential rocket was most likely to be next. Croker, the high priest of Tammany, was flirting with the idea of pushing into the Presidential chair the venerable New York State Supreme Court justice, Augustus Van Wyck, brother of Robert Van Wyck, New York's mayor. But he was also toying with the thought of choosing Harrison, and about the country were other potent Democrats of like mind. In Louisville "Marse Henry" Watterson had written in his *Courier-Journal* that the Chicago mayor was the "logical candidate." For this the *Tribune* spanked "Marse Henry" in its editorials and raised its hands to heaven lest the colonel be taken seriously. About this time, William Jennings Bryan, in Chicago to attend a meeting of the Democratic national committee, forswore his old friend Altgeld, and announced he would henceforth do business with Harrison, causing the *Tribune* to warn:

This makes Harrison supreme in Illinois. He can have the governorship in 1900 if he wants it. He is building an Illinois Tammany, great and powerful as Tammany in New York.

But the wily Harrison did not want the governorship. He allowed the *Tribune* the joy of reviling his Presidential ambitions and he remained quiet while Altgeld warned the Democrats that he was playing into Tammany hands. Croker sent emissaries to sound out Harrison on Van Wyck's chances, but the mayor kept them hot and cold and they prepared to return with empty hands.

One thing was sure, Croker did not want Bryan. Another thing was positive: Bryan would, under no circumstances, support a Tammany Hall candidate. If the two forces collided and Harrison remained in the clear, he would be, as Colonel Watterson had noted, "the logical candidate."

When the Tammany Democrats returned to New York, a Chicago Democrat went along with them to watch over the Van Wyck boom. He was Bathhouse John Coughlin.

THE DUDES' NEW KING

I

Coughlin had previously planned a tour of the East. "I'm goin' away for the summer," he told Harold I. Cleveland, the *Times-Herald* feature writer, on July 15. "I'm goin' away for a tour of the waterin' places and I'm really goin' to do 'em right."

Cleveland, assigned to do a story on the duties of a First Ward politician, had obtained the interview just after Bathhouse had returned from the funeral arranged by the First Ward club for the wife of a drayman and faithful voter. The Bath was sad and reflective.

"That little Dago girl has gone and died," he lamented. "I'm devilish blue. She gets sick from drinkin' th' bad water the city gives to the poor and warns the rich about. I don't know much about death, 'cause I'm too busy living, but I guess an alderman can't dodge its trolley any more than poor folks can. You know, if you ain't a lunkhead, that in wards where the poor have the chinch, next to the priest the alderman is their guardian angel."

Then the alderman brightened and went off to Meyer Newfield's, taking Cleveland with him. "I want a lot of new clothes, Meyer," he told the delighted tailor. "I'm going to make some radical changes to start with and one of 'em is to pass up this fad for gloomy dark clothes. What the boys want is a happy medium, a sort of cross between a Bowery drop curtain and a Quaker gray."

When the visit was over, Meyer Newfield itemized the wardrobe which Coughlin would take with him on his conquest of the East:

A mountain-green dress suit, "cut in conservative fashion."

One silk hat, "two-gallon capacity and liberal brim."

One straw hat, with blue band studded with white polka dots.

One striped Prince Albert coat, with plaid vest and plaid trousers.

One red vest with white buttons and six double-breasted white vests with black buttons.

One yachting suit with "double-breasted bright blue vest, white flannel trousers, and green leather belt."

One bathing suit of baby blue with heart's-blood polka dots.

One traveling suit, tuxedo coat of brown, white silk vest and duck trousers.

One brown business suit, a four-button cutaway and scarlet vest.

One pair of patent leather shoes with dark green tops.

One pair of russet shoes with bulldog toes.

Quipped Cleveland:

"All of the alderman's trousers will be rolled up from the bottom."

A few days later Coughlin donned the spectacular green dress suit and paraded before First Ward admirers invited for the preview. Tom McNally was reported to have marveled: "It's a peach. You look like an Evanston lawn kissed by an early dew!"

"The world is mine!" cried Bathhouse John as he pirouetted with elephantine grace. He prodded Cleveland in the chest. "I'll show them a thing or two in dress reform for the masculine gender. I want to be strictly original. I think that the Prince of Wales is a lobster anyway in his tastes. He may be all right playing baccarat and putting his coins on the right horses at the races, but when it comes to mapping out style for well-dressed Americans he's simply a faded two-spot in the big deck of fashion. People have been following his lead because no other guy has the nerve to challenge him for the championship. But I'm out now for first place and you'll see his percentage drop."

Cleveland returned to the paper and wrote his story and the

Times-Herald announced the good news for emancipated males under shrieking headlines:

DUDES' NEW KING!

HON. JOHN COUGHLIN TO
BECOME A SARTORIAL FASHION PLATE

BUYS ELEGANT WARDROBE

GOING TO SEASIDE RESORTS TO
STARTLE THE EASTERN MEN
WITH HIS MAGNIFICENCE

Alderman Coughlin, the account read, would gratify a new ambition. "He will pluck a few laurels in the field of fashion and become a 'lily of the valet.' His friends who have had a peep at his new wardrobe believe the alderman of the First Ward will dim the glory of J. Waldere Kirk and snatch from the latter's grasp the crown of fame which he has worn so many seasons as the King of the Dudes."

2

Following publication of this sparkling news Bathhouse John disappeared. It was a week before the public knew of his departure, and then none in Chicago guessed that he had gone in the company of the Tammany Hall delegation sent by Boss Croker to interview Mayor Harrison. Wrote the political reporter for the *Tribune:*

The mystery which shrouds the disappearance of the Hon. John J. Coughlin, statesman and broker, is still unpenetrated. The Chicago friends of the First Ward alderman are unable to solve the question of his whereabouts. All they know is that he left the city on Wednesday with the avowed intention of visiting New York. He has not been heard from since.

In a few days he was heard from. He was in New York, tread-ing up and down the Bowery, in and out of the Tammany headquarters and the city hall. He was gay and boisterous and everywhere he went the derby-hatted Manhattan reporters fol-lowed and hung on every word.

"Any time I get lost in this two-by-four village," was The Bath's indignant reply to the reports from back home, "I'll buy a suit of clothes and give a medal to the duck that finds me. I'm living at the Hoffman House an' they know me there. I'm known from Maine to California as a good fellow an' an all-around first-class man."

"Go on, go on!" cried the entranced newspapermen.

Bathhouse John glared at them. "Somebody told me I was reported to have had a green dress suit made for me an' a lot a pink gloves and a whole mess of other things. I am not a blasted idiot! However, if the boys can get a little glory in writin' such stuff about me I can stand it if they can. As I said, I am not an idiot! How many others are there on earth who can stand up an' say th' same thing?"

Then, as swiftly as he had appeared on the New York scene, he vanished again. While correspondents for the Chicago papers sought him to ask about the amazing green suit, he slipped off to Saratoga in the entourage of Justice Van Wyck. There, among the Vanderbilts and Drexels and eastern fashionables, Boss Croker hoped to snare for his current favorite the assurance of the Demo-cratic nomination and to launch the boom that would sweep the country and swamp Bryanism wherever it reared its head. To Saratoga's Grand Union Hotel were summoned the leading Democrats from the East and South. The newspapers called it "The Front Porch Caucus." Bathhouse was in the thick of it, although he was heard to utter the name of Carter Harrison more often than that of Augustus Van Wyck. To cronies in Chicago he dispatched picture postcards of the White House in Washing-ton, on which he had written in a scrawling hand:

"This is where we will have fun in 1900."

There was trading and maneuvering, talk of the possibilities in the pro-Bryan Midwest, exhortations in behalf of Van Wyck, discussion of Harrison's chances, and similar palavering until the night of July 31.

On that night Bathhouse John, having hearkened to the voices of political correspondents covering the Van Wyck conferences, invaded the prig Grand Union ballroom and marched to his table in the Van Wyck alcove as a one-man campaign for masculine dress reform.

The floor of the Grand Union Hotel was crowded with "fair women and brave men." The floor managers were hurrying to and fro, the music was already pulsating in the perfumed air.

Then entered Bathhouse Coughlin and Mrs. Coughlin. He was arrayed in a full dress suit of mountain green, his wife in turquoise foulard. Coughlin had a blood-red vest. "The Bath shone like an opal," noted a reporter in admiration. "He rivaled Solomon in all his glory."

Coughlin strode up to Justice Van Wyck and presented Mrs. Coughlin. He pirouetted several times for awed onlookers. The venerable Justice, candidate for the Presidency of the United States, was visibly nettled, but he exercised remarkable restraint.

"Mr. Alderman," he said solemnly, "I assume you have some serious purpose in mind in adopting a colored scheme for evening dress."

"Your honor," replied Coughlin, according to a sharp-eared *Times-Herald* man, "your assumption is not without reasonable warrant. It is my purpose to enlighten the effete East in the matter of proper attire of gentlemen upon festive occasions."

"Indeed!" answered Van Wyck coldly. "You interest me."

Coughlin was encouraged. "Now, when you are President of the United States I hope you will direct all ambassadors to foreign courts to wear coats of purple and fine linen."

"When I am President," harrumphed Van Wyck, "the United States ambassadors may, if they like, wear coats of as many colors as Joseph."

Coughlin proved the hit of the evening and all political discussion and planning were abandoned. The reporters from Chicago, and from other parts of the country as well, almost forgot the Van Wyck boom and devoted themselves to the astounding alderman from the First Ward. The Bath forgot about politics himself, except to mention now and then that Carter Harrison of Chicago would be a good man for President. He scurried from tailor to tailor in Saratoga, dashing off interviews as he made the rounds.

The time had come, he pontificated, for a reform in men's dress. He himself would lead the movement. "I didn't want to flash too red a vest at this early stage in the dress reform," said The Bath, "but I have a redder one and I'll wear it later on, right here in dressy Saratoga. If I had five or six others to join me now in the dress reform movement, I would show Saratoga. I have some suits of men's apparel that are great both in texture an' color an' have never been beaten for style and effect. They will be simply stunning."

The world could hardly wait. At the race course Bathhouse appeared one afternoon in a suit of clothes of which the coat was flannel with sky-blue lapels and lining. Running up and down were white lines "somewhat larger and wider apart than the bars of the Cook County jail" and at the breast pocket was a half-yard of cambric handkerchief embroidered with a large and vigorous monogram.

"The waistcoat worn by Bathhouse," wrote an astonished reporter, "was yellow, with orange spots. Miniature conch shells acted as buttons and to heighten the effect the waistcoat was ballasted with a massive watch chain. The trousers worn with this were a sort of check, somewhat quieter than the coat. However, the alderman might walk up and down the Bay Ridge front on Dewey day and no one would notice the absence of cannon."

To immortalize properly the precursor of the dress-reform movement, the new York *World* dispatched an illustrator to Saratoga to sketch Bathhouse in his bizarre regalia, and sent the paper's Chimmy Fadden* to interview the Chicago statesman.

"I believe," said Bathhouse heavily, "it is best for a change in full-dress ideas for men. They have prevailed until they are antiquated. I would suggest mountain green, royal purple, and lavender as successors to the somber, mournful black which men have worn since time immemorable. My idea is to wear coat and trousers of one color. I have several of these costumes and for an added vest have one of white silk and another of blood red, with blue and white figures. Yes, I shall wear one of these costumes the first time occasion requires."

Back in Chicago, the First Ward rubbed its head in bewilderment. On August 11, little Mike Kenna informed the reporters in his saloon that he was leaving at once for Saratoga. "I will wear a deep blue dress suit and a heliotrope vest," he said, his voice dipped in acid. The *Tribune* sarcastically editorialized:

A nation of men in somber black is watching the Hinky Dink and Bathhouse John dress reform movement with deep red hope for its success.

The Democratic *Times-Herald,* fearing quite reasonably that Coughlin's performance would besmirch the party generally, tried to read something purposeful into the antics at Saratoga:

Alderman Coughlin fain would have his name printed on the list of duly accredited delegates to the next Democratic national convention. By way of preparing for their plunge in behalf of William Jennings Bryan, he deemed it expedient to go to Saratoga and get acquainted with Dick Croker, Billy Whitney, Art Gorman, and "the boys." Therefore it was necessary to go appareled as he did, for the Honorable Bathhouse is a great hand for the proverb: The apparel oft proclaims the man. The secret

---

*Probably the late Edward W. Townsend, brilliant staff writer and creator of the character, Chimmy Fadden.

of Coughlin's eastern pilgrimage is to practice mixing with the "right guys." The Bath intends to go to the national convention and he may get his clothes messed.

On the same day this stern editorial appeared, Bathhouse John frolicked at the race track in a white silk pajama jacket, white yachting cap, and the waistcoat of red, white and blue.

"I'm agin two things," he proclaimed. "One of them is three studs with full-dress evening suits and the other is pink shirts with the same. I'm a quiet man but three studs is worse than heel-and-toeing to the last ace out of the box. Two is th' limit."

Someone informed Coughlin that Hinky Dink was on his way to Saratoga, and the next day Coughlin walked about the lobby of the Grand Union Hotel with the plaintive query: "You ain't seen nothing of Hinky Dink? I mean Alderman Mike Kenna. I'm lookin' for word of him. He changed his name and collar when he left Chicago and I ain't heard a word of him. He didn't tell me his Elias when he lit out an' they're beginning to worry in Chicago. You'd know him in a minute. He's about as big as a half-pint and if you hit him he'll holler first an' then slug you one. He ain't any bigger than your elbow, but Hinky Dink's th' real thing."

Then, simultaneously with Hinky Dink's arrival to put an end to the dress-reform movement, Boss Croker decided that the Van Wyck boom was over. "I have decided that Mr. Bryan would be the best man," Croker announced abruptly. "Mr. Croker is a fine man. He never asked me for anything and I never promised him anything," said Bryan. At the Harrison offices in Chicago there was silence.

3

When the Democrats convened in Kansas City the following July it was Bathhouse John and his dress-reform movement that saved the meeting from becoming a dull affair for Chicago Democracy. Kansas City awaited his coming with a fever not entirely induced by the summer heat. Said the Kansas City *Star:*

Bathhouse John is not only a politician but is keenly interested in dress reform. Being a gentleman of great pulchritude, it is his opinion that the adornment of the masculine form should be amplified and that the tailors and haberdashers should not be manacled by conventions. It is understood that Bathhouse is bringing his sartorial wonders with him, and, of course, Kansas City is wrought up to a feverish pitch of curiosity.

Coughlin and Kenna accompanied the Cook County Democratic Marching Club to the convention, but the occasion was not a happy one for Chicago party men. Mayor Harrison, it was conceded, had no chance for the Presidential nomination so long as Bryan wanted it. The Chicago mayor was being boomed for the Vice-Presidency by the Iowa, Kentucky and New York delegations, but he announced that he would refuse that position if it was offered to him.

The stage was left to Bathhouse John. He roamed the town, shaking hundreds of hands, and everywhere urged delegates to vote for Carter Harrison for President. Wherever he went a procession of reporters and gaping convention visitors followed him. When he appeared in the convention hall Coughlin wore a ventilated straw hat with a purple band, a white negligee shirt, checked trousers, and a coat of blue and white striped flannel. In the evening he wore his famous red and white polka dot vest, a summer suit lined with pink silk, a gold necktie, and a gray "flush of morning" hat. "Bathhouse Coughlin," wrote one perspiring correspondent, "is the coolest, gentlest and most refreshing sight to be found in Kansas City."

William Jennings Bryan won the nomination on the first ballot, after the convention had readopted the Free Silver plank over Harrison's protests. The mayor turned down the Vice-Presidential offer and took his delegation home, an unhappy crew which tried to cheer itself by speaking of the mayor's chances for the high office in 1904.

But for Bathhouse the trip was a success. His dress-reform movement had captivated writers from every part of the land, and for every word written about him he was grateful. Little Hink, with glum loyalty, permitted his partner to revel in the national publicity, but thenceforth the precinct captains in the ward began to understand that a clear definition of responsibility had developed in the Coughlin-Kenna alliance.

Little Mike would mind the organization, deal with the police, and devise the political manipulations that would keep the "little push" in power. Bathhouse would be the vocal front, braying in "the interests of the people" in the city council, trouble-shooting when collections went awry in the Levee, taking the bows and the blame while Hink worked quietly and effectively in the background.

POET LARIAT OF THE FIRST WARD

I

THE summer that year was so humid and the Kansas City triumph so enervating that Bathhouse John, much as he adored his First Ward, decided that he needed another pleasant vacation. Last year he had gone east, with gratifying results. This year he would investigate the vast expanses of the West.

For almost a decade the benevolent rulers of the First Ward had dispatched to the healthful climes of Colorado and California the favored among their charges who had become ill. The emigrés chiefly were girls from the brothels stricken with consumption. Occasionally a worthy barkeep or ward heeler went too, and in 1889, Ben Black, an efficient precinct captain, had been one of these. So, with young Arthur Haggenjos, a protégé he was seeing through law school, Bathhouse John scooted off to Denver, there to visit with Ben Black and other cronies and to delight the habitués of the Brown Palace with his red, white and blue vest, his green pants, and modest brown Prince Albert.

While he was gone, and favorable telegraph notices were coming back from Denver, sweating Chicago was diverted from the record heat wave by the antics of others attempting to outdo Bathhouse as a comic-opera politician. City Sealer Quinn invaded the costume realm and designed a new Scotch plaid waistcoat which was given a public showing in the city-hall corridors. Bobbie Burke fashioned a romper outfit for members of the Cook County Democratic Marching Club. Surpassing these attempts to snatch publicity, Alderman Charles Walker, who had been appointed acting mayor while Harrison rested in Michigan, announced the establishment of a free public bathhouse in the Second

218

Ward. "I think," he said, "I can be elected to anything on a program of free baths for the public. I've got class, I have. I'm right up there with Nero, Agrippa, and Diocletian. They were Romans and they gave free public baths. Free public baths! You can't beat it in politics."

Then, while these pretenders vied for the limelight, the train from Colorado drew into La Salle Street Station and on it was Bathhouse John.

"So?" he yelled. "They're going to change styles, are they? They're goin' to set up some more free bathhouses? Well, look me over boys, look me over. I'm hale an' hearty as I can be." He winked at the reporters and pounded on his valise. "I've got something here no alderman here or anywhere else has got."

During his stay in Denver, the newsmen learned, Bathhouse had set himself upon a spavined Pegasus, dipped his pen into the Pierian spring, and, of all things, had written a poem. "Yessiree, boys," said Bathhouse, "it's a sentimental ballad telling all about gratitude and love. That's what th' West does. Makes men an' poets. It's a great poem that tells about a mother's love an' gratitude. A mother's love, boys, is something wonderful. A mother feels love at midnight when she looks at her children in the cradle or when she is waiting for her boy or girl who may be out somewheres. That's it, see? I got a mother to support an' I know what a mother's love is. A fellow's love for a girl ain't nothin'."

"What are you calling it?" asked the happy reporters, forgetting at once about Burke and the rompers, Quinn and the waistcoat, Walker and the bathhouses.

"I'm calling it by a nice name," answered Bathhouse John. "I'm calling it 'Dear Midnight of Love.' Wait'll you hear it."

2

Before the palpitating public could hear this immortal ballad, the council convened and Bathhouse was soon in the thick of more serious business. Hinky Dink had apprised him of the great battle in progress between the Ogden Gas Company and the Municipal Gas Company, the latter firm having been launched by the People's Gas Light and Coke Company in competition with Roger Sullivan's firm. There was a price war on and Roger Sullivan was taking a drubbing.

When Ogden Gas received its franchise it was pledged to a low rate. When the Gas Trust refused to be sandbagged by the existence of such a franchise, Roger Sullivan had gone ahead, organized his company, and sold at 90 cents, a dime under People's dollar rate. Sullivan prospered, and Municipal was organized and sent into the field to undersell him. Municipal cut to 90, and Ogden dropped to 80. Then Municipal went to 70 cents and Sullivan came back at 60. Finally both companies were selling at 40 cents for 1,000 cubic feet and were rapidly going bankrupt. Half the city, served by Ogden Gas and Municipal, was enjoying the lowered rate, but the other half, still buying from People's, continued to pay the old rate of $1 and was furious.

Spokesmen for the public said that the gas war proved People's was charging an unconscionable rate, and there were rallies and demands for municipal ownership. The gas company bigwigs saw that the price cutting had gone too far. There was danger that an aroused populace might actually force a general reduction throughout the city. This was where The Bath and Hinky Dink came in. Some heads were put together, with that of Roger Sullivan notably missing.

On the night of September 24 Alderman Coughlin was well prepared. When his name was called, he bounded to his feet and damned all the gas companies, big and small. He spoke as a savior for the poor people. "We can stop this $1 outrage against our citizens," he shouted, "and I move this council be empowered to petition the state legislature for the right to build a city gas plant that will run them all out of business."

Hinky Dink arose. "I move that the Municipal Gas Company be restrained from obtaining any more street and alley openings."

The gallery roared happily. Here, if ever, were two true friends of the people. Not only did they want a publicly owned gas plant, but even dared to block a powerful company from further franchise rights.

Roger Sullivan knew better. That blast at Municipal was a smoke screen to cover the real purpose of the municipal ownership hullabaloo, but he was helpless to stop the onrushing steam roller. Other aldermen rose to get on the side of the people. They offered ordinances as fast as their names were called, all of them with the same purposes defined by The Bath and Hinky Dink. Ultimately the entire matter was referred to a special committee directed to petition the state for the right to adopt a municipal ownership ordinance. There was a sudden scramble away from Ogden Gas shares on the stock exchange and even the shares of People's Gas Light and Coke Company dropped a few points. The people's aldermen were lauded at public meetings and the municipal ownership advocates waited breathlessly for the great day.

Then the cat got loose. The Municipal Company held a stockholders' meeting and authorized an increase in capital stock from $500,000 to $5,000,000. Roger Sullivan saw the handwriting, but it was too late. In a few days, he was out as head of Ogden Gas, and the newspapers announced a big gas deal. "GAS WAR COMES TO SUDDEN END. OGDEN GAS BOUGHT BY MUNICIPAL. GAS WAR ENDED!"

And the rates? "RATES GO UP FROM 40 CENTS TO $1."

There was no further talk of municipal ownership of gas companies and Bathhouse John went back to his literary efforts.

3

Bathhouse John's poem, he had informed all who cared to listen, was being set to music. "We're going to get it sung at a big theater," he announced. "We got to have a big theater because it's the greatest thing ever written!"

Emma Calve, the operatic diva, had come to Chicago and The

Bath lost no time in asking her to accept the honor of being the first to sing his work. She glanced at the notes, raised her eyebrows at the lyric, and, according to a contemporary account, "snorted."

But her refusal failed to daunt Coughlin. He had another idea. John de Sousa, a detective who traveled the Levee beat with Fred Buckminster—the latter in later years a partner of the notorious confidence man, Joseph (Yellow Kid) Weil—often spoke to The Bath of his talented thirteen-year-old daughter May. On the proud father's recommendation the alderman swept into the child's classroom one day and, to the bewilderment of the teacher and pupils, asked to see little May. The girl arose and curtsied. "Lemme hear you sing," The Bath demanded. May sang a chorus of the school song and Coughlin, even before she had finished, nodded briskly. "You're gonna be th' one to sing this," he told her. He patted the girl on the head, bowed grandly to the teacher, and strode out again.

Coughlin's fellow aldermen pressed him to recite or sing his song. Each time The Bath declined politely and bade them be patient. Finally, on October 2 as the council was preparing to adjourn after voting huge sums for street repairs, the clerk intoned a resolution in which Alderman Coughlin, referred to as "The Silver-Tongued Nightingale," was asked to sing his "beautiful and far-famed song." Once more he declined, but this time he added, "All right, the little girl is goin' to sing it next Monday night at the Opera House. Everybody's invited. You too, Mr. Maar." The council rose and cheered its poet.

Dress rehearsals were rushed. At one, Hinky Dink, upon hearing May sing the verse, shouted, "Help! Help! Get me a drink!" and, insisted a *Journal* reporter who had crept into the balcony, fainted. The Bath was not shaken a bit at this but continued calmly with the rehearsal. When it was over the chorus and orchestra members hoisted him to their shoulders and paraded about on the bare stage.

"There's nothin' to it!" cried The Bath, once he was set on his feet again. "I'm certainly th' best there is, th' best anybody ever looked at. I'm doing a stunt right here now that no alderman can touch, no alderman in the world. Th' orchestra's all right, the singer's all right, the song's all right, the house will be all right. . . . And I—well, I'm just Jawn and I ain't swelled a bit because I got it all comin' to me."

Chicago's dramatic and music critics took mock cognizance of the impending cultural event. Amy Leslie, citing in the *News* that the week's features included Chauncey Olcott at the McVickers in *Mavourneen* and Joseph Jefferson as *Rip Van Winkle* at Powers', added:

These occurrences must not becloud the appearance of a contribution to poetic melody by Bathhouse John, the illustrious tyro who will have a hearing at the Chicago Opera house when his rhapsodic "Dear Midnight of Love" will blast upon an Indian Summer horizon. A chorus of fifty voices will help John put his serenade on the market and a brass band is to give "Dear Midnight of Love" a chance to be drowned.

The *Record's* critic wrote tersely that "just what this sentimental ballad will be it is difficult to say although its title is 'Dear Midnight of Love.' " In the *Journal* an irreverent scrivener described the creation as a "poem in dactylic tetrameter and hypercataleptic meter."

4

On the night of October 8 Chicago realized its great opportunity to hear the alderman's song of love.

The theater, with gallery space at ten cents and main-floor seats at a top price of thirty cents, was filled and the overflow crowded into the aisles and all available standing room. Each act of the preceding variety show—Gus Williams, the German comic, the Sohlke dancing troupe, the Wesson and Waters farce company—received lusty applause from the audience comprised of a horde of First Ward constituents, all the aldermen and Mayor Harrison, and a handful of regular theater-goers.

Soon a uniformed boy ran out on the stage and on the corner easel placed a placard reading:

> *May de Sousa and a Chorus of 50*
> *Singing Ald. Coughlin's*
> DEAR MIDNIGHT OF LOVE

Out tripped dainty May, in a white dress with ruffles. She sang a selection from Victor Herbert's *The Fortune Teller*. The crowd applauded as if that was The Bath's, too. Then the boy ran out again with another placard:

> DEAR MIDNIGHT OF LOVE

The front set opened, revealing De Baugh's Cook County Democratic Marching Club band in pyramid formation at the rear. Banked in front was a flower-garden arrangement in which girls in light-colored gowns and men in evening clothes—fifty in all—stood in impressive solemnity. The stage had been designed to resemble the interior of a garish palace, with dazzling lamps hanging from the rafters.

A mighty chord arose from the band, and May de Sousa danced from the wings to the center of the stage. Then, while the chorus swayed to the rhythm, she sang:

> When silence reigns supreme and midnight love foretells
>   If heart's love could be seen, there kindest thoughts do dwell.
> In darkness fancies gleam, true loving hearts do swell;
>   So far beyond a dream, true friendship never sell.

Then the refrain, in which the chorus joined:

Dear Midnight of Love,
   Why did we meet?
Dear Midnight of Love,
   Your face is so sweet.
Pure as the angels above,
   Surely again we shall speak,
Loving only as doves,
   Dear Midnight of Love.

In "hushed awe" the audience awaited the second verse.

When love hearts are serene, can wak'ning be their knell?
   Were midnight but between. . . . Sleep night, say not farewell
Stars! oh, what do you mean? For you to wake 'tis well;
   Look, mother, on the scene, For you my love will tell.

Again the stalwart men of the Cook County Democratic
Marching Club and their ladies took up the chorus and once more
May de Sousa cleared her throat and offered the third and most
astounding stanza of all:

Your promise, love, redeem; Your gentle words do thrill;
   Live as the rippling stream, Always, your friend I will
Now I must bid adieu. So cruel; why did we meet?
   List! love, what shall we do? Good bye, when shall we greet?

The massed voices finished in triumph and there was pande-
monium in the theater. The crowd shouted for an encore, and
May and the chorus obliged again and again. Finally the tumult
grew so great that a red-faced Bathhouse was forced to rise in his
box and wave his hands in appreciation.

Still the crowd cheered on, demanding that Bathhouse stand
beside May and sing a verse or two. "Good bye, when shall we
greet?" it chanted. "Sing it, alderman, sing it!" Coughlin strode
to the stage, embraced Miss de Sousa, and held up his hand for
silence.

"Gentlemen, friends, and ladies," he said. "I certainly appreciate this ovation. It is a pleasure and ambition of which every
young man should be proud. I appreciate it and I know you all
mean it because this is an unpartisan gathering."

He bowed to May de Sousa, waved his arms again, and the
crowd set up a shout for Hinky Dink. Kenna turned pale, clutched
his chair and remained still. Mayor Harrison took several bows
from his box. Baskets of red flowers were rushed to the stage
and heaped about May and Bathhouse John. More cheers and
more demands for encores. But an exasperated stage manager
ordered the curtain rung down and the debut of "Dear Midnight
of Love" and May de Sousa was over.*

5

All that week Chicago trooped to the theater to hear the fantastic song. There was plentiful praise for Miss de Sousa's voice,
but the critics pounced fiercely upon the alderman's ditty.

The *Journal's* man was succinct: "That settles it. From now on
it's Bathos John." The *Journal's* editorial writer chuckled:

"From the hocus pocus of ridicule and derision heaped on the
head of Bathhouse John, there arises a tremendous thought. This
statesman of Chicago has a soul above his surroundings and has
proved it. Other poets have sung amid sweet inspiration of hill-
sides green and waters white. That's far too easy. Anyone can
do it. The soul and song of John sprung skyward from a meaner
sphere. The purlieus of poolrooms and Clark Street feazed him
not. He saw visions in the council chamber and the alley. The
sacred haunts of the sandbagger titillated his muse. He could purl
tender thoughts to the stars as a bouncer assisted a penniless tout
into the street. The braying of the slot machine's music caused

*Miss de Sousa lists her debut date as 1901, when she appeared in the chorus of
The Chaperon. But her fame dated from the time she sang the alderman's deathless
song. She was later successful in London and Paris, appearing in *The Tenderfoot* and
The Wizard of Oz. At the outbreak of the war with Japan, she was living in
Shanghai, China.

him to thwang anew. He could detect the whisperings from Parnassus in the skiddings of Mamie Taylors over the bar.

Austin Dobson can write lyrics in a library. Our own Bathhouse writes doggerel in a doggery. Either achievement is magnificent."

The *Tribune's* critic refused to joke about the matter, noting sternly that while from a musical point of view the production was hardly a success, "Miss De Sousa deserved praise for her interpretation of a song decidedly lacking in musical merit."

But it remained for the *News* reporter who wrote under the pseudonym of The Inspired Idiot to make the most complete and penetrating analysis of the aldermanic poesy. Chicago, The Inspired Idiot pointed out, had a right to be proud of its new bard

". . . for Mr. Coughlin's latest effort shows that . . . we have time, we Chicagoans, to take a few sprints with the Muse. Some fellow with a clot on his brain said poets are not made. Mr. Coughlin is a living ha-ha to any such notion."

Then followed a comparison of the aldermanic technique with that of "the late Mr. Virgil" and Lord Byron. The Bath's style

". . . resembles his own more than any other poet's. His poetic feet trip lightly as if they were going from steam room to shower. There is some similarity at that, however, between 'Dear Midnight of Love' and the following from the late Mr. Virgil:

> "I go so
> Do you go so?
> I ride the ox
> Do you ride the ox?
> Does your brother ride the ox?"

In both, The Inspired Idiot detected a "directness of purpose and simplicity of thought." He continued:

"Bathhouse asking his Dear Midnight of Love, 'Why did we meet?' is as pointed in its terseness as Mr. Virgil's 'Do you ride the ox?' There is no sparring in either case. Both expect to have their man groggy in the next round. Let us take these oft-quoted lines from Byron:

> "I am
> Thou art
> He is.
>
> We are
> You are
> They are!
>
> I love!
> You love!!
> He loves!!!
> Everybody loves!!!!

"Mr. Coughlin's treatment excels that of Mr. Byron's. Mr. Coughlin starts off with the love business and Byron devotes two verses to biographies of the characters. Byron's statement that everybody loves is no doubt true but in all its sweeping scope is where it loses in comparison with Mr. Coughlin's more personal love affair.

"Perhaps if Mr. Byron had been a member of the Chicago city council he wouldn't be so ready to declare everybody in on a deal."

After all, concluded The Inspired Idiot, The Bath in his "rustling of the lodging-house vote has himself become a vast unwritten epic."

Others had other ideas of the worth of "Dear Midnight of Love." City Sealer Quinn sighed, "It's better to be a great poet than a great alderman. Why, I'd trade everything I have for one minute of John's renown."

That renown soon reached New York's Board of Aldermen, where Alderman Bridges responded with "The Day of Love," which, New York newspapers insisted, completely eclipsed the efforts of the Chicago poet. A typical stanza ran:

Sometimes I think I could sit and eat—
Even at thy feet.
Till hungry time had swallowed up my years,
And sure, substantial lunch at 1 for two,
When one of us is you,
The other I, is paradise for both.
So we renew our troth.
Bring me two more beers.

On the Levee the denizens of the houses accepted the melodic banality as it accepted everything about Bathhouse John. Copies of the song, published by Sol Bloom, (who later went to New York, where he was elected to Congress), showing the alderman's fine full figure and bristling mustache, with a church, a spray of flowers, and two doves wreathing him, promptly appeared on all whorehouse pianos and the professors thumped mightily.* At the newest house in the district—the one at 2131 Dearborn Street run by those two newcomers, Minna and Ada Everleigh—three orchestras played the composition as often as the house favorite, "Stay in Your Own Back Yard."

Mayor Harrison thought the creation an inane conglomeration of words, but whenever the joyful Coughlin and glum little Kenna came calling he would sit back and ask John to sing his famous song. The Bath would shoot a glance at Kenna, Hinky Dink would hunch himself in his chair and prepare stoically to listen. Then Bathhouse would begin, cautiously at first, but finally trilling forth in a cracked First Ward tenor. Once, when Coughlin was absent, Harrison asked Kenna: "Tell me, Mike, do you think John is crazy or just full of dope?"

"No," snapped Kenna. "John isn't dotty and he ain't full of dope. To tell you th' God's truth, Mr. Mayor, they ain't found a name for it yet."

Gibes and all, Coughlin was as happy as he had been in his life.

---

*The cover noted "Words and Music by John J. Coughlin." Although there is little doubt he wrote the words, the music was written by a Max Hoffman.

When the city-hall reporters told him, mockingly, that he was poet laureate of Chicago, he grinned and shook his head. "No, boys, not Chicago yet. Just th' First Ward, boys. Poet Lariat of th' First Ward. That's Jawn Coughlin."

For the rest of his fantastic life he took pride in that title.

VICE, CRIME, AND CORRUPTION

I

IN THE aldermanic election of 1901 Mike Kenna received 6,191 votes to a total of 502 for his three opponents. At the same time Mayor Harrison narrowly defeated Judge Elbridge Hanecy. Many of the Gray Wolves in the council had fared poorly, and Walter Fisher, secretary of the Municipal Voters' League, announced proudly: "There are now forty-four good aldermen to twenty bad ones. If enough pressure is put upon the remaining six, they may be good."

Johnny Powers and Ed Cullerton, a pair of contrite survivors of the MVL purge, publicly swore off fighting Mayor Harrison, and once more Bathhouse John Coughlin was adjudged the spokesman of the council Democrats. There was talk in some quarters that even the most evil of the burghers were going to give up their former ways. Hinky Dink, amusing the reporters one day, struck the proper note. Pointing to Cullerton, he grunted, "This is little Red Riding Hood. I am Jack and th' Beanstalk. Bathhouse is Prince Charming. We're all goin' to be good."

They could afford to be good, and furthermore, day by day, it was growing clearer that the great era of boodle was passing. The defeat of Yerkes had been a mortal blow, the day of the flagrant franchise was fading and the amounts to be obtained from sandbag measures were dwindling. Municipal Chicago had just about been sold out.

So dull were council affairs that April that Bathhouse John seized Mrs. Coughlin's arm and sped off to Colorado, traveling comfortably on his aldermanic pass. Although he intended to enjoy his vacation incognito, Coughlin was immediately recognized by Richard Harding Loper, a reporter for the Colorado Springs *Evening Mail,* when he registered at the Antlers Hotel.

"I'm going to be a farmer," Bathhouse John informed Loper. "I'm going to make Colorado Springs my second home." But events in Chicago soon disrupted the idyllic plans and Bathhouse came storming back to the city.

Throughout the spring and early summer, the insistent voices of the Municipal Voters' League and the churchmen had been heard inveighing against the three eternal curses: vice, crime and political corruption. Harrison bent at least one ear to the clamor and dismissed Police Chief Joseph Kipley, replacing him with a fire-eater named Francis O'Neill. Then he issued an order— "Clean up the town"—and hustled off to his summer retreat in Michigan.

O'Neill was a blunt and unimaginative Irishman who took his orders literally. He soon drove the expanding Levee from its northern outpost at the corner of State and Van Buren Streets, chased pickpockets and low criminals out of the city, ordered the buffet flats to close and even, in honest zeal, arrested John (Mushmouth) Johnson, a First Ward precinct captain and close friend of Hinky Dink's, for keeping his saloon open after hours. He also ordered all Levee females to remain indoors and the *Tribune* marveled: "For the first time in the history of the Levee women are kept out of the saloons."

The campaign against the Levee was going full blast when Bathhouse John returned, but it was short-lived. Simultaneously with the purity drive, a political revolt against Harrison had developed, when Bobbie Burke, irked by imagined slights, obtained the undercover support of the master turncoat, Powers, and, with the help of Tommy Gahan and Roger Sullivan, openly announced his intent to seize control of the Cook County Democratic Central Committee. Harrison cut short his vacation and ran back to Chicago to put into the race a ticket headed by Tom Carey for chairman and Bathhouse John Coughlin for vice-chairman. The raids in the First Ward decreased at once, despite the ululations of

Hearst's *Evening American,* which was claiming credit for the Levee drive. The Carey-Coughlin ticket promptly throttled Burke in the committee election. Bobbie Burke had suffered a near-mortal defeat; so had the campaign against the vice lords.

The sudden cessation of raids left the district wide open and encouraged a dark period of First Ward criminal activity. Within a few months daylight robberies on principal streets were commonplace occurrences and loose women moved into residential districts, soliciting from doorways and open windows of houses and flats side by side with those of horrified housewives. Gambling, chiefly in the horse-race books springing up not only in the First Ward but as far south as the stockyards district, thrived again. Hoodlum gangs, dire forerunners of others bigger and fiercer by ten times, reveled in terrorism and strong-arm robberies. Criminals and ruffians and confidence men began to streak into the city as in the days preceding the World's Columbian Exposition. Even the once innocent wine rooms in the First Ward's family districts seemed to have adopted the Levee technique, and the *News* clucked:

At the wine room tables any night may be found from eight to twenty women and girls. They are ready to pounce upon any stranger as he enters to induce him to buy drinks. For this they receive a rake-off from the house. Besides the regular habitués of the dives are many others who have respectable homes and families. Even young girls of tender years are grist for the mill.

The *News* also pointed an accusing finger at Coughlin and Kenna, charging that, among others, Augustus A. Karg, proprietor of a chain of infamous lodging houses, paid to the First Ward organization $10,000 a year for police protection. Less important establishments, it noted, paid from $100 to $300 a month.

The alliance between the presumably vile and the presumably righteous seemed more closely knit than ever. When Sime Tuckhorn was arrested by Chief O'Neill's detectives after the suicide of a young girl had brought his low brothel to public notice, Sime boasted the judge would free him in two hours. He was too conservative. Justice Thomas K. Prindiville, a regular attendant at First Ward balls, freed him in sixty minutes.

2

Such iniquities were a windfall for the determined members of the Municipal Voters' League. The whole effort of the MVL, declared Walter Fisher in February 1902, would be concentrated on crushing wicked Bathhouse John Coughlin forever.

"People of this city," advised Fisher, "do not realize the utter social and political debauchery in the First Ward. The way to beat Coughlin is to drive out the floating lodging-house vote. The tough saloons are great offenders too. It is these places that serve as pens for these colonizers, who sleep about the free lunch counters and the beer barrels."

Blithely, The Bath accepted the challenge. "I'll be re-elected. My friends who know me best appreciate me. The First Ward is a city and I know all the people in it. I have th' business interests with me. Because why? Because when anyone wants me to do anything I do it courteously. Marshall Field, Mandel Brothers, the First National Bank. They're all with me. I am not a man who talks Bowery slang. The people know me. I've lived in this here ward for forty years."

The League held its fire until after registration day early in March. Then Fisher approached Jacob Ball, deputy inspector for the state board of health, and called attention to the scores of men sleeping in saloons. "It's a terrible health menace," said the persistent Fisher. Early one morning, about an hour after midnight, Ball set out to see for himself. He visited eighteen saloons. In Hinky Dink's Workingmen's Exchange he found men sleeping on bunks and in chairs in the rooms above, while in the barroom proper there were seventy-five men, snoring on the floor and atop the bar. At 307 South Clark Street there were twenty-seven men, and 330 South Clark, thirty-seven—everywhere bums and tramps in beards and tatters drowsed blissfully. In all, Ball's horrified report to his superiors noted, there were nearly a thousand colonizers ensconced in the eighteen saloons.

The state board of health thanked Ball and filed his account away with other forgotten papers. But the MVL banded with the Iroquois, Standard, and Union League Clubs, employed Attorney Thomas Knight, and caused the arrest of Hinky Dink and four other saloonkeepers, who were jointly harboring more than three hundred men, on charges of violating the city ordinance limiting saloon hours.

The case was assigned to a young assistant city attorney named Thomas F. Scully. Hinky Dink demanded a jury trial. A hearing was ordered and Kenna then testified that the blinds of his saloon had been down, the door locked, and the establishment closed to business when Ball paid his late visit. Scully, it developed, had come to court unprepared to prosecute the case. The jury promptly found Hinky Dink and his associates not guilty. The MVL was furious, and Scully was ordered suspended for thirty days for dereliction of duty. It was remarked about the First Ward, however, that Scully's political future was a bright one.

Then began an even greater assault on the First Ward citadel. The *Record-Herald,* fighting in the front line with the Municipal Voters' League, assigned its chief cartoonist, John T. McCutcheon, to depict Bathhouse John in every possible guise from vicious scoundrel to cheap buffoon. Other newspapers joined the *Record-Herald,* and daily Bathhouse was hammered with drawings, editorials and screamer headlines. Parades and mass meetings were held each night in the First Ward. Money poured into the headquarters of David L. Frank, the Republican assigned to finish Goliath, and the ministers and civic organizations bent to the fray. Judge John Barton Payne, John M. Harlan and an up-and-coming young politician named William Hale Thompson spoke at Frank's ward rallies.

From the Municipal Voters' League came a crash of thunder as it reported on the qualifications of the aldermanic candidates:

Coughlin, John J.—Democrat. Resides at 1804 Michigan avenue; self styled "banker" with offices in room 210, 123 La Salle street; finishing fourth term; commonly known as Bathhouse; formerly a rubber in a Turkish bath, afterward saloon keeper, to which occupation he has lately added the toil of being a "banker" for graft and the protection of vice; is recorded to have voted right once, when his vote was not needed; his sole claim to even political strength rests on his being a parasitical partner of Michael Kenna; he deserves the contempt of good citizens and the hatred of the unfortunate and vicious, whom he has bled and abused; every citizen of Chicago and especially his constituents between 12th and 22nd streets, should take an active interest in his defeat, so that the center of the city shall not be misrepresented by such a travesty on common sense and representative government. If he must be supported by the public, there are several public institutions that can care for him at less cost in money and civic self respect.

This blistering diatribe, penned by Henry Barrett Chamberlain, then city editor of the *Record-Herald* and later head of the Chicago Crime Commission, was received calmly by the First Ward forces. Nor did the mass meetings in the Coliseum cause Bathhouse John great discomfort.

The shouts and cries were familiar ones:

Harlan, yelling: "Bathhouse John levies tribute on illegal business by using the police force to get blackmail. Bobbie Burke's own friends charge that Bobbie has stolen $250,000 in the last five years and I'll tell you how he did it. Burke didn't steal that money. Bathhouse Coughlin gave it to him as his share! Coughlin was once a rubber. Now he's a toucher. He keeps as much as he dares and gives the rest to Burke. No man in the ward can stay open without paying to Coughlin! When he first came into the council he was merely a grotesque fool. But now! Don't you know that Coughlin has every jail bird, crook and disreputable character in the ward? Don't you know they will do any service he requires of them?"

Fisher, shouting: "The kind of cattle upon whom Bathhouse John depends are human swine, literally penned before election in the tough saloons along Clark, State and Van Buren Streets, sleeping like hogs on the filthy floors and fed like hogs from the free lunch trough and the beer barrels piled against the walls."

The Reverend Frank Crane of People's Church: "John Coughlin is an octopus!"

William Hale Thompson, demanding: "Why doesn't Harrison do something to take this notorious man out of politics?"

First Ward voters, who did not attend the meetings, wearily regarded them as some kind of side show staged by people they knew nothing about, but Mayor Carter Harrison felt obliged to speak out.

"I shall not oppose Coughlin," he said. "My reason for this is that Coughlin stood by me on the fifty-year franchise fight and I do not propose to work against him now. On the other hand I do not propose to take any part in the fight."

"Do you think, Mr. Mayor, that Coughlin is an honest man?" asked the reporters.

"I have noticed no wings sprouting on John," was Harrison's reply.

Amid the hubbub, the work of organizing the First Ward for a Coughlin triumph was being handled quietly by Hinky Dink. Bathhouse John himself made his daily tours of the district, his pockets filled with quarters and half-dollars. Each morning he arose at 6:30, ate a liberal breakfast of four eggs, cereal, thick rye bread, three cups of coffee, and left his home about an hour later. First he visited the Harrison Street police station, where he shook hands with the desk sergeant, the captain, the patrolmen, the prisoners. Then he selected two stalwart officers and he was off on his journey through the First Ward.

He idled in the Italian neighborhood at Polk and Clark Streets, where he called out, *"Saluté! Buon Giorno!"* a phrase he had picked up from one of his precinct captains, a dark-eyed young Italian named Jim Colosimo, recently wed to Victoria Moresco, a brothel owner. Coughlin was big and handsome and regal in his morning coat and brown "dicer," but he spoke to everyone, from storekeeper and housewife to gutter drunk and bootblack. As he strode along, a motley throng grew large at his heels, and when the size of it satisfied him Bathhouse signaled his bodyguards to halt and he turned and faced his supporters.

"Men," he cried, "they call me Bathhouse. What of it? My answer is this. Read American history. Abe Lincoln was a rail splitter. What was Garfield? A canal boy and hewer of woods." Then he glared at the reporters, who had been tagging along with the crowd, and blustered: "I would like to know how these reporters would like it if some day when they rose above their jobs some man would turn like an adder and say to them, 'You was a reporter oncet.'"

At this, the crowd cheered in parched, anxious voices.

"C'mon boys," cried Bathhouse John. "Th' drinks is on th' alderman." There was a rush for the nearest saloon. Coughlin watched happily. "They's seven hundred people around here," he chortled, "an' there ain't one of them wouldn't go through hell for me."

By midafternoon Coughlin reached Hinky Dink's saloon at Clark and Van Buren where he conferred for two hours with saloonkeepers, whorehouse owners, the representatives of businessmen, the lodging-house keepers, the favor seekers and the thirsty. Then, another speech:

"I was born in th' First Ward at the corner of Franklin and Harrison. I never seen Waukegan till I was of age. Go out in your precinct an' brand this lie wherever you can. If it's a disgrace to be born in th' First Ward, then Carter Harrison is as much disgraced as I am. Tell all th' constituents that. I started life at the old Jones School and have been making friends since I was five years old."

The Bath's good friends did not fail him. In a speech at the campaign headquarters Tom McNally, a member of the state legislature now, rose brilliantly to the occasion.

"If our John was to put on a tin star and went and reported to the YMCA every time Maggie got a can of beer and wouldn't let Tom or Bill or Pat have a quiet drink when he wanted it, he would be the summer idol of them reformers," he shouted to two hundred ward captains and lieutenants. "Or, if he went and blew on every 4-11-44 policy game that he seen going on in basements, they would receive him with open arms. But, gents, he ain't that kind. He don't stick his nose where he ain't wanted. If you want a drink before twelve, or after twelve, go to it, says John, so long as you don't disturb your neighbor. We don't take no pointers from this Municipal League!"

And The Bath followed with cheery advice.

"Now, boys, go to your precincts and spread the joyful tidings of 5,000 majority. Be gentlemen, as you always are, an' carry your standard bearers' motto: HONESTY AND NO SLANDER. Put that in every American home!"

The battle raged hotly to election eve. Kenna made his customary prediction, a Coughlin victory by at least 3,000 votes. "If it's a fight, John can't lose. The vote will be about 7,500 to 8,000. Th' other fellow won't even know he's runnin'."

The *News* thought otherwise. "This unregenerate reprobate," it insisted, "is out of politics forever."

The *News* was wrong. When the votes had been counted under the eyes of thirty members of the University of Chicago football squad who acted as poll watchers, Hinky Dink's canny prescience was upheld. There were 8,065 votes cast and Coughlin was victor by 2,605.

Again had Bathhouse John been judged by his peers.

3

A maxim of First Ward philosophy was that it rarely forgave its foes or forgot its friends. When Mayor Harrison prepared to seek his fourth term, he found that his kindly reluctance to interfere in the First Ward had borne splendid fruit.

The city's conservatives detested the Harrison policies, and they were particularly irked by his recent espousal of a plan to hold a referendum on municipal ownership of traction companies. They lined up to a man behind Graeme Stewart, a wholesale grocer selected as the Republican candidate. Not only did the mayor face this expected opposition, but that dissatisfied trio— Burke, Powers and Gahan—were also working against him, behind scenes. Before Stewart had been named, the rebels had ordered their dupes to form a rump organization which unsuccessfully attempted to persuade Clarence Darrow to be their candidate. When he refused, they adopted a do-nothing policy throughout the campaign.

Not so Coughlin and Kenna. Little Mike faced no opposition for the council seat, but both men were as industrious as usual in the mayor's cause. Harrison had stood by them, and the ward was prospering; they would reward that loyalty. A reporter who slipped into a closed meeting of Coughlin saloonkeeper lieutenants soon disclosed the way the First Ward breezes were blowing. Coughlin, he reported, told the assemblage: "You support Mayor Harrison, or I'll put you out of business. There's a good chance that Stewart may win, but if he does I'll still be alderman and they'll be plenty of trouble for anybody who gets this wrong. Th' liquor interests have got to line up for their friends."

Harrison was returned to office by the slim majority of 7,388. More than half this margin of victory, 3,501 votes' majority, came from the First Ward alone, and the rest were scattered among staunchly Democratic areas. It was eloquent testimony to the worth of Aldermen Coughlin and Kenna in a tight campaign.

When the First Ward statesmen came to pay their respects to the victor, Harrison, who had been dubious about his chances, was properly grateful. "But honestly, boys," said the mayor, "I don't understand it. Why did I come out on top in this fight? Everything was against me. Why was it I won?"

There was a slight pause. Kenna chewed on his cigar and Coughlin pursed his lips. "Well, Mr. Maar," said Bathhouse thoughtfully, "I'd say you won because of the public satisfaction with the well-known honesty which has caricatured your every administration."

4

Harrison and his fond pair of aldermen grew closer as the days sped on. Rarely an afternoon passed that failed to bring a visit to his office from Bathhouse John and Hinky Dink. They would wait until the end of his day, just after the mayor had given his interview to the reporters from the morning papers. Then Hinky Dink would poke his head through the open doorway, step inside and stand for a long time without speaking. When Harrison motioned for him to come closer, he would vanish for an instant, returning with his swankily clad partner. The three would sit and talk then for an hour or so. Sometimes Bathhouse would recite one of his poems, at a suggestion from Harrison, while Hinky Dink grimaced. Sometimes the aldermen approached with requests for favors—pardons for friends in the Bridewell, permits, special licenses. Usually they had a few words about politics.

These tête-à-têtes horrified Harrison's friends in the reform circles. For them he had a ready reply. When a man went into city politics, he would insist, he had to take the cards as they fell and play them the best he knew how. Of Hinky Dink he once wrote:

Mike Kenna, with all his faults and failings, in those days at heart was a fine fellow, a good husband who led the quietest of lives, devoted to the home circle. . . . I never once knew him to lie. Our cards were always on the table face up, nothing ever held out.

And of Bathhouse John:

I verily believe he would have traveled far and high as a leader of men. Holier-than-thou human nature is too prone to dismiss as beneath contempt a type of man who, justly studied, is not to be blamed altogether in his derelictions.

THE PUBLIC CRIB

I

IN THE summer of 1904 many Democrats, among them Bathhouse John and Hinky Dink, still nourished the hope that Mayor Carter Harrison would be the next President of the United States. But they reckoned without John Hopkins and Roger Sullivan, who, buttressed now by an astute strategist, George Brennan, captured the support of downstate delegates, formed an alliance with the so-called Independence League of William Randolph Hearst, and combined those forces to torpedo Harrison's chances at the St. Louis national convention.

In vain did Bathhouse John plead with the Illinois delegation as it wavered between Hearst and Judge Alton B. Parker, while scorning Chicago's mayor utterly. "Look," he said, "I'm for Harrison. I can't see no one else but the mayor. He's a good Democrat and he don't go over the limit on anything. Hearst, he's too extremely radical. Parker, he's too extremely conservative. Cleveland, he's too extremely middling. I play Harrison as the par-excellence President."

But Tammany prevailed and the now forgotten Parker was the Democratic nominee. Back in Chicago the Democratic feud grew fierce. The Hearst press hammered Harrison, the Sullivanites conspired against him, and the radicals in the party assailed him for failing to espouse a plan for immediate municipal ownership of the traction lines. Finally—and it was a sad day for the two aldermen from the First Ward—Mayor Harrison announced that he was through. He would not again be a candidate.

The Republicans, led by the *Tribune,* that bitter foe of municipal ownership, sprang to the support of John Harlan, making his second try at the mayoralty. Municipal ownership was to be the issue, and the warring Democrats sought a man behind whom they all could march. They chose Edward F. Dunne, a judge of the Cook County Circuit Court and proud father of thirteen children. His candidacy had an electric effect. It solidified the Democrats and split the Republicans, drawing from them a radical wing, including, along with earnest theorists, visionaries, and crackpots, young Joseph Medill Patterson, son of R. W. Patterson, one of the owners of the *Tribune*. Naturally, the *Tribune* would not countenance such a defection, and Patterson, in youthful indignation, resigned from his father's newspaper while it endorsed Harlan with extra thunder.

None were more avid in their support of Dunne than the rulers of the First Ward. They plumped enthusiastically for municipal ownership, although neither had an especially clear idea of what such a system would mean to their bank accounts. Kenna informed the judge that he would carry the ward by a majority of at least two to one. Then, in his confidence, he ordered his helpers to institute an economy wave.

On registration day, March 14, the floaters, roused early from their filthy beds by the usual barrage of firecrackers, discovered as they lined up at the saloons that instead of the customary fifty cents a registration, they would receive only fifteen cents.

At once there was a collective howl and threat of revolt. "At the last election," protested Tom McKenna, an inhabitant of the cheap Palisades lodging house and a leader in the insurrection, "I don't remember how much I got because I was too drunk, but I know I was satisfied. Now they want us to register for fifteen cents! An' they're getting so strict I can't register in more than two places. Hell, that's a poor day's pay, only thirty cents, beer an' soup. Me, I'm holdin' out all day. The way to do this is for half a dozen of us right guys to stick together an' make a proposition. They'll have to come around."

McKenna ran to some other candidates willing to pay higher rates. Some of the rebellious habitués of the First Ward were crowded into wagons and driven to other wards where they were paid twenty-five cents for every registration. By late afternoon Hinky Dink gave in. He raised his price to twenty-five cents, and the revolt ended. "That's what birds like Billy Skakel do to politics," he grumbled, recalling the wild days of 1894.

2

"Immediate Municipal Ownership!"

This was the battle shout. Dunne believed it would be the solution of all traction ills. Harlan called it "anarchistic and socialistic!" Of the two, Dunne seemed to have the more potent arguments. The traction scandals had continued even after Yerkes had fled Chicago to build subway tubes in his native London. J. Pierpont Morgan and a crowd of New York and Chicago bankers had bought much of the Yerkes stock, and, charged the Hearst press, controlled the situation as fiendishly as "The Titan" ever had. The equipment of the companies had been allowed to deteriorate and the service was wretched. Thus the financial barons had hoped to provoke a public demand for franchise extensions. Instead the cry was, "Public ownership! Let the city own the lines!"

The words flew fast, from speakers' stands and in editorials. In the *American* and *Examiner,* Harlan was a fool, an idiot, a mountebank, a "tool of international financiers." In the *Tribune,* Dunne was a fool, an idiot, a mountebank, an "anarchistic-socialist."

Then Dunne was honored at a gala rally in the First Ward at which Hinky Dink advised his constituents: "Vote for the judge. He's gonna give th' streetcars to th' people!"

After responding to the cheers, the kindly judge extolled The Hink as a true friend of municipal ownership and urged his re-election.

"I want to have in the council," cried Dunne, "a man from the First Ward who is a true friend of municipal ownership. From the way he has voted in the past and from what he is doing now, I am satisfied that your candidate, Mr. Kenna, can be depended upon to support the cause. I ask your support and your votes for Michael Kenna for alderman in the ward."

By these kind words Judge Dunne pushed municipal ownership into the background and made Hinky Dink the campaign issue. His enemies were quick to seize upon his error.

"This," shrieked the *Record-Herald,* "is a blatant signal that the good old days of the Gray Wolves are to come back!"

"Here," chorused the press, "is the kind of man Dunne wants in his government. The issue is clear. It is Dunne and Hinky Dink against Harlan and decency!"

On their front pages, the anti-municipal-ownership newspapers emblazoned the current MVL estimate of the diminutive Democratic candidate for alderman of the First Ward:

A fit representative of the dissolute, vicious, criminal elements that infest certain resorts of the First Ward, but it is a disgrace that the great business sections of the city should be represented in the council by such an alderman.

Judge Dunne stood firm. "I don't like his business and I don't like his surroundings," he admitted. "But he helped to save the city from Yerkes and he has pledged his support to municipal ownership. I have not indorsed Cullerton, nor Powers. I want to say this about Kenna. A very close friend of William Kent of the MVL told me that Kenna was one of the two honest men he had met in politics."

Explanations and alibis did little good. A vote for Dunne, insisted the Harlanites, was a vote for Kenna. Kenna was not a true friend of municipal ownership. Kenna was a dangerous radical. Kenna was a friend of corporate interests. Kenna was bad, wicked, evil, a disgrace to the council, a disgrace to the city.

"Hinky Dink," shouted Harlan, "has become the vital issue in this campaign. And when I say Hinky Dink I mean Ike Bloom and all that rotten crew that dominates vice and corruption in the city. The Hink is the Prince of Grafters. Does my opponent endorse all the rest of the hungry crew that wants to get at the public crib?"

Mike Kenna was startled by the attention. "The council records show where I stand on municipal ownership," he retorted. "These reformers can talk all they want to, but my record speaks for itself. I have always voted for municipal-ownership measures. Judge Dunne will carry this ward and he will win the election by 40,000 votes."

Dunne hurled a last defiance at his tormentors by holding his final rally in the First Ward. As the precinct captains gathered they were handed bundles of pamphlets. These were printed in green ink—and in Chinese. "There's my answer to Harlan and those guys," Kenna explained. "Harlan has been throwing the harpoon into me for two weeks and I thought it was time to call him. I got old King Yen Lo, the manager of the Chink joint on top my place on Van Buren Street, to write the answer. I don't know what he said, but if it is anything like I told him it's a peacherino."

Voters on their way to the polls were bombarded with the pamphlets, whose only English wording was: "Ald. Kenna's Answer!" They laughed, jested over Little Mike's wit, and scrawled their X's. When all the thousands of X's over the city were counted Dunne had won by 30,000 and in the bailiwick of Bathhouse John and Hinky Dink his plurality was nearly 4,000 out of 6,000 votes. Hinky Dink won too, 6,006 to 656 for all three of his opponents.

3

The new mayor panted for action. In electing Dunne the city had also endorsed the principle of municipal ownership of traction utilities by a thumping count of 142,826 to 27,998, and Dunne, bolstered by such public support, promptly scrapped all pending negotiations for short-term franchises.

That fervent advocate of municipal ownership, Michael Kenna, left Bathhouse Coughlin to assist the mayor as best he could, and scooted off with his wife and Nick Martin, his secretary, to "make the high spots of Europe." Coughlin soon after departed for Colorado.

Neither of Mayor Dunne's First Ward supporters could understand the strange comings and goings at the city hall. Immediately after his election the mayor had sent out a Macedonian cry for James Dalrymple, engineer of the municipally owned tramways in Glasgow, Scotland. In preparation for the arrival of this expert he had surrounded himself with such advisors as Margaret Haley of the Chicago Federation of Labor, Adrian (Cap) Anson, erstwhile owner of the Chicago White Stockings, Chicago's leading ball club, Joseph Patterson, Clarence Darrow, and other high-principled but inexperienced citizens who proposed to build a new, Utopian Chicago overnight. This group was known derisively as the "Kitchen Cabinet" and it set out so energetically at cross purposes that the Dunne administration was quickly embroiled in vicious feuds which delighted the enemies of municipal ownership.

The opposing traction forces were readying for battle when Hinky Dink returned in November with glowing accounts of his trip:

"Rome? Most everybody you meet in Rome has been dead for 2,000 years.

"Monte Carlo? Great place. I spent two days there an' broke even. I didn't play. Game is on th' square and there's no limit, not even th' ceiling. That song about the man who broke the bank is just a bedtime story. The bunkerino.

"Paris? You sure get a run for your money in that man's town. There is no lid on that burg. Even th' stoves don't have lids in Paris.

"Philadelphia? She sleeps."

4

Both aldermen from the First Ward supported a proposed ordinance to give Chicago immediate ownership of the car lines, but so hot was the attack from the anti-municipal-ownership crowd that the council refused to bring the measure to a vote. The ordinance was returned to the Committee on Transportation for surgical attention, and the traction companies got busy. A fund of $500,000, railed Hearst's *American,* was being raised to buy out influential aldermen. This was denied by the streetcar barons, although two years later they admitted spending as much as $250,000 to prevent passage, that figure being disclosed when the companies tried to deduct it from their gross profits as "operating expenses."

Which aldermen were given gifts, which were given streetcar stock—if any—was never known, but three weeks later the Committee on Transportation reported it had scrapped the Dunne ordinance and brought forth one of its own. The terms were similar to those that had been advocated by Harrison, now seated on the sidelines. The companies were to be given a twenty-year franchise, but the city had the right to buy the lines at any time on six months' notice. While the companies continued the operation of the lines, they were to make various improvements. The city could buy at the base price of $50,000,000 instead of the $75,000,000 the companies wanted, plus the cost of improvements. Meanwhile the companies were to pay the city fifty-five per cent of the net receipts as the price of the franchise.

This seemed a happy compromise. The city was then in no financial position to undertake immediate ownership and, compared with the buccaneering past, the clauses for rehabilitation and compensation were magnificent. The negotiations had dragged along for almost a year and a half, and the public was weary of waiting for a settlement. But like Harrison his predecessor, Dunne would not give way to compromise and supported by Hearst, he pledged a fight against the ordinance.

Throughout the proceedings Hinky Dink and Bathhouse were blasted by the newspapers for their support of Immediate Municipal Ownership, and the IMO forces were attacked for having such supporters. In April 1906, while Coughlin was handily defeating one Frank Norton in the aldermanic race, Chicago voted again on IMO, this time on whether to approve the Dunne ordinance. A 10,000 majority voted with Dunne, most of the margin coming from the First Ward, but legal approval required a three-fifths affirmative vote, and this Dunne lacked by 17,000 votes.

This decision by the electorate gave Bathhouse and Hinky Dink an out. They clung to Dunne a few months longer, and then decided they had gone far enough along the road to municipal ownership. Amid horrendous cries from the *American* they deserted the cause. During a momentous session on the night of February 4, 1907, the council met for eleven hours, and on each test vote, on every resolution, the aldermen from the First Ward voted against the mayor. Alderman William Dever, blunt-jawed newcomer to the council, presented Dunne-sponsored amendments to the measure and these were consistently defeated by a count of 56 to 13. By that vote the committee-revised ordinance passed, subject to the approval of the voters the following spring. Coughlin and Kenna voted "Aye." At once Mayor Dunne vetoed the measure, and it was promptly passed over his veto.

Coughlin and Kenna were singled out for attack by Hearst, who had come to town to superintend the proceedings.

"Hinky Dink and Bathhouse John have sold out and betrayed the mayor. They are grafters!" he fumed in his *American*.

"Coughlin and Kenna and Powers sold out to Morgan!" yowled the *Examiner*.

"Hundreds of thousands of dollars were handed out as campaign contributions to buy such men as Coughlin and Kenna," raged Miss Margaret Haley.

But the strategy of their move soon became clear. They were finished with Dunne. Before the collapse of the municipal-ownership drive they had been writing letters to Carter Harrison in California. The two, conferring in their brusque, odd way in The Hink's saloon, had decided that Our Carter was needed to save Chicago Democracy and municipal ownership was something starry-eyed and incomprehensible anyway.

Early in February Harrison returned and announced he would again be a candidate. With Coughlin and Kenna he sought to round up all his one-time supporters. But they had reckoned without the solidity and strength of the Hopkins-Sullivan faction. On primary day, February 21, Hinky Dink and Bathhouse John gave to their Carter the entire thirty votes of their delegates, but the opponent organization elsewhere was barely dented. Harrison lost and Dunne again was the candidate.

5

One, two, three! The two aldermen pushed another button and, lo! they were for Mayor Dunne in a twinkling. Chicago this year was electing its mayor for a four-year term. The Bath and Hinky Dink hurried to the mayor, to Roger Sullivan and Johnny Hopkins even, offering their talents and money. They had to protect their valuable investment, these repentant sinners. Dunne's foe, the jolly federal postmaster, Fred Busse, had a reputation as a good sport and a liberal thinker, but you simply didn't trust a Republican in the First Ward.

"It's th' first time we're electing a mayor for four years, boys," Kenna told his precinct men. "Now you tell your people to vote as they please on traction. Write yes or no, but be sure you vote for Mayor Dunne."

"Th' mayor stands for our personal liberty," Bathhouse John bleated. "We may differ on the traction ordinance but we are with him first, last, and all th' time."

The mayor smiled and forgave. Into the First Ward he sent his corporation counsel, Ed Wade, whose quaver brought tears to the eyes of his audiences. "Alderman Michael Kenna," stated Wade, "is a reformer. He is not the kind that hollers reform with his right hand uplifted and his left hand reaching out for the coin. He goes into the home of the poor man who has no bread on the table and whose children have no clothes and no shoes. He goes into the home where the shadow of death has fallen and he calls the undertaker and says, 'Paddy Flaherty's mother is dead. Paddy is broke. I'll pay the funeral expenses.' He takes the little kids and leads them up to the light of education."

But glowing words and all the kissing and making up was in vain. Kenna, of course, received a tremendous majority, snaring 4,341 votes to 249 for his closest foe, Charles Espey, candidate of the Hearst-sponsored Independence League. But Dunne, swamped in defeat, had only a plurality of 751 votes in the First Ward, the smallest margin ever given a Democratic candidate since Coughlin and Kenna had become its rulers. The bitterest pill of all to the defeated mayor was the public's approval of the compromise ordinance he had so valiantly battled.

With considerable justification the *American* wept, "The Gray Wolves knifed Dunne." But the pleased *Tribune* rejoiced: "It was a great defeat of Hearstism and Dunneism."

6

Fred Busse settled into the mayor's chair and prepared "once and for all to settle the vexing traction tangle" and other municipal matters. He shook up the health department, the smoke-prevention bureau, and the board of education. He roared to Chief of Police George Shippy: "Get the big thieves! I'll back every honest copper!" He refused to close the saloons on Sundays, as the prohibitionists demanded, for he was well and unfavorably known as a saloon brawler himself, but he was credited with directing a movement in the state legislature to eliminate half the aldermen and lengthen the terms of the rest to four years. The *Tribune* claimed that this was a direct attack on Bathhouse John. But Alderman Coughlin was unruffled:

"I ain't dead yet an' anybody who thinks I am passing into the gloaming of the great political beyond don't understand higher statesmanship as you find it in the First Ward," he said. "Why, we're a hundred years ahead of our time in th' First. It will always take two aldermen to transact the business of th' First, but should the state legislature decide one alderman is enough, then I will be alderman in spiritus frumenti."

As the Busse regime got under way Chicago had a notable visitor, William Stead, returned to see what had become of the great reform movement he had created over a decade back. He visited the First Ward, spent time in Hank North's saloon and, with John Kelley, police reporter on the *Record-Herald,* toured the Levee and visited the Workingmen's Exchange where he listened again to the political philosophies of Aldermen Bathhouse John and Hinky Dink.

And when his stay was done he said to the reporters, with a wry grin: "Aldermen Coughlin and Kenna are typical of Chicago and it is to be regretted that their opinions on city government are not consulted more often." He put his tongue in his cheek and then, as he boarded his train to New York, added, "When I first visited Chicago I thought there was one in a thousand chances of reform succeeding here. Now I think the chances are one in two thousand."

SHE DRANK LIKE A LADY

I

As soon as the new council was sworn in under Mayor Busse, Bathhouse John and Mrs. Coughlin departed for Colorado Springs, where the alderman had purchased a handsome estate and where he was building an enormous zoo.

The Springs had become a second home to the Coughlins. On their return pilgrimage in the summer of 1902 they had been welcomed with such enthusiasm by the citizens that Bathhouse promptly retained agents to find for him a farm. They had arrived at the time of the annual Colorado Springs flower festival, and had been invited to participate as honored guests. Alderman Coughlin searched about and hired a huge, rickety carriage, which he and Mary decorated with blooms. With his wife beside him the alderman drove tandem in the parade, a resplendent cynosure for the eager western eyes. President Theodore Roosevelt, then in Colorado Springs on a tour of the nation, also had a place of honor, in the reviewing stand. As the Coughlins drew abreast, the grinning President waved and shouted: "Hi, John!"

There was an uproar from the crowd. Both Teddy and Bathhouse could touch the hearts of the people. The alderman was overwhelmed by the honor bestowed upon him. "Teddy! Teddy, me boy! Teddy!" he cried, raising his gray top hat and saluting. Tears of sentiment streamed down his face. Mrs. Coughlin flushed happily.

2

The Coughlins were welcome in Colorado Springs. They were

welcome also in the settlement of British prospectors and ranchers known to the natives as Little London. These outlanders found Bathhouse fascinating. They listened entranced as he boasted of the advantages of Chicago over a London he had never seen, and while he recounted the magnificent natural resources and wonders of a nation that gave hardworking and honest Irishmen such splendid opportunities in its political affairs. In the saloons, where Bathhouse moderately quaffed beer, or now and then tossed off awesome quantities of spirits, his prattling was regarded as rare entertainment.

One evening the boys were bending elbows over discussion of the recent scaling of the Matterhorn by an Englishman. Bathhouse was contemptuous of the feat. "Let' em try to climb Cheyenne Mountain!" he cried, slamming down a stein. "Now, there's a hill! Ain't a man can climb Cheyenne, except, maybe, myself."

Slight, thin-haired Winston Dunraven took up the challenge. Backed by his British compatriots, he dared Coughlin to a race to the top of Cheyenne, the loser to set up a champagne dinner for the whole of Little London. The Bath accepted eagerly. He had confidence in his physical prowess, and from the distance Cheyenne didn't look so high. "I'll ride my Arabian steed right to th' top, and plant th' American flag," he boasted. "You better rustle up that champagne."

The contest caught the imagination of the country. The Colorado Springs reporters were kept busy filing dispatches to newspapers in a dozen states. They interviewed Coughlin daily, and meticulously and somewhat imaginatively chronicled his preparations for the ascent. The Bath had discovered that he could better negotiate the six miles of mountain trail aboard a burro than on an Arabian steed, and he found also that he would have to climb most of the last mile afoot. Still, he was undaunted.

"Say, I'll beat that guy in a walk," he told reporters. "I'll hand him a bunch so hot it'll burn him, see! He don't know. Dunharen or Dunraven, whatever his name is, might as well come up with the goods now for the supper. I'm a guy that always stands a call, an' I don't never come up with a four flush, I'll tell you those."

But Frank R. Van Meter of Colorado Springs, after inspecting The Bath's preparations and observing the efficient way in which Dunraven and his backer, J. L. Conway, were preparing for the climb, began to be worried. It would be a humiliation the natives of Colorado Springs could never live down if the British colony planted its own flag atop lofty Cheyenne first. So Van Meter started out alone. While the two contestants were entertaining the press with their stories of what they would do to each other, Van Meter in three and a half hours rode and climbed to the summit of Cheyenne and planted the American flag. "It's a record that will not be bettered easily," boasted the Colorado Springs *Evening Mail,* which seemed to have been in on the plot. "Van Meter has guaranteed that the record will remain American."

Coughlin was furious when he heard of Van Meter's accomplishment. "I had that thing won!" he roared. "Who does that Van Meter think he is, anyway? Now who's goin' to buy the champagne dinner?" The Bath and Conway and Dunraven finally supplied it together. It was, said the *Mail,* one of the nicest parties Colorado Springs had ever witnessed.

In December of 1902 Alderman Coughlin purchased from Mrs. Mary E. Johnson of Colorado Springs a 100-acre tract in Cheyenne Canyon, near the foot of Cheyenne Mountain, where he proposed to build his summer home. The price was $88,560. Later he added 100 acres. It was a beautiful site, cut through by Cheyenne Creek, rugged and wooded, looking out upon the purpled heights of Pike's Peak and Manitou Mountain, six miles away to the northwest.

The Coughlin home, a rambling, stained-shingle dwelling of nine rooms, was constructed far back among the trees of this pretentious estate. To the west, a few hundred feet from the house, the alderman built a great round barn, where he proposed to stable his racing horses and to keep a string of saddle ponies. He bought 200 Leghorn hens, which he pronounced the finest in the land, and announced that he was not going to play rancher but intended to get down to real business. When the house was completed Coughlin invited twenty-five guests for a flag-raising ceremony, and made a brief speech on Americanism. "Always carry th' American flag with you, wherever you travel," he advised his audience. "That's what I do. There's no flag like the good old stars and stripes."

Bathhouse dearly loved animals, and Colorado Springs citizens, always heartily welcomed when they visited the estate, soon began bringing him pets. The first were two eagles. Then came two coyotes. Then a deer. Then Bathhouse bought a half-dozen mountain burros. One of these he crated up and sent to Mayor Harrison. Harrison, however, soon became tired of this symbol of his party, and he presented the beast to Ed Lahiff, his secretary, who took the little animal to his home in Ravenswood. There it was discovered that the donkey considered Ravenswood poison ivy the most palatable of foods. The children of the neighborhood rented him out as an exterminator. The burro grew fat at his work, and soon became famous throughout Chicago.

So pleased was Bathhouse with the quiet life in Colorado Springs that he and Mary spent every possible vacation there. For a time the alderman toyed with the idea of converting his land into a huge sub-division which he would call Little Chicago, and which, he predicted, would be quickly settled by prominent citizens from the First Ward. The Colorado Springs *Gazette* naïvely assumed that this would be a tremendous boon for the town, and spoke feelingly of Coughlin as an upstanding citizen and entrepreneur.

But the increasing size of Coughlin's zoo eventually began to alter his plans. A streetcar line had been constructed through his estate to the Broadmoor Hotel in the foothills of Cheyenne Mountain, and the zoo was readily available to the townsfolk. Visitors from all over Colorado soon began coming to look at his animals, and the zoo became a popular attraction for the summer tourists.

John M. Harland, owner of Pabst Park in Milwaukee, visited the place and suggested to Bathhouse that it would be an ideal spot for an amusement park. The coaster slides, said Harland, could be built on the hills at practically no expense, the private lake could be converted into a swimming pool, and transportation was available.

The idea of a Coney Island in the wilderness appealed to Bathhouse. He informed the weekly *Gazette* that he would change the name of his sub-division to Cheyenne Springs, and that he would construct the most magnificent amusement park in the United States, at the same time selling small parcels of land to those desiring to live in "the true heart of God's country." Cheyenne Springs will not be inhabited by Chicago people alone, The Bath said. "Everyone will be welcomed, so long as they got th' spondulix." He hired forty men to plant 6,000 trees on the estate.

3

The news that Coughlin planned a real zoo reached his friends about the country. Circus trainers, who had met the alderman on their visits to the Levee, big-game hunters, park superintendents, and mountain trappers sent him animals for his collection. The crates of birds and beasts included parakeets, a bedraggled parrot that some in Chicago said was once Carrie Watson's, a hyena, a cub lion, a tiger and a brown bear. Coughlin brought out Hinky Dink and Mrs. Kenna to inspect his zoological quarters, and The Hink declared that perhaps he had a good thing.

"What I need for this zoo," said Bathhouse, "is an elephant."

"H'm," said Hinky Dink. "An elephant! That would be something." He thought a moment. "They is an elephant in Lincoln Park."

"That is just what I was thinkin'," said Bathhouse happily. "They is two elephants in Lincoln Park, eating up th' taxpayer's money. One elephant is enough. Maybe I should take the other elephant off th' hands of th' taxpayers."

Borrowing an elephant from Lincoln Park was not an easy accomplishment. But fortunately for Bathhouse, Princess Alice, smaller of the two pachyderms in the Lincoln Park zoo, had caught her trunk in a trap door, and the tip was torn off. This distressed Cy DeVries, veteran keeper of the Lincoln Park zoo, who felt that Princess Alice no longer met the zoo's esthetic requirements. Bathhouse was not so particular. All he wanted was an elephant. Princess Alice was crated up and shipped to Colorado Springs. The taxpayers, however, were not informed of the removal.*

Princess Alice became the pride of Coughlin's life. She was an affectionate beast and would follow The Bath all about his estate, poking into his pockets for peanuts. The reputation of the zoo shot up enormously when an elephant became domiciled there, and Bathhouse pressed his plans for the construction of his full-scale amusement park.

While the rides and stands were building, the alderman decided to establish a stage line to carry tourists on trips to Pike's Peak and through the Garden of the Gods. He imported rigs and horses from Chicago, and on the day this equipment reached the zoo, Walter Colburn, sun-tanned, sandy-haired Colorado Springs youngster, arrived with it. Colburn wanted a job, taking care of the stage line. He got it, at a salary of four dollars a week. The alderman, having no children, took a fancy to young Colburn, and one day after Walter had pursued a tourist to the Rio Grande station and forced him to pay for the hire of a rig he had used Bathhouse announced:

"Walter, that settles it. I can use a wide-awake young fella like you in Chicago. You go tell your mamma you're going t' live with me from now on." Thereafter Walter was a fixture in the Coughlin household, and Bathhouse made him manager of the amusement park.

---

*Lincoln Park records do not show that there were ever two elephants in the zoo. The men who helped transport Princess Alice insist, however, that she came from Lincoln Park.

The Zoo Park, as it was called, was finally completed in 1905 and was known as the most impressive establishment of its kind west of Omaha. To the animal collection The Bath added an elk, a tiger, a zebu or sacred cow, and a camel. There were bear pits and monkey cages, birdhouses and a string of burros and Shetland ponies for the children to ride. The shoot-the-chute curved down from a hillside into Coughlin's private lake. There was a roller coaster, a swimming pool, a miniature railroad, an aerostat, a dance hall, a motion-picture theater, a fun house, and a roller-skating rink. When Lincoln Park dismantled its famous "Old Mill," Bathhouse John obligingly carted it away and installed it in his park, over Cheyenne Creek. There were shooting galleries, cane racks, one of the most beautiful merry-go-rounds in the country, a figure eight, a refreshment pavilion, a stable with eighty riding horses, a ball park, a wild-west show, and a trained-animal exhibition under the personal direction of Professor McGuarren, once of Ringling Brothers, or in any event so advertised.

But, above all these attractions, Alderman Coughlin delighted most in his loving, snub-nosed elephant. In the winter of 1906 Princess Alice was comfortably stabled among the horses in the big round barn when Coughlin arrived for his winter vacation. He did not immediately go to the barn, and Princess Alice, sniffing his presence, could not wait. She snapped her chain, crashed through a wall of the barn, and went out in search of her master. Once outside, the Princess was distracted by the wonder of a fresh snowfall, and she wandered about, becoming thoroughly chilled. That night she had a bad cold.

Colburn summoned Bathhouse and suggested that they should send for a veterinarian.

"Listen, Walter," answered the alderman. "When I get a cold, what do I do? I take me a good drink of whisky. Now what is good for humans is good for elephants, only they need more of it. What Princess Alice needs is a quart of good Egandale whisky."*

Colburn produced the whisky, and he and Coughlin forced it

---

*A product of Sol Friedman's distillery.

down the throat of a squealing Princess Alice. Halfway through her ordeal, Princess Alice suddenly relaxed and began to drink of her own accord. The next morning when Bathhouse decided to renew the treatment, Princess Alice seemed positively eager. As the morning sun came out and the barn warmed, the Princess became lively. She squealed and trumpeted, tossed straw on her head, and looked belligerently upon the workmen who were repairing the hole she had made in the barn. Then suddenly the Princess, unchained this time, went swaying along the stalls, snorting gleefully at the frightened horses and cattle, aiming at the hole. The workmen scattered, and a moment later Princess Alice was gamboling in the snow at the top of a little hill, defying all who would come to claim her.

Thereafter Princess Alice was a confirmed alcoholic. In the summer she was given the run of the ball park. On rodeo days a good many of the patrons came in high spirits, redolent of liquor, and with a bottle or two on the hip. Princess Alice would sniff eagerly, then mince coyly up, and choosing a particularly sodden customer, beg for a drink. Never again did Princess Alice become intoxicated. She drank like a lady. After a few dainty gurgles, she would go swaying off into the outfield, her poor, crippled trunk curved proudly, her little eyes shining, thinking the thoughts elephants think when they are particularly happy. Princess Alice never got back to the Lincoln Park zoo. In 1913 she again caught cold during a winter storm, and died.

4

Oddly, in spite of his indulgence of the misbehavior of Princess Alice, Alderman Coughlin had one iron-clad rule for his Zoo Park proper: No Drinking. Enforcing this order during part of every summer was Sol Friedman, who had the whisky-selling concession in the Chicago Levee. Sol fancied himself an animal trainer and loved to visit the park. When the animals refused to perform for him he blistered them with a sizzling blasphemy that left veteran Colorado bullwhackers pop-eyed with envy. During times when Alderman Coughlin was away Sol assisted Colburn in the management of the park, and frequently produced a roll of bills when the money ran short. For the zoo continually lost money, in spite of the fact that Coughlin never ceased to expand and improve it. Still, he was happy to enjoy at once the healthy air of the open spaces and the honky-tonk noises of his First Ward's gayer regions. Coughlin never quibbled over expenses. He counted his losses and grinned.

The alderman's attempts to inveigle Chicagoans other than politicians to his Colorado Springs retreat were not very successful. At one time he proposed to establish a travel bureau which would organize tours of the nation, said tours to stop a few days at Colorado Springs as one of the country's chief spots of interest.

"My main object in these trips is to educate a lot of yaps who thinks Chicago is th' only place in the world," Bath confided to Hinky Dink. "Most of them New Yorkers, when they get a hundred miles from Broadway, think they're campin' out. Let me tell you they ain't th' only ones. There are more yaps to th' square inch in Chicago than there are in Oberlin, Ohio. Why, there's lots a people in Chicago who ain't never been west of th' Desplaines River, or south of Grand Crossing.

"My idea is to take a few of these yaps around th' country and show 'em a few things. We could go to Colorado Springs and to the zoo and to the Garden of th' Gods and to Pike's Peak. Then, maybe next summer, we could go to New York and Atlantic City. And in th' winter I could take a tour to New Orleans and Florida."

The Bath's scheme, announced in the newspapers, didn't work. Most Chicagoans lacked aldermanic passes to travel on.

Still, many politicians did visit the Zoo Park, and even former President Theodore Roosevelt invited Coughlin to call on him at the Antlers when he again stopped in Colorado Springs. The Bath became interested in placer mining on his estate, industriously worked a cradle, and then dug a shaft believing he would find gold in one of the foothills. No gold was discovered, but the Chicago politicians enjoyed healthy outings with pick and shovel, working up splendid appetites for Bathhouse John's home-grown steaks.

5

In the summer of 1908 Carter Henry Harrison was again in California, leaving leaderless his wing of the Cook County Democrats. Roger Sullivan seized the opportunity to take control of the Illinois delegation to the Denver convention of the party, although loyal followers of Harrison forced him, in the Springfield state convention, to pledge himself to the third-time candidacy of William Jennings Bryan. Thus pledged, Sullivan had the nominal support of Bathhouse John and Hinky Dink, and even that of former Mayor Dunne. A kind of peace had descended upon the Cook County Democrats, disturbed only by the activities of fat little Bobbie Burke, who, also supporting Bryan, sought to muster up all malcontents for a trip to Denver to contest the Sullivan delegation.

Sullivan himself, who loved automobiles and whose red Studebaker was considered one of Chicago's finest machines, organized a motor caravan to Denver, a daring move, and one successful only after twelve days of driving through parched hinterlands. Hinky Dink and Bathhouse, duly considering the wide desert to the west of Chicago, would risk no such unreasonable strain on a man's throat. A special train with a bartender in every car was indicated. They joined with Johnny Powers to charter such a train.

Bathhouse John for years had been imploring loyal First Warders to visit his Colorado Springs estate. The time had come. Hinky Dink selected thirty trusted followers who should witness the wonders of the Zoo Park, and Bathhouse went out ahead to prepare for their coming. For his delegation Hinky Dink had reserved two cars of the special train, and he took a private car for himself. It was called the $50,000 Special, and, boasted Johnny Powers, it cost $15,000 before it even turned a wheel.

The evening of July 4 the convention Special stood in the Burlington station, bedecked from cowcatcher to rear platform and back again with bunting, flags, Bryan and Sullivan banners, placards lettered "Boost Chicago!" and a few blazing likenesses of Mlle Chooceeta, brown-bellied hoochy dancer then performing with much success at the Trocadero burlesque. Aboard, in the baggage car, in preparation for the journey, were 800 quarts of champagne, 150 quart bottles of whisky, 100 boxes of cigars, 40 packs of cards, 20 quarts of gin, and 8 crates of lemons. Said Henry Carroll, Jackson Street bridge tender and quartermaster for the trip: "It's a long, hard and dusty run. We don't want to have to drink water out of the Platte."

It seemed that most of downtown Chicago had turned out as the Kenna-Powers boys marched to the train. First there was a forty-piece band blaring, "There'll Be a Hot Time in the Old Town Tonight." The band was followed by the white-shirted, whiskered Lakeside quartet, singing its version of "Illinois," which ended with three rousing cheers for Roger Sullivan for Vice-President. Behind this musical van marched the party chiefs, Hinky Dink and Powers, gorgeous in swallow-tailed coats, white ties and top hats. They carried furled umbrellas, with which they made marching signals to their 200 followers, similarly garbed and equipped, who strung out behind them. The ranks were closed by stay-at-home Democrats of the two ward organizations, followed by some of the ladies of the politicians, who rode in motor cars. A few of the county leaders, among them ex-Mayor Dunne and Alderman Dever, sneaked to the train alone.

As the procession reached the station, red fire was lighted, aerial bombs burst, skyrockets sizzled through the evening heavens, and roman candles belched furiously. Four little boys carried the big bass drum to the baggage car, men laughed and shouted and waved to their women, leaders were hoarsely cheered as they mounted the train steps, and finally a series of whistle blasts climaxed the din. The trip to Colorado was on.

In Omaha the caravan halted for a brief, but uproarious, parade and then proceeded on to Lincoln where Bryan, the Colossus of the West, was astride the great highway to Denver, meeting all delegates and pledging them securely in advance of the convention. Most delegations called at surburban Fairview to inspect Bryan's farm and drink his buttermilk, but such bucolic delights had no attraction for the Chicagoans. They sent word asking would Mr. Bryan please come down to Lincoln to see them. Bryan would. He had advance reports of the mob descending upon him. The meeting with The Peerless One in Lincoln was quiet and brimming with dignity, however, and Mr. Bryan was promised that he would be the next President of the United States. When someone in the Powers group cried that Roger Sullivan would be the Vice-President, Mr. Bryan stared stonily and said nothing.

A few hours after the Kenna-Powers Special had left Chicago, Bobbie Burke and a mob of bawling followers departed aboard another chartered train, similarly provided against the great drouth areas, but led by a band of fifty pieces and brightened by tiny "flags of all nations" at the tips of their umbrellas. The news of the size, the enthusiasm, and the mutual dislike of these contesting delegations aroused all Denver. Thousands waited at the Union Station on July 6 to witness the battle expected when the two trains came puffing in.

The Kenna-Powers Special was delayed, and Burke arrived first. The convention crowds cheered lustily as his blaring procession swung snappily through Seventeenth Street to the tune of "Ain't Dat a Shame" and found its quarters in the Albany Hotel. In a short time the Kenna-Powers express steamed into Union Station. Hours before, the ward heelers and other batmen carried along had been rousing the bleary delegates for their supreme moment. When the train ground to a stop they poured out, emblazoned with banners and badges, flags flying, the band crashing wild tunes. Captain Farrell marched in the lead, a strapping drum major beside him. Directly behind was Hinky Dink and his squad of First Warders.

"Along the route Hinky Dink was immediately recognized and pointed out as one of the celebrities," wrote Arthur Evans for the *Record-Herald*. "He was the smallest man—in stature—in the bunch. He is so short a silk hat doubles his height."

Down Seventeenth Street, amid applauding Denver citizens and convention visitors, the parade moved. As it passed the Albany it was greeted with catcalls and boos, paper bags filled with water, and little receptacles that came down in a veritable shower. The marchers yelled angrily from the street, but the Burke men upstairs advised one and all: "Listen, cul, go soak your heads."

Into the Brown Palace Hotel went the marching club. There it met and conquered the band of the Rose Club of Milwaukee in a battle of music that sent hardened miners and cattlemen screaming for the open air.

Finally the demonstration was over. "Wasn't that a wonder?" said Hinky Dink proudly to Powers. "It reminds me of the First Ward ball. This is the handsomest bunch of men that ever went out of Chicago to a convention. There are real guys in this crowd, no pansies. Think of it! We had a car full of bubble water and not a soak in th' bunch! And another thing," he added, "you notice not a geek in this crowd eats with his knife? I been at conventions where they thought the fork was for spearing bread and eatin' looked like an exhibition of sword swallowing. But not these boys!"

While the rest of the delegation repaired to hotel rooms for alcohol rubs and to stuff cotton pads between their toes, Hinky Dink, his pale eyes alight, marched his thirty First Ward men back to the train.

"Now, boys!" he cried. "Th' real fun starts. Bathhouse is waiting for us."

While the First Ward cars were detached from the train and hooked to a fresh locomotive, The Hink dispatched a message to Bathhouse: "Get us the wagons and the keys to the town. We're coming."

6

Bathhouse, clad in corduroy, his big sombrero held high, his iron-gray pompadour at attention, his black mustache trembling with happiness, met them at the Rio Grande Station. He was flanked by the mayor and elders of Colorado Springs, and an eager, excited delegation of citizens. Beside the station stood six shiny automobiles.

"Hooray!" bellowed Bathhouse. "Hooray for th' First Ward! Hooray for Kenna! Welcome to Colorado Springs!"

The reception The Bath had arranged suddenly turned loose. Six-shooters began popping, a band of Indian warriors that hailed from Little London howled, pranced in a war dance and charged down upon the visitors. Little Hink stood his ground. "Say, Jawn," he demanded nervously, "what th' hell is this anyway? Sounds like home."

Into the cars were packed the thirty, for a trip to the summit of Pike's Peak, from which vantage point Bathhouse, in husky oratory, declaimed the glories of the West. Upon their return, the good folk of Little London had prepared for the Chicagoans' coming at the Zoo Park. Among the carrousel and shoot-the-chutes, the deer and bears and howling venders, popping rifle ranges and screaming calliopes, a picnic feast had been spread, champagne bottles chilled, and pails of foamy beer nestled among big blocks of ice.

"Barbecue and corned beef and cabbage!" shouted Bathhouse. "Eat up, men!"

While The Hink and his friends sported in Colorado Springs, convention affairs proceeded in Denver. Bobbie Burke's delegation was refused credentials, as even Burke must have expected, and an Illinois caucus was held in the Brown Palace. Sullivan was candidate for national committeeman, but he was opposed by the loyal Bryan followers, who had been instructed by Bryan himself to vote against him. To the caucus went one Pat White of the

First Ward, carrying a proxy to act for Delegate Kenna. Sullivan, after a battle, was elected national committeeman.

"My God!" cried Hinky Dink, when he returned to town with Bathhouse and learned of the vote in the caucus. "When I went up to Jawn's I appoint Pat White my proxy to vote against Sullivan. An' what did the son-of-a-bitch do? He mixes his orders an' helps elect him!"

7

But it was Bryan's convention. He was nominated on the first ballot following a demonstration that shook the Denver auditorium to its foundations. The quick nomination of The Great Commoner left the town hungry for more excitement. It seized upon Bathhouse and Hinky Dink. Wherever the First Ward aldermen went they were pursued by noisy throngs, until finally the city assigned them for their protection an honor guard of Denver Boomers, eagerly hospitable men in white felt hats and white linen dusters who represented the Denver Chamber of Commerce. Visiting newsmen sought out Hinky Dink for interviews. "What," they asked him with reportorial slyness, "do you think of water as a drink, Mr. Kenna?" The Little Fellow had an answer.

"Water is the greatest thing we have today," he told them, "and I'm in favor of more of it. Especially I'm in favor of more in the sprinkling carts of Denver. I love water. Why, I owe my nickname to th' old swimmin' hole. Th' boys called me Hinky Dink. If it wasn't for me swimmin' in good old water as a kid, th' chances are I'd be plain Mike Kenna today. And you take Bathhouse here. He couldn't of got his start without water, could he? Water certainly made him.

"Of course," the Little Fellow added with a grin, "now an' then we like to mix a little of it."

EVERYBODY IN SOUP AN' FISH

I

THE summer had been a gay one. The winter of 1908 promised to be even gayer.

What if Bryan had lost to William Howard Taft in November? There would always be other elections. Mayor Busse had shown signs of becoming a liberal, and Bathhouse John and Hinky Dink were riding high. And the war chest was about to be replenished. The First Ward ball—Bathhouse John's "Derby"— was drawing nigh, was it not? For a lush decade and more, this ball had been a symbol of wickedness to those so persistently eager to regenerate The Bath and Hinky Dink, but despite denunciations and railings it only got bigger and worse. The First Ward statesman looked hopefully forward for the new campaign against it to begin.

The conflict soon renewed. Even as the tickets were being printed the reform drums began to thunder savagely, and Arthur Burrage Farwell, fervent president of the Chicago Law and Order League—the scornful First Warders called him Arthur Garbage Farwell—drew up for the edification of Mayor Busse a scorching report on the 1907 ball, of which the *Tribune* had written:

If a great disaster had befallen the Coliseum last night there would not have been a second story worker, a dip or plug ugly, porch climber, dope fiend or scarlet woman remaining in Chicago.

At that ball, Farwell indignantly noted, some 20,000 guests had slopped up 10,000 quarts of champagne and 30,000 quarts of beer. Riotous drunks had stripped off the costumes of unattended young women, maudlin inebriates collapsed in the aisles, a madam named French Annie had stabbed her boy friend with a hat pin, several toughs suffered broken jaws when they tried to rush a filthy "circus act" in the Coliseum annex, and a thirty-five-foot bar was smashed to bits in one of a hundred free-for-all fights. All but two of the aldermen—and those two were ill at home—had attended, and the profits for Bathhouse John and Hinky Dink had been over $20,000.

This, stormed Farwell, must not happen again. He led a delegation of church men and civic leaders into Mayor Busse's offices.

"A real description of the 1907 ball is simply unprintable," said Farwell. "You must stop them from putting another on this year. You must stop this disgrace to Chicago. You must stop it in the name of the young men who will be ruined there."

"What do you want me to do, gentlemen?"

"You can refuse a liquor license. That will stop them. Mr. Busse, you cannot in good conscience issue the liquor license for this affair. Suppose you had a young friend whose character and life you prized highly. How would you like to have such scenes of debauchery as are allowed at this ball to bring degradation and perhaps destruction to your friend? Prevent a repetition of this vile orgy!"

The mayor squirmed and considered the First Ward's voting power, which extended even to enfranchised Republicans. He was sorry, he told the visitors, but a liquor license already had been issued. Privately Busse confided to intimates he thought Farwell was exaggerating the evils of the affair. Could a broad-minded city like Chicago afford to be prudish when in Berlin Olga Desmond had danced in the nude before the Society for the Propagation of Beauty, with the approval of Kaiser Wilhelm?

The reformers refused to be stopped. Farwell's plaints were echoed by the Christian Endeavor League, the Chicago Methodist Social Union, the Episcopal City Missions, Dean Charles T. Sumner of SS. Peter and Paul, a two-fisted crusader against vice, and the Reverend R. A. White, fiery pastor of the People's Liberal Church. The Reverend Mr. White turned the attack on former

Alderman Charles Gunther, who headed the board of directors of the Coliseum. "What's the use of berating Hinky Dink and Bathhouse John, the prostitutes and dive keepers?" he demanded from his pulpit. "You don't blame a lot of hogs for wallowing in the mire and mud. Go after the Coliseum directors who make a sty for the swine in your civic parlor!"

But Gunther held that a contract was a contract. The Bath and The Hink had paid their $1,000 fee for the use of the hall and there was nothing to be done about it. Farwell threatened to ask Governor Charles S. Deneen to call out the state troopers, but Coughlin and Kenna, scorning the tumult and the mound of petitions daily rising higher in Mayor Busse's office, went jubilantly ahead, ordering supplies, personally selecting the decorations for the bars and bandstand, and supervising even the smallest details, such as collecting five-dollar fees from each of 200 waiters eager to work the night of the ball.

2

A few days before the gala occasion, the *Tribune* decided to come to the assistance of Farwell and his group. On December 7, there appeared on the newspaper's front page this announcement, bold and black:

The Tribune wishes to announce that it will print a list of every respectable person who attends the First ward ball next Monday night. Every effort will be made to make the "among those present" as complete as possible.

The opponents of this affair believe that publishing the names of attendants will keep business men and the better grade of politicians away and come pretty close to making the affair a failure from a financial standpoint. All of which might mean the abandonment of the ball in the future and force Kenna and Bathhouse to resort to other means to raise campaign expenses.

"OK," muttered Kenna. "Let 'em stay away." But he feared

the *Tribune* had struck a potent blow, for the big money circulated at the balls had in the past been brought by respectable sports who came to see the demi-monde frolic, to look over new girls the madams might have on display, and to spend with complete abandon. To insure as large an attendance as in 1907 The Hink took charge of the ticket sales himself, with Ike Bloom second in command.

Quotas were doubled and redoubled. If a house had two more girls than in the prior year, it received fifty more tickets. If a provisioner had increased his sales in the Levee, he got a greater number. If a barber had been given the free right to set his peppermint pole on the sidewalk, he dispensed tickets to his customers to show his appreciation of such favors. Every saloonkeeper and theater owner in the district was handed an extra block of tickets to be sold to their friends and patrons. Bloom even shipped pads of tickets to resorts miles from Chicago on the theory that businessmen patronizing houses in such distant areas need have no fear of recognition by *Tribune* reporters.

Here and there in the Levee a stubborn resident defied the order to buy. Harry Thurston, manager of the Palace of Illusions, a low South State Street burlesque house, was a newcomer to Chicago and ignorant of First Ward tradition. When Bloom's aide called, Thurston flatly refused the tickets and threw his visitor into the gutter. Two hours later a squad of police swooped down upon the Palace of Illusions, seized Thurston and fourteen ebony and lightly clad "Devotees of the Danse Oriental," and hauled them to the Harrison Street station where all were charged with presenting an indecent performance. After a few hours in a stuffy cell, during which time a policeman who often accompanied Bathhouse on pre-election tours described the wonders of the First Ward ball and the First Ward club's great need of money, Thurston pleaded for an opportunity to buy tickets. He was accommodated almost at once, and half an hour later Thurston's terpsichoreans were again receiving the plaudits of the clientele at the Palace of Illusions.

Big Jim McCallum, a State Street saloonkeeper notorious for his ugly disposition, also refused his quota. On the next day the brewers who financed his establishment sadly informed him that restricted finances forced them to foreclose on a $16,000 mortgage. McCallum closed his saloon and disappeared.

The aldermen had other obstacles than balky constituents. The Reverend William O. Waters of Grace Episcopal Church sued in Circuit Court for an injunction to restrain the Coliseum Company from fulfilling its contract to rent the hall. Hot arguments were heard by Judge Albert Barnes, but he finally held with Levi Mayer, appearing for Coughlin, that a contract was indeed sacred and inviolable. The Reverend Mr. Waters, was the judge's wry suggestion, should himself go and censor the Derby.

"That vindicates the ball," chortled The Bath. "Let 'em censor. We're willin' to let anyone come down and see how good a ball is run by good fellows."

Then, on December 13, two nights before the party, a bomb was hurled at the rear of the Coliseum. Bathhouse John immediately blamed the reformers. Farwell said the deed was the work of First Ward hoodlums. The explosion did little else than shatter a few windows up and down Michigan Boulevard and Wabash Avenue, but it did throw fears into some of the law-enforcement officers. State's Attorney John E. Wayman and Chief of Police George Shippy both asked The Bath to make some kind of compromise with the reformers.

Coughlin pondered a bit and shouted to the reporters who came to see him, "All right, we'll compromise." He winked broadly. "We won't let parents bring their children. There! No kids allowed. What's more, we don't want any disorderly characters, people who get a load up somewhere else and try to say they got it at our Derby." He winked again and laughed loudly. "Yah, even preachers can come—if they behave themselves and promise to stick by the rules."

Such effrontery sent the town's ministers into greater rage and a hasty final protest rally was called in the Church of the Covenant at Belden Avenue and Halsted Street. The crowd heard vigorous denunciations of the ball, sang "Abide with Me" spiritedly, but could arrive at no plan for effective action. On the Levee the henchmen of The Bath, called together to receive final instructions, warmed up to the rollicking strains of "Mariutch, she danca da houtcha ma coutch, down on Coney Isle!"

"Boys, this Derby is gonna have tone," The Bath announced. "You guys all got soup an' fish?"

"Nah, nah!" was the shout. "Dey cost t'ree bones," yelled a slugger at the back of the room.

"Well, you gotta dig up," replied Bathhouse John. "Everybody in soup an' fish. This Derby's gonna have tone."

From the force assembled Coughlin made careful choices, preparing for possible trouble with the reformers. Pickpockets were detailed to duties outside and informed they would be run out of town if a single complaint was received against them. Two hundred husky young ward heelers, professional collectors and sluggers were given jobs as bouncers and handed red ribbons to pin to their lapels. Trusted precinct captains and First Ward job holders, among them a quaint character named First Search Hansen—so called because, as coroner's deputy, he was always first to go through a corpse's belongings—were named cloakroom custodians and given blue ribbons. Over all these save the pickpockets, who answered to William (Billy) Skidmore, Ike Bloom was general factotum. All was ready.

3

On the day of the ball Hinky Dink was sunk in habitual gloom, but The Bath never had been livelier. He went early to Meyer Newfield's for a final fitting for his specially designed costume, and devoted most of the afternoon to personal preparations for the festivities.

In the evening, while thousands already were jamming Wabash Avenue clamoring for the Coliseum doors to be opened, The

Bath hastened to a meeting of the city council. It was imperative he attend, since he was conducting a battle to prevent unanimous award to a low bidder of a $3,000,000 contract for a new city hall.

The council was assembled and in order before the alderman arrived. Business halted abruptly as he entered the chambers, and the council members watched expectantly while he strode to his seat near the rostrum. His long thick form was wrapped in a huge greatcoat. A red muffler was wound about his neck. He carried his shining silk topper in one hand and his pink kid gloves in the other. Quite unaware of the awesome effect of his splendor, he seated himself.

His colleagues gasped. The Bath intended to sit through the meeting without removing his greatcoat, notwithstanding the heat of the hall and the affront to aldermanic decorum. There was a moment of whispering among a little knot of aldermen and then Councilman Mike McInerney arose. He cleared his throat and began:

"I have a resolution which I wish to address to His Honor, the Mayor. 'Whereas, the splendor of Alderman Coughlin's dress has not only delighted his friends but has made the city council famous the world over and, whereas, it is reported that Alderman Coughlin has spent the last four hours adjusting his wardrobe for use at the famous First Ward ball, therefore, be it ordered: that the mayor be and he is hereby directed to appoint a committee of three to cause Alderman Coughlin to remove his overcoat.'"

A hasty vote was called and the resolution carried. Coughlin rose with great dignity while his colleagues and the gallery craned to catch a glimpse of his newest creation.

Alderman Bathhouse John flung aside his cloak and stood revealed. The council cried out in amazement. For The Bath was in a dress coat of somber black, in trousers as conservative as those of the most prosaic usher at Dean Sumner's cathedral. The only bold effects were his lavender cravat and a wide red sash across his broad bosom. At first the aldermen applauded and then they burst into wild cheers. The Bath sat down, voted against the con-

tract award, then hastily seized his coat, hat and gloves and sped
to his waiting carriage.

4

When Alderman Coughlin reached the Coliseum more than
15,000 persons were packed into Wabash Avenue and the streets
and alleys about the building. Trolleys on Wabash and State
were stalled, and 100 extra policemen sought to control a mob
that pushed and jostled and chanted in unison, "Let us in! Let
us in!"

Passage ultimately was cleared for The Bath. He entered, conferred briskly with Kenna, checked the ticket-takers, ran a quick
eye over the festooned boxes, saw that the bartenders were ready,
spotted the ushers and bouncers in their proper places, and then
joined The Hink again.

They exchanged pleased glances. "OK!" shouted Bathhouse
John. "Let 'em in."

The doors of the Coliseum swung open and the tremendous
pack outside poured in like a debris-laden flood breaking its gates.
The revelers swarmed over the dance floor in wild disorder, pushing and stomping, screaming and cursing at their slower neighbors
ahead. It was a madhouse at the very beginning.

Some guests, already drunk, sang ribald songs and others
bawled out for their favorite ladies of the Levee. Ticket-takers
were overwhelmed, bouncers were swept into the mob, ushers ran
about howling "Order! Order!" The railings of the gaudy boxes,
as yet unoccupied by the madams and the various entourages,
cracked and crashed. The crowd surrounded all the bars, pushed
into the annex, thronged the narrow aisles, upset ferns and palms,
packed the bleacher seats and balcony, and even overflowed into
the basement. Tables were overturned, wine glasses smashed,
chairs broken. Some of the guests climbed girders for better views
of the action and some rode piggy-back through the melee. Those
still on the outside tried to smash through the exits and the police,

disregarding the fire hazard, were forced to lock them out. Women fainted and were passed over the heads of the crowd to the barred exits. "Gangway! Dame fainted!" was a recurring cry.

"So close was the press," recorded a *Record-Herald* reporter, "that even those already drunk were forced to stand erect."

In the midst of the human swirl the waiters were marooned and guests snatched food and drink from their trays. All the careful instructions given the bouncers and ushers were useless. No one could dance, eat, drink, nor buy at the champagne bars. The bartenders at the beer tables passed out schooners of suds under threats of the mob and the cash drawers never once opened. Clouds of smoke grew so thick it became impossible to see across the hall. Fights developed when amorous drunks sought to fondle supposedly helpless women, who defended themselves with hat pins. As the air and noise grew oppressive, the crowd inside surged to the doors. But the crowd outside still wanted to get in. The two groups roared and fought, cursed and blubbered. The Bath wrung his hands and bellowed for the police. The Hink retreated to his box and watched helplessly.

Finally the pressure became so great a side door burst open and a sector of the mob spurted into the street. The Bath and his guards streaked for the opening and hurried out to attempt, in some way, to restore order. Outside they were confronted by Lyman Atwell, a photographer for the *Record-Herald,* who with Wyncie King, the paper's cartoonist, had just set up a tripod and camera to record the wild scene. As Bathhouse approached, Atwell set off his flash powder.

"Help! Help! I'm shot! They got a bomb!" yelled The Bath, leaping upon Atwell and throwing him to the cobblestones. His hoodlums manhandled King and the tripod and camera were broken and shattered.

The cry of "Bomb!" helped to scatter some of the crowd and others inside were able to force their way out. By eleven o'clock, a comparative calm prevailed and Henry Erlinger's band struck up "Dear Midnight of Love." A few couples ventured to the dance floor, and bartenders began demanding money for their liquor and got it—or else motioned for a bouncer.

5

Soon the ladies of the Levee began to arrive, fresh and pert despite a half-day shift in their respective establishments. Minna and Ada Everleigh, the perennial queens of the ball, drove up in their broughams, which were drawn by pairs of handsomely matched bays. Beside them was the pick of their house, and the lesser attractions followed in hansoms and hacks. Then came the other people of the red-light district: Frankie Wright, mistress of the famed Library; Maurice Van Bever, the white slaver, and his wife, Julia, of the *Sans Souci;* Big Jim and Victoria Colosimo; Mont Tennes, the gambler; Georgia Spencer, Vic Shaw, Madame Francis, Irene Woods, Zoe Willard, French Emma, the ingenious inventor of the famed mirror rooms.

Each group of madams and girls was escorted by the police as they flounced into the Coliseum, greeted by bawdy tributes from the horde lining the entrance. When they marched into their reserved sections, they stimulated renewed rioting. Men jammed the dance floor and the corridors behind the boxes to be near and ogle the girls from the brothels and perhaps to lay a hand on a soft shoulder. Waiters and ushers fought them back and bouncers formed a gantlet to an exit through which were dragged the most obstreperous of the revelers. At the end these were tapped lightly but expertly on the head and then tossed outside for a breath of air. The Levee queens, in their *mousseline* waists and daring directoire gowns, Merry Widow and floppy plateau hats, sat proudly in their boxes and inspected the scene. Most of them wore huge gleaming rings and heavy strands of pearls. Even the Everleighs, always modest in their dress, had expensive gems pinned to their quiet gray gowns.

At midnight the moment for the Grand March arrived. There was a flourish from the band, and the crowd, quieted from sheer exhaustion, settled back. The Bath elbowed his way to the Everleigh box, bowed to the sisters, who rose gracefully to take his arm. Then, flanked by Minna and Ada, a covey of the demimonde and a bouncer corps, The Bath withdrew to the south end of the hall. The various madams, pimps, and prostitutes lined up behind. Hinky Dink sidled into front-line position and the Grand March, the exuberant display of the best the Levee had to offer, began.

Down the floor the procession advanced slowly, twenty-five abreast. The crowd, forming a great semicircle, pushed in for a better view. Ahead of the marchers pranced The Bath, his elegant black pumps treading daintily on the polished floor. He loosed his hold on the Everleighs and extended his arms, keeping time to the martial music with a delicate waving of his hands. On they came, madams, strumpets, airily clad jockeys, harlequins, Dianas, page boys, female impersonators, tramps, panhandlers, card sharps, mountebanks and pimps, owners of dives and resorts, young bloods and "older men careless of their reputations." From the annex came the spawn of the city, cheap and dissolute women and whining seedy bums who gamboled and gallivanted on the outer fringes of the march.

As the procession approached the palms and ferns at the north end of the hall, The Bath signaled to Bandmaster Erlinger for the evening's theme. "Hail! Hail! The Gang's All Here!" sang thousands of voices. The turbulent crashing of these robust strains marked the end of the march, the general unmasking: the revelry was ready to begin in earnest.

6

Now the wine merchants started the pace by stacking the champagne bottles high on the tables. Each merchant had a quota of $1,500 to spend. Free drinks were dispensed to all who could press near the railings and provide containers for the precious stuff. One young woman draped herself over the edge of a box, like a clothesline wash, and commanded: "Pour champagne, cul, pour champagne into me mout'." The wine merchant ignored her and she continued to dangle until a policeman dragged her away.

In the royal aldermanic boxes were various men who seemed to be having a gay time but took special care not to be recognized by any *Tribune* reporters. These men, who remained masked, were important lawyers, railroad executives, prominent businessmen. Here, too, were Johnny Caverly, Johnny Powers, Bob Cantwell, one of Coughlin's lawyers, little Andy Hoffman, The Bath's boyhood chum, and other special friends of the First Ward monarchs. Matrons of the Harrison Street police station, all of their expenses of the night paid by Coughlin, giggled in an adjacent box.

The Everleighs spent at the rate of fifty dollars an hour and the city's young rakes clamored about their box, demanding a sip of champagne from a lady's slipper, a rare innovation said to have been introduced on a memorable visit to the famous brothel by Prince Henry of Prussia. Ike Bloom, noting the growing pyramid of empty bottles, rushed over. "Keep it up, Minnie!" he shouted. "You're th' only live ones here!"

But there were other live ones. Big Jim O'Leary, the southside gambler who had hired a hundred women to sell First Ward ball tickets to out-of-town stockmen in his South Halsted Street saloon; Big Jim Colosimo, Polack Ben Zeller, Matt Hogan, Fred Buxbaum, Ed Weiss, Tom McNally and other lordlings of the First bought plentifully and the bottles stacked high. It was a custom of the ball that an empty bottle was never removed from a table. Piled tier upon tier, the mounds of empties permitted the aldermen to see at a glance how the evening and the finances were progressing.

As the party drew on to a hectic finish, the beer drinkers in the annex began to venture toward the boxes. The girls in peek-aboo waists, slit skirts, bathing suits and jockey costumes relaxed and tripped to the floor, where they danced wildly and drunkenly with their overjoyed bumpkins. One harlot, in sheer waist and tight-fitting velvet trousers, reeled to the box in which sat, like a Sphinx, Dean Sumner, who had come to observe and report to his reform crusaders. She stared at the good dean and winked, beckoning him to follow her to the dance floor. He waved her away sternly.

"I intend to stay until it's all over," Dean Sumner told a near-by reporter. "You can say the ball is an ever-increasing drunken revel."

Hinky Dink, preparing to leave, for it was past three o'clock in the morning and long after his habitual bedtime hour, was less critical.

"Why," he snorted, just the least bit tipsy from too much champagne, "it's great! It's a lallapalooza! There are more here than ever before. Those reformers tried to blow up th' place an' look what they got for it. The *Tribune* thought people was gonna stay away. Well, look at it! All th' business houses are here, all th' big people. All my friends are out. Chicago ain't no sissy town!"

The bedlam raged on. In the annex men and women sprawled together on the tables and the floor. In the main hall fights broke out every two minutes. Drunken men sought to undress young women and met with few objections. Policemen stood at the side watching the vicious scenes and interfered only when the fighting grew too violent. Men in women's costumes conducted themselves in manner described later by Dean Sumner as "unbelievably appalling and nauseating."

Finally The Bath, a bit bedraggled, rose in his royal box. "Give 'em 'Home, Sweet Home,'" he ordered.

Two choruses of the song and the ball was over. The crowd began to disperse, a few to their homes, many to Freiberg's dance hall to prolong the festivities, others to the Pacific Street resorts. Hackmen were kept busy as the weary, maudlin crowd burst into the streets and clamored for transportation.

The Bath was worn and sleepy but he stayed to check receipts.

The result was sad; too many had crashed in without tickets, too many had failed to spend. The profits, he lamented, would be well below $20,000. Well, maybe next year . . . Bathhouse shrugged and clambered into Kidney Bill Tucker's hack and headed homeward.

7

However lurid and lawless the ball seemed to newspaper readers the next morning, the one hundred extra policemen assigned could hardly be accused of neglecting their duties. The police blotter showed eight arrests during the long hours of the Derby. Seven of the malefactors were released without punishment, but Bernard Dooley was convicted and sentenced to work out a fine of twenty-five dollars for trying to enter a building through a rear door.

LEVEE PENANCE

I

THE Levee chuckled at the fulminations of the reformers following the First Ward ball; it laughed uproariously when the police,
hearkening once more to general criticism, raided a few lowly
buffet flats and found nobody home. It doubled with glee when,
in October 1909, Gipsy Smith, the British evangelist, came to the
city, took one look and inveighed, "A man who visits the red-
light district has no right to associate with decent people in daylight. No! Not even if he sits on the throne of a millionaire!"
It laughed the laugh of the unhealthily fat, the sodden and glut-
tonous.

Like Chicago's politicians and businessmen, the masters of the
city's lust had been far-seeing. With changes in population and
the physical characteristics of the city, the vice area had shifted its
place and malignantly expanded. When the old Levee on the
southern fringe of the Loop district was outgrown, a newer and
more elaborate and infinitely viler section sprang up in the choice
area bounded by Clark Street, Wabash Avenue, Eighteenth and
Twenty-second Streets, its vicious tendrils still extending into
other parts of the town. Here was the new Levee, the notorious
Levee, the internationally infamous home of sin and evil, combin-
ing the worst features and elements of the old Bad Lands and
Little Cheyenne. Here were the brothels and peep shows and dime
burlesque houses, the cheap saloons and smelly cribs. And when
the Levee moved south, the boundaries of the First Ward, by the
grace of the council and the state legislature, moved southward
with it, so that Bathhouse John and Hinky Dink reigned on as the
omnipotent lords of this sordid domain.

Around the hub of Twenty-second Street and Wabash Avenue

were concentrated the holdings of the lesser lords. Big Jim Colosimo thrived in his bordellos—the Victoria, at Armour and Archer Avenue, managed by Sammy Hare, and the Saratoga on Twenty-second Street, whose manager was a baby-faced hoodlum named Johnny Torrio, alias Turio, whom Colosimo, growing rich and soft, had imported as a bodyguard from the Five Points gang in New York a year earlier. Along the streets jutting west from Michigan Avenue whore houses lined the cobblestones and pimps and panders and streetwalkers plied their ancient trades. On Armour Avenue there were resorts like the Bucket of Blood, opposite the string of low cribs appropriately called Bed Bug Row— Black May's; Silver Dollar, a name appropriated from Coughlin's saloon; the House of All Nations, with girls from every land purveying to every type of human depravity; a unique establishment blithely named Why Not?; subsidiary houses of Van Bever, the white slaver, who ranked as a foremost patron of the First Ward balls; and Frankie Wright's famous Library. From Cullerton Street to Twenty-second along Dearborn Avenue was brothel after brothel, duplicating in detail the notorious stretch that thirty years before had ranged along Customs House Place from Polk to Harrison Streets. Ed Weiss, leading light in the Coughlin-Kenna organization, who had begun as a pimp in Freddie Buxbaum's Marlboro Hotel, now wed to Aimee Leslie, one of the Everleigh house girls, was prospering next door to the Everleigh establishment. Vic Shaw, the Levee perennial, was a dweller on this street, among such other neighbors as Madam Zoe Millard; Louis Weiss, Ed's brother and manager of the Sappho; Mike Monahan, an ex-footpad; Roy Jones; Harry Guzick, a greasy white slaver; French Emma Duval, and Mesdames Leo and Francis.

Eclipsing all these in fame and splendor was the internationally known house of the sisters Everleigh, set solidly between the brothels of Ed and Louie Weiss. By 1909 the scarlet sisters had been operating nine years, having opened their place shortly after they arrived in Chicago from Omaha where they had thrived in the brothel business during the Trans-Mississippi Exposition. The

284

Everleigh house, at Nos. 2131-2133, was a three-storied, fifty-room mansion erected in 1890 by Madame Lizzie Allen and her man, Christopher Columbus Crabb, a wizened old red-light rooster, at a cost of $125,000. Lizzie enjoyed indifferent success during her tenure and shortly after she died in 1896 Chris Colombo looked about for likely tenants. He found them in Minna and Ada Lester, who chose the name of Everleigh and used their profits from the Omaha venture to refurbish the building as an exclusive and expensive bordello.

The opulence of the place, its choice girls, its exotic reputation among visitors from foreign lands had by 1909 actually made many Chicagoans proud of having such a famed landmark in their midst. During its heyday and since, millions of words, words sentimental, scathing, and neutral, have been written of its wonders.* And those wonders indeed were remarkable, including an amazing gold piano costing $15,000, rare books, costly statuary, rich rugs, oil paintings, golden silk curtains and draperies, gilded bathtubs, solid silver dinner service, twenty gold-plated spittoons each costing $650; gold-rimmed china and glassware. There was a huge ballroom, with chandeliers of cut glass and a hardwood floor of rare woods in mosaic patterns. And the parlors, twelve of them, each soundproof and ornate, one the Gold Room, with furniture encrusted in gilt; another the Copper, its walls paneled with brass; a third the Blue Room, with collegiate pennants and pillows of blue leather on which were pictures of ravishing Gibson girls.

The Everleigh girls were the best in the Levee, "best in the world," said their patrons, comely and skilled in their profession and each selected personally by Miss Ada. No amateurs were permitted to work; a girl had to be a harlot of reputation to join the Everleigh staff and the house's waiting list was filled with some of the choicest talent in the country. For the favors of these women customers paid the highest rate on the Levee. The lowest

*Best accounts are in Herbert Asbury's *Gem of the Prairie,* and Charles Washburn's *Come Into My Parlor.*

charge, ten dollars, was nothing more than an entrance fee to the wine rooms. Fifty dollars for an evening was routine; those who spent less were rarely admitted again unless they happened to be newspaper reporters, for whom the sisters professed great admiration and to whom, though their thirst and ardor were great and their purses thin, larger privileges were granted than to the offspring of the wealthiest State Street merchants. Wine was twelve dollars a bottle in the parlors, and three dollars more in the bedrooms. Dinners started at fifty dollars a plate, including wine but no sirens. Rich men came, less wealthy men too, when they could scrape up enough for one memorable night.

Everywhere the names of the sisters Everleigh and the names of Bathhouse John and Hinky Dink, their reputed protectors, were intertwined. You no sooner said, "Yes, I'm from Chicago," than your companions wanted a full description of the fabulous Everleigh club, the remarkable sisters, and the even more remarkable aldermen.

All his life, Bathhouse John maintained he had never passed beyond the front doors of the Everleigh house. Whether he did was never quite established, although it was always possible in the city-hall corridors, when the aldermen were bored, to stir up quite a discussion on this point. What was important, however, was the protection which Coughlin and Kenna afforded the two girls—and how well they were repaid for it. When Lizzie Allen had lived she and Crabb made their payments regularly and without fail to the bland men of the Coughlin organization. So it was with the Everleighs. So it was with the Ed Weisses, the Harry Guzicks, the Vic Shaws and the others. All of the plans Mike Kenna had carefully laid back in 1897 had progressed splendidly, and by 1909 with the district thriving, everybody paid. No longer were the collectors thrown into the street. They no longer needed even to make calls; the pimps and madams brought their payments in. They paid to Jim Colosimo, to Andy Craig, to Jakey Adler, to Hank Hopkins. They even paid to Bathhouse John personally. Minna Everleigh in the nine years had contributed

$65,000, not including special assessments. Once Bathhouse John himself called for such an extra payment. "We're tryin' to get a bill stalled down in Springfield that wants to make you stop selling booze or wine in this place," was his excuse. Minna paid Bathhouse by check, the appropriate arrangements were made with the legislative pirates, and the bill was defeated.

A personal payment, however, was rare; by check, rarer. Kenna, whose proudest boast was that he never entered a house of ill fame and never permitted women to enter his saloons, did not himself receive a direct payment. Usually the agents of the brothel keepers, as they had once come to Bill Gaffney's, now trekked to Ike Bloom's grimy office in Freiberg's hall, where Ike and his brother-in-law, Sol Friedman, welcomed them and snatched the envelopes. When they were tardy Bloom, who had no scruples about entering a brothel, would stalk in and make his demands. If they still were remiss there was a word or two at the city hall, and it was highly likely that a police raid would follow. From the thousands of dollars collected, weekly or by the month, all in the organization got their shares. The amounts varied with each collection, sometimes a few hundred dollars, sometimes a thousand. But the money rolled in regularly, the fame of the Levee increased, the houses became larger and more numerous, white slavers scoured the country for women, new lures and charms were devised to attract patrons.

2

Upon this welter of whoredom, Gipsy Smith gazed and pronounced it wicked, vile, outrageous. God, preached the fervent evangelist, was on his side, and God and he together would bring the people of the Levee to a realization of their sins.

The Levee jeered on. "De guy's bats," sneered Andy Craig. "He's th' nuttiest yet," chorused the ladies of the red lights. "He's a nuisance," sighed the madams and the pimps. Even many of those who attended the evangelist's meetings wondered what good words would do. Action was needed. Action, it developed, was what Gipsy Smith planned.

At a revival meeting held in the Seventh Regiment armory on October 18, 2,000 faithful joined Gipsy Smith in singing evangelistic hymns, heard him pour brimstone upon the rulers of an iniquitous Chicago. Then, led by a Salvation Army band, the 2,000 swarmed into the street and tramped purposefully the mile north toward Twenty-second Street, the bass drum booming a hollow tocsin to the righteous and the curious of the neighborhood. As they marched they were joined by hundreds, then thousands, and when they approached the outer limits of the brothel district there were nearly 20,000 persons in the throng, good churchgoers, simpering scoffers, stiff-jawed reformers and callow youngsters, cynical men who leered at the women marchers, and honest men with the gleam of the crusade in their eyes.

Once inside this "Hellhole of Sin," chants for the damned souls within came from the lips of Gipsy Smith's flock. "Where Is My Wandering Boy Tonight?" and "Where He Leads Me I Will Follow" they sang. And, more in bewilderment than respect, the Levee remained mute. The professors ceased tinkling on their pianos. The women stayed in their rooms, the window shades were drawn, the doors remained closed. The gratified evangelist led his weird procession to the Everleigh house where he knelt and prayed and his followers sang hymns. Then Gipsy Smith led those still interested to the near-by Alhambra Theater, there to offer further prayers for the denizens of the Levee.

But thousands of men and boys, many of them inside the forbidden city for a first time, stayed behind. In a twinkling, the Levee became itself again. Up went the window shades, the doors swung open, the pianos began to jangle, the women leered and lured from their portals. The night, which had begun on such a spiritual plane, became the busiest in many years. The happy mongrels who kept the brothels were delighted. Among them only Minna Everleigh seemed to keep any perspective. "We are glad for the business of course," she admitted, "but I am sorry to see so many nice young men coming down here for the first time."

So were many other citizens. They deplored the evangelist's sensationalism. They called Gipsy Smith a crank, and his followers misguided, harmful zealots. "Bosh!" they replied to Gipsy Smith's firm assertion: "My experiment has been worth while. Great good has been done."

The immediate results were perfunctory. Police Chief Leroy T. Steward pretended to be greatly disturbed at what he saw in the spotlight thrown on the vice district and he ordered the usual "cleanup." So a few houses on the western fringe of the district were raided and a threat was made that Ike Bloom's place would be closed. The newspapers professed to take a serious view of the situation, the august *Tribune* praising Chief Steward's action in a front page story headlined:

VICE LOSES POMP

IN LEVEE PENANCE

The reporters went to hear the one voice which, when it spoke, carried authority in the district. "I don't know what they want from us here," said Hinky Dink Kenna. "Me, I don't have a thing to do with the women. When it comes time for elections I go down there and go around the bars, but never into the houses where the women are. But the women have to be somewhere and they might as well be where they bother the least people. You can't put them out into the residential districts."

That, he hoped, was that.

3

Hinky Dink was wrong. By the day public feeling against his empire grew more bitter. The march of Gipsy Smith had been a jab in the city's arm, awakening it as Stead's fulminations had done in 1893. The reformers grew alert once more, and when Bathhouse John Coughlin in November announced his plans for the annual First Ward ball, protesting committees converged angrily upon the city hall. So great was the pressure on Mayor Busse that he refused to issue a liquor license. Bathhouse John and Hinky Dink held their Derby nevertheless, the saddest, most colorless, dullest affair the First Ward had ever seen. Tony Fischer's band played a benefit concert in the Coliseum, and only 3,000 persons came.

That disastrous Derby was the last ever held in the First Ward. But if the Levee thought that the reformers would be content with this victory it erred woefully. The righteous element had drawn blood, and it intended to move in for the kill.

Unable immediately to force decisive action by Mayor Busse, the crusaders paraded again. This time nearly 4,000 members of the Women's Christian Temperance Union, with Mrs. Emily C. Hill, chairman of the Cook County chapter, at their head, marched through the Loop streets and into the city hall. The ladies wasted no time. They crowded into the office of Mayor Busse and demanded that he fulfill his duties.

"Mr. Busse," cried Mrs. Hill, "you are the mayor and you must abide by the laws. There is a city law which forbids the operation of one of these—these houses of ill fame. Obey that law and carry it out!"

"Yes," said Busse, "I've already decided on an investigation."

"The Lord be praised!" beamed Mrs. Hill. "Oh, Mr. Mayor, Mr. Mayor, pray for divine guidance and you will conquer all!"

"Yes, yes," snapped the mayor. "I plan to do so, but at the proper time and at the proper place."

Four days later from another quarter, at a mass meeting of the Church Federation comprising some six hundred congregations in Chicago, came a further blast against the Levee. There Dean Sumner, reporting on his personal investigation into life in the district, concluded his talk by demanding that the mayor appoint a committee of men and women to make a complete report and to devise realistic means for exterminating the evil. A resolution to this effect was unanimously passed and acclaimed as "the first sure step toward the eradication of this blot upon the city."

On March 5, 1910, Mayor Busse was forced to act. He selected thirty persons of prominence to form a Vice Commission, with Dean Sumner as its chairman and United States District Attorney Edwin W. Sims as secretary. On the roster of the commission were upright and upstanding men of the community, among them Dr. W. A. Evans, city health commissioner, Julius Rosenwald, Professor Herbert L. Willett of the University of Chicago, Judge Harry Olson, chief justice of the Municipal Court, and Merritt W. Pinckney of the Juvenile Court.

The committee was handed an appropriation of $5,000 by unanimous vote of the city council, even Coughlin and Kenna voicing no objections. What, mused these statesmen, could anyone clean up with $5,000? One single block on Armour Avenue cleaned up more than that on a Saturday night. Besides that, the political winds were blowing favorably. Bathhouse John had been apprised by their long-time mayoral favorite, Carter Henry Harrison, that he would make another attempt to win a fifth term. With Carter Aitch back in the city hall, they reasoned, it would put a stop, once and for all, to this talk of smashing the Levee. Carter Aitch was a man who recognized the impossibility of driving sex under cover, was he not?

So, while the detectives of the vice commission scurried about town, probing into every parlor house from the expensive Everleigh club to the reeking cribs in the Maxwell district on the west side, Kenna and Coughlin steamed ahead with their political plans.

4

The Democrats, as usual, were split wide by the Harrison candidacy. Former Mayor Dunne, backed by the so-called radical elements, promptly entered the race, and Roger Sullivan, growing stronger year by year, put up Andrew J. Graham, who was supported also by Johnny Powers, George Brennan, and Hot Stove

Jimmy Quinn. Only Coughlin and Kenna of the gang aldermen remained to besmirch the candidacy of Harrison. Dunne, lacking the support of any of the Gray Wolves, was proclaimed "clean as a hound's tooth."

As the battle within the party progressed there appeared to be no serious campaign issue. Vice was evidently going to become a thing of the past, now that the Vice Commission was digging up the facts. The traction problem had been settled during Busse's tenure for at least twenty years by the public's approval of the compromise ordinance, first launched in the Harrison regime. The Gray Wolves were in hopeless minority, although the MVL still yearned for an absolutely pure council. It seemed that the campaign would merely offer the voters their usual alternatives of two absolute evils: Democrats or Republicans. But The Bath and The Hink soon changed that by making themselves the chief issue in the contest.

For the primary election, the two aldermen loaded the rooming houses as usual. Voters were brought in from the Oak Forest poor house and from the Hospital for the Insane at Dunning. It was The Hink's candid opinion that the Dunning inmates were more perspicacious politically than the most erudite of Republicans. When the voting was over it was evident that the First Ward, once again, had secured Harrison's nomination, for he had defeated Dunne by a city-wide margin of 1,556 votes, and in the First Ward alone his majority was 2,424 votes.

Immediately Dunne demanded a recount. "The crooked First Ward nominated my opponent," he declared. "His whole margin of victory can be counted in fraudulent First Ward votes."

"That's all a lot of talk," replied Kenna. "We had all the university investigators, civic leaders and uplift politicians in town guarding the polls. Believe me, if anyone had tried any fraud in the First Ward, there would have been twenty people to tell about it in no time. It was as clean as could be."

Alderman Charles E. Merriam, the University of Chicago professor who was the Republican nominee, thought otherwise. He made the First Ward support of Harrison the campaign issue.

"The First Ward, under the guidance of Hinky Dink and Bathhouse John, encompassed the defeat of Mayor Dunne," said Merriam. "Now they are at it again. They are going to attempt to repeat. This time I am going to be the victim. But if I am elected mayor I will ruthlessly smash the powers they have exercised so insolently and defiantly and I will put an end to their domination of vice and gambling. Hinky Dink," he added, "has put aside his mask of humility and buffoonery and has come out to name Chicago's mayor. Hinky Dink and Bathhouse John must be crushed."

Hinky Dink and Bathhouse John could not afford to be crushed. Their empire was at stake. In recent elections they had not exerted themselves to a great extent to keep their council seats. They had been too busy with other matters, Coughlin with his zoo and his "poetry," Kenna with his collections, his trips to the Mount Clemens baths, and his real-estate interests at Hot Springs, Arkansas. Now, with Harrison as a candidate, they determined to make their finest showing. Hinky Dink at once raised the price of votes from twenty-five to fifty cents, ordered the saloonkeepers to increase their quotas of floaters, and summoned to his board of strategy the most impressive gathering of politico-criminal brains since Prince Hal Varnell had directed the nomination of Bathhouse John in Billy Boyle's loft in 1892. In addition to Coughlin, McNally and Andy Craig, the First Ward campaign committee listed such luminaries as Ike Bloom, Sol Friedman, Ed Weiss, Big Jim Colosimo, George Little, Andy Begg and Mike Boston, the last three small-time brothel keepers; Pat O'Malley and Mont Tennes, saloonkeeper and gambler; Harry Williams and Jim Leathers, bartenders; Ike Rodrick, professional bondsman and secretary of the First Ward Democratic Club; and John Griffin, a Kenna protégé and the Republican representative in the state legislature. Griffin's inclusion was a blatant admission of the reform charges that the First Ward, through bipartisan deals, elected not only Democrats, but Republicans as well.

Harrison defeated Merriam in a close fight, by a majority of 5,193 votes. In the Coughlin-Kenna ward he garnered 4,283 votes, 3,647 more than his Republican foe and the largest plurality in any of the city's thirty-five wards. Hinky Dink was returned to the council by a majority of 4,886, and the *Tribune* headlined:

CARTER HARRISON ELECTED
THE SAME OLD FRAUDS IN RIVER WARDS
HINKY DINK LEADS THE RAIDS

But William Randolph Hearst, with whom Harrison had made his peace, predicted, "Harrison's election means new, clean Democracy in Illinois. I rejoice in his election." And Blind Billy Kent, inveterate foe of the aldermanic plunderbund and once head of the MVL, sighed: "Well, after all, Carter Harrison is an honest man."

WAYMAN'S CRUSADE

I

In June Dean Sumner's Vice Commission presented its report. It listed 1,020 resorts, operated by 1,880 keepers and madams, and housing at least 4,000 prostitutes, most of these in the segregated district in the First Ward. The commission's totals were not to be disputed. It had dispatched its representatives into every district and building suspected of purveying to the city's sex hunger—brothels, wine rooms, dance halls, call flats, buffet flats, assignation houses, saloons, lake excursion boats, cheap cafés, and even ice-cream parlors and amusement parks. They seemed to have interviewed nearly everyone engaged professionally in the sordid business—veteran madams, inmates, panders and street walkers, department-store and factory girls who augmented their low wages in the call houses, white slavers, saloonkeepers, bartenders, managers of cribs and brothel chains.

Crime and vice, boomed the report, yielded an annual revenue of $60,000,000, with net profits of $15,000,000 a year to the men controlling the system. "Chicago's vice annually destroys the souls of 5,000 young women," it said, estimating that hundreds of young women were ruined by the system in addition to those accounted regular professionals. It condemned the segregation of vice in the First Ward and called for the extermination of the Levee. It demanded the establishment of a police morals squad and a morals court to receive the cases of derelict women. It recommended the teaching of sex hygiene in the schools. It dug deep into the causes of the civic cancer, citing the "Economic Side of the Question." "Is it any wonder," asked the commission, "that a tempted girl, a girl who receives only six dollars a week working

294

with her hands, sells her body for twenty-five dollars per week when she learns there is a demand for it and men are willing to pay the price?"

On and on, for nearly 400 flaming pages, went the report, reciting case after case, remedy after remedy. It indicted no one city or police official, but demanded a realistic appraisal of a serious problem, to be followed by action to solve that problem and, once and for all, to eradicate the evil.

2

Coincident with the issuance of Dean Sumner's report, an aroused public forced the Civil Service Commission to open hearings into charges that the crime-vice-gambling syndicate centering in the First Ward had on its pay rolls practically every high and intermediary police official in all the infamous sections of the city. The finger was promptly put on Hinky Dink by one Ben Hyman, who testified that he and three other men had been forced to pay to the First Ward syndicate a total of $1,700 a month in order to get Hinky Dink's permission to operate out of Chicago the gambling boat, *City of Traverse.* Another witness, Henry Brolaski, who described himself as a "reformed gambler," said that a brief but turbulent war a few years back between Mont Tennes, handbook king and close friend of Kenna, and Big Jim O'Leary and Tim Murphy, who were rebelling against Tennes' rule, was ended only when Hinky Dink intervened as mediator. "Some guys said Little Mike got $40,000 out of it," mumbled Brolaski, who immediately was denounced by Kenna as a "big liar." The commission, from other witnesses, learned that Tennes now was the virtual monarch of all the handbooks, poolrooms, crap and poker games in Chicago and that the good friends of the Tennes syndicate were the Big Fellow and the Little Fellow.

The public, fortified by such revelations, demanded a shutdown of gambling and vice. Honest Herman Schuettler, who had been protesting the fix in the police department, was empowered to close the handbooks, and in five days he had arrested 1,825 operators. Then Mayor Harrison issued the first of many fateful orders: "Move all disreputable women from Michigan Avenue at once and close all disorderly flats."

Along this boulevard, from Twelfth to Thirty-fifth Streets, were some 1,000 prostitutes, ensconced in call houses and disorderly hotels, among them the notorious Arena at No. 1340. For years dwellers in adjoining residences had complained of the indecent activities. Now the mayor decreed that all this must cease. He informed the Levee that further brazen taunting of the decent element would not be tolerated. The loose women were to remain off the streets and out of the saloons. Solicitation by pimps and cadets had to stop at once.

The police struck, the girls moved to other neighborhoods, and for a week or more there was a breathing spell. Then the mayor, eager to deliver a telling blow, obtained a brochure published by the Everleigh sisters detailing the attractions of their peerless house. It was about as lurid as a well-written travel guide, but it was filled with photographs of the house, its hallways, and the famed parlors. Said a sedate preface:

THE EVERLEIGH CLUB

While not an extremely imposing edifice without, it is a most sumptuous place within. 2131 Dearborn street, Chicago, has long been famed for its luxurious furnishings, famous paintings, statuary, and its elaborate and artistic decorations. "The New Annex," 2133 Dearborn street, formally opened November 1, 1902, has added prestige to the club, and won admiration and praise from all visitors. With double front entrances, the twin buildings within are so connected as to seem as one. Steam heat throughout, with electric fans in summer: one never feels the winter's chill or summer's heat in this luxurious resort. Fortunate indeed, with all the comforts of life surrounding them, are the members of the Everleigh club.

This little booklet will convey but a faint idea of the magnificence of the club and its appointments.

The deliberate advertisement of a brothel was, of course, an unspeakable assault upon public decency, and on October 24 came the command to an astonished Chief John McWeeny: "Close the Everleigh club."

There was a collective gasp from the city, from the residents of the Levee to the plump housewives usually sheltered from news of the resorts by their solicitous spouses. Mike Kenna rushed to Mayor Harrison's office. His visit was perfunctory.

"On the square, does this go?" he asked. "For keeps?"

"As long as I am mayor."

"O. K."

Emissaries of Ike Bloom sought to convince the sisters that if they would contribute $20,000 they could escape closing, but they refused. They attempted to reach Mayor Harrison directly, and, failing, sought Chief McWeeny. He was not to be found.

"Well," sighed Minna, "I know the mayor's order is on the square. But I'm not worrying about anything. You get everything in a lifetime."

On the last day of its existence, the club was filled with the feverish gaiety of the doomed. Couples pranced about, ran up and down the broad stairways, danced with abandon in the gleaming ballroom. Ada and Minna brought out champagne for their favorite newspapermen, the orchestras played merry tunes, patrons drank toasts to the morose professor. At midnight the guests were in a high humor, insisting that the closing order was merely another false alarm. But an hour later, four squads of police arrived from the Twenty-second Street station. A burly lieutenant stepped forward.

"Sorry, girls," he said. "If it was us, you know how we'd be."

"All right," shrugged Minna. "What do we do now?"

"Better clear out. Tell everybody to go home."

So it finally had happened. The "ultimate sanctuary of vice," the symbol of everything wicked in the very wicked city of Chicago, had toppled. In a few hours the Everleigh club was a tomb. Its girls—"the best in the world"—wept floods of tears that streaked their painted faces, then they sped away to accept offers from brothels all over the country. And the sisters packed their belongings, locked the front doors, and went off on a jaunt to Europe. Before they left, they were comforted by Ike Bloom and Big Jim Colosimo. "You ain't got a thing to worry about," advised these gentlemen. "We'll have you back in no time. We'll get the Little Fellow and Johnny Coughlin to work on the mayor."

3

But the mayor was unyielding. "Vice in Chicago," he intoned, "can exist only under the most stringent regulations. The Everleigh club has been advertised far and wide. I am against this advertisement of Chicago's dives and I intend to close up all such places. Proprietors of dives must remain in certain restricted districts."

His forays continued. Chief McWeeny was handed a list of fifty flats in the Cottage Grove Avenue area and instructed to clean them out. The Civil Service Commission plagued McWeeny too, and demanded that he draw up a list of disorderly houses and then take proper action. Women without escorts in saloons and cafés were ordered to leave, and if they refused were arrested.

This continuing harassment of the Levee was beginning to dull some of the Coughlin-Kenna enthusiasm for Harrison. You couldn't reason with a man who was obeying the edicts of the reformers, they lamented. You couldn't be sure of a man who, forgetting his past quarrels, had now allied himself with William Randolph Hearst, whose newspapers constantly belabored the aldermen of the First Ward. What was more, it was poor politics to stay with a sinking ship, and despite his brave stand for decency Carter Harrison's craft had sprung some leaks in the fall of 1912.

And Roger Sullivan, he of Ogden Gas, seemed the man who would fire the inevitable torpedo.

During the strife preceding the national Democratic convention in Baltimore, Harrison, backed by Hearst, had pledged himself to the support of Champ Clark of Missouri, veteran speaker of the House of Representatives. Roger Sullivan would not commit himself to a choice, but he entered his own slate of convention delegates in opposition to the Harrison-Hearst crowd. Both delegations, each claiming victory in the election, descended upon Baltimore, but it was Sullivan, the adroit manipulator, who made a back-room compact with the supporters of Woodrow Wilson. With their aid his delegates were seated, and when the endless balloting was tensest, Sullivan clinched the nomination for Wilson by bringing up a battery of Illinois support.

Sullivan was a kind of hero of the convention, and the new political boss of Illinois. For he had dealt Harrison a deadly blow by his maneuvering, and the mayor's delegates, Hinky Dink and Bathhouse among them, had left Baltimore long before the voting sessions were under way.

"The only good thing about this convention," growled Hinky Dink, "was the people of Baltimore. Wherever you went, someone mixed a mint julep for you."

4

Back home again, the portent was inescapable. Harrison was slipping. And Harrison was attacking the Levee. For Bathhouse John and Hinky Dink the choice was fast becoming one of deserting the "little push" or deserting the mayor. They did neither, and both. They accepted the blandishments of the Sullivan crowd, but they also exhibited a kind of perplexed steadfastness to Harrison. But their hopeful search for signs that "Our Carter" would eventually relent were unrewarded. The plaguing of the underworld continued, although in quieter vein, sparked to a minor climax now and then by the exhortations of the Committee of Fifteen, which could always find indecent saloons and dives when the police could not.

Then, from across the Indiana line, came young Virginia Brooks, as fervent an anti-vice crusader as Gipsy Smith. She had launched a successful war in her home town of Hammond by handing her women followers axes and promising to chop down any brothel which refused to obey police orders. The keepers jeered, but, with public indignation marshaled behind the virtuous Virginia they had been cowed into a condition of semi-respectability. In Chicago Virginia employed her talent for the dramatic again. She organized a huge parade of more than 5,000 men, women and children, who marched in a torrential rain through the streets of the downtown district, while a band blared and a chorus of preachers sang "Onward, Christian Soldiers!" and Boy Scouts, Campfire Girls, Bible students, Epworth League members, Catholic Temperance Society boys, and children of members of the W. C. T. U. tramped along. There was an enthusiastic rally in Orchestra Hall, at which the fiery Miss Brooks insisted that Mayor Harrison, Chief McWeeny and State's Attorney Wayman should be driven from their offices in disgrace for their failure to clean up the Levee.

Wayman responded almost immediately. He had been denied renomination for his office by the Republicans, and thus had nothing to fear. "There is an apparent effort to lay the blame for Chicago's vice at my door," he declared. "Nobody is going to be able to say that I protected the social evil."

He obtained warrants for the keepers of 135 resorts, called in his own detective force, and told them to raid and keep on raiding. "Go into every place you find open," he ordered. "Every place in town will be closed when I go out of office."

He was as good as his word. On October 4 the raids began, and they continued for a week. Every day and night Wayman's police stomped into forbidden territories and were met by humble and puzzled women or found empty flats, hastily deserted. None was untouched. Ed Weiss, Roy Jones, even Big Jim Colosimo were seized, then released on bail. Every house, from the largest to the tiniest, yielded up a quota of prisoners. The ruck fled, or cowered and snarled, hoping for help. But none came.

Mayor Harrison, however, refused to participate in Wayman's crusade. He announced that his police were not taking part in the raids. A referendum should be held, he suggested, to determine whether Chicago wanted segregated vice, but no one paid him any attention. In the churches there were prayers for Wayman, who a week before had been condemned for failing in his duty.

One last gesture of defiance the crumbling Levee did offer. In the midst of the raids, Ike Bloom and the other bosses organized their own Committee of Fifteen and advised the girls cast from their shelters to don their most strident clothes, paint more gaudily than usual, then parade up and down the residential and business streets, ringing doorbells of respectable dwellings and asking for lodgings. This order the unfortunates of the district carried out promptly, beginning with an invasion of several hundred into the staid Hyde Park neighborhood. The strumpets were rebuffed by the scandalized housewives, but even if they had been accepted they would have laughed and fled, for the strategy was to direct attention to the need for a segregated vice section and the probable consequences for the residential districts if Wayman should succeed. A few public shelters—the Beulah Home, the Florence Crittenden Anchorage and the Life Boat Home—offered sanctuary to the women, but only one of the bedizened thousands applied for entry.

Finally Mayor Harrison joined once more in the drive. In November he threw all political considerations overboard. His first objective was to clean out the Levee, and house after house was padlocked. Curiously, Freiberg's hall was unmolested, but the wiseacres predicted it would soon go. The girls fled to other areas, or temporarily left the city. "Lay low!" was the order from the First Ward. The newspapers sent out their reporters, who came

back with the unanimous report: "The Levee is dead forever."
Trumpeted the *Tribune:*

The end has come. Their women are scattered. The open, tolerated, police regulated, segregated district is gone from Chicago. A single smashing blow ... has accomplished the task.

5

Such satisfaction was premature. No single blow was going to smash the Levee. Men like Ike Bloom and Big Jim Colosimo rarely surrendered their shrievalties with a shrug and a sigh. Ike had Bathhouse John and Hinky Dink; Big Jim had them and more. He had the pasty-faced, sad-eyed lad named Johnny Torrio. And Johnny Torrio had his cousin, Roxy Vanilla, alias Vannelli, alias "The Yellow Kid," the plug-ugly murderer from Montana; Mac Fitzpatrick, alias W. E. Frazier, the bad man from the Barbary coast; Mike Merlo and Joie de Andrea, homicidal Sicilians; Jew Kid Grabiner, Billy Leathers and Chicken Harry Gullet, a pimp and bribe-passer. This cozy gang of specialists in mayhem and murder had protected Big Jim from the violence of the Mafia which was beginning to plague him, they guarded his whore houses and his Wabash Avenue café, they jack-rolled drunks, they slugged and killed in the newspaper circulation wars, they kidnapped and enticed girls for Big Jim's white slave ring, they hired professional rapists who prepared the innocents for the horrors of the brothels. They operated with the connivance and co-operation of the First Ward police.

For the commander of the Twenty-second Street district now was Michael F. Ryan, called White Alley for some obscure reason. Ryan was beholden to none but Michael Kenna. "Police Chief of the First Ward," the boys called him, and he loved it. He took his orders from Hinky Dink, and his advice from Big Jim. If they conflicted with orders from the city hall, the city-hall instructions were ignored. "Mike Kenna is my friend and he's a good fellow;

he gives food to the hungry and feeds the poor," White Alley Ryan explained to his friends.

Under such a protector the scum of the Levee began to creep back. Frieberg's hall continued on its merry way, Jim Colosimo's café opened its doors again, and the brothels quietly began bidding for business. Roy Jones opened a new saloon, which quickly gained notoriety when a police stool pigeon named Ike Henagow was shot and killed there by a quaint character called Duffy the Goat. The call flats worked furtively, but busily. Chief McWeeny continued to issue frantic orders and White Alley Ryan tossed them into his wastebasket.

Mayor Harrison might have thwarted the resurgence of the Levee by removing White Alley Ryan, but he was still attempting desperately to retain the political allegiance of Coughlin and Kenna. Little Hink, however, was definitely straying. In the summer of 1913 County Judge John E. Owens, a close friend of Harrison's, had brought down the wrath of the Little Fellow when he summarily erased hundreds of names from the First Ward poll lists on the ground that many of the men whose signatures appeared were either completely fictitious characters, or long deceased. Hinky Dink had sworn vengeance, and now, in the midst of the inchoate resurrection of the Levee, when Harrison began forming his political slate, both The Hink and Bathhouse refused to support Owens. Harrison insisted they must. But still he delayed any final attempt at force.

As the mayor dallied, Roger Sullivan entered the fray. He visited Hinky Dink, promised him aid in his fight against Judge Owens, and then asked for the support of the First Ward for his candidacy for the United States Senate. A bold proposal this, but Kenna and Coughlin, casting sentiment aside, promised their help to Sullivan. For the first time in seventeen years, they were arrayed against Harrison!

The mayor was furious. Sullivan he regarded as his arch-enemy, a conniving scoundrel who would sell out the party for his own gain. In unison with Senator James Hamilton Lewis, runner-up to Bathhouse John as the peacock of the Democratic party, and former Mayor Dunne, Harrison declared for the candidacy of Congressman Lawrence Stringer. He invited the aldermen of the First Ward to participate in the Stringer boom, but they stood by Sullivan. This was their reply to the raids on the Levee, to the command to back the detested Judge Owens.

A showdown fight loomed, but action was delayed as the politicians prepared for the spring municipal campaign.

THE CHALLENGE OF MARION DRAKE

I

Nor once in twelve years, not since the tempestuous campaign of 1902, had Bathhouse John's claim to a seat in the council been seriously threatened. Every two years the Municipal Voters' League indicted him on his record. Every two years an aldermanic hopeful was led to the sacrificial altar and ignominiously slain thereon, amid pagan shouts from the followers of Alderman Coughlin.

But by 1914 a long fight of women suffragists for the franchise had reached a victorious climax in Illinois. Governor Edward F. Dunne, the former mayor, had signed the bill giving the women the right to vote and the ladies undertook their new duties with an alarming eagerness. Not only could they vote but, joy of joys, they now were permitted to run for office. At once, they organized the Cook County Suffrage Alliance, they infiltrated into scores of newfangled political movements, and in Chicago they vied with Harold L. Ickes in running the affairs of the Progressive party.

It was inevitable as the aldermanic elections approached that the girls would fight the boys for places in the city council. In eight wards the women filed their petitions. Harriett Vittum, president of the Woman's City Club, told the Poles of her home ward, where she was head resident at Northwestern University settlement, "I stand for free immigration." Mrs. Bernice Napieral-ski, a one-time seamstress and mother of six children, was candidate in the Twelfth Ward, and Mrs. Julia Agnew of the Thirty-first was another Progressive party hopeful. The Socialists entered women candidates too—Josephine C. Koneko, Lida E. McCermut, Gertrude R. Dubin and Maude J. Ball.

But all these were soon shoved from the spotlight by the startling announcement that the Progressives would do battle against Bathhouse John in the First Ward with a woman candidate! She was Marion Drake, firm chinned and tight lipped, intelligent, a woman of experience and character, and a woman of great self-reliance and energy. She once had been a stenographer and court reporter for various attorneys. Later she took and passed the bar examinations. She was an early suffragist and first president of the Cook County Suffrage Alliance. She was animated in conversation, spoke rapidly, earnestly and to the point, and swayed crowds with her eloquence as did Bathhouse John with his ungrammatical ramblings.

Merry, indeed, was the reaction in the First Ward to the challenge of Marion Drake. In the Workingmen's Exchange and at Freiberg's hall the jests flew, many of them indecent, most pointless as whistles in the dark. Hinky Dink and Bathhouse sneered in public, schemed in private. Soon after Miss Drake filed her petition for the Progressive nomination a young unknown named Karl N. Wehle announced that he, too, was seeking that party's support.

"I gotta lotta pals want me t' run in tha Foist Ward," said Wehle, dumping a bundle of petitions on the desk of an election-board clerk. "I t'ink I got a chanct."

Miss Drake and her fellow candidates went to work. They checked every name on Wehle's petition, interviewed hundreds of alleged signers. Then Miss Drake rushed with her evidence of fraud to the election commissioners. Hundreds of the names were those of people not in the Progressive party. Other persons said they had never signed the petitions. John Longnecker, Miss Drake's attorney, alleged that young Wehle was a minion of Bathhouse John's. Carefully the election commissioners examined proof, found that of the many names only three were legitimate, and erased Wehle's name from the ballot. The action was acclaimed by the newspapers. Said the *Tribune:*

The decision of the board assures the nomination of Miss Drake and provides the setting for one of the most strenuous campaigns in the city. Miss Drake's supporters propose to bend every energy to secure her election and in so doing will seek to enlist the women of the entire city in making the campaign in the First Ward.

2

"We're turning the searchlight on the First Ward!" was Marion Drake's first cry. She had no money to start with, but friends loaned her enough to rent headquarters in the heart of the ward. She strode into Freiberg's hall and dared Ike Bloom to rent her an adjacent vacant store. He chased her and her stiff-collared followers into the street, and she finally obtained space at 2222 Indiana Avenue. There, in a big-windowed store front, she placed a live drake which sat complacently eating corn and lettuce leaves.

Hundreds of women rushed to Marion Drake's banner, some of them giddy socialites looking for excitement, others serious-minded social workers and suffragists thirsting for the defeat of Bathhouse John. Miss Drake used them all, sending the bravest to canvass the toughest precincts, the Bloody Ninth and the Terrible Fifteenth, where derelicts from the Levee had settled. Before the fight was a week old Miss Drake charged that her supporters were being threatened and warned to stay away from her. An Italian janitor at the headquarters was slain in a mysterious assault and Miss Drake declared: "I'm not saying he was killed in connection with the campaign. I simply make the flat statement that he was murdered. As a result lots of people are afraid to work for me."

But there seemed to be no dearth of people anxious to see The Bath vanquished. The Progressive club passed a hat at its meetings and collected $200. A phonograph company sent a record player, and a piano maker sent a piano upon which the Drake

campaigners thumped victory songs. One unidentified man printed 50,000 campaign dodgers without charge. A loop store donated
cloth for banners. Into the headquarters from hundreds of citizens poured letters, each with one and two-dollar bills.

All was not bright and easy for Miss Drake. Adamant dry
leaders frowned upon her because she was considered a liberal
and was known to approve the sale of beer, and free lunches.
Miss Drake made her position clear early in the campaign.

"We are not fighting the saloon," she declared. "We are fighting commercialized vice and all that it implies. We are seeking
to regulate conditions which have made the First Ward notorious." All she wanted, asserted the woman candidate, was to be
an honest alderman, to give the city and the First Ward a clean
record. Bathhouse John, Miss Drake told audiences that marveled
at her courage, was a symptom of a terrible disease and would
cease to exist once crime and vice were strictly suppressed. And
she promised to suppress crime and vice.

"Do the voters of the First Ward relish having their ward
known the country over as a place where it is dangerous for citizens to walk abroad at night? Where the young, the decent and
the pure are enmeshed in the web where all that is good, decent
and pure is dragged out of them?" This was typical of the Drake
attack, and it seemed effective.

Still the Coughlin cohorts pretended to laugh. A red-nosed
precinct captain, asked for a statement by Mary O'Connor Newell,
of the *Record-Herald,* spat vigorously and scoffed: "We ain't
worryin' about Miss Drake. We don't even know she's runnin'.
That's our man!" And he directed Miss Newell's gaze down along
the Clark Street saloons, where from every window shone huge
posters with handsome likenesses of Bathhouse John:

WE KNOW HIM BEST!
JOHN COUGHLIN, OUR FRIEND

Hinky Dink soon arranged for a rally in Central Hall, near

Ike Bloom's establishment. A big band led a parade through the ward to the auditorium, whose pink walls were blazing with green banners urging, "VOTE FOR JOHN J. COUGHLIN FOR ALDERMAN OF THE FIRST WARD." The South End Volunteer Band played martial music and a First Ward quartet, accompanied by a weird assortment of two banjos, a guitar and cello, struggled with the latest ragtime number, "Bobbin' Up and Down." For the occasion, The Bath wore conventional black. After the hall was well filled, Alderman Bathhouse John stepped to the platform. He gazed a moment in conscious dignity. Silence enveloped the room.

"Fellow Democrats," he called out, "permit me to present as your presiding officer the Hon. James J. Ahearn. Gentlemen, I present James J. Ahearn."

A portly, smooth-shaven man rose and stood by the alderman. "Fellow Democrats," he said modestly, "I feel all swelled up on myself to be chairman of this meeting. I present for your approval the Hon. Frank Childs."

A tall, dark-eyed man stepped forward, and after a curt word of endorsement for Bathhouse John yelled: "Are a lot of outside reformers gonna tell you who's gonna be your alderman when Alderman Coughlin has so ably represented you for twenty-two years?"

"No! No!" shouted the constituents.

"All right then!" said Childs. "Go into the ward and tell the people to vote the right way, the Democrats' way!"

3

Undaunted by the increasing activities of the First Ward organization, Marion Drake slashed and fought her way through the campaign. She flooded the district with posters on which Coughlin was caricatured as a horrible beast, shown sucking money from defenseless women. This excited Coughlin and he ran to the federal post-office authorities, demanding that Miss Drake be arrested for distributing obscene printed matter. "I never did that to no woman!" wailed Bathhouse. "I'm a good family man." But the federal officials turned down the plea. "It's not obscene, but you might try suing for libel," was their advice.

There was no time for lawsuits. The election was only a week away and every moment had to be consecrated to winning at the polls. "All right, I'll get that skirt," threatened The Bath. "No man'll vote for a woman. I'll get her at th' polls."

From the MVL came a blast presumed to aid Miss Drake:

Coughlin, John J.: An insurance broker with other sources of income; one of the original gray wolves of the council; finishing eleventh term with notorious record; . . . held in office by special interests and commercialized vice; once ran a Turkish bath patronized by race horse touts and later was proprietor of the notorious Silver Dollar saloon, a hangout for low characters.

Eastern newspapers and magazines sent their best writers to report on the struggle. The *Outlook* found that the kind of partnership between vice and politics which had made Tammany a byword in New York was highly specialized in the First Ward. Its correspondent paid a visit to a Coughlin mass meeting and reported that the famed alderman's most impressive characteristics were his "size and bushy white hair." In meeting him, the writer observed, "You get the impression he is a kindly character. His arguments are unsound, his grammar inexcusable, his political ideas unintelligible, and yet it is apparent he has the confidence and even the affection of his constituents. He talks their language and he thinks their thoughts and so he gets their votes." The *Outlook* had high hopes for Miss Drake, of whom it said:

Her magnetism is evident at first sight. . . . She is far from being experienced in political matters and she had no idea up to within recent months that she would ever take such an active part in politics.

If Miss Drake was indeed inexperienced politically, she was

learning fast. Her women aides continued to make their house-to-house and flat-to-flat calls; she herself scanned the registration lists for fraudulent entries, and on the speaking platforms she grew fiercer with each oration.

"Bathhouse John and Hinky Dink, his midget partner, are the heads of the terrible vice ring in the city," she shrilled. "Decent citizens should drive them out of the council and make it so hot for them that both would decide a more congenial residence would be on Coughlin's immense estate in Colorado. I am not sure that Bathhouse would not earn more in his amusement park in Colorado by exhibiting himself and his colleague than by the exhibition of the elephants, tigers and jackals he has."

Not only at Coughlin, but at her Republican opponent, a First Ward undertaker named Philetus I. Orme, did she shoot her darts.

"Mr. Orme is not a factor in the campaign and never was intended to be! Mr. Orme was nominated in the interests of Coughlin. He is a straw man, a dummy candidate to be set up and knocked down in the interests of Bathhouse John." Thus she disposed of the silent Mr. Orme, who never uttered a word throughout the campaign.

To her charges that Coughlin was a thief and grafter the First Warders responded feebly. A newspaper writer had promised a story about any shop which presented Miss Drake with a campaign hat. Several did and the Coughlin speakers jeered:

"Yah, graft! Graft! She don't have to talk about graft. That hat she wears on her head is graft. It was just plain given to her, an' if that ain't graft I'd like to know what is."

Miss Drake ignored this attack and kept to the main theme. "The report is that Alderman Coughlin owns a valuable farm in Iowa and is reputed in addition to be possessor of great wealth. *Where did he get it?* From his literary efforts?

"Knowing that Bathhouse John is a modest man in the one particular of any statement concerning the source of his wealth, I will undertake to answer my own question. Alderman Coughlin has wrung his wealth out of the poor, the unfortunate, the vice-

ridden and the criminals of the First Ward. He has capitalized
the misfortunes of a certain class of his constituency. Vice and
crime have flourished to a degree they have not been able to flourish in any other part of Chicago. The First Ward has become a
byword and a reproach!

"Debauchery has replaced virtue, and vice has driven out respectability. There are certain sections of the First Ward where
the chances are against the decent rearing of children and which
self-respecting men and women, unless driven by necessity, will
shun as they would shun the plague."

The Bath's response was fierce. "That dame. I'll beat that skirt
by 8,000 votes, see if I don't! I inherited my wealth. That farm
I inherited from two of my cousins that got killed in a railroad
accident.* What's wrong with me? Not a thing! I'm in favor
of raisin' teachers' salaries and don't have no bad feelin's for anyone. Voters, mark your cross in th' ballot where you see it says
Democratic!"

Miss Drake had one last rally at which the women screamed
for the downfall of Bathhouse John. In the American Music
Hall on the day before election Grace Abbott, leading social
worker and teacher at the University of Chicago, spoke as a representative of the Immigrants' Protective League, declaiming: "The
immigrants are easy for Coughlin to exploit! Negroes are defenseless! Women hate him!" Jane Addams of Hull House,
Charles Merriam, Robert Morss Lovett and Harriet Vittum raged
against The Bath, and a Mancha Bruggemeyer, calling attention
to his remark about beating "that skirt by 8,000," shrieked: "His
mouth is foul. It should be washed with soap and water. Won't
you do it for him tomorrow?"

4

Ninety-five thousand strong, the women voters of Chicago

*Coughlin's farm in Polk County, Iowa, was inherited in July 1912 from George
and James Hanley of Des Moines, his cousins who were killed in an automobile accident near Geneva, Illinois.

marched to the polls. Everywhere there was a new activity, the occurrence of incidents which caused hardened campaigners and poll watchers to shake their heads in bewilderment. In the Sixth Ward, Mrs. George A. Soden, vice-president of the Illinois Equal Suffrage Association, carried sandwiches and milk to precinct workers. In other sections the women bustled about challenging voters, ejecting drunks, making the most of what Mrs. George Bass, another leading suffragist, called "the first day of our full citizenship."

But, as Marion Drake had shouted in the early days of the campaign, the searchlight was still on the First Ward. Early in the morning the Coughlin workers hustled their floaters into the ward from outlying districts. Miss Drake's protests went unheard, likewise her plea to the police for special officers. "Carloads of bums are being delivered at intervals in the Fourth Precinct," she charged. "There," she added, "they stumble out and are greeted by a man in green who hands them specimen ballots."

They were not specimen ballots. It was Hinky Dink's chain-voting system in operation. Genuine ballots had been obtained and were marked for Bathhouse John. A floater deposited one of these in the ballot box, and brought back with him the ballot he had received at the polling place. This he surrendered for a fee, and it was marked and given to another floater. That insured that every vote paid for was really cast for Coughlin.

Two Australian suffragists, Dorothy Pethick, an aide of Mrs. Sylvia Pankhurst, the patron saint of all suffragists, and Margaret Hodge came to the First Ward to watch the election. They offered the prediction that the woman's vote would curb the liquor traffic in the United States. "One-sixth of New Zealand," Miss Hodge disclosed, "has been voted dry and it is the happiest and most prosperous part of the country."

All over the First Ward Coughlin's workers hustled out the vote. Those in charge on this important day were such gun fighters, sluggers, whore-house keepers and saloon owners as Squiggy Monahan, Andy Craig, Pat O'Malley, Chink Crosby, Joe Buffalo, and the more important Levee leaders, Ike Bloom, Judy Williams, Sol Van Ulm, Jakie Adler and Jew Kid Mendelsohn. In the Italian district, Big Jim Colosimo ran from poll to poll telling the dark-eyed voters, *"Colonna seconda, colonna seconda!"* Pat O'Malley, stationed at the old Jones School in the Fifth Precinct, stood at the head of a line of Democratic workers with a basketful of taffy kisses and invited all the women to dip in as they passed inside to cast their votes. In a brothel precinct the girls came in hordes, still in their working costumes. They swore quite blithely they could neither read nor write and asked the judges for instructions, thus affording a pretext to have Democratic judges enter the voting booth to mark the ballots for them.

Whenever suffragettes or Drake workers appeared at the polls, they were pushed aside while the police stared elsewhere. At the end of the day Marion Drake knew that her valiant fight had been a losing one. The first sign that Coughlin had won—though by 5,000 fewer votes than his boastful prophecy—was the shouting in the streets and the extra din in the Clark Street saloons. Ike Bloom came personally to the Drake headquarters to sneer at the downhearted women. "G'wan, take those figures back to your girls," he said, flashing an election bulletin. "That's what we do to 'em when they run against our friend."

Elsewhere in the city the other lady candidates had fared as poorly. But in the rest of Illinois saloons were closed in a thousand districts by the feminine vote on local option. And Marion Drake, after she surveyed the good done, made a last defiant gesture. "I and thousands of others," she vowed, "will go after Hinky Dink next year. If necessary these women will move into the ward. We must make the women realize that this is their problem and that they must fight on the side of civic righteousness!"

THE LEVEE'S LAST STAND

I

FOLLOWING the arduous campaign against the women, Bathhouse John sped to his peaceful retreat in Colorado, after spurning the suggestions of his friends that he effect a compromise with Mayor Harrison. The mayor meantime had installed Captain James Gleason, famous for breaking up the notorious car-barn-bandit gang, as chief of police, and, at the suggestion of the Committee of Fifteen had placed Major M. C. L. Funkhouser and W. C. Dannenberg in charge of a special Morals Squad, specifically instructed to resume raids on the reviving red-light district. Then the mayor revoked Roy Jones's saloon license and Jones, drinking heavily, soon blurted out to a police stool pigeon that Big Jim Colosimo and Maurice Van Bever had entered into a plot to kill both Funkhouser and Dannenberg.

On July 3 Chief Gleason decreed that Colosimo's place and others still operating in the Levee must be closed. White Alley Ryan ignored the order. Irate, Chief Gleason told Major Funkhouser to make a grand cleanup. "We're going to drive out this unofficial Levee," Funkhouser promptly announced. He nodded to Dannenberg. "It's time for a showdown," he said.

Dannenberg, a hot-headed and fearless detective, was anathema to the district. As director of the Chicago federal agents in 1905 he had directed the smashing of the Colosimo-Van Bever white-slave ring and sent Van Bever and his wife, Julia, to prison. State's Attorney Wayman had employed his services in the 1912 cleanup and no man lived who was more detested by the brothel keepers. Captain Ryan had fumed at the appointment of Dannenberg to the Morals Squad, and he was downright indignant when he learned that the red-haired detective had been given special instructions to invade his district. "This district has never been clean," blustered Ryan, "and it never will be. We keep order as well as possible. We don't want no Dannenberg around here. He uses stool pigeons. I won't stand for it."

The Committee of Fifteen, thoroughly approving the assignment to Dannenberg, called upon Gleason to congratulate him on his intended campaign. "Don't worry," the chief assured them, "the Levee will go. It's a fight to the death. It's the Levee's last stand."

The Levee accepted the challenge. Big Jim Colosimo assembled his gangsters at a banquet, attended also by Detectives Big Ed Murphy and Johnny Howe, and Maurice Van Bever, recently released from prison. After champagne had been drunk and the guests had picked the chicken bones clean, Colosimo calmly suggested, "We gotta get rid of that Dannenberg bastard. Let's try th' easy way first, eh? A little cash on d' line." So Chicken Harry Gullet approached Dannenberg and offered him more than $2,000 a month if he would betray Major Funkhouser and protect the dives. Dannenberg promptly arrested Chicken Harry on a charge of proffering a bribe.

Then the raids became routine daily affairs. In a week Dannenberg's squads had seized 2,000 vice mongers and women and cost the district $20,000 in fines. He himself invaded many of the houses, despite the threats and the fact that Detectives Michael McFadden and John Cook of the Twenty-second Street station had carried about the Levee pictures of the morals inspector and his squad members so that the keepers and inmates could recognize them. Dannenberg closed up buffet flats, call houses and all-night saloons and then began to move into the heart of the district, where the larger brothels had reopened.

On July 16 Dannenberg took off from the city hall with a squad, and the news spread swiftly through the vice district. Women were hustled away from the resorts through the labyrinth of interconnecting tunnels, but Dannenberg and his men reached The Turf, a dive at 28 West Twenty-second Street, ahead of the alarm and arrested the women inmates. Then he called the Twenty-second Street station for a patrol wagon. When the squad left it was followed by a mob of cadets, pimps and hoodlums, yelling: "We'll get you next time, you bastard."

The squad proceeded on foot toward Michigan Avenue. Trailing it was the big red automobile of Johnny Torrio, in which rode Roxy Vanilla and Mac Fitzpatrick. The crowd at the heels of the policemen grew larger, the curses came thicker and finally some of the men began throwing rocks. Dannenberg's men stopped in front of the Swan poolroom off Michigan Avenue and drew their guns, while their chief went on ahead. Around the corner came two men from the Detective Bureau, Sergeants Stanley J. Birns and John C. Sloop. Mistaking the plain-clothes men of the Morals Squad for hoodlums, Birns and Sloop opened fire. In the furious exchange of shots, in which some of the bystanders and Vanilla and Fitzpatrick joined, Birns was killed, Sloop was critically wounded, and Joe Merrill and Fred Amort of Dannenberg's squad were shot in the legs. Also wounded were Johnny Caroll, a Dannenberg informer; Frank Langan, and Roxy Vanilla. Edward P. O'Grady of the Twenty-second Street station said later that he had come upon Torrio and Fitzpatrick helping Vanilla into their car and had let them proceed when they said they knew nothing about the shooting.

The tragedy brought disaster in its wake—disaster for the Lords of the Levee. The whole city was aroused. Blame for the shooting was shifted about by the hour. White Alley Ryan insisted that Dannenberg's men were at fault. "They're green cops, looking for someone to pick on them," he said. "They saw the plain-clothes men coming, got scared and cut loose." Some witnesses said that the first shots came from the big red automobile, and when the bullets were extracted from the victims some were found to be dum-dum cartridges, not the .38-caliber type usually used by the police. This development sent officers into the Levee, scouring the joints for the leaders. But all of them seemed to have vanished.

Chicago blamed the shooting upon the vicious Levee, but it was not upon the heads of Colosimo, nor Torrio, nor Van Bever that the real wrath fell. Shrilled the *News:*

This is the answer of the Coughlin and Kenna vice ring to the decent citizens.

And the *Examiner:*

The life of this policeman is part of the price Chicago pays for the dominion of the Kennas.

And the *Evening Post:*

This vicious empire gave Bathhouse Coughlin $25,000 to beat Miss Drake. Now it is collecting by violence and it is the decent people of Chicago who are made to pay.

And the *Tribune:*

There are three reasons why the tragedy of the Levee could not be avoided.

First, in order of importance, is Ald. Hinky Dink Kenna, the absolute overlord of Chicago vice.

The second is Bathhouse John Coughlin. He it is who rubs elbows with that powerful source of graft and revenue, the red-light district. Coughlin takes his orders and does not fear to rush in where Kenna fears to tread.

The third is Captain Michael Ryan. He is Chief of Police of the First Ward. The Hink put him there. The Hink and The Bath keep him there.

The new state's attorney, Maclay Hoyne, opened a grand-jury investigation into the link between vice and politics, and listed

Colosimo, Torrio and Van Bever as the leaders among the vice lordlings. The Civil Service Commission began its own inquiry, at the request of Chief Gleason. Colosimo, returning from his hideout, was arrested by Hoyne's police and lodged in a cell, but was released when neither Vanilla nor other hoodlums would testify against him. Raiders stormed the Levee only to find that Captain Ryan was "raiding" ahead of them, allowing the inmates and keepers to escape. The Christian Endeavor Society called a mass meeting of young people and demanded a final, complete cleanup of the district, and the Committee of Fifteen issued a strong statement:

The Hinky Dinks, Bathhouse Johns, Dago Franks, Polack Bens, Jim Colosimos, Jew Kids, and Mike the Greeks must go! War has been declared on the Levee and commercialized vice. It's a war to the finish!

2

The empire of Bathhouse John and Hinky Dink tottered groggily. State's Attorney Hoyne vowed to emulate his predecessor, Wayman, but Mayor Harrison stepped in ahead of him. The mayor shifted White Alley Ryan to the west side and installed hard-hitting Captain Max Nootbar, one-time student at Heidelberg University and German army veteran, who had a reputation as an efficient and honest policeman. Nootbar was a man who could not be bought. Both Bathhouse and Hinky Dink knew that it would be useless to approach him, so they remained away, calmly oblivious to the dangers, Bathhouse lolling in Colorado while The Hink soaked himself in the baths at Mount Clemens. And the days of the Levee were numbered.

Captain Nootbar shut the remaining smaller dives and then singled out Ike Bloom's establishment for a frontal attack. "Close at one o'clock," was the command. "Balls!" retorted Ike Bloom. "You make a deal, an' we'll be friends." Captain Nootbar replied by kicking little Ike down the stairs of the Twenty-second Street station. Then the doughty German strode to the squad room and tore a handsome picture of Bloom from the wall, hurling it through an open window. He repeated the order: "Close." Bloom rushed into court to seek an injunction restraining the police from raids upon Freiberg's hall. Various lieutenants from Twenty-second Street station, who had been ordered reprimanded by the Civil Service Commission for taking money from the vice lords, appeared in court to testify that they had never seen liquor sold in Freiberg's after 1:00 A.M. While the court pondered the case, Captain Ryan resigned from the department, saying: "I have been made the goat. All I did was carry out my orders." When the court turned down Bloom's plea for an injunction, moody Ike promised he henceforth would bow to the law. "It's all off," he wept. "The profits are falling off because of the fight against vice. We're not even paying expenses. I'll close at one o'clock."

Then came a voice from the Levee's heyday, calling further attention to the workings of Alderman Bathhouse John. It was Minna Everleigh, speaking through the *Examiner,* which had obtained a copy of a statement Minna had made to Chief Justice Harry Olson of the Municipal Court after her club had been padlocked. She had intended previously to offer her disclosures to the newspapers in vengeance for the closing, but had been dissuaded by Colosimo gangsters who vowed to kill both sisters if the affidavit were ever made public. She entrusted the document to Justice Olson, who decided to release it in the interests of public policy.

"In the days when the Everleigh club was being openly conducted with huge profits," began the statement, "all orders came from Hinky Dink Kenna and Bathhouse John Coughlin through the person of Sol Friedman, to whom the aldermen assigned the whisky, taxicab, groceries, and clothing privileges in the segregated district. Insurance had to be taken from Coughlin's company and a choice of four provision stores was in force.

"After the club was closed Ed Little, owner of ten resorts on Federal and Dearborn Streets, came and told me it could be reopened for $20,000. I refused to pay, and others visited me. I insisted I must have the personal promise of the aldermen, and this was refused. Alderman Coughlin telephoned me personally one time for $3,000 to help stop legislation in Springfield. Hank Hopkins and Jakie Adler came and got the check, which was made out to the alderman." The canceled check, she added, was still in her possession. Other payments, totaling over $100,000 in twelve years, had been made in cash.

"I always entertained state legislators free in the club," the statement continued. "George Little (a brothel owner who once managed Jack Johnson, the Negro heavyweight champion) made the collections at the club and took the money to the office in Freiberg's hall. Two detectives from the Harrison street station also collected regularly."

Minna Everleigh estimated that $15,000,000 in graft had been collected in the Levee since it was established in the Twenty-second Street area. Andy Craig, she said, handled problems of legal defense and bonds, with the aid of Aaron Andrews, Hinky Dink's personal lawyer. The price for stopping an indictment on a charge of pandering was $1,000; on a complaint of harboring a girl, $2,000; and on a charge of grand larceny against a client of a panel house, $500.

Minna laid her troubles at the door of Ed Weiss who had enticed some of the Everleigh girls into his brothel, thus violating the Levee code that no other house should vie with the club so long as the protection payments were kept up. Ed Weiss, charged Minna, had influenced the aldermen, urging them not to expend themselves in efforts to save the house from destruction.

"We were supposed to have real protection," she said. "When the Ridgeway and Devonshire Hotels opened on Prairie Avenue, outside the Levee, complaints were made by the Levee keepers to Alderman Coughlin. The hotels were closed."

A scale of protection prices on the Levee also was printed by the *Examiner:*

Massage parlors and assignation houses, $25 weekly. Larger houses of ill fame, $50 to $100 weekly, with $25 additional each week if drinks were sold. Saloons allowed to stay open after hours, $50 a month. Sale of liquor in apartment houses without licenses, $15 a month.

Poker and craps, $25 a week for each table.

Bathhouse John Coughlin and Sol Friedman personally controlled sales of liquor in the Levee, the *Examiner* charged, storing their products in a new $60,000 warehouse in East Chicago. Alderman Kenna, the paper declared, was an important stockholder in a big brewery. That, it sneered, was why the alderman could afford to sell such large schooners for a nickel in his Workingmen's Exchange.

3

The city gasped and watched to see what would befall the aldermen of the First Ward.

County Judge Owens knew what he wanted. He decreed the time was propitious to cleanse the Democratic party by driving Coughlin and Kenna from their well-worn seats on the Cook County central committee. Was Harrison ready for action too? The *Tribune* sent Charles Wheeler, its able political reporter, to Huron Mountain, Michigan, where the mayor was vacationing. They fished, ate a steak dinner prepared by the mayor himself, and then Wheeler put the question: "What about The Bath and Hinky Dink?"

"Coughlin and Kenna," replied Harrison, "are through unless they will support Judge Owens and the entire Democratic slate. I will support Lawrence B. Stringer for the United States Senate.

I am going to cut loose from every politician who will not sign up for the Harrison program. Coughlin and Kenna must go. I have reached the final conclusion that my ideas on the vice question have been wrong. Segregation is not the way. It corrupts the whole law-enforcement agency."

The last thin strands binding the aldermen to Carter Aitch had snapped. Bathhouse and Hinky Dink stood indicted, not because they had organized and sheltered the greatest vice ring in the city's history, not for affording protection to an army of thugs, killers, grafters and hoodlums who for twenty years had preyed upon the city, but because they intended to back the wrong political candidates.

Wheeler's story vied on the front page with the threatened outbreak of war in Europe. Now Bathhouse, thoroughly frightened, hastened home, and on July 28, the day Austria declared war on Serbia, he drove up to the city hall in a shiny automobile and demanded to see Harrison.

The mayor put his case bluntly. "John," he warned, "either you support the Harrison ticket or get out. You must support the entire slate and that means Judge Owens, too. There's nothing personal in this, John. I'm sorry we have to come to a parting of ways. I'm also sorry that Mike Kenna is not here. I would like to tell him just what I've told you."

A week later Kenna slipped into the city, his little eyes ablaze. "I see by the papers the mayor has beat me to it," he cried. "Well, we've been on the outs for a couple of months, ever since I told him I couldn't support Owens for renomination. And the man don't live who is big enough to make me break my word and Mayor Harrison knows that better than anyone else. I won't support Owens or Lawrence Stringer."

"That," nodded Bathhouse John, "goes double in spades for me."

As for his relations with the Levee, Hinky Dink went before the grand jury and readily admitted that Colosimo and Torrio and others of the brothel keepers were his friends. "These conditions was in the First Ward before you an' I were born," he shrugged, "an' they'll be there after we're dead."

In response to public demands that Freiberg's hall be shut down forever, Bathhouse John roared: "Why are they always talkin' about the Levee district? Why am I never asked about the district north of Van Buren, where the world's greatest buildings, the world's greatest department stores, the world's greatest railroad terminals are? Why always harp on the Levee district? I am alderman for more millionaires than all the other aldermen combined. I represent the wealthiest ward in the world an' neither Mayor Harrison nor all the newspapers can put me out of it. I'm here for a fight, if there's going to be one, even if it wasn't of my asking. I won't run away."

Into the Roger Sullivan camp went this experienced pair, and their act sparked a general rebellion against Harrison. Johnny Powers, who was grooming Alderman Jim Bowler, a former professional bicycle rider, for county sheriff, joined up. Hot Stove Jimmy Quinn swore his allegiance. A rising young man in Cook County Democracy named Anton J. (Tony) Cermak, once a pushcart peddler and later secretary of a saloonkeepers' league called the United Societies' League for Personal Liberty, supported Sullivan for the senate in the Bohemian wards, but reserved the right to back Harrison county candidates, a neat bit of political legerdemain. Chicago would some day learn that Tony Cermak was quite a political magician.

In payment for First Ward support Sullivan allowed Hinky Dink to name Judge Owens' opponent in the primary. He named Thomas F. Scully, then a Municipal Court judge but once the assistant city attorney who was suspended for forgetting to prepare his case against the erring Kenna.

While the politicos lined up, the vice raids continued. Nootbar was an amazing mass of energy, and he refused to let up. Ike Bloom's license was withdrawn, then Colosimo's, Torrio's, Johnnie Jordan's, and more than twenty others. Some of the red-light leaders deserted Hinky Dink, and sought to help Owens, a maneuver on which Kenna spat with disgust.

"I had one of my men at an Owens meeting the other day," he said. "It was awful. The biggest gathering of crooks, gunmen, and lousy guys he ever saw. See, they figure th' houses'll get open if Owens is re-elected. Look at those yellow bellies he's got in th' ward—Johnny Adler, Frankie Webber, Joie McGraw, Kid Newman, Jake Wolfson and that Van Bever. I know 'em all. Whore-house keepers and second-story men, every one of 'em!"

Kenna labored like a beaver and on election day he grinned for the first time in months. Scully defeated Owens for county judge, winning the nomination by 1,116 votes, almost exactly his margin in the First Ward. Sullivan, garnering 1,903 votes to Stringer's 419 in the ward, won the senatorial nomination by 70,-000 votes. And, though jolly Roger lost the subsequent election to Lawrence Y. Sherman, his position as Democracy's chieftain was unquestioned, and Mayor Carter Harrison, who had defied the anger of Aldermen Coughlin and Kenna, was a political has-been.

4

But when the city elections approached in the spring Carter Harrison would not acknowledge his downfall. In the primary he contested with Sullivan's choice, Robert M. Sweitzer, and was beaten. In the First Ward, which had furnished his margin of triumph in so many campaigns, he received only 1,098 votes to Sweitzer's 6,105. In the aldermanic fight, the threat of the suffragettes to invade the First Ward was only a memory. But the campaign did not lack fire, for the Municipal Voters' League was out to finish Alderman Kenna as usual. First Ward voters might have been excused for some confusion as to Kenna's real personality when they viewed, side by side, the two most notable broadsides of the fight. The first was a statement from the MVL, the second, from the Sullivan publication, *Public Safety:*

Michael Kenna (Hinky Dink). In council since 1897; utterly unfit; bellwether of the council goats; known to the underworld as the little fellow; "what he says goes"; voted against putting "soft snap" policemen to traveling beat; against protecting street laborers from soliciting jobs from public service corporations; against having a civilian police chief; against city hall investigations by the bureau of public efficiency; for Johnny Powers' building ordinance violation; for Home theater whitewash; for suspending enforcement of theater violation ordinance; for loading park consolidation bill with tax increase; every vote a bad one; listed here not so much to throw light on the workings of Hinky Dink's mind as to show how other aldermen's votes can be appraised by their constituents.

Like his colleague, he has been the target for envenomed shafts and abuse, vituperation and calumny. He has been made the butt for the marksmen of every professional "reform" organization, every cabal of goody-goody cranks, every scheming gang of civic righteousness buncombe that has existed in Chicago for the last 20 years. . . . The mendacious scribblers of the MVL and similar organizations have howled in chorus against him as regularly as election day rolled around and Alderman Kenna has just as regularly been reelected by the electorate of the First Ward.

Alderman Kenna, shouted his speakers, stood for shorter hours and better pay, he had fought hard for the interests of the people in traction matters, and he had the welfare of the humblest of his constituents always in his heart. "It is this quality of inherent justice and true Democracy," sang the paeans, "that has gained for

Alderman Kenna the esteem, confidence and support of the rich
and poor alike."

The voters read and heard these pearls of persuasion, they pe-
rused the indictments by the MVL, they even read, with wide eyes,
the *Tribune's* astounding advice that the only man to vote for in
the First Ward was the Socialist, Lester Phillips. And they voted
for Hinky Dink.

Sweitzer, though, was opposed by a man with great personal
appeal, the ex-football star and former ranch cook who once had
inveighed against the iniquities of Bathhouse John. William Hale
Thompson promised the folks a wide-open town, which meant, to
the Levee, uninterrupted prosperity. So the people voted for Big
Bill Thompson too, and, on election night, the victorious Big Bill
beat on his desk with a beefy fist and yelled, "The crooks had
better move out of Chicago before I am inaugurated!"

The crooks guffawed and set up their gambling outfits, the
men of the red lights sighed in relief and looked for the keys to
the rusty padlocks, and Carter Harrison began to interest himself
in the war in Europe.

THE COLOSIMO INCURSION

I

BIG BILL THOMPSON puffed out his fleshy cheeks and scanned the police lists. Honest old Max Nootbar was lifted from the Twenty-second Street station and shunted to the hinterlands. The new mayor turned aside the plaints of the Committee of Fifteen that the forces of vice were rising again. He curtailed the powers of the Morals Squad and looked down his ruddy nose at Major Funkhouser. He switched police captains like chessmen, and ladled out jobs to deserving adherents. And then he settled his ample haunches into his big red leather chair for four years of roistering rule.

Bathhouse John and Hinky Dink watched bug-eyed as Big Bill, their avowed enemy, reopened the sluice gates for First Ward graft. But they were quickly disillusioned. Big Bill's policy was not made in deference to their power. In October the mayor abruptly and noisily ordered the Sunday closing of Chicago saloons. A wail of anger went up from the First Ward, and Tony Cermak and his United Societies members paraded the Loop in protest. Bathhouse and Hinky Dink scurried to the city hall, and were shown the door. If the town was going to be wide open it was only because Big Bill said so, and when he said so. The police raided, or ignored violations as they pleased, and to the First Ward came again the terror of insecurity.

Over the scattered remains of the Levee Big Jim Colosimo now took command. As a hedge against the uncertain future he began the dispersal of his empire. Burnham, a dull town to the southwest of Chicago, became, through the bold invitation of its boy mayor, Johnny Patton, a new citadel of vice, in which Johnny

Torrio, Jakie Adler and Jew Kid Grabiner, Big Jim's brain trust-
ers, set up cribs, two-dollar houses, cheap saloons and gambling
dives. Another retreat was established in Stickney. Even within
the confines of the old Levee there was new activity. Organized
segregation had been smothered, but with watchful Nootbar gone,
the shady hotels and call flats dusted their front steps and flung
out their mats of welcome. Established places of infamy were
transformed into cabarets which the Committee of Fifteen
promptly denounced as "recruiting stations for the promotion of
vice." Ike Bloom's dance hall was renamed Old Vienna, and
later, Midnight Frolics. Colosimo's tavern was enlarged and
remodeled and catered again to the wealthy, the epicures, the
curious, and the underworld elite. Johnny Jordan and others
thrived in new, cheap all-night cafés on South State Street. Dennis Cooney, chubby-faced aide to Hinky Dink, was deputized
chief of the disorderly hotels in the First Ward, centering his
operations in the Rex, 2138 South State Street.

As the czar of vice, Big Jim Colosimo took on an importance
surpassing that of Bathhouse and Hinky Dink. He wielded voting
power among the Italians he had organized into social and athletic
clubs, and he controlled a retinue of thugs who did not hesitate
at violence. Big Jim grew fatter and happier, wore a dozen diamonds as he passed among the guests in his splendid dive, kept a
horde of relatives on his pay rolls, bought huge houses and stuffed
them with garish *objets d'art,* and counted his friends among the
best people, the judges, police officials, senators, congressmen,
heads of important city departments.

As his purses were filled to bursting and his realm made more
secure by the efficiency of the sad-eyed Torrio, Big Jim Colosimo
found less and less need for his political fathers. What Bathhouse
John and Hinky Dink could do for him Big Jim could do ten
times as well himself. What need was there of middle men to
smooth out your troubles with officials when your stubby fingers,
decked with sparklers and clutching green dollars, could reach
into the city hall itself, eh? No hard feelings. No rancor. No

bitterness. Only the tacit and certain understanding that Big Jim, with soft-spoken Torrio ever in his shadow, would see to the interests of the vice elements, and Bathhouse John and Hinky Dink could, by taking a realistic view of this situation, go on being "Lords of the First Ward."

Bathhouse John and Hinky Dink had no choice but to accept the unspoken conditions. Politically, within their own territory, they were firm. Big Bill Thompson was too astute a strategist to attempt any direct onslaught against the Coughlin-Kenna fortress. Big Jim, given control of vice, regularly furnished his voting strength to the aldermen as needed, and with Italian immigrants pushing the Irish beyond the ward boundaries, this strength had grown formidable. Coughlin and Kenna were solid with the Sullivan-Brennan organization, where Kenna's advice was solicited, and they controlled the county judge. With the burden of vice control off their hands, and their whisky-selling rights generously respected by Colosimo, both, especially Coughlin, could concentrate on other interests.

Bathhouse John turned his attention to his flourishing insurance business, and devoted more time to the race tracks and his thirty-five excellent horses on his farm near St. Charles. Hinky Dink continued to sit, a diminutive patriarch, in the important political conferences, managed his two saloons and his brewery interests, dabbled in his Arkansas real estate, and provided acceptable assistance to Big Jim.

In his office across from the city hall Alderman Coughlin gave increasing thought to the expansion of revenue that might be had from the legitimate business men of the First Ward. The day of big franchises was over, and Bathhouse, remembering the advice of Billy Mason, had to turn again to the little stuff. One of his favorite devices was the sale of insurance under a neat form of duress. The businessmen were constantly in need of minor council permits. These Coughlin gladly granted, but first he sent Walter Colburn to the applicant to inquire into the state of his insurance. If the suppliant found he could take his policies from Coughlin, he discovered that city permits and licenses could be readily obtained. If not, he was required to wait until he was in a more suitable frame of mind. Colburn passed so frequently before the eyes of Samuel Insull on visits of this kind that the irascible utility magnate finally pretended to take a fancy to him, and gave him a permanent job driving a repair truck. Colburn's new duties did not interfere with his insurance activities and Insull thereafter had no difficulties with his First Ward permits.

In the winter of 1916 Alderman Coughlin's home at Colorado Springs burned to the ground. A few months later Colorado Springs voted to close its saloons. These two untoward events so infuriated the alderman that he announced he would never visit the Springs again. He forthwith closed his zoo, and offered the equipment to the highest bidder. In return for his investment of over a million dollars he now was offered only $30,000. He sold the equipment, and in disgust rejected a bid of a Methodist Temperance organization for the grounds. He gave the zoo park land to Colburn, who later converted it to a tourist camp.

Bathhouse John was growing old and testy. His stiff pompadour was graying and his paunch drooped below his mauve waistcoat, for he still insisted on eating like four men, especially when Mary served his favorites, roast beef and boiled potatoes. He continued to rise promptly at six in the morning, arriving at his insurance office ahead of the rest of the staff. At noon he took lunch in Mangler's saloon, and then he journeyed leisurely about the ward on political business until four o'clock, when he repaired to Hinky Dink's to remain for an hour or so. At those afternoon meetings First Ward policies were decided, The Bath offering suggestions galore, Hinky Dink voting yes or no with a nod or a grunt. There was rarely a disagreement between the two, for The Bath always bowed to the will of the Little Fellow. After a dinner at home with Mary, Walter Colburn and Etta Kiley, Mary's favorite sister, Bathhouse and Colburn would wander to Ike Bloom's to sit about until ten o'clock, drinking beer and receiving reports on the Levee. Sometimes they went to Colosimo's, where Big Jim welcomed them effusively. But The Bath was not wholly comfortable among the slick young hoodlums who frequented these establishments. He liked violence no better than did Hinky Dink, and the swaggering, itchy-fingered thugs who now comprised the Levee push under Colosimo frightened him a little. He was treated with respect, however, and the policemen and political big shots sat at his table with him and listened politely to his pronunciamentos on politics, business and racing.

The Bath's voice thundered only sporadically in the council chambers; in the committee meetings, where he was largely ignored, he relapsed into a morose, suspicious silence. When new aldermen twitted him about his dress—for he continued to affect the brand of raiment that had won him glory at the turn of the century—he puffed out his lips and glared defiantly. He rarely accompanied Kenna to the conferences at the Sullivan-Brennan headquarters, for he had discovered that his advice was not welcome.

For a time he puttered in business and farming with unfortunate results. In 1916 he bought 100,000 bushels of corn at thirty-five cents a bushel and fed beef on his Iowa farm. The market dropped, and he sold his steers for less than he paid for them. He established a pig farm on River Road, near Chicago, and arranged to have the city garbage men haul out their daily collections in payment for their city contracts. His pigs became tubercular, political opponents exposed his garbage arrangement, and the venture failed. He tried to grow mushrooms and discovered too late that he didn't have the proper technique.

2

The joys remaining to Bathhouse were his home, his horses, and his fame as a "poet." This reputation he steadfastly maintained, despite his political tribulations and financial setbacks. Always his verses seemed to find first publication in the newspaper currently employing the services of John Kelley, usually on a Monday morning when news was scarce and the columns were open to novelty. Typical of the poetical effusions was this ode:

To a Hod Carrier

'Tis not a ladder of fame he climbs
This rugged man of bricks and mortar;
The mason gets six for laying the bricks
While the hod carrier gets but two and a quarter.

National magazines gibed at Coughlin as "Chicago's poet-alderman," but published his verses and his photographs, for which he posed eagerly, frequently appearing with a white kerchief about his neck, sleeves rolled, and a quill in his hand. But this bubble was burst when Jack Lait, writing a column for the *Herald,* told Coughlin's public what every newspaperman in town knew, that John Kelley, then on the *Tribune,* was the real author of the poems attributed to Bathhouse. Kelley, Lait related, had arranged with the alderman shortly after the debut of "Dear Midnight of Love" to act as his creative amanuensis, and subsequently had written all of the verses that had given Bathhouse John national fame and caused so many visitors to Chicago's city hall to demand, "Where does Bathhouse John sit?"

"This kindly Kelley," wrote Lait, "when he saw that Bathhouse John's heart was breaking under the tease of a muse that itched for utterance, but stuttered, took in hand the commissariat pencil of his profession, and he indited the verses."

All of the poems that had been credited to The Bath—"Ode to a Bath Tub," "When the Moonbeams Kiss the Roses in the Glow of Eventide," "Why Did They Build the Lovely Lake So Close to the Horrible Shore?" "An Ode to a Bowl of Soup," "Oh! for the Life of an Alderman," "I'm Poor but I'm Honest, Goodness Knows," "Suds and Spuds," "When the Silver Moon Shines over Smiley Corbett's," "Farewell to the Wellington Hotel," "Two Thirsts with but a Single Drink," "Tramp, the Traffic Squad is Going Off Duty," "They're Tearing Up Clark Street Again,"

334

"Ode to a Lower Berth," "She Sleeps at the Side of the Drainage Canal," "Perhaps," "On with the Dance," "Welcome to the Press," "Why Did They Build Lake Michigan So Wide?"—all, all were the creations of Kelley.

Bathhouse John roared indignantly that Lait was "talkin' through his hat!" "Nobody writes my stuff. It comes natural to me. I dash it off before I know it," he puffed.

Kelley maintained a discreet silence; the city, seeking surcease from the darkening war clouds, chuckled merrily over the literary controversy, and the poems kept appearing under Coughlin's name.* The Bath, unashamed, continued to pose as the council's "poet lariat." On the twenty-fifth anniversary of his first election to the council, the *Tribune* published what it called his own "ode to his lily-like life." Its high spot was this verse:

> In all the years I served as member from the First,
>   I've never lamped a crooked dime, not e'en a weinerwurst;
> I've heard a lot of foolish talk regarding 'easy mon'
>   But I my colleagues will defend from slander's flippant tongue.

"This poem," breathed The Bath, "is not only my first poem of the new year. It is the best."

The comedy continued. On one occasion, when Alderman Merriam made use of the word "apparatus" in a council address, giving it the long "a," Bathhouse promptly called upon the corporation counsel to produce an opinion on the correct pronunciation of the word. He himself held for the short "a." He was overruled, and snorted disgustedly: "That Merryman! That college perfessor! Now he has ruined my best poem." At another time the *Tribune* announced that Bathhouse was preparing to publish a volume of verse, which he proposed to dedicate to Hinky Dink.

"If he does he'll never get another vote," threatened Hink.

The Bath then determined to honor Henry Carroll, bridge-tender and precinct captain.

---

*In 1932, Kelley finally confessed.

"My Gawd!" exclaimed Carroll. "I couldn't stand that. They'd run me outa th' ward. If Bathhouse does that I'm gonna challenge him to a duel."

All this seemed a bit of *Tribune* press-agentry preliminary to its publication of Coughlin's collected works in a Sunday supplement, and in color. The Bath's choicest verse was printed, together with a heroic picture of the alderman strumming a guitar, yodeling from a balcony before his entranced council colleagues.

3

The war years were quiet and mildly prosperous for Bathhouse and Hinky Dink, although the Colosimo incursion had curtailed their revenues. Into the south end of the ward poured thousands of Republican-voting Negroes, attracted from the South by high war wages. These Hinky Dink promptly converted to Democracy, wherever possible, or in any event made them part of his organization, casting their votes in his interests even if they were in the Republican primaries.

In the spring of 1919 the Sullivan-Brennan organization again selected Sweitzer to run against Big Bill Thompson for mayor. Maclay Hoyne entered the race as an independent, and was endorsed by Carter Harrison, then a captain with the Red Cross in France. In their efforts to destroy Thompson some of the newspapers charged that he had the support of Bathhouse and Hinky Dink, particularly in the colored district.

"Bunk," said Kenna, in reply to a story in the *Journal*. "I have never made a statement that Thompson should be re-elected. I don't know where they could have heard it. I don't know when they could have heard it. And I don't know what earthly reason or any kind of other reason anybody could have for saying it—because, because it is false."

Thompson agreed completely. He promised to drive Hinky Dink out of the First Ward. He failed, of course. Sweitzer got 6,502 votes to 3,557 for Thompson and 1,041 for Hoyne in the

First Ward, while Hinky Dink romped to victory almost without opposition. Big Bill, however, carried the city by a plurality of 17,600, and the First Ward was in for four more years of Republicanism, under a now definitely unfriendly mayor.

4

And then came a new blow—prohibition. Chicago and the First Ward had always and invariably voted dripping wet, but in the Springfield state house and at Washington the drys were in ascendancy. Bathhouse and Hinky Dink were soon to be up against a new era, one that they neither appreciated nor understood. The Bath's Silver Dollar had long since closed, its site taken over by the Hotel La Salle, but Hinky Dink's saloons, on which he had lavished a lifetime of affection, were going strong. Even the imperturbable Hink was upset by the prospect of a national drought. No saloons? Where could a man go? Where could a man's friends gather? How could the business of politics be conducted without the friendly barroom? The Hink couldn't and wouldn't understand it.

His Workingmen's Exchange had always been the joy of Kenna's life. It was his philanthropy, wherein he distributed happiness to the poor and unfortunate. It had a national reputation as a place to see, and famous sociologists and noted writers had come there to study the stew bums and talk with Hink and leave with an improved opinion of saloons and the Little Fellow. Among these were Rudyard Kipling, Lincoln Steffens and H. G. Wells. Wells wrote of Hinky Dink:

Now, Alderman Kenna is a straight man, the sort of man one likes and trusts at sight, and he did not invent his profession. He follows his own ideas of right and wrong, and compared with my ideas of right and wrong, they seem tough, compact, decided things. He is very kind to all his crowd. He helps them when they are in trouble, even if it is trouble with the police; he helps them find employment when they are down on their luck; he stands between them and the impact of an unsympathetic and altogether too-careless social structure in a sturdy and almost parental way. I can quite believe what I was told, that in the lives of many of these rough undesirables he's almost the only decent influence. . . . He tells them how to vote, a duty they might otherwise neglect, and sees that they do it properly. And whenever you want to do things in Chicago, you must reckon carefully with him."

The visitors doted on the fine, beery smell of the place, the polished bar, just two inches under 100 feet, and the crystal-clear mirror. The Exchange had established a firm tradition: the largest schooners in town, the best free lunch, no orchestra, no women, no selling to minors. Once when Hink's bartender, Georgie Rosenbaum, was hailed to court for selling beer to two youngsters and fined twenty dollars, Kenna insisted that the fine stand, paid it, and took the money out of Rosenbaum's salary. On another occasion Johnny Crossen, a First Ward character, bought two beers and took them to two sailors who waited outside the saloon. The Citizens' League brought charges against Kenna and Rosenbaum, who were accused of violating a city ordinance and the Navy's dry rule. This time Hinky Dink fought the case, while the Coughlin muse, tickled by Kelley, sang:

> The drag of politics, the boast of power,
> All the pull the dear old Foist could sport
> Before the Navy's bone dry rule must cower
> And bring e'en Hinky Dink to court.

Charges against Hinky Dink were dismissed, but Rosenbaum again was fined. This time Kenna paid the twenty dollars himself.

The Workingmen's Exchange was the social club for some of the most sordid derelicts in the First Ward, appreciated by them as such far beyond recognized shelters like the Pacific Garden

Mission and the Salvation Army havens. Upstairs, in the Alaska Hotel, there was always a horde of bums sleeping in coops lined with chicken wire. Every morning they would slip down and scrub the floors and bar, shine the hefty beer mugs and polish the rails and spittoons. Then each was given a little dinner pail and a line was formed at the end of the bar, so that each might receive his reward—an explosive pick-me-up known as "a rub of the brush." Beneath the bar was a huge vat into which the drippings of beer, bourbon, Scotch, wine, ale and all other beverages sold the night before had collected. Their little pails clutched in trembling hands, the bright-eyed rum pots presented themselves to Rosenbaum and he ladled out the weird brew. The happy recipients then would rush to Grant Park, sipping the lethal concoction while sunning themselves. Then they rested the forenoon, awakening in time to return to Kenna's place for free lunch.

Incipient prohibition focused attention on Hink's saloons as symbolic of a happy, carefree era. After September 15, 1918, when a whimsical reporter joked that Kenna's Workingmen's Exchange would become an ice-cream parlor where little Mike would dispense grape juice, pineapple flips and strawberry floats, the speculation as to its fate seemed to occupy the whole city. Finally, on July 1, 1919, the famous saloon was transformed into a near-beer emporium, in conformity with Illinois law, and Kenna disgustedly refused to enter the place. Six months later, on the eve of the passage of the prohibition law, the Workingmen's Exchange was closed forever and transformed into a combination candy, sandwich and cigar store.

"Yes, dear reader," lamented a *Tribune* writer, "the scuttle, the gold fish bowl, the schooner, the tankard, the flagon which held the amber fluid that was quaffed by ye merrie hobo have been relegated to the basement. These scuttles—now relics of a past age—will never again be filled with the nectar that made a certain western city more or less famous. Farewell to wassail! Bacchus, adieu!"

As news of the shutdown spread, there was a clamor for the

huge schooners. Even many who had frowned upon the Kennas and the Coughlins made formal requests for the tubs, Arthur Burrage Farwell declaring he wanted one to use as a goldfish bowl. Kenna complied with Farwell's plea, and Mayor Thompson, Chief of Police William Garrity and numerous society women also received the souvenirs. Another was given to the Chicago Historical Society. One precisionist produced a tape measure and announced to an amazed public that the famous schooners were eight inches high, sixteen inches around the bowl, weighed three pounds, eight ounces when empty, were four inches deep, had a four-and-a-half-inch diameter, and a content of one pint, nine fluid ounces. Thirsty Chicagoans sighed and wiped away nostalgic tears.

Kenna kept one last tub for himself, but later presented it, much to the country's amusement, to Miss Anna A. Gordon, president of the national and international Women's Christian Temperance Union. She installed it in Rest Cottage, Evanston, the national headquarters, and filled it with packets of tea, which were distributed to visitors. Noted the Coughlin muse:

Dear, gentle, gracious, efficient president of the WCTU,
 This souvenir of pre-Volsteadian days I beg to present to you
My sentiments go with it, and as you gaze upon it filled with flow-
  ers sweet
 I prithee remember that it oft contained Manhattan suds on
  Clark Street.

5

Death came that year to others beloved of Bathhouse John and Hinky Dink. Chesterfield Joe Mackin, once lord of the First Ward and sponsor for Coughlin, passed away in Dunning Insane Asylum, a raving maniac who spent his final days hurling furniture and dishes at imaginary foes. Pat O'Malley, the gambler, cashed in his chips. Then, on November 24, 1919, Mary Coughlin, following a short illness, died in the Coughlin home at 120 East Twenty-first Street. Mary had kept to the background. Many of The Bath's closest political associates were unaware that he had been wedded for thirty-five years, for the Coughlins' home life, quiet, sedate, devoted to talk of church socials and charities in St. John's parish, had remained far removed from the gaiety of the First Ward. Even the Coughlins and the Kennas had not mixed socially, and their friends in politics were rarely invited to either home.

Mary's death was recorded with some surprise by newspapers that had for years referred to Bathhouse as a bachelor, and the weeping alderman told reporters, "We were brought up together. We were companions, you might say, since we were six months old. We were sweethearts all our lives, children together from the time we could walk. She was a homebody, that's what she was, just a good plain homebody. Her home was her life. Her church work and her home were all she cared for."

Quiet little Mary left an estate of $86,959, mostly in gems, and she bequeathed good-sized gifts to the charities of her parish.

Six months later came another tragedy to sadden Bathhouse and push him farther along the road of frustration and oblivion.

Amid the filth of his sordid business Big Jim Colosimo had fallen in love—with Dale Winter, a singer in a church choir. And she, inexplicably, fell in love with uncouth Big Jim. The friends of neither could understand. "This," Colosimo assured his gangsters, "is the real thing." He would divorce Victoria, who had helped him to greatness in the brothel business, and wed his choir flower. Johnny Torrio shrugged. "It's you' funeral, Jim," he commented. Johnny Torrio was a prophet.

In March Big Jim obtained his divorce, settling $50,000 upon Victoria. Two weeks later she married Antonio Villano, twenty years her junior. Three weeks later Big Jim and Dale were wed in Crown Point, Indiana, and after a honeymoon they returned to Jim's mansion on Vernon Avenue.

Prohibition had added to Big Jim's enormous wealth. He was

the leader of the Italian community that had promptly and profitably gone into the alcohol-cooking business, and his gangsters were beginning their control of the wholesale bootlegging racket. On May 11, Colosimo went to his café to keep a "business appointment." He spoke for a few minutes with his secretary, Frank Camilla, and his chef, Tony Cesarino. His expected visitor, he grumbled, was late. He was leaving. He went into the lobby, preparing to step outside. There were two shots. Camilla ran into the lobby. Colosimo lay dead, sprawling on a bloody floor.

For four days the underworld trembled at its first great slaying. The Mafia, which had often threatened Big Jim, and Victoria and her Sicilian husband were immediately suspected. Victoria's brothers, whom Big Jim had sponsored in the poolroom business, were questioned, but shrugged their way out. Johnny Torrio wept bitterly. "Big Jim and me were like brothers," he told the police. A greasy, scarred young hoodlum, one Alphonse Caponi whom Torrio had brought in from New York to act as Colosimo's bodyguard, was taken into custody, and quickly released.

Bathhouse John and Hinky Dink went nightly to Big Jim's wake, The Bath sobbing openly. He was the chief comforter for Dale Winter, and even had a cheering word for Victoria. When Archbishop George Mundelein refused to permit a church funeral for Big Jim, Bathhouse John, following a prayer by the Reverend Pasquale de Carol, a Presbyterian clergyman, knelt beside Colosimo's coffin, reciting Hail Mary's and the Catholic prayer for the dead.

At the head of the funeral procession, first of the endless, gaudy corteges to mark Chicago gangland deaths in the next decade, strode 1,000 men of the First Ward Democratic Club, led by Bathhouse John and Hinky Dink. Among the pallbearers and honorary pallbearers were ten aldermen, three judges; Giacome Spadoni, Francisco Daddi and Titta Ruffo, of the Chicago Grand Opera company; Congressman John W. Rainey, Michael L. Igoe, Democratic leader in the state legislature, other politicians and businessmen, and all the big shots of the vice district.

Thus in honor was the master pimp and white slaver, the czar of the street cleaners, the politician and restaurant host and Chicago's first big-time gangster laid to rest. Bathhouse and Hinky Dink, though they did not quite know it, were in the thick of new and hectic times.

THE GLORY THAT WAS THE FIRST

I

WHILE the Colosimo rites occupied the politicians, Johnny Torrio took over Chicago's vice and gambling empire. He chose as his first assistant the swart young gunman he had brought from New York to act as Big Jim's bodyguard, and to enforce the edicts of the syndicate among the brothel keepers. He was Alphonse Capone, sometimes Caponi, sometimes Al Brown, "dealer in second-hand furniture."

Young Capone had already proved himself. His first job in Chicago was to lounge against a wooden fence at the north end of the district and flash an alarm when raiders were on the way. An electric switch, set off by a nail pushed through a keyhole, was connected with buzzers in all the organized bagnios, and Capone's signal sent keepers and inmates fleeing into the tunnels that connected the houses. After that assignment Capone traveled with Colosimo, and shared with Dago Mike Carrozzo, later a Chicago labor czar, the duty of guarding the alley behind Colosimo's café. Now, at twenty-three, Capone became Torrio's office manager and chief torpēdo, ensconced in the general headquarters on the second floor of the Four Deuces, a four-story red brick saloon and brothel at 2222 South Wabash Avenue. Capone's word became law in the district, and his income was estimated at $25,000 a year.

Al Capone was an organizer, ruthless and bold. As dapper Torrio had outstripped Colosimo, so Scarface Al rose above his frightened boss. His gun-crazy hoodlums, directed by Capone himself, soon poached on the territories of other outlaw leaders

343

and touched off ghastly gang wars that made the depredations of the Quincy Street boys and the other old-time First Ward hoodlums seem as child's play. A murder a day for five days running was not unusual. Election days were more terrible than ever. Rival gangsters cruised the precincts, kidnapping and killing and bombing in the interests of their favorite candidates. And, out of it all, emerged Scarface Al triumphant, new Lord of the Levee, and lord of everything else illegal and vicious in the city of Chicago.

2

As Capone rose, the fortunes of Bathhouse John and Hinky Dink descended. In the heart of this new gangland empire they existed only by sufferance. Had he wished, Capone could have ousted either or both from politics. But although Al Capone could function without the legal processes represented by The Bath and The Hink, he could use them too. He respected the organizing genius of the shrewd little First Ward committeeman. He loafed often in Hinky Dink's cigar store, accompanied by snap-waisted gunmen who stood stonily about while Al and the Little Fellow passed the time of day. He gave Kenna's right-hand man, Dennis Cooney, a key place in his organization as lieutenant in charge of brothels. Cooney (The Duke) was little, bland, and pink, and a master at his profession. He kept the owners in line, increased collections, established new houses, made strict rules and saw that they were kept. He produced rich profits—for the pockets of Al Capone.

Capone loafed at Hinky Dink's, but he made it clear that Coughlin and Kenna would get the gangland vote and remain clear of interference as long as—Capone was never the most eloquent of men—"Ya keep ya nose clean, see?" He had even taken the trouble to summon Coughlin to his suite in the Metropole Hotel where, after guards shut the steel door behind the quaking alderman, the gang chief informed him, "Alderman, you was a good pal of Big Jim's. You stood in wid Torrio. Well, they gone now an' we runnin' things, an' we don't want no trouble wid you. Let it git aroun'. I'm tellin' you 'cause I like you."

The alderman, sweating through his extra suit of underwear, nodded rapidly and was ushered from the sanctum. For days afterward, he told all who would listen, "My God, what could I say? S'pose he had said he was goin' to take over th' organization! What could we do then? We're lucky to get as good a break as we did."

There were a few compensations for Bathhouse John and Hinky Dink, however. Capone's obvious friendship rather increased their political stature in the day when many politicians were fawning upon the gangster. Too, Kenna was high in the Brennan councils, an equal then with rising Tony Cermak, president of the county board and known as "The Mayor of Cook County," and Patrick J. Nash, sewer contractor, neighbor and follower of the late Roger Sullivan.* When the state legislature passed a redistricting act in 1923, creating fifty wards in Chicago and limiting representation to one alderman for each ward, Hinky Dink had stepped aside for Bathhouse John. But he still was powerful as ever in his position as ward committeeman, in his control of patronage, and in his reputation as the wisest of all Chicago ward politicians.

Bathhouse John, alone once more in the council, found that better days had returned. He improved his friendship with Samuel Insull, the utility czar, and discovered that his vote had been enhanced by the action of the legislature. Chicago was expanding once more, business was on the march, there were franchises and ordinances to be passed upon, and in such matters Capone took little interest. All seemed good in the best of all possible wards.

Kenna, who had no taste for council meetings anyway, professed to be snugly happy in his little two-by-four cigar store on Clark Street. He had opened it, he said, as a place for his friends to gather. The walls were hung with pictures of the First Ward elite

---

*Roger Sullivan died April 14, 1920.

and the big-time politicians friendly with the Little Fellow. There Hinky Dink repaired, day after day, to transact business, fill political jobs, and gossip with his cronies who sat about chatting of the good old days.

Kenna was rich, the possessor of sound stocks and government bonds, and Bathhouse had some money still, although it was slipping away rapidly. The Bath had women friends, one of them a comely matron he established in a lingerie shop. He engaged in business ventures and was pointed out on the streets as a friend of Capone, and the Nestor of the city hall. He still shone as a "poet," and was a willing foil for all the publicity stunts the city-hall reporters could invent.

They decreed, among other things, that Bathhouse John should designate the official Straw Hat day for Chicago, insisting that he was "the recognized stylist for male attire in the city council." So early each June the picture editors dispatched their photographers to Coughlin's dingy office, where he posed gladly as he donned his headpiece of jungle straw. There would be a big day in the council, when Bathhouse John rose to orate: "Our beautiful city is ready to accept the warmth of the sun and our citizens are appreciative of the opportunity afforded them to cast aside their dreary clothes of winter. Therefore, be it resolved, that the city council designate June 12 as acknowledgment of the new season and put forth its headwear regalia of straw."

Then, after the council had hilariously approved such a resolution, The Bath would recite some couplet written for him by one of the reporters:

Come sun, come rain, come snow, come thaw,
The hat to wear right now is straw.

Never did Bathhouse give up his right to the title of best-dressed man. Editors, ever reluctant to let loose of a readable idea, kept up the fiction. When council matters became dull with the eternal discussion of traction, taxes and ward trivia, there was always good old Bathhouse to furnish a smile or two. Time after time he was voted the council's best-dressed man; his colleagues never wearied of it. Coughlin, now weighing a loose 250 pounds, would oblige with new creations. Sometimes he appeared in a fawn-colored striped cutaway, with deeply slashed breast pockets on either side, the edges of the coat and sleeve cuffs sewed with silver bands. There was also his double-breasted vest with cat's-eye buttons, the lapels braided in silver to match the coat. His trousers were wide and roomy, with two-inch cuffs. He usually wore gleaming black shoes, buttoned, with gray kid tops. His collar was low, turned down, his shirt striped in gay colors that invariably clashed with his raucous, polka-dotted ties.

When he came to the council thus garbed it was usually a sign of a poem. The aging alderman would acknowledge his ovation gravely, and then rise to spout some new, inane verse:

> Dear Paree, O gay Paree
> Why should I cross the sea—
>   To thee?
> Here by the lake,
> The winds blow soft,
>   My thirst I slake
> Both bold and oft.
> The girls are fair,
> Their smiles are sweet;
> They trip along on twinkling feet.
> *A bas* Paree!
>   Boul Mich for me!

"Bathhouse John's appearance," wrote a *Herald and Examiner* reporter on one such occasion, "is that of the perfect well-dressed man. He is superb." The writer was describing Coughlin's latest creation, a delicate gray cutaway coat with trousers to match, a waistcoat with orange stripes, each an eighth of an inch wide and lambent against a green background.

3

Bathhouse poured out money on his horses, year after year, with indifferent success. He maintained a training farm near St. Charles, managed by Trainer Will Curran and a clutch of First Ward bums, and he annually rented stables at Churchill Downs. He could never get enough of racing, and proposed in 1925 that the city build a track in Grant Park, live off the proceeds, and abolish taxes. The chuckling aldermen discarded the proposal as they did most other Coughlin suggestions. They had learned to expect nothing from him. When people wanted serious business put through the council they consulted Hinky Dink, but they soon learned to deal with a more responsible alderman.

Bathhouse adored his horses as another man might love his children. Every one he bought was a particular pet for which he predicted splendid triumphs. He would go to the track early in the morning, help to curry and brush his steeds, feed them, give them sugar, and then solicitously see them work. At the races he had his clubhouse pass, but he usually preferred a position at the end of the grandstand where he could watch, with jowls drooping, his hopefuls hit the stretch last. But he was a perennial optimist, like all who follow the tracks, and inevitably looked forward to happier days.

These came—and went—in 1928. By that time, the aces of his stable were his two-year-olds, Roguish Eye, sired by Flittergold and dammed by Sly Wink, and Karl Eitel, named for the Chicago hotel man and restaurateur. Coughlin called them "The Eye" and Karl. By September "The Eye" had won three out of seven starts for $23,430, and Karl Eitel five of nine for $21,470. Bathhouse John had finally arrived as a horse owner, and he eagerly pointed for the Belmont Futurity and its purse of $97,990. Although the odds were 15-1 against Roguish Eye, Alderman Coughlin had confident hopes. Roguish Eye got away beautifully, ran neck and neck with High Strung, the Marshall Field entry, and left the favorite, Colonel E. R. Bradley's Blue Larkspur, in tenth position. There was a photograph finish, and the judges decreed High Strung the winner.

Bathhouse John was desolate, refusing to be cheered even by the fact that Roguish Eye took $12,600 for second place. "I don't want to be unsportsmanlike," he moaned, "but I think I won the race." He obtained pictures of the finish, taken from an angle that showed Roguish Eye to be the winner by half a nose. This picture he hung on the wall at Hinky Dink's, labeled: "Who Win?" He struck off copies and used them on his insurance calendars and his stationery. Ever thereafter most of The Bath's business literature bore that repining question: "Who Win?"

The unfortunate decision sent Roguish Eye toppling, and he soon acquired a reputation as the greatest hard-luck horse in history. Immediately after the Futurity one of his knees gave way and for weeks failed to mend. Nevertheless, Bathhouse planned to enter both horses in the Kentucky Derby the following spring. To Churchill Downs went a big, noisy, drunken entourage from the First Ward. Many of the old-timers professed to think that no horse would dare run against Roguish Eye, but some of the slick newcomers thought differently and prepared to bet against him. The sports writers were flatly discouraging. Both steeds were fat and showed signs of laziness, they said.

At race time Bathhouse had to scratch both entries. Not even Hinky Dink could cheer him. He squirmed as a wag suggested that Roguish Eye would soon be seen at the corner of State and Madison, carrying pencils and a tin cup. But after a riotous ride back to Chicago aboard the First Ward special, Bathhouse John revived his hopes. He retracted his statement that he was through with racing, and continued to spend his dwindling funds. In 1932, Roguish Eye did make a brief comeback, pushing through at 5-to-1 at Hawthorne. But Coughlin's plan to enter the horse in the Cuban Grand National at Oriental Park collapsed, and Roguish Eye was retired to the farm to graze beside Karl Eitel and Sly Wink.

"Anyhow," said Bathhouse, "it was a great life. I enjoyed every minute of it. There was only one thing wrong—Lady Luck played me false."

4

While The Bath played about with his horses, almost wholly oblivious to politics, the Democrats of Chicago won their way back to power. George Brennan, high priest of the party after the death of Roger Sullivan, became convinced that a reformer was needed to whip Big Bill Thompson, and he selected Alderman William E. Dever, square-jawed and honest. By some miracle, Dever won. Chicago raised its head hopefully. Dever went into office with the best of intentions, announced what everybody knew, that there were 20,000 protected speakeasies in the city, and promised to close them. Al Capone chuckled, the police and the federal agents stumbled about in the dark, and the syndicate continued to grow rich and fat.

In 1927 Big Bill Thompson was again elected mayor, and the following year George Brennan died, leaving control of the Democratic organization to Tony Cermak, the veteran spokesman for the organized liquor interests. In 1931 Cermak decided that the time had come to end Thompson Republicanism in Chicago. Big Bill sought vigorously to beat off the challenge, sneering at Cermak, "Whyn't you go back to your pushcart, Tony?" But Cermak, who indeed had once been a pushcart peddler, became mayor of Chicago.

Upon Cermak's ascent to the mayor's chair, Kenna and Coughlin, his ardent supporters, thought they could breathe more easily. Al Capone had been convicted by the federal government for income-tax evasion. Frank Nitti, his ulcerous cousin, had succeeded to the overlordship of the syndicate. Perhaps, mused Coughlin, who considered Cermak his close friend, and Kenna, who was a political advisor of the new mayor, Tony Cermak would take away the syndicate's powers and once again the original Lords of the Levee might come into their own.

Their thoughts remained wishful. Had they forgotten that when Cermak was head of the county board, Capone gangmen had thrived in the country towns under the board's jurisdiction? Had they forgotten, too, that the syndicate campaigned as heartily as anyone for the election of Tony Cermak? Chicago became an open town, with handbooks and speakeasies in every other block in the First Ward, but Hinky Dink and Bathhouse John did not operate the cash registers.

Mayor Cermak was a dictator who refused to tolerate the ward feudalism that had characterized Chicago politics for generations. The aldermen and ward committeemen took their orders or else. The old-fashioned politics of Kenna and Coughlin were too slow for the new order. All they retained in return for the privilege of delivering the vote was a limited amount of patronage, and their man Cooney as czar of vice. Gambling went wholly to Billy Skidmore, liquor remained in the hands of the Nitti crowd, and city business in general was handled by the high command in the mayor's office.

Kenna, nevertheless, still talked of the First as "my ward."

"My ward is Democratic," he told Judge Edmund K. Jarecki when he was hauled up on ballot-stuffing charges. "We have the finest organization in the city. It's an absolute lie that I delivered any votes by fraud. I go around on election mornings and see that the clerks and judges are on duty. I preach to them to be honest, give every man his correct count, and see that the tally sheets are taken care of. I got the cleanest and most respectable ward in the city."

"You know," said Judge Jarecki, "that it's been said for the last twenty-five years that your ward has been a plague spot so far as election frauds are concerned?"

"Yes," exploded Kenna, "by the racketeer reformers! Who cares a damn for the reformers? We don't care what they say as long as we have a clear conscience!"

Clear conscience or no, it was easy to prove that Kenna was

persisting in his ancient methods. An enterprising *Tribune* reporter spent a day in the lodging-house district. One of the first of his encounters was with a Patrick Sheehan, who wore a long, black overcoat, a derelict cap, a badge boosting pink-whiskered James Hamilton Lewis for United States senator, and a tomato nose.

"You vote yet, son?" wheezed Sheehan. "You want to make fifty cents?"

"But I vote in another precinct."

"Well, I voted myself in th' Twenty-seventh Ward and then voted here. I voted in the Twenty-seventh for me son. He's in Minnesota." Then Mr. Sheehan scooted off, whispered a few words to a voting prospect and escorted him to the door of the Eighth-Precinct voting place. The voter emerged five minutes later and grinned at the reporter, "I've voted six times today an' I'm gonna vote four more times. That'll be five dollars for th' day's work."

5

Mayor Cermak pushed his way into the national political scene, backed Roosevelt and repeal, and died gloriously in Miami from an assassin's bullet meant for the President-elect. Pat Nash succeeded him to leadership of Chicago Tammany, and put Edward J. Kelly, former chief engineer of the Chicago Sanitary district, into the city hall as mayor, a job to which he has been returned in triumph at every election since. The Democratic organization of Cook County became the Kelly-Nash machine, bearded successfully now and then only by Henry J. Horner, whom it had lifted from judge's bench to governor's mansion; bearded rarely, since his death, by anyone.

Under Kelly and Nash the ward committeemen were given a new measure of power, not enough to get them anywhere should they disobey orders but sufficient to keep them content and hardworking. Discipline became perfect, party stalwarts advanced or were demoted and punished as the bosses saw fit. Armies of pay-rollers went to work at campaign time, and the riddled Republican opposition could not stand up against them. Hinky Dink, through Cooney, renewed the old friendship with the Capone-Nitti syndicate, expanded now to control not only vice and gambling, but racketeer labor unions as well. Nitti got the illegal privileges of the First Ward; Kenna and Coughlin got funds and organized support at election time. City-hall business was the property of the organization.

Coughlin, in these last years, had no voice of his own in the city-council proceedings. Like most other aldermen he voted as the organization directed, and on the whole the orders were for the general good of the city. Consequently the Municipal Voters' League, in 1933, saw fit to say of the erstwhile Gray Wolf: "He has seemed to improve his bad record of many years' standing. Perhaps he has mellowed with age." And again, in 1935: "Either age, experience, conscience, or conditions beyond his control have resulted in a fair record during this last year."

The Bath responded with characteristic gruff indignation. "Why," he grumbled, "until this staggering report came out th' worst thing th' MVL said about me was that I was born in Waukegan, which was a malicious lie. But this endorsement by th' MVL is just too much!"

Snapped Hinky Dink: "You oughta sue 'em."

6

Bathhouse was a lonely figure those final years. The brisk young men in the First Ward organization sometimes even forgot to be respectful. Only their fear of Hinky Dink kept some of them from trying to take the coveted council seat in advance of Coughlin's death. With the repeal of prohibition his insurance business prospered, especially among the tavern owners. But the cost of his stables was too much for his limited income. He began borrowing money. He was pursued by men with unpaid feed bills. He failed to raise the entry fees for his horses. He could not afford a new automobile. He still attempted to pose now and then in the council, ranting loudly on some bit of legislation that seemed to affect directly his ward. Occasionally he tried his hand at legislation himself. He advocated a law requiring separate trolley cars for women. "In the rush hour young girls and frail women are jammed in with a lot of rough men," he complained. He offered an ordinance to set definite limits for women's skirts. "We are of the firm opinion that any additional abbreviation of the skirt would be a menace to the health of the wearer with winter coming, and everything," he explained, inexplicably adopting the regal plural first introduced by King John of England. "We are equally sure that any lengthening of the skirt would tend to destroy an important element of civic beauty." There was a losing fight against prohibiting U-turns by automobiles in the Loop district. There was a battle to prevent women from wearing knickers. "Oskaloosa and Keokuk are sufficiently civilized to prohibit women from parading in male attire," said Bathhouse John. "Why shouldn't Chicago be?"

The council snickered at his ordinances, but it honored him with a dinner and mock ceremony in which he was dubbed "Knight of the Bath." Among the guests were Mayor Kelly and Big Bill Thompson. Big Bill leaned close to the mayor and whispered: "Everything I ever learned about politics I learned from John Coughlin."

Bathhouse grew fatter, his clothes drooped, his gray pompadour yellowed with inattention, his arthritis bothered him, he watched the world move away from him through sad, suspicious eyes. The friends and enemies he had known were finally gone— Johnny Powers, old and mellowed; Ed Corrigan, broke and unhappy; Sol van Praag, bitter to the end; Big Sandy Walters, George Silver, Paddy O'Malley. . . . Of the old crowd there were left only Hinky Dink, who sustained him, Joe Friedman, his faithful precinct captain, and Carter Harrison, now collector of internal revenue and still unforgiven.

Carter Harrison wrote his autobiography, and said acridly of "Dear Midnight of Love"—"the most inane, outlandish conglomeration of words I've ever seen." The Bath rose wrathfully to the insult.

"Twenty-five years ago, when a little verse of mine put him back in the mayor's chair, I wasn't such a bum poet," he said. He quoted himself:

> Safe and best, tried and true,
> He stood the test, now it's up to you.

Thus aroused, Bathhouse had one last fling at poetry. He rose in the council, just before Christmas, and recited to Mayor Kelly:

> I love you more tomorrow
>   Is the answer that I give
> I will cause you no sorrow
>   Just as long as I live.
> And when we are old and gray
>   And in life's boat we will row
> I will love you more tomorrow than
>   I did yesterday.

The same tremolo in his voice, the same fancy clothes, a bit dirty and tattered, the same thrust of the hand into the waistcoat. But no John Kelley. The council applauded politely.

Now and then, on the street, an old crony found him. "Alderman, I need a job, see?" "Get out to the farm an' see my trainer, Will Curran." "Alderman, I need a little t' get me on me feet." A search of the wallet, and then . . . "M'boy, you come aroun' tomorrow." "Alderman, me mudder is sick, gotta get her to a hospital." "Well, m'boy, send her out to County. Tell 'em I sent ya."

And then it all ended. It began as a line in the newspapers: "Ald. John (Bathhouse John) Coughlin ill." For weeks, then months, in the Lexington Hotel, once the Metropole, in the same

356

room according to some sentimentalists where Al Capone once held forth, Bathhouse John lay sick. The sun beat through the windows, the steam was on day and night, it was unbearably hot for anyone save a former rubber in a Turkish bathhouse. Visitors came—horse trainers, little, unshaven bums from Clark Street, a few aldermen, Hinky Dink once or twice a week, a reporter or two.

Even Carter Harrison came. The two old men shook hands. "Carter, m' boy, Carter!" cried Bathhouse John. He insisted on rising from bed to pose for photographs, setting between himself and "Our Carter" the framed display of badges he wore as alderman during the Columbian Exposition. (*Mr. Maar, I'd sure like to get on some of them committees. . . .*) He gave his collection to Carter Harrison and their peace was made.

Soon, on November 8, 1938, it was over, and the political reporters sharpened their memories and told of the long rule of Bathhouse John. The rulers of the city draped the city-hall entrances in mourning, and over the seat Alderman Coughlin had occupied for forty-six years they spread black and purple crepe, and on his desk they set a vase of roses.

7

Bathhouse John Coughlin died a poor man. His debts were $56,000, and his assets were largely his insurance business and a string of broken-down race horses. The horses, sold at a tenth and a twentieth of the prices Bathhouse John had paid for them, finally reduced the claims against the estate to $18,000. Of this amount Fletcher Robinson, chauffeur and secretary to the alderman during his final years, assumed an obligation of almost $10,000 in return for the privilege of continuing the insurance office. For Kate Coughlin, who had hemmed the towels for her brother's first bathhouse, little was left.

The boys in the First Ward clucked their tongues and shook their heads and forgot. For the death of Bathhouse John soon loosed in the ward a turmoil of factionalism not known since the days of Billy Skakel and Sol van Praag. The prize was only Coughlin's aldermanic seat and the petty privileges not gobbled up by the Nitti crowd, but the contenders squared off for battle with the viciousness of a group of kinsfolk fighting over a legacy. The prospect frightened the party bosses. There could be no breakdown in the iron discipline. Only one solution could be considered: Hinky Dink, aged and weary, must return to the city council.

Hinky Dink had no desire to return. He was rich, he was eighty years old, his sight was failing, he no longer thrived on the rigors of a campaign. He was assured he need do no more than present himself at the ward meetings. He need not even attend the sessions of the council. But he had to restore peace among his followers.

The voice of the party was still law to the Little Fellow. He emerged from his suite in the old Auditorium Hotel, filed his petition, ran for office, and, although he attended few rallies and made no speeches, he won again.

For a time he attended the council meetings, huddling in a big chair, his blue eyes dulled now, the stub of a cigar clamped cockily in his teeth, his pale face expressionless. Once or twice he would lean to one side and spit deftly on the floor, ignoring the brass cuspidor. He uttered no word. Then he stopped coming. He sent his orders to the council by Joe Clark, his secretary, a merry, energetic little man who had become heir apparent to the fading First Ward empire.

At least once a month in recent years some of the older politicians liked to bring up the hoary tale that Hinky Dink was as sharp as ever. But the facts were otherwise. His power was nominal, his presence, beyond the magic of his name, unnecessary. Dennis Cooney, liaison man with the Nitti crowd, was the general fixer. State Senator Daniel A. Serritella, friend of Capone, controlled the Republican vote and made the bipartisan compacts. Dago Mike Carrozzo. who died in 1941 while under federal indictment on charges of income-tax violations, handled the Italian vote and grew rich on fees from the city's day laborers and street cleaners. Joe Clark took charge of the patronage and the normal aldermanic business.

The glory that was the First is gone. And soon the ward itself may disappear. For now that the Little Fellow is weary of further service to the city, he has stepped down for another and it is planned that Chicago will have the redistricting that has been demanded for years. If Joe Clark and his friends cannot prevail, the old First Ward will disappear, the south end going to form a new colored unit, the Loop allocated to other adjoining wards.

Then the legend of Hinky Dink will really begin.

BIBLIOGRAPHY

BIBLIOGRAPHY

Books

Abbott, Willis John, *Carter Henry Harrison, a Memoir.* New York, 1895.

Ahern, M. L., *Political History of Chicago.* Chicago, 1886.

Andreas, A. T., *History of Chicago.* (3 vols.) Chicago, 1884.

——, *History of Cook County, Illinois.* Chicago, 1894.

Asbury, Herbert, *Gem of the Prairie.* New York, 1940.

——, *Sucker's Progress.* New York, 1935.

Barnard, Harry, *Eagle Forgotten: Life of John Peter Altgeld.* Indianapolis, 1938.

Bennett, Fremont O., *Politics and Politicians of Chicago, Cook County and Illinois.* Chicago, 1886.

Bennett, James O'Donnell, *Chicago Gangland, the True Story of Chicago Crime.* Chicago, 1929.

Bonney, C. L. (compiler), *Who Owns the Streets?* Chicago, 1896.

Bright, John, *Hizzoner Big Bill Thompson.* New York, 1930.

Bross, William, *History of Chicago.* Chicago, 1876.

Brown, Waldo R., *Altgeld of Illinois.* New York, 1924.

Burns, Walter Noble, *The One-Way Ride.* New York, 1931.

Bryan, William Jennings, *The Memoirs of William Jennings Bryan.* Chicago, 1925.

Conroy, Rev. Joseph P., *Arnold Damen, S.J.* New York, 1929.

Currey, J. Seymour, *Chicago: Its History and Its Builders.* (3 vols.) Chicago, 1912.

Darrow, Clarence, *The Story of My Life.* New York, 1932.

Dennis, Charles H., *Victor Lawson, His Time and His Work.* Chicago, 1935.

Dobyns, Fletcher, *The Underworld of American Politics.* New York, 1932.

Dreiser, Theodore, *The Titan.* New York, 1914.

Dunne, Edward F., *History of Illinois.* (5 vols.) Chicago, 1933.

Ellis, Elmer, *Mr. Dooley's America.* New York, 1941.

Flynn, John J., *History of the Chicago Police.* Chicago, 1887.

362

———, *Standard Guide to Chicago*. Chicago, 1891-1892-1893.

Gilbert, Paul Thomas, and Bryson, Charles Lee, *Chicago and Its Makers*. Chicago, 1929.

Goodspeed, Weston A., and Healy, Daniel D., *History of Cook County, Illinois*. (2 vols.) Chicago, 1929.

Gosnell, Harold F., *Boss Platt and His New York Machine*. Chicago, 1933.

———, *Machine Politics: Chicago Model*. Chicago, 1937.

———, *Negro Politicians*. Chicago, 1935.

Hamilton, Henry Raymond, *The Epic of Chicago*. Chicago, 1932.

Harrison, Carter, *Stormy Years*. Indianapolis, 1938.

Hendrick, Burton J., *The Age of Big Business*. New Haven, 1919.

Herrick, Genevieve Forbes, and Herrick, John Origen, *The Life of William Jennings Bryan*. Chicago, 1925.

Hibben, Paxton, *The Peerless Leader, William Jennings Bryan*. New York, 1929.

Johnson, Claudius O., *Carter Henry Harrison I*. Chicago, 1928.

King, Hoyt, *Citizen Cole of Chicago*. Chicago, 1931.

Kirkland, Joseph, and Moses, John (editors), *History of Chicago*. (2 vols.) Chicago, 1895.

Landesco, John, *Organized Crime in Chicago*. (Illinois Crime Survey.) Chicago, 1929.

Lewis, Lloyd, and Smith, Henry Justin, *Chicago, The History of Its Reputation*. New York, 1929.

Linn, James Weber, *James Keeley, Newspaperman*. Indianapolis, 1937.

Masters, Edgar Lee, *The Tale of Chicago*. New York, 1933.

Matby, M. R. (editor), *Street Railways of Chicago*. Chicago, 1901.

Merriam, Charles Edward, *Chicago, A More Intimate View of Urban Politics*. New York, 1929.

Nevins, Allan, *Grover Cleveland, A Study in Courage*. New York, 1932.

Norton, Samuel Wilbur, *Chicago Traction, A History, Legislative and Political*. Chicago, 1907.

Palmer, George Thomas, *A Conscientious Turncoat: The Story of John M. Palmer*. New Haven, 1941.

Pasley, Fred D., *Al Capone, The Biography of a Self-Made Man*. New York, 1930.

———, *Muscling In*. New York, 1931.

Pierce, Bessie Louise, *As Others See Chicago*. Chicago, 1933.

——, *History of Chicago*. (vols. 1-2) New York, 1937.

Reckless, Walter, *Vice in Chicago*. Chicago, 1933.

Robertson, Mrs. Harriet M. (editor), *Dishonest Elections and Why We Have Them*. Chicago, 1934.

Stead, William T., *If Christ Came to Chicago*. Chicago and London, 1894.

Steffens, Lincoln, *Shame of the Cities*. New York, 1904.

——, *The Autobiography of Lincoln Steffens*. (2 vols.) New York, 1931.

Sterchie, John C. (compiler), *Public Officials of Chicago*. Chicago, 1896.

Stuart, William H., *The 20 Incredible Years*. Chicago, 1935.

Sullivan, Edward Dean, *Chicago Surrenders*. New York, 1930.

——, *Rattling the Cup on Chicago Crime*. New York, 1929.

Sullivan, Mark, *Our Times*. (vols. 1-2) New York, 1926-27.

Sullivan, William L. (compiler), *Dunne: Judge, Mayor, Governor*. Chicago, 1916.

Tallmadge, Thomas E., *Architecture in Old Chicago*. Chicago, 1941.

Tannenbaum, Frank, *Crime and the Community*. Boston, 1938.

Thrasher, Frederick, *The Gang*. Chicago, 1927.

Van Every, Edward, *Sins of America as "Exposed" by the Police Gazette*. New York, 1931.

Washburn, Charles, *Come Into My Parlor*. New York, 1936.

Weber, Harry (compiler), *Outline History of Chicago Traction*. Chicago, 1936.

Wells, H. G., *The Future in America*. New York, 1906.

Wilson, Samuel Paynter, *Chicago and Its Cess Pools of Vice and Infamy*. Chicago, 1910.

Zorbaugh, Harvey W., *The Gold Coast and the Slum*. Chicago, 1920.

Newspapers

Chicago *American* (1901-40)
    Chronicle (1895-1907)
    Daily News (1890-1942)
    Dispatch (also Chicago *Democrat*) (various dates)
    Evening Journal (various dates)
    Evening Post (various dates)
    Examiner (also *Herald and Examiner*) (1902-39)
    Graphic (various dates)

Illustrated Graphic News (1890-91—various dates)
Inter-Ocean (1890-1906)
Mixed Drinks: the Saloon Keepers' Journal (1892-4)
Public Safety (1914-18)
Record (also *Record-Herald* and *Times-Herald*) (1892-1905)
Saturday Record (1894-5)
Tribune (1885-1942)
The Day Book (1914—various dates)
The Voter (1903)
Colorado Springs *Gazette* (1901-07)
Evening Mail (1901-2)
Evening Telegraph (1903-07)
Denver *Evening Mail* (various dates)
New York *Herald* (various dates)
Times (various dates)
World (various dates)

Reports, Pamphlets, Documents

Annual Report of the Civil Service Commission of Chicago (1911-14).
Blue Book of Cook County Democracy, and History and Record of Organization. Chicago, 1902.
Chicago City Manual (1908-16).
Chicago Police Problems, The Citizens Police Committee. Chicago, 1931.
Chicago Recreation Survey (Vol. 2), The Chicago Recreation Commission. Chicago, 1939.
Chicago Vice Commission Report. Chicago, 1912.
Citizens Association of Chicago, Annual Report. (1897-1924).
Hodes, Barnet (editor), *Municipal Code of Chicago*. Chicago, 1939.
Estate of Mary Kiley Coughlin (File of the Cook County Probate Court).
Estate of John Joseph Coughlin (File of the Cook County Probate Court).
Illinois Crime Survey (1902).
Proceedings of the Chicago City Council. (1889-1920).
The Everleigh Club Illustrated (pamphlet).

It is not possible for the authors to acknowledge their indebtedness to all the scores of persons who generously sat for interviews on the subject of Bathhouse John and Hinky Dink. Many, in fact, specifically requested that they be not mentioned for reasons obvious. We want to thank Mr. Samuel A. Rinella for reading the manuscript, Mr. John T. Mc-Cutcheon for permission to republish many of his cartoons of Bathhouse John and Hinky Dink Kenna, and the staffs of the Chicago *Tribune* morgue and reference library, the Chicago Public Library, Newberry Library, the University of Chicago Library, and Mr. Frederick Rex, librarian of the Chicago Municipal Reference Library, and his staff for their generous co-operation. We are grateful too to Mr. L. E. Dicke, who opened his fine collection of Chicagoana to us, and to Corporation Counsel Barnet Hodes, and Mr. David J. A. Hayes for special assistance.

The following newspaper people, many of them directly familiar with the era concerned, gave us invaluable help: John Astley-Cock, August Bartz, Newberne A. Browne, Parke Brown, Frank Cipriani, Charles Collins, Will Davidson, James Doherty, Arthur Evans, Joseph R. Garrett, Eddie Johnson, the late Moses Lamson, John A. Menaugh, Edward L. Wilson and Percy Wood, all of the *Tribune;* Justin Forrest of the *Herald-American;* Clarence R. Dore and Charles N. Wheeler, of the *Daily News;* Miss June Provines and Will O'Neil, of the *Sun;* Edward Groshell of the *Times;* W. L. McKay, of the New York *Daily News;* and Richard Harding Loper, formerly of the Colorado Springs *Evening Mail.*

For especially useful interviews we are grateful to Alderman Kenna himself and his close friend, John Kelley, former veteran Chicago police reporter, now living in Erie, Pennsylvania; to Arthur Haggenjos and Robert E. Cantwell, Sr., once attorneys to Alderman Coughlin; to Walter Colburn, Mrs. Kate Coughlin, sister of Bathhouse John and widow of Sergeant William Coughlin, Miss Anna Coughlin, niece of Bathhouse John, former Mayor Carter Henry Harrison, George Grubb, Kenna's present office manager; Andrew Hoffman, Hoyt King, James E. Foster, and W. C. Dannenberg.

We wish also to make acknowledgment of permission to quote from *The Future in America* by H. G. Wells, published by Harper and Brothers.

INDEX

INDEX

369

374

380

384

A selected list of MIDLAND BOOKS

(continued on next page)

MIDLAND BOOKS